Charles Edward Stuart

David Daiches has been Professor of English at Sussex University since 1961. Born in Sunderland in 1912, he was educated at George Watson's College, Edinburgh, Edinburgh University, and Balliol College, Oxford, where he later became an Andrew Bradley Fellow. Since then he has held posts at many universities both in Britain and the United States. His many other books include *Virginia Woolf, A Study of Literature, Robert Burns, A Critical History of English Literature, Walter Scott and His World*, and *Robert Burns and His World*.

D0932172

Charles
Edward Stuart

The life and times of Bonnie Prince Charlie

David Daiches

Pan Books Ltd London and Sydney

First published 1973 by Thames and Hudson Ltd
This edition published 1975 by Pan Books Ltd,
Cavaye Place, London SW10 9PG
ISBN O 330 24349 7
© David Daiches 1973

Printed in Great Britain by
Richard Clay (The Chaucer Press) Ltd, Bungay, Suffolk

Conditions of sale: This book shall not, by way of trade
or otherwise, be lent, re-sold, hired out or otherwise circulated
without the publisher's prior consent in any form of binding or cover
other than that in which it is published and without a similar condition
including this condition being imposed on the subsequent purchaser.
The book is published at a net price, and is supplied subject to the
Publishers Association Standard Conditions of Sale registered
under the Restrictive Trade Practices Act, 1956

Contents

List of Illustrations

Acknowledgments

By gracious permission of Her Majesty the Queen, 11, 15; by kind permission of the Duke of Atholl, 13 (photo National Galleries of Scotland); British Museum, Department of Coins and Medals, 5; British Museum, Department of Prints and Drawings, 1, 10, 16, 18–22, 25; the Duke of Buccleuch and Queensberry K.T., G.C.V.O., 6 (photo Victoria and Albert Museum); F. Harrison, 14; A. F. Kersting, 7; by kind permission of Prince Jean Charles de Ligne, 9 (photo Dupé); Donald B. MacCulloch, 17, 23; Mansell Collection, 30; National Portrait Gallery, 26, 27; by kind permission of the Countess of Rosebery D.B.E., LL.D., 2 (photo Courtauld Institute of Art), 8 (photo National Galleries of Scotland); Scottish National Portrait Gallery, 3, 24, 29; Galleria degli Uffizi, 28; Victoria and Albert Museum, 4; West Highland Museum, Fort William, 12 (photo Studio Nevisbank)

The maps were drawn by Hanni Bailey

Note on the Spelling of
Highland Place Names and
Personal Names

THERE is no consistency at all in the eighteenth-century spelling of Highland place names and personal names. In particular, Gaelic place names are rendered in the most extraordinarily diverse ways. In general, I have followed four principles: in quoting from eighteenth-century sources I have used always the spelling of the original; in referring to Gaelic place names, apart from their mention in original sources, I have used the spelling of the modern Ordnance Survey map; in deciding whether to capitalize the part of the name which follows 'Mac', where there is no consistency in either eighteenth-century or modern practice, I have made an arbitrary choice in the light of what seems to be the more usual modern practice, but here again in citing eighteenth-century sources I have used the original spelling; I have preserved differences in spelling between place names and personal names which derive from those places where these differences have now become traditional – e.g. Glen Garry for the name of the place and Glengarry for the name of the person.

Prologue

The visitor to Rome is likely to find more interesting things to do than to turn up the narrow Via dei Santi Apostoli which goes off to the right shortly after the Via del Corso commences its long straight course up to the Piazza del Popolo. If he does, however, he will soon find himself at the north end of the Piazza dei Santi Apostoli, where he may notice a shabby baroque building which houses a language and business school, a *pensione*, a restaurant and a barber's shop, among other things. If he goes through the archway to enter the small courtyard whose high walls exclude the afternoon sun, he will hear the clatter of dishes and smell the odours of cooking from the open windows of the restaurant kitchen, which now occupies one of the ground-floor rooms of the palazzo. On a plaque on the left-hand wall he will find the following inscription:

ABITÓ QUESTO PALAZZO
ENRICO DUCA POI CARDINALE DI YORK
CHE FIGLIO SUPERSTITE DI GIACOMO III D'INGHILTERRA
PRESE IL NOME D'ENRICO IX
IN LUI NELL' ANNO MDCCCVII
S'ESTINSE LA DINASTIA DE' STUARDI

('There lived in this building Henry, Duke later Cardinal of York, who, surviving son of James III of England, took the name of Henry IX. In him in the year 1807 the Stuart dynasty became extinct.')

If the visitor then proceeds round to the long east side of the Piazza he will easily find the splendid Basilica dei Santi Apostoli whose origins go back to the sixth century and whose present baroque appearance is the result of eighteenth-century additions. If he enters the church and goes up the aisle, he will soon find on a pillar on the right, underneath a complex of baroque statuary, the following inscription:

HIC CLEMENTIÆ REMANENT PRÆCORDIA: NAM COR
CÆLESTIS FECIT NE SUPERESSET AMOR
MARIÆ CLEMENTINÆ
MAGN. BRITANN. ET C. REGINÆ
FRATRES MIN. CONV.
VENERABUNDI PP.

('Here rests the outer part of the heart of Clementina, for heavenly love did not allow the heart itself to survive. To Maria Clementina, Queen of Great Britain etc., the convent of Franciscans reverently placed this.')

The last of the Stuart dynasty in a faded Roman *pensione* and the heart of a Queen of Great Britain buried by the Franciscans in a Roman church! Nobody in the Piazza dei Santi Apostoli knows anything about either character, and neither friar (for the building next to the church still houses the order of Fratres Minores or Franciscans) nor caretaker can explain how they came to be there. But if the reader then crosses the Tiber and proceeds to St Peter's, he will find, on the left after entering the church, over the doorway that leads up to the dome, a mosaic portrait of this same Clementina, after a painting by Ignazio Stern, upheld by an angel and by a figure representing Charity, sculptured (as the guide-book will tell him) by Pietro Bracci. Below is the following inscription:

MARIA CLEMENTINA M. BRITANN.
FRANC. ET HIBERN. REGINA

('Maria Clementina, Queen of Great Britain, France and Ireland.') And on a pillar opposite, below the delicately executed busts of three male figures, is the following inscription:

JACOBO III
JACOBI II MAGNAE BRIT. REGIS FILIO
KAROLO EDVARDO
ET HENRICO DECANO PATRUM CARDINALIUM
JACOBI III FILIIS
REGIAE STIRPIS STVARDIAE POSTREMIS
ANNO M·DCC·XIX

('To James III, son of King James II of Great Britain, Charles Edward, and Henry, Dean of the Cardinal Fathers, sons of James III, the last of the royal house of Stuart. 1819.') Below are two finely modelled weeping angels. The monument is by Canova.

The history books know no James III of Britain, while the concept of a Henry IX is positively bizarre. Why are these characters so described in Roman inscriptions? And what were the last of the Stuarts doing in Rome?

It is a strange story. The building which now houses the restaurant and the barber's shop (and also, for that matter, the '*opera nazionale per gli invalidi di guerra, direzione provinciale di Roma*', the Rome branch of the national organization for war wounded) was once the Palazzo Muti where the hero of this book was born and spent his early years. (No one can explain why only his younger brother Henry and not Charles Edward himself is mentioned in the plaque.) His mother, Maria Clementina Sobieska, who died virtually in the odour of sanctity in Rome in 1735 and had her heart buried in the Basilica dei Santi Apostoli and the rest of her body in St Peter's, never in fact visited Britain. The Canova monument, erected by order of the Pope and contributed to by George IV when he was Prince Regent, commemorates the son and the two grandsons of James II of England and VII of Scotland, the last Stuart king to reign in Britain, the man whose exile in 1688 started the whole story. A main cause of his exile was his Roman Catholicism, and Catholic Rome received him and his family in death as it received his son and grandsons in life.

The expulsion from the British throne of James II of England and VII of Scotland produced the Jacobite movement, the term 'Jacobite' deriving from 'Jacobus', Latin for James. The story which begins in England and ends in Rome has its memorable middle scenes set in Scotland, where James's grandson, Prince Charles Edward, made his spectacular attempt to regain the ancestral Stuart throne for his father. It is the Scottish part of the story which explains why Prince Charles Edward has come down to us as Bonnie Prince Charlie, wearing a kilt and accompanied by Highland chiefs. In any attempt to follow the Jacobite story, Scotland is the real clue, which is why the following pages will centre so often on Scotland.

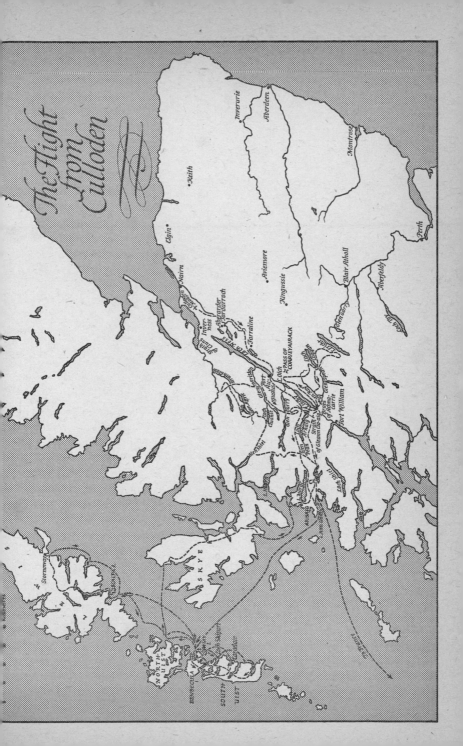

The Flight from Culloden

CHAPTER ONE

From Stuart to Jacobite

THE MARQUIS DE DANGEAU, aide-de-camp to Louis XIV whom he attended in all his campaigns, kept a voluminous and detailed diary from 1684 until shortly before he died in 1720, and though his younger contemporary the Duc de Saint-Simon said that the diary was so dull it would make you sick (it certainly cannot compare with his own brilliant memoirs), it has its moments of interest. The entry for 3 September 1701 noted that King James, the deposed King of England, was sinking fast, and dying like a saint. He was still alive on 11 September, but, Dangeau noted, past hope of recovery. On 13 September, as again Dangeau duly noted, James was visited by Louis XIV who told him that he might die in peace for he (Louis) would recognize James's son as King of England, Ireland and Scotland. Three days later the diary records James's death, at about three o'clock, and on the 20th King Louis visited the dead man's son, whom he now regarded as King James III of England.

James II of England and VII of Scotland had fled to France in December 1688 after the triumphant landing on the southern English coast of William of Orange. William, married to James's daughter Mary, had been invited by the Protestant nobles of England, who had become increasingly worried by James's Roman Catholicism and the part played by his Catholicism in his policy as king. The Scots, from whom, as the last Stuart king to reign, James traced his descent, also objected to James – at least the Protestant Lowlanders did. James thought that Catholic Ireland might help him regain his throne, but his defeat at the Battle of the Boyne in July 1690 ended that hope, and he left Ireland hastily for permanent exile in France.

The English Parliament (strictly, not a parliament but a convention, because there was no king on the throne), proclaimed William and his wife Mary joint sovereigns of England in February 1689, and then proceeded to settle in their own favour the terms governing the relationship between king and parliament. The situation in Scotland was more tricky. Though there was fierce anti-Catholic feeling among devoted Presbyterians in the Lowlands, many of whom had suffered bitterly from the attempts of the Stuart kings in the seventeeth century to impose an episcopalian church rule on them, there was a widespread national feeling that Scotland, still an independent kingdom, did not necessarily have to choose the same king as England had just done; there was also a feeling for the Stuarts as a Scottish line, a feeling especially strong among the Catholics of the Highlands and the Episcopalians who were particularly numerous in the north-east of the country (notably in Aberdeen). So, while the convention parliament of Scotland proclaimed on 11 April 1689 that King James VII had forfeited the Crown of Scotland ('being a profest Papist' and having 'by advice of Evil and Wicked Counsellors invaded the Fundamental Constitution of the Kingdom, and altered it from a Legal, limited Monarchy, to an Arbitrair and Despotick Power') and resolved 'That *William* and *Mary*, King and Queen of *England*, *France* and *Ireland*, Be, and Be Declared King and Queen of *Scotland*', there was at the same time a counter-movement in favour of the deposed and absent James. The leader of this movement was the debonair John Graham of Claverhouse, first Viscount Dundee, hated by the Covenanters for his part in putting down their holy and intolerant extremism, and beloved by the Highland clans for his courage and panache.

Claverhouse was the first active Jacobite, the first to lead a military campaign to restore the exiled James to the throne. When the Estates of Scotland were meeting in their convention at Edinburgh, Claverhouse left the city, collected a Highland army in Lochaber, and prepared to fight for the man he still recognized as his lawful king. When he first left Edinburgh with his fifty troopers all he knew was that he didn't like the Whig atmosphere and the seeming certainty that the Convention would proclaim William and Mary as joint sovereigns. His immediate intention was simply to get out of the hostile city and then consider what was to be done:

> To the Lords of Convention 'twas Claver'se who spoke,
> 'Ere the King's crown shall fall there are crowns to be broke;
> So let each Cavalier who loves honour and me,
> Come follow the bonnet of Bonnie Dundee.' ...
>
> Dundee he is mounted, he rides up the street,
> The bells are rung backward, the drums they are beat;
> But the Provost, douce man, said 'Just e'en let him be,
> The Gude Town is well quit of the Deil of Dundee.' ...

With sour-featured Whigs the Grass Market was pang'd [stuffed]
As if half the West had set tryste to be hang'd;
There was spite in each look, there was fear in each e'e,
As they watched for the bonnets of Bonnie Dundee. . . .

'The air of "Bonnie Dundee" running in my head to-day, I wrote a few verses to it before dinner, taking the key-note from the story of Claverse leaving the Scottish Convention of Estates in 1688–9.' So wrote Walter Scott in his Journal on 22 December 1825, registering the continued appeal for him of Claverhouse's Jacobitism and for the first time transferring the name 'Bonnie Dundee' from the city to the Viscount. But Claverhouse had no romantic appeal for the Convention sitting at Edinburgh. They cited him to appear in his place in Parliament, and required him to disarm, under pain of being declared a traitor. He neither appeared nor disarmed, but went north to gather Highland support and eventually met in battle the government's force under another Highlander, but a Whig one this time, General Hugh Mackay of Scoury (in Sutherland), a veteran officer who had commanded the Scots Brigade in Holland and who now led a mixed Scottish and Dutch force against the enemies of King William. The battle was fought on 27 July 1689, in the picturesque Pass of Killiecrankie. Mackay's forces were unable to resist the wild charge of the Highlanders, who, in their characteristic manner, first came on slowly to draw the fire of the enemy, then fired themselves while the enemy were screwing on their bayonets, and finally threw away their guns and rushed madly on to the foe with drawn broadswords. Claverhouse himself was shot dead while waving on his troops, so that, while his army won, it was a vain victory, since the Jacobite forces were quite ineffective without their brilliant leader.

This was virtually the end of the first Jacobite revolt. But it does not mean that Scotland was now dependably behind William and Mary, nor indeed was England as a whole enthusiastic about the new régime. The 'Glorious Revolution' of 1688 was the work of a resolute and efficient minority, and in general there was more annoyance with James than enthusiasm for William, who was a cold fish with nothing at all of what is now called *charisma*. With skill and imagination James could easily have retained his throne. He lacked the political cunning of his brother Charles II, whom he succeeded. At the end he seems to have given up, fleeing to France against the advice of his friends to stay and face it out, and again after the Battle of the Boyne fleeing precipitately to France, to the disgust of his followers. Yet earlier in life he had shown that he was a man of conspicuous courage. It has been argued that the

3

desertion to the other side of his two daughters – Mary, married to William, and Anne, who was to succeed William as sovereign – so upset him as to destroy his judgment, but this is perhaps a romantic interpretation.

In Scotland, where Jacobitism was mainly nourished for another sixty years, there was simultaneously a great fear of Popery and a detestation of James on religious grounds, especially by the extreme Covenanters of the south-west, and a suspicion that the new king they had brought in would devote himself more to the welfare of his larger and richer kingdom, England, than to the welfare of Scotland. In the 'Articles of Grievances' that the Scottish Convention drew up to present to King William, nationalist grievances against limitation of their freedom as a nation went side by side with religious grievances against Popery. Another grievance was 'the not taking an effectual Course to Repress the Depredations and Robberies by the Highland Clans' – a significant indication of the split between Lowlands and Highlands of which Jacobitism was continually to take advantage. If the new king had read these articles carefully, he would have realized that one certain way of uniting much of Scotland against him would be to co-operate in measures that would exacerbate Scottish national feeling. As we shall see, there was a moment soon after the turn of the century when Lowland Protestant and Highland Catholic, anti-monarchist nationalist and monarchist patriot, came together in a mood of high Scottish feeling against the betrayal of Scottish interests by a monarch and his advisers in London.

Not that the Stuarts had done particularly well by Scotland since James VI of Scotland inherited the throne of Queen Elizabeth in 1603, to become also James I of England. James's great-grandfather, James IV of Scotland, had married the daughter of Henry VII of England in 1502; Henry VII was Elizabeth's grandfather; so, Elizabeth having remained unmarried, the Scottish James became heir to the English throne. Two kingdoms ruled by a single king – it did not augur well for the smaller and poorer of the two. Naturally enough, the king preferred to devote himself to the interests of the larger and richer kingdom. James II of England and VII of Scotland had been twice in Scotland when Duke of York. The first time was in 1680, when his brother Charles II was annoyed at his embarrassing return from Holland, where he was supposed to stay until the end of the session of the English Parliament which wanted to exclude him from the succession since he had declared himself a Roman Catholic in 1672. Charles got him out of the way by appointing him Lord High Commissioner in Scotland. James worked hard at making himself agreeable in Edinburgh, and played golf on Leith Links. (The eighteenth-century Edinburgh historian William Tytler wrote many years later: 'I remember in my youth to have often conversed with an old man named Andrew Dickson, a golf-club maker, who said that when a boy he used to carry the Duke's clubs, and to run before him and announce where the balls fell.') Gilbert Burnet, later Bishop of Salisbury, who was a fair-minded observer of events in the 1680's, wrote that 'The Duke behaved himself upon his first visit to *Scotland* in so obliging a manner, that the Nobility & Gentry who had been so long trodden on by the Duke *Lauderdale* [Charles II's Secretary for Scottish Affairs from 1660 to 1680] and his party, found a very sensible change: So that he gained much on them all.... It was visibly his interest to make that Nation sure to him, and to give them such an essay of his government, as might dissipate all the hard thoughts of him with which the world was possessed: And he pursued this for some time with great temper and as great success. He advised the Bishops to proceed moderately, and to take no notice of Conventicles in houses; ... In matters of Justice he showed an impartial temper, and encouraged propositions relating to trade: And so, considering how much that Nation was set against his Religion, he made a greater progress in gaining upon them than was expected.'

James came again to Scotland as Commissioner in 1681, and was active in passing through the Scottish Parliament an Act to secure his own succession to the throne. Many Scots fought bitterly against this, as they did not want a Catholic king. James was willing to accept a clause establishing the Protestant religion in Scotland, so long as the succession was determined in his favour. But the irony was that, on the question arising how to define Protestantism, it was agreed to define it in a Test Act in terms of the confession of faith enacted by the Scottish Parliament in 1560, 'a book', says Burnet, 'so worn out of use, that scarce any one in the whole Parliament had ever read it'. That confession made it obligatory on the subscribers to 'represse tyrannye' and 'defend the oppressed'. Many in this Parliament thought that James was preparing a tyranny for when he succeeded to the throne, so they found the Act self-contradictory. The powerful Earl of Argyll, who offered James, in Burnet's words, 'all possible assurances that he would adhere to his interest in every thing, except in the matters of Religion' (he was a zealous Protestant), provoked James's implacable enmity. 'The Duke,' says Burnet [i.e. James, Duke of York] 'seeing how great a man the Earl of *Argyle* was in *Scotland*, concluded it was necessary for him either to gain him or to ruin him'. Since he couldn't gain him, he ruined him.

Argyll said that he would subscribe to the newly enacted Test Act so far as it was 'consistent with itself'. This qualification was considered treasonable, and Argyll was brought to trial and condemned to death. But his step-daughter managed to smuggle him in disguise out of Edinburgh Castle, where he was imprisoned awaiting execution, and he escaped to Holland: he was, however, executed later, without a further trial, after returning to Scotland to support Monmouth's rebellion against James in 1685.

So James's two periods of residence in Scotland were not all sweetness and light. He showed no sympathy at all with the Highlands, where later Jacobite support was to be found, and he had nothing whatever in common with the extreme Covenanters, or Cameronians, of the south-west. And his second wife, Mary of Modena, seems to have alienated Scottish sympathy by her snobbish behaviour: she refused, according to one story, to sit down to dinner with the veteran royalist General Thomas Dalyell, on the grounds that it would be beneath her dignity, whereupon the General said: 'Madam, when I last had the privilege of dining with the Emperor, your father was standing behind my chair.' (Her father was Alphonso IV, Duke of Modena.)

Scottish Protestants tended to associate in their minds Popery and arbitrary power, and once James succeeded to the throne in 1685 they were convinced of the correctness of this association. They viewed with the greatest suspicion the Indulgences which he issued 'by our sovereign authority, prerogative royal, and absolute power, which all our subjects are to observe without reserve,' both because they issued from the royal 'prerogative' (an English concept which traditionally had no counterpart in Scotland) and because they afforded complete toleration to Roman Catholics. It is true that successful attempts were made to widen the Indulgences to embrace dissenting Protestants as well as Catholics, but this was generally regarded as a mere device, reluctantly employed by the King to enable him to impose a Catholic tyranny on the country. At the same time it can be maintained with some justice that, in the words of that noted historian of the Jacobite movement Sir Charles Petrie, 'what brought about the downfall of James was his attempt to secure toleration, which was interpreted by his enemies as a circuitous method of securing the return of England [and Scotland] to the Church of Rome'.

There is no reason to suppose that James was a religious bigot, though it would have been more politic if not more moral for him to have concealed his adoption of the Roman Catholic faith, as Charles II had done until he lay on his deathbed. It is true that after he lost his throne and settled down to exile in France he underwent some kind of conversion at the hands of a Cistercian abbot and changed his self-indulgent way of life into one of great austerity. But his life had hitherto been as self-indulgent as his brother's had been, the only difference being, as his brother observed, that his mistresses were so unattractive. He had two wives, the first Protestant and the second Catholic, and among his mistresses were Arabella Churchill (sister of the future Duke of Marlborough) and Catherine Sedley. He had children by both wives and both mistresses but a surviving legitimate son only by Mary of Modena. It was the birth of this son to his Catholic wife on 10 June 1688, thus apparently securing the eventual succession to the throne of another Catholic, that precipitated the revolution which brought in William of Orange and his wife Mary, the Protestant daughter of James's first and Protestant wife. It was widely put about and for some time popularly believed that this son and heir of James, who was christened James Francis Edward, was a fake, smuggled into the Queen's bedroom in a warming pan in order to secure a Catholic succession. But this belief only increased opposition to James.

James's faults as a man were egotism and lack of sensitivity: his numerous marital infidelities caused his wife Mary much suffering. As a king he lacked tact and political understanding. But he was a highly efficient administrator, and Samuel Pepys is only the most important and detailed of many witnesses to his hard work and efficiency as head of the admiralty. He had a fine record as a naval commander. He was a coarser-grained man than his father Charles I (who might have kept his head as his son might have kept his throne if he had shown more tact and imagination) and he did not have his brother's political cunning and social liveliness. He had the Stuart obstinacy without the Stuart charm. Still, he *was* a Stuart, scion of a great Scottish royal house, and it was this fact that made the Jacobite movement possible and which associated Jacobitism so significantly with Scotland.

The origins of the Stuarts were not, however, Scottish. The first Stuart was King Robert II of Scotland (1316–90) who succeeded to the throne in 1371 on the death of his uncle David II. He was the son of Marjory, daughter of Robert Bruce, king and liberator of Scotland, and her husband Walter, Steward of Scotland (hence the name Stuart or Stewart). Now Scotland's great national hero Robert Bruce, who defeated the English King Edward II at the Battle of Bannockburn in 1314 and thus secured Scotland's independence, was himself the descendant of a Norman knight, Robert de Brus, who had come over to England from Normandy in 1066 with William the Conqueror, who granted him lands in Yorkshire. His grandson, Robert de Bruce, frequented the Court of the English King Henry I, where he met the Scottish Prince David. When David succeeded to the Scottish throne, he granted Bruce substantial lands in Annandale, in south-west Scotland. But Bruce repudiated his Scottish allegiance to fight against the Scots with the English, and so forfeited his Scottish estates. His son, however, yet another Robert de Bruce, fought for the Scots, and eventually succeeded to both the English and the Scottish estates of the family. *His* grandson, Robert Bruce, who died in 1245, founded the Bruce family's claim to the Scottish throne by marrying Isabella, daughter of David, Earl of Huntingdon, younger brother of two successive Scottish kings, Malcolm IV and William the Lion. Their son, still Robert Bruce, claimed the throne of Scotland in 1290, though in fact the rival claimant, John Balliol, had a better right for he was descended from an older sister of Isabella. It was now that King Edward I of England was invited to settle the dispute, and chose Balliol. Robert Bruce died in 1304, and his claim was inherited by his son, the great Robert Bruce (1274–1329) who was also Earl of Carrick in view of his father's marriage to the daughter and heir of the last Celtic Earl of Carrick. This Bruce was crowned King of Scotland at Scone in 1306, when he was still in the middle of his epic struggle to free Scotland from English overlordship. Balliol, who had the better claim to the Scottish throne, had submitted to the English king, so that Scottish national feeling was all on the side of Bruce. This is an important point, as it showed that the King of Scotland was the choice of the people, not necessarily the most direct heir.

It was King Robert Bruce's daughter Marjory who married Walter the Steward to found the Stuart dynasty. Walter's family hailed originally from Brittany, his ancestors having held the office of *dapifer* or steward to the archbishops of Dol, near Mont St Michel. (The first of his family to come to Britain was apparently called Flaald, and this gave the opportunity of later Stuart genealogists to identify him with that Fleance, son of Banquo, whom we find mentioned in Shakespeare's *Macbeth*: but this was sheer romancing.) Thus the Bruces were originally Normans and the Stuarts originally Bretons.

The son of Marjory and Walter was Robert II of Scotland, who was succeeded by Robert III (whose troubles and deficiencies as a king are vividly shown in Scott's novel *The Fair Maid of Perth*), who was in turn succeeded in 1406 by the first important Scottish Stuart King, James I. There followed a succession of Stuart kings of Scotland – James II, James III, James IV (killed at the disastrous Battle of Flodden in 1513),

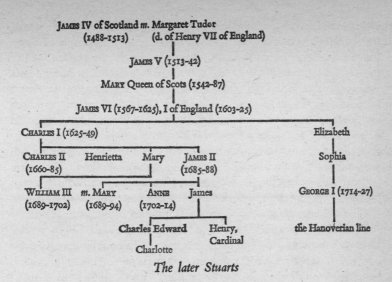

```
JAMES IV of Scotland m. Margaret Tudor
   (1488-1513)        (d. of Henry VII of England)
                    │
              JAMES V (1513-42)
                    │
          MARY Queen of Scots (1542-87)
                    │
       JAMES VI (1567-1625), I of England (1603-25)
        ┌───────────────────────────────────┐
   CHARLES I (1625-49)                    Elizabeth
        │                                    │
   ┌────────┬─────────┬──────────┐        Sophia
CHARLES II  Henrietta  Mary    JAMES II        │
(1660-85)                     (1685-88)    GEORGE I (1714-27)
   │                             │             │
WILLIAM III m. MARY   ANNE    James      the Hanoverian line
(1689-1702) (1689-94) (1702-14)
        Charles Edward    Henry,
              │           Cardinal
          Charlotte
```

The later Stuarts

James V. James V left only a daughter, who became Mary Queen of Scots, but she was dethroned by the emergent anti-French Protestant party in Scotland, in favour of her son, James VI. By this time the Reformation and a variety of political factors had separated an important political group in Scotland from her traditional ally France; this group turned towards a now Protestant England. When James VI inherited Elizabeth's throne in 1603 and came south to become James I of England, he thought of his two kingdoms as bound to unite eventually. But the Civil War, which broke out in the reign of James's son Charles I, brought Scotland into new kinds of conflict with England, and when Cromwell succeeded Charles I as the head of a now non-monarchical English government he thoroughly defeated the Scottish army and forcibly incorporated Scotland with England in a single Commonwealth. Though most Scots regarded this enforced union as 'usurpation', it must be said that Cromwell's men governed Scotland sensibly and justly. General Monk's pacification of the Highlands was achieved with both efficiency and imagination; he showed an understanding of the traditions and sensibilities of the clans.

The restoration of the monarchy in 1660 with the return of Charles II brought an end to the united Commonwealth and a return of the separate kingdom of Scotland. But the problem of how a king of both England and Scotland was to handle his northern kingdom remained: indeed it became more vexatious than ever. Charles ruled Scotland by Commissioners, who represented the policy of the King's ministers in

England or, when Charles was 'going it alone', his own policy, marked by sending his brother as Commissioner. The religious conflicts in Scotland during this period, and the hounding by the government of the more extreme Protestants, the Covenanters who suspected any compromise with the state as Erastianism and the beginning of a return to Rome, is no part of the present story: it is told with great vividness and understanding in Scott's *Old Mortality*. That understanding was lacking in the last Stuart kings, who were interested in Scotland only in so far as their Scottish policy could help to implement their policy in England. They were to learn in adversity the importance of cultivating Scottish national feeling, and they were helped in this by some terrible mistakes made by their successors.

Charles II, leaving no legitimate offspring on his death in 1685, was succeeded by his Catholic brother James, and it took less than four years for James to find himself an exile in France, with his daughter and son-in-law on his throne. He was welcomed in France by Louis XIV, who had his own political reasons for keeping a lively Jacobite movement going as a constant threat to the new régime in Britain. He was given the Chateau of Saint-Germain-en-Laye, overlooking the Seine some thirteen miles west-north-west of Paris, where he could live and hold his exiled court. His wife and baby son were already settled there when he arrived, and Louis XIV was there to greet him, and to grant him an annual pension of 600,000 livres. The quondam King of England was now a pensioner of the King of France.

James long remained confident that he would be recalled by his people, as Charles II had been after the death of Cromwell. Before leaving England he had addressed a letter to the Earl of Middleton, his Secretary of State and strong supporter (who vainly tried to persuade him to stay in England and summon Parliament). 'I have thought fit to withdraw myself,' he wrote, 'but must not tell you where it shall be; if honest and loyal men will declare for me, and stand by me, I shall soon come to them.' Throughout his exile it was clear that he had learned nothing and forgotten nothing. After the Battle of La Hogue in May 1692, when a French squadron was defeated by the British navy in the English Channel, under the very eyes of James (who, as former head of the British navy, could not help admiring the conduct of what were now his enemies: 'none but my brave English could do so brave an action,' he exclaimed), Louis gave up active attempts to restore James. Expected revolts in England had failed to materialize, and Louis would do better to oppose England on the Continent. But James still refused to compromise. He spurned William's suggestion, made in July 1696, that in return for James's recognition of William's right to reign until his death, William would recognize James's son as his heir. He refused to be a candidate for the throne of Poland on the death of John Sobieski on the grounds that it would prejudice the restoration of his regal position in Britain. When, by the Treaty of Ryswick signed in September 1697 between France on the one hand and England, Spain and the Netherlands on the other, Louis XIV acknowledged William as *de facto* King of England and so bound himself to abandon the cause of the restoration of the Stuarts, it was clear that James's chance of restoration with the help of France was over. Up till now his claim had been politically useful to Louis, so that, while being the French King's pensioner, he could with some justice claim really to be his ally. Now he was his pensioner merely.

James realized well before his death that the struggle for restoration would have to be carried on by his son. As early as 1692 he drew up written instructions for him. They began, significantly:

> Kings being accountable for none of their actions but to God and themselves, ought to be more cautious and circumspect than those who are in lower stations, and as tis the duty of Subjects to pay true allegiance to him, and to observe his Laws, so a King is bound by his office to have a fatherly love and care of them; ...

There followed advice about religion:

> In the first place serve God in all things as becomes a good Christian and a zealous Catholick of the Church of Rome, which is the only true Catholick and Apostolick Church, and let no human consideration of any kind prevaile with you to depart from her; remember always that Kings, Princes and all the great ones of the world, must one day give account of all their actions before the great tribunal where every one will be judged according to his doings. ...

He went on to advise his son to 'secure his own right' as a precondition of being able to protect his subjects; 'therefore preserve your prerogative, but disturbe not the Subjects in their property, nor conscience, remember the great precept, Do as you would be done to, for that is the law and the Prophets'. He should not oppress or torment his people with vexatious suits or projects; he should be a father to them. He must not engage in foreign wars in order to enlarge his territories, but live in peace and quiet with all his neighbours. 'Endeavour to settle Liberty of Conscience by a Law.'

This last piece of advice sounds very enlightened, and up to a point it is. True, he adds later: 'Be never without a considerable body of Catholicke troops without which you cannot be safe, then will people thanke you for Liberty of Conscience'. But he also observes: 'Our Blessed Saviour whipt people out of the Temple, but I never heard he commanded any should be forced into it; 'tis a particular grace and favour that God Almighty shews to any, who he enlightens as so to embrasse the true Religion, 'tis by gentlenesse, instruction, and good example, people are to be gained and not frightened into it, and I make no doubt if once Liberty of Conscience be well fixed, many conversions will ensue, which is a truth too many of the Protestants are persuaded of, Church of England men as well as others, and so will require more care and dexterity to obtaine it.'

He then goes on to warn his son strongly against 'the forbidden love of Women', and to admit 'with shame and confusion' that he himself has erred grievously on that score. He expatiates at great length on this 'fatal Vice', to which, he adds, 'the late King my Brother had the misfortune to be much addicted'. A King must not be extravagant and learn to 'live within his Reveneu'. He should try to improve trade, and maintain mastery of the sea, without which 'England cannot be safe'. He then proceeds to talk about Scotland, in a passage which is particularly interesting in view of the part Scotland was to play in the history of the Jacobite movement:

As to our Antient Kingdom of Scotland, take all care to let no alterations be made in the Government of that Kingdom, they will stand by the Crown, and the Crown must stand by them for tho there has been Rebellions and Revolutions, as well as in other Countrys, the body of the Nobility and Gentry, and the Gen: of the Commons are very Loyal and Monarchical especially the Com: be North Forth and all the Highlanders, except the Campbells; the rest of Scotland being the only place where there are numbers amongst the Commons of ridged Presbyterians, and Enthusiasts and feild Conventiclers, the first of which are the most dangerous, and will be allways bitter enemys to the Monarky and so ought to be well observed, and kept out of any share of the Government; the others, tho now and then troublesome, are lesse to be feared, hardly a Gentleman amongst them, and of so extravagant principles as they can never agree amongst themselves.

He goes on to advise his son to beware of any who propose the union of England and Scotland. 'Tis the true interest of the Crown to keep that Kingdom [Scotland] separat from England, and to be governed by their own laws and constitutions.' Later, after the Union of England and Scotland in 1707, it became a normal part of the Jacobite programme to redress the grievances caused by the Union and to restore the ancient rights and privileges of Scotland. But James never really understood how Scottish national feeling could be harnessed to the Jacobite cause. Still less did he understand national sentiment in Ireland. In view of the feeling for James among some Irish Catholics today (comparable to the Orangemen's feeling for William), it is worth quoting from what he says about Ireland in this document:

> Great care must be taken to civilise the ancient familys, by having the Sons of the Cheef of them bred up in England, even at the charge of the Crown, when they have not where with all out of their estate to do it, by which means they will have greater dependance on the Crown, and by degrees be weaned from their natural hatred against the English, be more civilised, and learne to improve their Estats, by making plantations and improving their Land as the English and Scots have done wheresoever they have settled; this with the charge the Crown should be at in setting up Scholes, to teach the Children of the old Natives English, would by degrees weare out the Irish language, which would be for the advantage of the body of the Inhabitants, . . .

> None but trusty men ought to be put into the garrisons, which need be but few, as Kingsale, Duncannon, Galloway, London Derry, Athlone and Charlemont, which last place should be enlarged to serve for magazine for all the North.

> 'Tis not safe to lett any of the Natives of Ireland be governors of these above named places, nor to have any troops in them but English, Scots or Strangers, not to tempte temper, and easily led by their Cheefs and Clergy, and bear with great impatience the English yoak, and one cannot beat it into their heads, that several of the Os. and Macks, who were forfited for Rebelling in King James the firsts time, and before, ought to be keept out of their Estates and will allways be ready to rise in arms against the English, and endeavour to bring in Strangers to support them. . . . No Native to be Lord Lieut. nor no Englishman that has an Estate in that Kingdom or great relations there, to be changed every three yeares, to buy no land there.

So far as the Irish were concerned, it was clear that it would have made no difference who won the Battle of the Boyne. As for Scotland, her role in the prosecution of the Stuart cause becomes extremely interesting after James's death and the death of William, which followed soon after in March 1702. To understand that role, we must look at what happened to Scotland in William's reign and in the reign of his successor, Queen Anne.

CHAPTER TWO

Glencoe and Darien

WHEN James II and VII was in Ireland in 1689, in the vain hope of winning back his crown with the help of an army of Irish Catholics, he sent an appeal to the Highland clans for help against 'the oppression of antimonarchial and ill men'. What cause had he to expect the gratitude of the Highland clansmen? From one point of view it can be argued that he had no cause at all. Ever since James VI had inherited the throne of England the Stuarts had neglected their northern kingdom and as far as the Highlands went they tended to regard the clansmen as wild trouble-makers who required suppressing. At the same time an understanding of the causes of the wild behaviour of the Highlanders can help us to see why, in spite of everything, their loyalty to the House of Stuart outlasted that of any other section of the population of Britain. The trouble with the Highlands was that a feudal system of land tenure, with the accompanying rights of the person holding the land, was superimposed on an older patriarchal social system in which personal status and hereditary familial relationships meant everything. The feudal system came up from the south and challenged the traditional Highland clan system; the feudal superior, with his rights of feudal jurisdiction, was not necessarily the patriarchal chief, and feudal charters granting land ownership were suspect in the eyes of clansmen who had been brought up to believe in the rights of kindred rather than of legal ownership. A hereditary monarch was the natural superior of a clansman living in a patriarchal society, while a feudal land-owner coming between him and the monarch, represented a kind of superiority that he found puzzling. As a modern historian of the clan system has put it: 'Freedom from existing superiorities or feudal jurisdictions, and resistance to the establishment of new ones, were the constant preoccupation of highland diplomacy; and the ambition of this freedom became one of the mainsprings of highland loyalty to the monarchy'. There were some clan chiefs who used devices of feudal law to gain possession of new territory – notably the house of Argyll – and these on the whole accepted the Revolution of 1689 and did not remain loyal to the Stuarts. But for most clansmen, whether they came out actively in rebellion after 1689 or not, the Stuarts were the legitimate hereditary kings of Scotland whose claims they could understand in the light of their own familial organization. The clans tended to see James VII as the King who understood their social organization and who stood for a direct relationship between king and chief against the oppressive mediate figure of the feudal superior. Whether James would have done anything about this if he had not lost his kingdom remains a matter of conjecture.

In dealing with the clansmen, earlier Scottish kings had often adopted the old Celtic custom of taking hostages: that is, a member of a chief's family would be kept at the King's court as security for the clan's good behaviour. This provided some kind of historical authority for the later detaining in Edinburgh of influential clansmen suspected of Jacobite activities. Another traditional policy was to restore direct clan dependence on the monarch by the buying up of feudal superiorities: William III himself at one time proposed this, though unaware of all the implications. But William was in any case suspect in Highland eyes as he was not the legitimate hereditary monarch. His wife, of course, was a Stuart, but the clansmen did not recognize succession through the female line and indeed had much reason to complain of feudal manoeuvrings whereby the daughter of a clan chief who had no sons was married off to a stranger who thus acquired superiority over the clan lands. As far as the Highlands were concerned, William started out with built-in disadvantages. But they were not insuperable, until he made them so by his own policy or at least by his acquiescence in the policy of others.

William had little real interest in or knowledge of Scotland, which for him was a troublesome and backward country in the northern part of his new realm; the sooner it was united to England the better. When the Scottish Estates were meeting at Edinburgh to consider the question of the succession to the Scottish throne after James's departure, William had addressed a letter to them, of which the second paragraph runs:

> We are glad to find, that so many of the Nobility and Gentry, when here at *London*, were so much inclined to an Union of both Kingdoms, and that they did look upon it as one of the best Means for procuring the Happiness of these Nations, and settling of a lasting Peace amongst them, which would be advantagious to both, they living in the same Island, having the same Language, and the

same common interest of Religion and Liberty, especially at this Juncture, when the enemies of both, are so restless, endeavouring to make, and increase Jealousies and Divisions; which they will be ready to improve to their own Advantage, and the Ruin of *Britain*; We being of the same Opinion, as to the Usefulness of this Union, and having nothing so much before Our Eyes, as the Glory of GOD, the Establishment of the Reformed Religion, and the Peace and Happiness of these Nations, are resolved to use Our utmost Endeavours in advancing every thing which may conduce to the effectuating the same.

Quite apart from the fact that much of the Highlands did not have the same language as England, but spoke Gaelic, this virtuous-sounding paragraph made no attempt to address itself to specific Scottish problems. The enemies to whom William refers are as much the French as the supporters of James (who of course included the French): one of his principal objectives as King of England and Scotland was to use the power and influence this position gave him to prosecute his own long-standing quarrel with Louis XIV. True, his reference to the reformed religion was calculated to please Scottish Presbyterians, and in due course the Scottish Parliament passed an 'Act Ratifying the Confession of Faith, and settling Presbyterian Church-Government' (an enormously long act full of biblical references and theological definitions) which restored the Presbyterian establishment first set up in 1560 and consistently refused under the Stuarts. (It was James I and VI who had said: 'No bishop, no king,' and his son, grandson and great-nephew all agreed with him that a non-episcopal church structure was a threat to the monarchy.) Perhaps he did not know, or did not consider it relevant if he did know, that a considerable part of the Highlands was inhabited by Catholics.

When 'the Estates of the Kingdom of Scotland', as they called themselves, otherwise the Convention, offered the crown to William and Mary jointly they had included in the declaration a 'Claim of Right', setting forth 'their ancient Rights and Liberties', and followed this up with 'Articles of Grievances represented by the Estates of the Kingdom of *Scotland*, to be Redressed in Parliament', curiously enough neither acceptance of the rights nor promise to redress the grievances was made a condition of the offer of the Crown. The oath administered to William and Mary was much more general. Most of it was a verbose and imprecise definition of the religion 'now Received and Preached within the Realm of *Scotland*', which the monarchs had to promise to maintain. The imprecision was the more surprising because the oath concluded with the promise to 'be careful to Root out all Hereticks and Enemies to the true worship of GOD, that shall be Convict by the True Kirk of GOD, of the foresaid Crimes out of Our Lands and Empire of *Scotland*'. William demurred at this, saying that he would not be a persecutor, but he was assured that the words were a mere matter of form, and so he signed. The oath also involved a promise 'to preserve and keep inviolate the Rights and Rents, with all just privileges of the Crown of *Scotland*'. The officers sent down from Scotland to administer the oath to William and Mary were instructed simply to read over the Claim of Right to them and to present the list of Grievances to the King, for him to read at leisure and presumably to act on or not as he thought fit. These officers, the Earl of Argyll, Sir James Montgomery of Skelmorlie and Sir John Dalrymple, though they represented respectively the three estates of the realm, the peers, the barons and the burgesses, between them represented only one section, though an influential one, of Scottish opinion. They were all Presbyterian and Whigs, though Montgomery later went over to the Jacobites.

Montgomery's defection to the Jacobites indicates the precariousness of William's hold even on Scotsmen of impeccable Whig Protestant credentials. Indeed, it was precisely because Montgomery had been a strong supporter of the Covenanters (he had been imprisoned for harbouring Covenanters in 1684) that William preferred a more moderate Presbyterian as his Scottish Secretary of State, and he selected the Earl of Melville, to Montgomery's great disappointment. Montgomery refused the consolation prize of the office of Justice-Clerk and founded an opposition political group in Edinburgh called 'The Club' which at first consisted both of Whigs disappointed of office under William and of Scottish patriots worried about the preservation of Scottish rights and privileges, and later had dealings with Jacobites also. In this combination of dissident Whigs, Jacobite Tories and Scottish nationalists there emerged the possibility of an inter-party Scottish Jacobitism which was to give new heart to the Jacobite movement.

The Jacobites rubbed their hands over any evidence of Whig dissatisfaction with the Dutch King whom they (the Whigs) had brought in. William's policy in the Highlands did not help him there either. George Mackenzie, first Viscount Tarbat, who had been a royalist during Charles II's exile and had been the King's chief minister in Scotland from 1682 to 1688 but who had accepted William and joined the Williamite Scottish government in 1689, was anxious to prove his ability to pacify the Highlands in order to show his capacity for high office in the government. Melville, the Secretary of State for Scotland, had helped to persuade William to pardon Tarbat's earlier pro-Stuart activities for he too needed to show what he could do in the Highlands and needed Tarbat's help in this. For Tarbat had a plan for buying peace from the Highland chiefs by distributing among them a sum of 'five or six thousand pounds' which William professed to be ready to supply for this purpose. But Claverhouse's success in raising a Highland army for James prevented this plan being put into execution. John Campbell, first Earl of Breadalbane, another supporter of the House of Stuart who had submitted to William, who had a stormy career in the Highlands and knew the country and its people, took over Tarbat's suggestion on the understanding that he himself would deal with the chiefs and distribute the money. He obtained from King William a commission 'to meet, treat and correspond with any of the Highlanders in order to reduce them to submission and obedience'. But William delayed in sending the money, and Breadalbane, who was deeply mistrusted both in the Highlands and in Edinburgh, dragged his feet. Jacobite activity as well as miscellaneous raiding continued in the Highlands. Then early in 1691 William once again commissioned Breadalbane to treat with the Highland chiefs. By this time Sir John Dalrymple, the Master of Stair (later Viscount, then Earl of Stair), was joint Secretary of State for Scotland with Melville, and shortly afterwards he managed to oust Melville and keep the secretaryship for himself alone. Dalrymple and Breadalbane worked closely together, not out of any friendship but because each thought the other could be of help in his personal ambitions: Dalrymple wanted the pacification of the Highlands as a preliminary to the complete union of England and Scotland, while Breadalbane wanted to make his branch of the Campbells the most powerful and important in the country.

Breadalbane met the chiefs at Achallader in Argyllshire at the end of June 1691, and he talked confidentially with them as a fellow Highland chief. He succeeded in getting them to promise to refrain from hostilities until the following first of October. Thomas Buchan and Sir George Barclay who described themselves as 'General Officers of King James the Seventh his Forces within the Kingdom of Scotland' signed an agreement on 30 June to refrain from 'all acts of hostility or depradation' both in Scotland and England until 1 October, provided that 'no acts of hostility or depradation' were committed against any of the Jacobites whom they had been leading. Breadalbane in his turn signed a statement that in the light of the undertaking given by the Chieftains of the Clans to refrain from acts of hostility and depredation he certified that the officers and Chieftains had signed such an undertaking and in return declared that 'it's most necessary, just, and reasonable that no acts of hostility ... or depradations be committed upon the said officers, or any of their party whom they do command, or upon the Chieftains, or their kinsmen, friends, tenants or followers' until 1 October. The idea was that by 1 October the chiefs loyal to the exiled James could obtain from him an agreement to absolve them of the allegiance they had previously sworn to him.

One man who remained highly suspicious of Breadalbane was Alasdair Macdonald of Glencoe, commonly known as MacIain, twelfth Chief of Clan Iain Abrach, an immensely tall red-headed man, now in his sixties, who had fought with his clan for Claverhouse at Killiecrankie. His clan had a long record of depradations and bloody raids not only against the Lowlands (which were regarded as a legitimate target by most Highlanders) but against other Highland clans, among whom the Campbells figured conspicuously. At least from the sixteenth century they had been giving trouble by their raiding. They had fought for King Charles in the Civil War less out of loyalty to the Stuarts than for their own hand, but it was as raiders, pillagers and cattle-lifters that they were most widely known. Time and again they had been proclaimed as such by different governments. It may be that when MacIain and Breadalbane faced each other the bitter knowledge of generations of Macdonald depradations against Campbell territory prevented Breadalbane from exerting his customary double-faced charm, but whatever the reason, the fact is that the two men quarrelled bitterly, and MacIain went home with his sons without signing anything. There were other chiefs who also refrained from signing.

Breadalbane gave no account of the money he had been given to distribute among the chiefs, and when asked about it replied simply: 'The money is spent, the Highlands are quiet, and this is the only way of accounting between friends'. Many believed that he kept much of the money himself, but this persistent belief has never been proved, and it is now thought that William in fact never sent the money, or the bulk of it, at all. Anyway, Breadalbane seemed both sure of himself and pleased with himself, and even when it was discovered that he had secured the agreement with the Jacobite chiefs by some secret provisions which allowed for a Jacobite rising if William went abroad and actually committed Breadalbane himself, with a thousand of his men, to join such a rising if William and Mary did not agree to the articles proposed in the main agreement, he managed to survive. He stoutly denied the charge, alleging that it was a malicious invention, and William, who had no illusions about the nature of politics, does not seem to have been particularly disturbed when the matter was brought to his attention. The question of who was double-crossing whom remained for later developments to clarify.

Messengers were sent by the Jacobites to James at St Germain, explaining the nature of the agreement that had been made between the chiefs and Breadalbane and asking him to release them from their allegiance. Time was of the essence, because on 17 August King William issued a statement declaring that it was his gracious pleasure 'to pardon, indemnify and restore all that have been in arms who shall take the oath of allegiance before the 1st day of January next'. William was also willing to absolve the Highlanders from crimes other than Jacobitism of which they stood accused: a specific crime officially pardoned in this way on 20 August was 'a slaughter' committed by MacIain of Glencoe and a cousin of his. James hesitated and dithered, and it was not until 12 December 1691 that he issued a letter to 'General-Major Thomas Buchan' authorizing him to allow his loyal subjects in Scotland 'to do what may be most for their own and your safety'. It was brought to Scotland in haste by Major Duncan Menzies, who arrived in Edinburgh on 21 December, almost dead from exhaustion. Messages were sent north to inform as many of the clans as possible.

Chiefs loyal to the exiled James would not be able to take the oath of allegiance to William before James's letter of discharge arrived. As the autumn wore on and no news arrived from St Germain, many of the chiefs became restless and suspicious. At the beginning of December Dalrymple became sole Secretary of State for Scotland. He contemplated the situation in the Highlands with frustration and anger. There were chiefs who had not yet taken the oath of allegiance; the deadline was drawing near; someone had to be made an example of. He thought of the Macdonalds of Glencoe, and took a savage pleasure in contemplating severe measures against them. The nature of these measures was suggested to him by Breadalbane: writing to Breadalbane, Dalrymple talked of 'your scheme for mauling them' (the recalcitrant chiefs).

By 1 January 1692 most of the chiefs had taken the oath of allegiance, after a proclamation announcing 'the utmost extremity of the law' against all who failed to meet the deadline. They came in one by one and subscribed to the oath before the Sheriff of the county, as by law required. But some kept delaying and one of these was Macdonald of Glencoe. Dalrymple, worried lest he might be baulked of his plan of 'mauling' Highlanders as more and more chiefs subscribed, was glad to see MacIain holding out. His would be a most suitable clan for mauling, with their record of marauding and killing.

MacIain, having heard of James's letter of release, turned up at last, but at the eleventh hour. The weather was bitterly cold, with heavy snow falling, when the old man made his way across the wild country that separates Glencoe from the River Lochy to present himself before Colonel Sir John Hill, the veteran military governor at Inverlochy. It was the very end of December 1691. He had come, he told Hill, to take the oath. Hill, who understood the clans and was sympathetic to them, was astonished. Didn't MacIain know that the oath had to be subscribed to before the Sheriff of his county, Argyllshire? He would have to go to Sir Colin Campbell of Ardkinglass, Sheriff of Argyll, at Inveraray. So on 31 December MacIain set out in bitter winter weather on the difficult journey from Inverlochy to Inveraray. He was arrested by government troops on the way, and held for twenty-four hours. He finally arrived at Inveraray on 2 January, to find that the Sheriff was on the other side of Loch Fyne, at Ardkinglass, still celebrating the New Year with his family. He returned on 5 January, and, after having soundly berated MacIain for coming so late – it was now well past the deadline – administered the oath to him the following day on MacIain's entreating him with tears to do so and promising future loyalty to the government on the part of all his people.

Meanwhile, Dalrymple and Breadalbane were both in London, discussing punitive action in the Highlands. Dalrymple prepared instructions for King William to sign. To the Privy Council of Scotland: 'We do consider it indispensable for the well of that our kingdom to apply the necessary severities of law.' To Sir Thomas Livingstone, commander of the government forces at Cromdale: 'You are hereby authorized to march our troops which are now posted at Inverlochy and Inverness, and to act against these Highland rebels who have not taken the benefit of our indemnity, by fire and sword and all manner of hostility; . . .' The King read and signed both documents. On 16 January Dalrymple brought further instructions for King William's signature. Glengarry (who had also delayed taking the oath of allegiance) was to be promised 'entire indemnity for his life and fortune, upon the delivering of his house and arms, and taking the oath of allegiance', but if MacIain and his clan could be separated from the rest it would be 'a proper vindication of the public justice to extirpate that sept of thieves'. Dalrymple heard of MacIain's belated submission on 30 January, and wrote to Livingstone that he was 'glad that Glencoe did not come in within the time prescribed'. He wanted them totally destroyed, not just their cattle harried and their houses burned but the whole tribe 'rooted out and cut off'. He wrote to Colonel Hill at Inverlochy about the Glencoe affair: 'let it be secret and sudden'.

The man put in charge of the sudden and secret rooting out and cutting off of all the Macdonalds of Glencoe was Robert Campbell of Glenlyon, a sixty-year-old impoverished drunkard whose land had previously been raided by the Macdonalds. The actual massacre was planned by Major Robert Duncanson of the Argyll Regiment and Lieutenant-Colonel James Hamilton who was second-in-command to Colonel Sir John Hill and Deputy Governor of Fort William. Unlike Hill, he had no sympathy with the Macdonalds and their like, and Dalrymple dealt directly with him rather than with his more humane superior. On 12 February Major Duncanson wrote to Captain Robert Campbell of Glenlyon a letter which began: 'You are hereby ordered to fall upon the rebels, the MacDonalds of Glencoe, and to put all to the sword under seventy'. This was to be done 'at five of the clock precisely'. 'This is by the King's special command, for the good and safety of the country, that these miscreants be cut off root and branch.' By this time two companies of the Earl of Argyll's Regiment, under the command of Robert Campbell of Glenlyon, were already quartered in Glencoe. They had arrived on 1 February, saying that they came as friends and wanted quarters till the weather improved, since the fort was full. In spite of the suspicion between MacIain's men and the Campbells, MacIain welcomed the troops with Highland hospitality. They were his guests, and were to be treated as such: this was a matter of sacred honour among Highlanders, Campbells and Macdonalds alike.

At five o'clock on the morning of 12 February, the guests turned on their hosts with the intention of murdering every single one of them. MacIain himself, being awakened at that early hour with the news that the soldiers had to leave and wanted to say goodbye, hastily got out of bed and started to dress so that he could give a parting dram to Lieutenant Lindsay, the officer who had called ostensibly to take a kindly leave. He was shot dead in the act of putting on his trews. Everything was indeed 'secret and sudden'. Men, women and children were shot and bayoneted. But the Macdonalds of Glencoe were not in fact 'rooted out and cut off'. In the cold darkness of the winter morning many escaped into the snowy hills. Thirty-eight was the figure finally reported as killed, which was no more than about a tenth of the Glencoe Macdonalds.

This was the infamous Massacre of Glencoe, suggested by Breadalbane, obsessively planned by Dalrymple, approved (however unthinkingly) by King William. It may have cowed a part of the Highlands for the time being, but it was a gift to the Jacobites. The Highlands, which had known much bloody inter-clan warfare, were in some respects less shocked than the Lowlands, in spite of the fact that most Lowlanders regarded the Highland clans as an incorrigible race of cattle-lifters and depredators. The Scottish Parliament held an inquiry, the report of which blamed Dalrymple and others and laid down the principle that even in the face of absolute commands of a superior officer 'no command against the laws of nature is binding', a principle that was to be reiterated in a later age at Nuremberg. But nobody was punished. William himself, however, could not altogether shake free of guilt in the matter, and his chance of showing that the new order was more understanding and compassionate in Highland affairs than the old was lost for ever.

The most guilty men in the Massacre of Glencoe were Scotsmen, so there was no question of its uniting Scottish national feeling against England. It was another and more wide-reaching mistake in King William's policy with regard to Scotland that went far towards achieving such a unity. This was the affair of 'The Company of Scotland Trading to Africa and the Indies'. It began very promisingly. Scotland had benefited in trade under the Cromwellian union, but on the Restoration, particularly after the passing of the English Navigation Acts in 1660 and 1663 which excluded Scotland from any participation in England's profitable commerce with Asia, Africa and America, these benefits disappeared and Scotland felt herself ill-used. The powerful East India Company jealously guarded its rights and privileges not only against Scottish competition but also against any attempt to form a rival company in England. Perhaps a company based in Scotland, established by act of the Scottish Parliament, would enable Englishmen and Scotsmen together to break the East India Company's monopoly. Already in 1693 the Scottish Parliament had passed an Act for the encouragement of Scottish trade; now in 1695 it passed an 'Act for a Company Trading to Africa and the Indies':

> Our Sovereign Lord taking into his Consideration, that by an Act past in this present Parliament, Intituled, *Act for encouraging of Foreign Trade*, His Majesty for improvement thereof, Did, with Advice and Consent of the Estates of Parliament, Statute and Declare, That Merchants more or fewer may Contract and enter into such Societies and Companies, for carrying on of Trade ... to the East and West *Indies*, the *Streights*, and to trade in the *Mediterranean*, or upon the Coast of *Africa*, or in the *Northern* Parts, ... Which Societies and Companies being contracted and entred into ... His Majesty

... did allow and approve, giving and granting to them and each of them, all Powers, Rights and Privileges, as to their Persons, Rules and Orders ... And His Majesty understanding that several Persons as well Foreigners as Natives of this Kingdom, are willing to engage themselves with great Sums of Money in an *American*, *African* and *Indian* Trade to be exercised in and from this Kingdom, if enabled and encouraged thereunto, by the Concessions, Powers and Privileges needful and usual in such Cases: Therefore, ... his Majesty ... Doth hereby make and constitute [here come the names of a number of prominent Scotsmen and of a number of Scottish and English merchants living in London] with such others as shall joyn with them ... shall admit and joyn into their Joynt stock and Trade, who shall all be Repute, as if herein originally insert to be one Body incorporate, and a free Incorporation with perpetual Succession, by the name of *The Company of* Scotland *Trading to* Africa *and the* Indies: ...

The Act gave the new company many privileges, including a permanent monopoly in Scotland of trade with Asia and Africa and a thirty-one-year monopoly in America. For twenty-one years all goods imported by the company except sugar and tobacco were to be duty-free. The King himself was to intervene to obtain redress if any foreign state inflicted injury on the company. A capital of £600,000 was fixed, with half assigned to England, where the required £300,000 was quickly subscribed. Everything seemed to be going swimmingly, and the economic prospects for Scotland looked magnificent. But the supporters of the new company had reckoned without the English vested interests, notably the East India Company. Their power was soon manifested. As soon as news of the Scottish company was known in England, the House of Lords drew up an address to the King pointing out 'the great prejudice, inconvenience, and mischiefs' that the Act of the Scottish Parliament would entail for English traders. On 17 December representatives of both Lords and Commons waited on the King to present the address. 'I have been ill served in Scotland,' William replied, 'but I hope some remedy may yet be found to meet the inconvenience that may arise from the Act.' He claimed to believe that the Scots had jumped the gun by incorporating the company's charter in the Act instead of waiting for him to grant a patent and that the company had disregarded certain limitations they had been warned about by James Johnstone, who had been Secretary of State for Scotland since 1692. Johnstone was now dismissed as Secretary and the Marquis of Tweeddale was simultaneously dismissed as Commissioner, to show the King's displeasure about the new company (though he had officially approved the Act that set it up) as a sop to English commercial feeling. Now that it was made clear that both the King and the Lords and Commons of England opposed the new company, the English subscribers hastened to withdraw their share of the capital. What had begun as a promising Anglo-Scottish venture was now reduced to being a purely Scottish venture, desperately in need of capital.

Scottish national feeling was deeply affronted at this deliberate attempt by the English Parliament to strangle Scottish trade. In anger and pride the Scots determined to go it alone, and decided to raise the amount of capital to be subscribed in Scotland from £300,000 to £400,000. Incredibly, this poor country raised that sum, subscribers straining to contribute every penny they could, both to show the English that they could do it and in the confident expectation of eventual rich returns. A further £200,000 was still needed. They tried to raise it in Amsterdam, but the Dutch, having their own East India trade to protect, put a stop to that. They then tried Hamburg, where subscribers were tempted by prospects held out by the company. But again they had reckoned without English commercial jealousy. Sir Paul Rycaut, English Resident at Hamburg, was determined to prevent the Scottish company from raising money in that city. 'I hope', he declared, 'with God's grace and help so to manage this businesse that the businesse of the Scotch East India Co. shall get no footing in my province.' He went so far as to send (in French) a 'Memorial' to the Senate of the City of Hamburg assuring them that if they allowed the recently arrived 'Commissioners from an Indian Company in Scotland' (so runs the official English translation) 'to open to themselves a Commerce and Trade in these Parts' this would be regarded by King William 'as an Affront to his Royal Authority' which 'he would not fail to resent'. As a result the Scottish representatives had to leave Hamburg empty-handed. Rycaut appeared to be a bit nervous about Scottish reactions to his manoeuvre, and he hastened to assure his master in England, Secretary of State Sir William Trumbull, that he had the King behind him: 'but you knowing how well I am fortifyed and warranted by his Majesties command, I feare not their menaces'. The Scots in vain petitioned King William to repair the damage done by Rycaut to a company formed under an Act that had royal approval.

Shut off by English manoeuvring from trading in Africa, India and America, and prevented by the English from raising money outside Scotland, the company decided on another scheme, more limited in immediate scope but (they believed) boundless in its possibilities. This was to found a trading colony on the Isthmus of Darien, which connects North and South America and separates the Caribbean Sea from the Pacific Ocean. The Scottish-born financial wizard William Paterson had long dreamed of such a project: he saw the Isthmus as a natural centre of world trade, drawing on both east and west and north and south, and his vision of an expanding Scottish community thriving there and producing enormous wealth for Scotland was eagerly accepted throughout the country. Even though the territory was claimed by Spain, it was thought that by gaining the good will of the native inhabitants there would be no trouble from that quarter. The colony was to be called 'Caledonia', in honour of the mother country.

A first expedition of three armed vessels and two tenders left Leith harbour amid scenes of great enthusiasm on 14 July 1698. But from the start things went wrong. A terrible error had been made in the matter of provisioning. And soon after their arrival early in November a circular letter sent by the English government to all their colonial officials asking them to ensure that no supplies reached the Scottish colonists prevented more provisions from being obtained. Then the Spaniards asserted their claim to the territory, a claim supported by the English government for their own reasons. Ill, under-nourished and under attack from Spain, the survivors left Darien in June 1699. But news of their misfortunes had not yet reached Scotland, which had sent a second expedition of two ships, with three hundred new colonists and abundant stores, in May. When they reached Darien they found the settlement deserted. One ship and her cargo were destroyed by fire; the other went on to Jamaica where most of the colonists died of fever. A third expedition set out in September and was much troubled by divided counsels. Another ship arrived in February 1700, bringing not only provisions but its captain, Alexander Campbell, an experienced soldier who decided to anticipate the threatened Spanish attack by attacking first. But though the colonists (ably assisted by the Indians) won, a Spanish fleet soon arrived to cut off the colony. Food, water and ammunition ran low, and people died daily of fever. At length, on 30 March, honourable terms were offered by the Spaniards and the colonists were allowed to sail off in their own ships 'with colours flying and drums beating'. None of these four ships ever reached Scotland: three sank in a storm and the fourth, putting into Cartagena after springing a leak, fell into the hands of Spain. Those on board were sentenced to death as pirates but, prodded by Lord Seafield (who had succeeded Johnstone as Secretary of State for Scotland), William interceded with Spain for their release. But William did nothing else to help the Darien colonists or the Scottish company, and flatly refused to approve an Act asserting the Scottish colonists' right to settle in Darien.

The utter failure of the Darien scheme caused enormous indignation in Scotland, where all the misfortunes of the colonists were attributed to English malice. William, who already bore the onus of Glencoe, now had this new source of unpopularity. Some Scotsmen, and many Englishmen, now believed that the only way to solve Scotland's economic problems was to bring about a union of England and Scotland into a single country and so remove English discrimination against Scottish trade. But for very many Scotsmen England was now demonstrably the enemy, and association with England only meant increasing Scottish humiliation. There now developed a struggle in Scotland between unionists and nationalists. If the unionists were to win, disgruntled nationalists, whatever the differences among them in religion and constitutional ideas, might turn to the King Over the Water.

CHAPTER THREE

'Farewell thou ancient Kingdom'

QUEEN ANNE succeeded to the throne on 8 March 1702. In England, the Declaration of Rights of 1689 had settled the crown on her after William and Mary and their children (but there were no children, and Mary had died in 1694), while in Scotland the Claim of Right of the same year had similarly named her as inheritor of the 'Crown and Royal Dignity' of the Kingdom of Scotland after William and Mary and any children of Mary. The English Parliament had gone further, after the death in 1700 of the only one of Queen Anne's numerous children to survive infancy: by the Act of Settlement of 1701 the Crown of England was settled on Sophia, Electress of Hanover, and her descendants. Sophia was the daughter of the beautiful and unfortunate Elizabeth, Queen of Bohemia, daughter of James VI of Scotland and I of England and once the toast of England. Scotland was not involved in the English Act of Settlement: so far as Scotland's Parliament was concerned, the succession after Anne still remained open. It at once became a major objective of English politicians to make sure that Scotland would permanently have the same sovereign as England, and the most certain way to achieve this was an 'incorporating union', as it was called, which would bring the two countries together in a single political unit in which England, as the larger, richer and more powerful country, would always call the tune. To a considerable extent England already called the tune, for the Queen's ministers in Scotland were appointed by her on the advice of English politicians. But the Scottish Parliament still remained.

Queen Anne's accession took place without fuss. She was after all a Stuart, daughter of James II and grand-daughter of the man whom Jacobites considered a royal martyr, Charles I. But she had deserted her father and, in spite of a chequered relationship with her sister Mary and her brother-in-law William, had in general supported the settlement of 1689, so that she was acceptable equally to the Whigs. Of course, the Jacobites considered Anne's half-bother James as the true heir, but most of them were willing to leave the question of the succession in abeyance until Anne's death. After all, James was twenty-three years younger than his half-sister and was only a boy of fourteen when she came to the throne. Indeed, if it were not for the religious question it would not have been difficult to arrange for James to succeed Anne, in spite of the Act of Settlement. But both the English and the Scottish Parliaments were adamant about securing the Protestant succession, and James was to remain a devout and determined Catholic who would not change his religion even to secure a kingdom.

Anne was not a very interesting queen, although interesting things happened during her reign. Politically, she represented a pause, a breathing-space, in dynastic conflict. Personally, she has been accused of spitefulness, inconsistency and vulgarity, and certainly she does not seem to have had much royal charm. Her ineffective husband George, brother of King Christian V of Denmark, was an agreeable enough blank, of whom Charles II is supposed to have said: 'I have tried him sober, and I have tried him drunk, but there is nothing in him'. Charles advised George to stick to his conjugal duties by Anne, which he did to considerable effect: it was not his fault that his wife had numerous miscarriages and that none of her seventeen children survived.

Meanwhile, back at St Germain, the young James Francis Edward was under the regency of his mother, Mary of Modena, until he reached the age of eighteen on 10 June 1706, when the regency was dissolved and James took over. The Court of St Germain during his father's last years had not been without its internal stresses, a characteristic feature of any court in exile. A major division was between Compounders, who were willing to accept certain conditions for the restoration of James II to the throne, and Noncompounders, who held that the royal dignity admitted of no compromise and he should be restored unconditionally. The Catholic Duke of Melfort, the older James's Secretary of State, was an ardent Noncompounder and influenced his master against any realistic policy, but when the Compounder Charles Middleton, second Earl of Middleton, a tolerant and cultivated Protestant lover of the classics, joined the Duke of Melfort as joint Secretary of State in 1693 and became the exiled king's chief adviser, the Compounders came to the ascendant and James issued declarations promising pardon to all who should not oppose his return, together with the maintenance of the Church of England and of all laws passed since 1689. But few now took the possibility of his restoration seriously, or even took what he said very seriously, and most Jacobite hopes now centred on his son.

The Duke of Melfort later lost favour at the exiled Court and was replaced by his brother the Earl of Perth (later created titular Duke of Perth in James II's will), an unpopular character, described by the English government agent John Macky in his *Memoirs* as 'always violent for the party he espoused, and ... passionately proud; tells a story very prettily; is capricious, a thorough bigot, and hath been in each religion, while he professed it'. He had held high office in Scotland under Charles II and James II, and introduced the use of the thumb-screws in interrogating Covenanters. Later he became a Roman Catholic convert. At the beginning of the regency of Mary of Modena, Perth represented the uncompromising faction and Middleton the compromising. But after he had had a vision of the dead James II, who told him that he had secured his salvation by his prayers, Middleton suddenly became an ardent Roman Catholic and as such a person of great influence with the Queen. But the arrogant and narrow-minded Perth had charge of the young James.

Across the Channel, plans for effecting a union of England and Scotland, and so closing the 'back door' to England so feared by English politicians, were now proceeding apace. The Scottish Parliament met at Edinburgh in June 1702, with the Duke of Queensberry Her Majesty's High Commissioner. It passed an Act enabling the Queen to appoint Commissioners to treat for a union between the two kingdoms, something the English Parliament had already done, and on 25 June sent the Queen a letter announcing this:

> The Estates of Parliament, in the due and chearful Prosecution of what Your Majesty so graciously recommended as to the Union of both Kingdoms, have past an Act enabling Your Majesty to Appoint Commissioners for Treating thereforeof in the same Extent, and almost in the same Terms with that past in the Parliament of *England*. ...

This was Queensberry's work, the union between Scotland and England being the prime object of his life. But he was to meet with much opposition in Scotland, and Parliament in Edinburgh was to witness a momentous struggle and justify itself as a chamber of significant debate in a way it had never done at any other period in its history, before it finally voted itself out of existence on 16 January 1707, by voting to ratify and approve the Treaty of Union.

There were both Whigs and Tories in Scotland, both Presbyterians and Episcopalians, both supporters of the 1689 revolution and Jacobites who opposed an incorporating union on the grounds that it would whittle away important Scottish rights, traditions and institutions. The Presbyterian Whig journalist George Ridpath argued in his *Discourse upon the Union of Scotland and England*, published in 1702, that proposals for a union of the two kingdoms that had been made on various occasions before the union of crowns in 1603 had in fact been fairer to Scotland than proposals made since 1603. He argued also that 'ever since that time [1603] to the beginning of this Reign there has been a prevalent Party in that Court, who have been for imposing upon us in relation both to Church and State, and instead of allowing us a share in anything of their Constitution, which was better than our own, they have been for obliging us to a Compliance with that which was worse than our own.' The great independent Protestant liberal Scottish nationalist Andrew Fletcher of Saltoun made similar points again and again in the Scottish Parliament. 'When our Kings succeeded to the Crown of England, the Ministers of that Nation took a short way to ruin us, by concurring with their Inclinations to extend the Prerogative in Scotland; and the great Places and Pensions confer'd upon Scots-men by that Court, made them to be willing Instruments in the work.' According to the report of the proceedings of the 1703 Parliament in Edinburgh given in the Diary of Sir David Hume of Crossrigg, the Protestant anti-unionist Lord Belhaven, on 9 June 1703, 'had a long discourse on the attempts of Union with England, both before K. James 6, and since, and that kingdom's encroachments ever since, and their endeavours to exalt the prerogative here, to sett up Episcopacy to enthral us, not on a religious account: He was by some desired to print his discourse'.

Both Ridpath, Fletcher and Belhaven argued that ever since 1603 Scotland had been *imposed upon* by English interests with respect both to Church and State. These three were at the opposite extreme from the Jacobites in their views of monarchy, yet on the question of union they had much Jacobite support. George Lockhart of Carnwath, Member of Parliament for Edinburgh and a most ardent Jacobite admired Fletcher of Saltoun as a Scottish patriot, referring to him as 'that worthy and never to be enough praised Patriot' and echoing his sentiments with respect to the union again and again. In his powerfully Jacobite-oriented *Memoirs Concerning the Affairs of Scotland, from Queen Anne's Accession to the Throne to the Commencement of the Union of the Two Kingdoms of Scotland and England in May, 1707*, published anonymously without the author's knowledge and consent in 1714, and republished from the original manuscript in 1817, Lockhart attacked Queensberry, the great advocate of union, as 'the first *Scots Man* that disserted over to the Prince of *Orange*, and from thence acquir'd the Epithet (amongst Honest Men) of *Proto Rebel*'. He accused Queensberry of 'having undertaken and promoted every Proposal and Scheme for Enslaving *Scotland*, and Invading her Honour, Liberty, and Trade, and rendring her Obsequious to the Measures and Interest of *England*'.

Sir David Dalrymple anonymously introduces the 1714 edition of Lockhart's *Memoirs*, which he presents as an awful warning and a horrid example of the mind of a Jacobite traitor. In this introduction he makes quite clear why, in the minds of many politicians of the time, the union was inextricably bound up with the succession question:

> I shall pass by the Union without any Remarks upon the Author's Relation, only beg leave to say, That tho' some Rights and Privileges in *Scotland* may have been weaken'd by this Conjunction, yet they have their Religion and Liberty secur'd to them by it, for it had been impossible to have defeated the Attempts of the *Jacobites*, or extinguish'd their Sanguine Hopes, without Declaring the Succession to the Crown of *Scotland* to be in the Illustrious House of *Hanover*. This is evident from the Alarum it gave the whole Party; for no sooner was the Union settled, but Projects were concerted for Restoring their King, as they call'd him.

Once again we note the paradox: the House of Stuart, on succeeding to the throne of England, allowed the rights of their original kingdom of Scotland to be encroached on in favour of English interests, yet among those who complained of this were those who were dedicated to the restoration of the direct Stuart line to the throne. By seeing the Union as a guarantee against Jacobitism, Hanoverians not only ensured that most Scottish Jacobites would be anti-Union but also that they would be led to dwell more and more on the Scottish aspect of the Stuarts. So when Bonnie Prince Charlie made the last, memorable attempt to regain the throne for the Stuarts in 1745 he started off in the Highlands, determined to show himself in dress and bearing above everything else a Scottish Prince.

But the road that led to 1745 was a tortuous one. Part of it leads through the debates about the Union in the Edinburgh Parliament between May 1703 and January 1707.

When a new session of the Scottish Parliament opened on 6 May 1703, the Queen's High Commissioner was again Queensberry and the Lord Chancellor (roughly the equivalent of the modern Speaker) was James Ogilvie, fourth Earl of Findlater and first Earl of Seafield, also an ardent advocate of union between England and Scotland and an accomplished political trimmer who had held a great variety of offices since 1693. Seafield had made himself unpopular in Scotland by opposing the Company of Scotland Trading to Africa and the Indies and taking the official English view about Darien. He looked to the Court in London rather than to the people of Scotland for his instructions. Lockhart of Carnwath gave the Jacobite view of him: 'He was finely Accomplished; a Learned Lawyer, a Just Judge, Courteous, and Good-Natured; but withall, so intirely Abandon'd to serve the Court Measures, be what they will, that he seldom or never Consulted his own Inclinations, but was a blank Sheet of Paper, which the Court might fill up with what they pleas'd.'

There were three parties in the Scottish Parliament at this time. There was the Court Party, who supported the Government; then there were Jacobite sympathizers, mostly Episcopalian, who called themselves by the old name of Cavaliers; and there was the Country Party, who were Presbyterian but who had become increasingly dissatisfied with the results of the 1689 revolution on account of their outraged Scottish national feelings, exacerbated after the failure of the Darien scheme. The coming together of the Cavaliers and the Country Party in the 1703 Parliament in a common Scottish nationalist feeling was the most significant development of that year.

The way the wind was blowing first became apparent on 26 May 1703. On 13 May the Earl of Home had presented an Act of Supply, which provided much needed supplies for the Government and which Queensberry knew was a vital measure in the eyes of his masters. Immediately the Marquis of Tweeddale, leader of the Country party, submitted what was called an 'Overture' resolving 'that before all other business the Parliament might proceed to make such conditions of government and regulations in the Constitution of the Kingdom to take place after the decease of Her Majesty and the heirs of her body as shall be necessary for the preservation of our religion and liberty'. No money without prior guarantees, in fact. Queensberry was not worried, because he counted on having the Cavaliers with him in opposing this. But he was mistaken. When the matter was taken up again on 26 May an extraordinary scene took place. The Duke of Hamilton, leader of the Cavaliers and spokesman for Scottish nationalism, made a speech suggesting that with the best will in the world the advice given to the Queen by an English politician would naturally be in England's rather than Scotland's interest, and then Fletcher of Saltoun, in the words of Hume of Crossrigg's Diary, 'proposed the state of a vote, Whether to give the Act for the Cess [land tax] a first reading, or proceed to make Acts for the Security of our Religion, Liberties, and some added, Trade.

There was long, and tedious, and nauseous repetitions in debate, till candles were brought in, and it was moved, The debate be adjourned.' But it was not tedious in the eyes of the Jacobite Lockhart of Carnwath:

'Tis needless, and would be endless to repeat, suppose I could, the Discourses that were made *Pro* and *Con*, whilst the Parliament was upon Overtures to secure their Liberties, and redeem the Nation from the Oppression it groaned under: 'Tis sufficient to say, That the Court opposed every Thing that could be proposed for that End, and, in Return, were so baffled in all their Schemes and Designs, That on the Fifth of *December*, when a Motion was made for Granting a first Reading to the Act for a Supply, the Parliament flew in the Face of it, some Demanding the Royal Assent to the Act of Security, others asking, If the Parliament met for nothing else than to drain the Nation of Money, to support those that were Betraying and Enslaving it? And after many Hours warm Debates on all Sides, a Vote was stated, *Whether to proceed to Overtures for Liberty, or a Subsidy*? And the House being Crowded with a vast Number of People, nothing, for near Two Hours, could be heard but Voices of Members, and others (it being late, and Candles lighted) requiring *Liberty* and no *Subsidy*.

Lockhart's account captures something of the passion and the drama of the debate, which was essentially about Scotland's insistence on making her own conditions before she would accept as her sovereign the same monarch who succeeded to the English throne. The Government ('the Court', in Lockhart's term) was determined not to concede this, but a majority in the Scottish Parliament, much to Queensberry's dismay, were determined on making the passing of such an Act of Security, as they called it, a condition of voting the supplies the Government were so desperate for. The Cavaliers and the Country party, now united on this issue under the leadership of the Duke of Hamilton, presented a solid front. Fierce debate continued, the Earl of Roxburgh declaring at one point that 'if there was no other Way of Obtaining so natural and undeniable a Priviledge of the House as a Vote [on the Act of Security], they would demand it with their Swords in their Hands'. Lockhart's account is echoed by the Whig Sir John Clerk, who tells us in his *Memoirs* that 'at times we were often in the form of a Polish diet with our swords in our hands, or, at least, our hands on our swords'.

The fiercely patriotic Fletcher of Saltoun produced further excitement by putting forward a draft of an Act containing 'limitations' – twelve conditions governing the succession to the Scottish Crown 'in the case only of our being under the same King with England'. These, which included annual elections, changes in parliamentary representation, and specific new powers to the Scottish Parliament side by side with limitations of the royal power in Scotland, went further than the majority were willing to accept, and Fletcher's proposal was rejected by 26 votes. But the debate on the limitations helped to formulate the terms on which the Act of Security was drawn up and finally passed. Each clause was debated, every issue fought out. The Act which emerged contained nearly 2,000 words. It put the succession to the Scottish throne, on the death of Queen Anne without heirs of her body, firmly in the hands of the Scottish Parliament, and made the significant provision 'That the same be not Successor to the Crown of *England*, unless that in this present Session of Parliament, or any other Session of this or any ensuing Parliament during Her Majesty's Reign, there be such Conditions of Government settled and enacted, as may secure the Honour and Sovereignty of this Crown and Kingdom; the Freedom, Frequency, and Power of Parliaments, the Religion, Liberty and Trade of the Nation from *English*, or any other Foreign Influence; with Power to the said Meeting of Estates, to add such further Conditions of Government as they shall think necessary, . . .'

The Act of Security was finally passed by a majority of sixty ('A vast Plurality of Voices,' commented Lockhart of Carnwath). But before any Act became law it had to be 'touched' with the sceptre on behalf of the Queen by the Commissioner, and this at first Queensberry, acting on instructions from London, refused to do. So debate went on as fiercely as ever in the House, with members demanding to know why royal approval was not given to the Act in the usual manner. Meanwhile the people in the streets of Edinburgh showed their approval of the passing of the Act of Security. On the day it was voted, says Lockhart,

> The Temper and Inclinations of the People were very remarkable on this Occasion; for after the Parliament was that Day adjourned, the Members that had appeared more eminently in behalf of the Resolve, were caress'd and huzza'd as they pass'd in the Streets, by vast Numbers; and the Duke of H———n was after that Manner convoyed from the Parliament House to the *Abbay*, and nothing was to be seen or heard that Night, but Jollity, Mirth, and an universal Satisfaction and Approbation of what was done, and that by People of all Ranks and Degrees.

Queensberry was finally instructed by the Queen, on the advice of the Earl of Godolphin, to 'touch' the Act. This was done on 5 August 1704, and the House immediately proceeded to pass an Act of Supply. Three days after this, discussion of the nomination of commissioners for a treaty of union with England was inaugurated, but it soon got bogged down in angry exchanges about the so-called 'Scots Plot', a curious affair involving the strange and volatile Simon Fraser, Lord Lovat, who had been flitting between the Court of St Germain, England and Scotland apparently in the Jacobite interest and apparently also on the other side, playing both ends against the middle in a very odd way: he had professed to let Queensberry into secrets of a proposed Jacobite rising and had tried to involve the Duke of Atholl, but his deviousness was exposed and his double-dealing suspected. Members of Parliament who considered they had been unjustly besmirched in talk about this plot angrily demanded that their names be cleared before the question of commissioners was taken up. The session ended in what Hume of Crossrigg's Diary describes as 'a great hubbub'.

A new session of Parliament met in Edinburgh on 28 June 1705. By this time both Houses of the English Parliament, outraged at the Scottish Parliament's passing of the Act of Security and thus declaring the succession to the Scottish throne to be entirely in Scottish hands, had passed the vengeful Alien Act. This Act provided once again for the nomination of Commissioners to treat for a union between England and Scotland and talked of the desirability of 'a nearer and more complete union' between the two countries, but went on to provide that unless the succession was settled in Scotland in the same way as it had been settled in England by 25 December 1705, then all Scotsmen normally resident in Scotland were to be treated in England as aliens, with all the disabilities this implied: further, Scottish coal, linen and cattle were to be totally excluded from the English market and no English horses, arms or ammunition could be sent to Scotland. 'This', commented Lockhart of Carnwath, 'was a strage Preamble and Introduction towards an Agreement, First, to propose an Amicable Treaty to remove Grudges and Animosities betwixt the two Nations; but at the same Time threaten the *Scots* with their Power and Vengeance, if they did not comply with what was demanded of them: And truly all true *Scotsmen* looked upon it as a gross invasion of their Liberties and Sovereignty, and an insolent Behaviour towards a free and independent People; and 'twas odd so wise a Nation as *England* should have been guilty of so unpolitick a Step; for they could not have proposed a more effective Way to irritate the *Scots* Nation, . . .'

Queensberry was in temporary disgrace with his English masters for not having prevented the voting of the Act of Security, and when the new session of Parliament met in Edinburgh in 1705 he was no longer Commissioner, that office now being held by the Duke of Argyll. The Marquis of Tweeddale replaced Seafield as Chancellor. It was clear now what was in the Government's mind. They would hold out the bait of a complete union between the two countries, which would of course give Scottish merchants access to English markets at home and abroad, and would be prepared to agree to temporary measures that seemed to strengthen Scottish independence in the confidence that a complete union in the near future would render such measures nugatory. And this is what happened. The Act of Security was the law of the land, but with all Government efforts now concentrated on an incorporating union, it did not look as though it would remain so for long. An incorporating union would make sure once and for all that the succession question would be automatically settled in Scotland as it was in England; the 'back door' to England would be permanently shut; and the threat of a separate Stuart king of Scotland after the accession of George of Hanover to the English throne would vanish.

The high drama of Scottish parliamentary debate now shifted from the security question to the union question. Queensberry was reinstated in the Government as Lord Privy Seal, in which capacity he returned to Edinburgh and directed the unionist tactics in Parliament. His followers there were Protestant Whigs committed to the Protestant succession and to an accommodation with England that would prevent another Darien disaster as well as providing recompense for the one that had occurred: an incorporating union with England would accomplish both purposes. His opponents were the Cavaliers, led by Hamilton, mostly Jacobites and Episcopalians, and often voting with the Cavaliers was a group representing the nationalist wing of the old Country party, and of these Fletcher of Saltoun was the dominating figure. Between the Queensberryite Government party and the Cavalier-cum-Country-party opposition stood an independent group, the New party known also as the *Squadrone Volante*, the flying squadron, most of whom had hived off from the Country party.

The Duke of Hamilton set the ball rolling again on 17 July when he re-introduced a resolution he had first brought forward the previous year: 'That this Parliament will not proceed to the Nomination of a Successor, until we have had a previous treaty with England, in relation to our commerce, and other concerns with that Nation.' This was carried, obviously meaning different things to different voters, for both the Cavaliers and Queensberry's men voted for it. The Earl of Seafield, who sat in this Parliament holding a watching brief on behalf of the Earl of Godolphin, Lord Treasurer of England (who was once a firm friend of James II and an active Tory Jacobite, but was now associated with the Whigs and a driving force in favour of an Anglo-Scottish incorporating union), tried to explain to his master exactly what was happening, but he was not clear about Hamilton's intentions. 'The Duke of Hamilton does say', he wrote to Godolphin just after this vote, 'that he is for a treaty and against breaking up the Parliament, and sayes he heartily wishes a good correspondence betwixt the two kingdomes. If he concurr and act in this, it would be of great advantage. A little time will now discover what he and others will doe, ...' On 1 August Seafield was writing to Godolphin in some distress that while he and Queensberry were trying hard 'to obtain such ane act of treatty as her Ma^{ty} could give her royall assent to, ... the high Cavaleer Party and New Party ... did reconcile ... to prefer limitations to a treatty'. He went on: 'Att first, wee mett with nothing but high and studied speeches complaining of the English act of treatty, and that it was inconsistant with our soveraignety and independancy to treat untill the menaceing clausses in the English act [the Alien Act] were recinded.' He complained that Fletcher of Saltoun and the Duke of Hamilton were bringing up the matter of limitations again. 'Att last, the vote was stated, 'proceed to limitations or to the act of treatty,' and, the Cavaleer and New Party having fully conjoyned, it was carryed by a majority of three votes only to proceed to limitations.' He enclosed a copy of a resolution presented by Fletcher stating that 'notwithstanding the unneighbourly and injurious useage receaved by ane act lately past in the Parliament of England, intituled an Act for the effectuall securing of the kingdome of England, etc.,' the Scottish Parliament was 'still willing, in order to a good understanding between the two nations, to enter into a treaty with England, but that it's not consistant with the honour and interest of this independent kingdome to make any act or appoint Comm^{rs} for that end, untill the Parlia^{tt} of England doe propose the same in a more neighbourly and friendly manner'. On 11 August he was complaining to Godolphin that 'wee are as yet very diffident of success as to the treaty and supplies, for the New Party and Cavaleer Party have joyned in almost every thing since Queensberries friends concurred with us.'

And so it went on, well into September. On 3 September Seafield told Godolphin that the Cavalier Party had proposed Commissioners for the Union 'might be restricted by the act for treating of any thing but a federall union and spoke much against ane incorporating union'. It was becoming increasingly clear that the Government wanted a complete incorporating union while many Scotsmen who thought a union would be to Scotland's benefit were thinking of a federal union, which would preserve a larger measure of Scotland's national identity.

Further, the Alien Act stuck in Scottish throats, and there could be no agreement to any kind of union while that gun was levelled at Scotland's head. 'Wee found that all parties were lyke to unite not to treatt whilst wee were declared aliens,' wrote Seafield to Godolphin on 3 September, 'so wee were necessitat to argue only that it was unfitt to have such a clause in the act of treatty, and that, as to the other clause in our trade, wee did not doubt but that, if a treatty were set on foott, these would be adjusted. Att last, wee found it necessary to aggree that by ane address or instruction we should so order it that the Comm^{rs} should not enter on the treatty till the clause declaring us aliens be rescinded. . . .'

Seafield and Queensberry between them, arguing, cajoling, promising, threatening, both inside and outside the House, gradually built up a majority for the Government. The extreme nationalist fervour of Fletcher of Saltoun – the most thoughtful and the most disinterested spokesman for Scottish nationality in the course of all these proceedings – gradually came to seem to be speaking for a lost cause. But the turning point came on 1 September, when the Duke of Hamilton, to the astonishment and anger of other members of the opposition, moved that the nomination of Commissioners for the Treaty of Union should be left wholly to the Queen. Fletcher of Saltoun, noted Hume of Crossrigg laconically, 'opposed most bitterly'. He added: 'Put to the vote, and carried by about 40, It should be by the Queen'. This made an incorporating union certain, for the Queen would, of course, nominate commissioners who could be trusted to recommend such a union.

Hamilton's *volte face* was, in the words of Lockhart of Carnwath, 'very surprising to the Cavaliers, and Country party; 'twas what they did not expect should have been moved that Night, and never at any Time from his Grace, who had, from the Beginning of the Parliament to this Day, roared and exclaimed against it on all Occasions; and about 12 or 15 of them ran out of the House in Rage and Despair, saying aloud, 'twas to no Purpose to stay any longer, since the D. of H———n had deserted, and so basely betrayed them'. Whatever Hamilton's motives (and he was a devious character with his own fish to fry, and indeed his own claim to the throne), he had served the interests of the Government. Seafield concluded his letter to Godolphin of 3 September triumphantly: 'so there is now voted a plain act of treatty leaving the nomination to her Ma^{ty}, qch I am very hopefull, if rightly managed, may be the foundation of a lasting settlement betwixt the two nations'. He did not forget his promise about the Alien Act. 'All that remains to be done is that her Ma^{ty} effectually prevail with the English Parliament to rescind that clause in there act [*sic*] declaring us aliens, . . . and, if this is refused by the English Parliament when wee have desyred it in the most discreett manner and att the same time left to her Ma^{ty} the nomination of the Comm^{rs}, then it will be thought universally in this kingdome that the English doe intend no good correspondence with us, and I am perswaded that now yor Lo^p may have the honour of compleetting what you have been sincerely endeavouring these sērall years past.' It was a fair exchange.

'From this Day may we date the Commencement of Scotland's Ruine,' wrote the Jacobite Lockhart of Carnwath of the vote on 1 September 1705, and whether one agrees with him or not it certainly marked the commencement of an irreversible move towards an incorporating union. The Commissioners – one group from Scotland and one from England – were duly appointed by the Queen's Ministers, and, in Lockhart's words, all of them 'were of the Court or *Whigg* Interest, except Mr *Lockhart*, in the *Scots*; and the Archbishop of *York* in the *English* Commission'. (Lockhart says that he was surprised at being appointed, and did not want to accept, but his friends [the Jacobites] persuaded him to remain, in order to observe what happened: he took no part in discussions but 'sat quiet, and concealed his Opinion'.) The Commissioners met in London on 16 April 1706 and by 22 July presented to the Queen their agreed articles of union. Scotland was to send 45 members to the British House of Commons at Westminster (where England and Wales had 513) while the Scottish Peers would elect sixteen from among their number to sit beside the 190 English Peers in the House of Lords. There were complex financial proposals including (as the Act approving these articles later phrased it) 'That an equivalent shall be answered to *Scotland*, for such Parts of the *English* Debts as *Scotland* may hereafter be liable to pay by reason of the Union, ...' of the amount of £398,085 10s. And the succession to the throne of Great Britain was to be the Electress of Hanover and her heirs.

The fourth session of Queen Anne's Scottish Parliament, and the last session of any Scottish Parliament, met in Edinburgh on 3 October 1706. The main business was to debate the articles of union agreed by the Commissioners and, the Government hoped and expected, to pass an Act embodying them. There were twenty-five articles in all, taking up twenty-six folio pages, and they were read out on the opening day of the session, after the reading of a letter from the Queen and the delivery of speeches by the Commissioner (now once again Queensberry) and the Chancellor (now once again Seafield). 'The union has been long Desired by both Nations,' said the Queen in her letter, 'and We shall Esteem it as the greatest Glory of Our Reign to have it now Perfected, being fully perswaded, That it must prove the greatest Happiness of Our People'. She renewed earlier assurances 'to maintain the Government of the Church, as by Law Established in Scotland'. Queensberry's speech echoed the Queen's sentiments and Seafield's concluded, according to the official report, by asserting that 'it must be of great Advantage to have this whole Island Unite under one Government and Conjoyned Intirely in Interest and Affection, having Equality of all Rights and Privileges, with a free Communication and Intercourse of Trade, which must certainly establish Our Security, augment our Strength, and Increase Our Trade and Riches'.

As one reads through the minutes of Scotland's last Parliament one gets a succinct picture of the fight over the Union, less vivid and picturesque than the highly emotional and far from objective account given by Lockhart of Carnwath and more official in tone than the quietly objective summaries given by David Hume of Crossrigg in his Diary. What the minutes give that we do not find in the other sources is the actual names of the voters on each side, every time a matter was brought to a vote. Again and again we find, voting against approval, the Duke of Hamilton (who, in spite of his earlier *volte face*, voted regularly against an incorporating union), Lockhart of Carnwath and Fletcher of Saltoun, among others. The stubborn rearguard action fought clause by clause notably by Fletcher was not mere destructive opposition. Nobody contested the proposition that it would be for the advantage of all for England and Scotland to be united in peace and amity, but a federal union preserving Scotland's individuality as a nation was what the majority of Scottish believers in union wanted. And day by day, as the debate proceeded, addresses were handed in protesting against an incorporating union – from the Merchants and Trades of the City of Glasgow (who were in fact to benefit significantly from the union) on 15 November, from barons, freeholders and householders of Kirkcudbright, Cupar-Fife, Lanark, and the Presbytery of Lanark on the 18th, from Paisley on the 21st, from Roxburgh on the 26th, from the 'Shire of Midlothian' on the 27th, and more and more came in at each day's sitting; but nothing was done about them. The Articles of Union were burned at Dumfries on 11 December. The Scottish people left no doubt that, whatever Parliament might decide, they did not want an incorporating union.

The Duke of Hamilton took a high patriotic note. 'What,' says he, 'shall we in Half an Hour yield what our Forefathers maintain'd with their Lives and Fortunes for many ages; are none of the Descendents here of those worthy Patriots who defended the Liberty of their Country against all Invaders, who assisted the great King *Robert Bruce*, to restore the Constitution and revenge the Falshood of *England* and Usurpation of *Baliol*? Where are the *Douglasses* and the *Campbells*? Where are the Peers; where are the Barons, once the Bulwark of the Nation? Shall we yield up the Sovereignty and Independency of the Nation, when we are commanded by those we represent, to preserve the same, and assur'd their Assistance to support us?' (Lockhart's report.)

The most astonishing reaction, and the strongest proof of the unpopularity of the Articles of Union, was that of the Cameronians, those extreme Calvinist Covenanters of the south-west, who hated with equal ferocity Popery, Episcopacy and Jacobitism. They actually talked of joining the Jacobites to restore the exiled James Francis Edward, the Catholic Stuart whose immediate forebears had so persecuted them. There were fierce demonstrations in the streets of Edinburgh and Glasgow, and elsewhere, and Daniel Defoe, sent by Robert Harley, Queen Anne's Secretary of State and Lord Treasurer, to help facilitate passage of the Act of Union in Edinburgh, wrote nervously to Harley in November of danger from rabbles and mobs.

But too many members of the Scottish Parliament had been persuaded that it was in their interests to vote for the Articles of Union, and though the debate was often fierce and sometimes splendid, the conclusion was not really in doubt, especially after the Duke of Roxburgh, earlier a passionate defender of Scotland's independence, and the *Squadrone Volante* had gone over to the Government's side. One by one the Articles were carried. And finally we read in the official minutes:

> In the Parliament the 16 of *January* 1707, A Vote was put, *Approve of the Act Ratifying and Approving the Treaty of Union of the two Kingdoms of* Scotland *and* England, *Yea* or *Not*, and it carried *Approve*: And the List of the Members Names as they Voted, *Approve* or *Not*, (ordered to be Printed) is as follows.

One hundred and ten names appear under 'Approvers' and 68 under 'Noe's'. Hamilton and the indomitable Fletcher of Saltoun voted 'no'. Lockhart of Carnwath could not bring himself to be present at all. In his *Memoirs* he turns from the scenes in Parliament with a kind of relief 'to give an Account of what happened after the Commencement of the Union, particularly of the Projects that were on Foot to subvert the same, and restore the King [i.e., young James].' This makes crystal clear the relation between Jacobitism and anti-Unionism at this time.

Three attempts were made to frustrate the Union after the passing of the Act (the passing of a similar Act by the English Parliament was, of course, a foregone conclusion: the only significant opposition to the Union was in Scotland). There was a plan for a joint Cameronian-Cavalier rebellion, but the Duke of Hamilton, who was to lead it, withdrew at the last minute, and it came to nothing. There was a plan to address the Queen, pointing out that she had been grossly misinformed about Scottish affairs and public opinion in Scotland, but this, too (in Lockhart's briefly eloquent phrase) was 'broke by the Duke of Hamilton'. And there was a proposal for those Members of the Scottish Parliament who opposed the Union to withdraw from Parliament so as to 'startle the English' and 'convince them that the Union would not be founded upon a secure and legal Basis', and to accompany the withdrawal with a protestation, but this plan too, again in Lockhart's words, was 'broke by the Duke of Hamilton'.

The Union became effective on 1 May 1707. Henceforth there was no Scottish Parliament, and though the history of that institution had not been glorious it had sprung nobly to life in its last phase and shown what its potentialities were. 'The end of an auld sang,' remarked Lord Seafield, Scotland's last Lord Chancellor. The Scottish regalia – the old crown and sceptre and sword of state – which used to be borne in procession at the picturesque opening ceremony of 'riding the parliament' which Edinburgh would now never see again, were lost to view, not to emerge until Walter Scott arranged for their recovery and public exhibition in 1818. While he was planning the ceremony of the regalia Scott pondered much on the Union and its significance. 'I remember,' he wrote to the Duke of Buccleuch, 'among the rebel company which debauched my youth there was a drunken old Tory who used to sing a ballad about these same Regalia at the time of the Union in which they were all destined to the basest uses, the crown for example

> To make a can/For brandie Nan
> To p—— in when she's tipsey.

The rest of the song is in a tone of equally pure humour the chorus ran

> Farewell thou ancient Kingdom
> Farewell thou ancient Kingdom
> Who sold thyself
> For English pelf
> Was ever such a thing done.'

The recovery of the ancient kingdom and the restoration of the direct Stuart line were now seen by the Jacobites in Scotland as part of the same operation.

CHAPTER FOUR

Jamie the Rover

DURING the reign of Queen Anne the possibility of her being succeeded by her half-brother was never out of the question, in spite of the Act of Settlement, and most of her leading statesmen maintained some kind of communication with the court-in-exile at St Germain. In spite of a general desire to have the Protestant succession secured, there were few who relished the succession of a German princeling with little or no knowledge of England and its language. But in England at least those who were dubious about the Hanoverian succession were prepared to wait until the Queen's death. In Scotland, especially after the Union of 1707, the situation was, as we have seen, different. There was discontent among many different sections of the people. And less than a year before the Union came into effect, with the ending of the regency of Mary of Modena, the existence of a real live young Stuart heir across the water had become difficult to ignore.

That Stuart heir himself was growing anxious to regain the crown he regarded as lawfully his. James Francis Edward, otherwise the Chevalier St George, who was now recognized by true Jacobites as King James VIII of Scotland and III of England and who later came to be known by supporters of the House of Hanover as the 'Old Pretender' – and whom we shall from now on simply call 'James' – has always been a bit of a puzzle so far as his character goes. There can be no doubt of his personal courage, of which there is much concrete evidence, but he altogether lacked the panache that his son was to exhibit in his youth and he tended to be withdrawn and melancholy. A supporter who was with him in Scotland during the rebellion of 1715 recorded that he never saw him smile and that 'we saw nothing in him that look'd like Spirit; he never appear'd with Chearfulness and Vigour to animate us: ... his Countenance look'd extremely heavy'. A non-Jacobite account of that rebellion recorded that, after it became clear that it was going to fail, James complained that 'instead of bringing him to a Crown, they had brought him to his Grave'. (The same writer, Peter Rae, has this footnote: 'This being told Prince *Eugine* of *Savoy*, His Highness reply'd, *That Weeping was not the Way to conquer Kingdoms*.') He had grown up in exile since earliest infancy. His schemes for re-possessing his crown were hounded by every kind of bad luck and bad management. His confidence that the French King or the Pope or the Swedish King or the Spanish King would assist him lavishly with money, arms and men was never borne out by events. Even the weather was always against him. 'Jamie the Rover' became 'Old Mr Misfortunate', doomed to a life of permanent frustration and exile. (He spent a total of 45 days on Scottish soil, all in 1715–1716.)

James at St Germain and Louis XIV at Versailles sniffed the air in 1707 and thought they smelled the prospect of successful Jacobite rebellion. France had been at war with England since 1701 on the question of the succession to the Spanish throne which Louis, counter to treaty obligations, wanted for his grandson Philip of Anjou, while England and her allies were determined to prevent such a huge accretion to French power; for Louis civil war in Britain was always a helpful diversion. James was encouraged by news of Scottish discontent at the Union and rumours that he was imminently expected in Scotland.

Colonel Hooke, a Jacobite exile who had already undertaken an earlier mission to the Jacobites of Scotland in 1705, set out from France for Scotland in the early spring of 1707 to make contact with the Jacobite nobility of Scotland. His object was to negotiate with the Scottish Jacobites and report on their strength and readiness to take action. Louis's object in sending Hooke was, as Lockhart of Carnwath suspected, less to help the Jacobite cause than to advance French interests: 'the French King only minded our King in so far as his own Interest led him, and made use of him as a Tool to promote and be subservient to his own private Designs'. Hooke reported on his mission to M. de Chamillart, French Secretary of State, and an English translation of this report, together with a variety of other documents relating to Hooke's mission, was published in both Edinburgh and London in 1760. It gives a detailed account of how the Scots 'demanded what succours they might expect from his most Christian majesty' and how Hooke replied to their demand for 5,000 men by saying 'that the question was not whether the King could send 5,000 men to Scotland; but whether they had need of them to deliver them from the yoke of the English; that they had not proved their want of them, and to put an end to the dispute, I would propose a difficulty which I believe they would find it very hard to answer; that the English had their eyes upon them, being well apprised of the general discontent of their nation; that as 5,000 men could not be embarked without some bustle, on the first news of the preparations the English would not fail to suspect some commotion, and would immediately seize the leading men in Scotland, which would entirely break all their measures, ...' Eventually the Scots compromised with the statement 'that they needed some troops, but would refer themselves to the King as to their number, and likewise as to all their other supplies, excepting the article of arms, which they said they could not do without'.

Among the Scottish peers who talked with Hooke and who sent back with him the promise of a national Jacobite rising in Scotland were the Earls of Errol and Panmure, and Lords Stormont and Kinnaird. The Duke of Atholl was cagey, and communicated with Hooke only through intermediaries. The Duke of Hamilton, as he wrote to James in code, did not like the idea of a purely Scottish enterprise. 'It is not worth while to come for Scotland only. England is the object. ... If you come, come strong.' But it is clear from the terms in which Hooke wrote his report that his mission was to set Scotland against England, not to aid a joint Scottish-English Jacobite rising. That he could write in such terms, which assume that Jacobitism and anti-English Scottish nationalism are to be equated, is but one more piece of evidence of the cumulative effect of Glencoe, Darien, and the articles of Union, on Jacobite feeling in Scotland.

Hooke's mission bore no immediate fruit, but early in the following year a French fleet was fitted out in Dunkirk with 6,000 men and 13,000 stand of arms [a stand of arms consisted of musket, bayonet and sling] to aid a Jacobite rising in Scotland.

James sent Charles Fleming, brother of the Earl of Wigtown, to Scotland to inform the Jacobites there that a French fleet was on its way and to instruct them on how to co-ordinate their activities with James's landing. But nothing went right. The command of the French fleet was entrusted to the Comte de Forbin, who has left his own account of the expedition which makes it quite clear that he regarded the whole enterprise as futile and believed that it never had the slightest hope of success. He complained that his chief, M. de Pontchartrain, French Minister of Marine, never mentioned any Scottish port that was in a condition to receive the expedition and that anyway it was madness to land 6,000 men without an assured means of retreat. Pontchartrain brushed aside his objections, insisting that far from being 'calm and tranquil', as Forbin had maintained, Scotland was ready to rise as soon as a French fleet arrived. Forbin even protested to King Louis himself, but the King dismissed him abruptly, wishing him a successful voyage and saying that he was busy and couldn't stay to listen to him. Preparations continued. The soldiers arrived at Dunkirk before the sailors, and Forbin was worried lest the arrival of so many troops would become known to the British Government (it did). Finally, the sailors came and then James himself, who was to sail with the expedition to Scotland. But just at the critical moment he fell ill with measles, and everything had to be delayed until his recovery. This delay, as Forbin later complained, 'allowed the enemy to reconnoitre our position'. But of course the British Government knew very well what was going on all the time. As early as 25 February the chamberlain to the Earl of Seafield, who though no longer Chancellor of Scotland still served the interests of the Government and was a Scottish representative peer in the House of Lords, received a letter from London telling of the government's alarm 'with a ffrench invasion from Dunkirk'. An English fleet under Sir George Byng was anchored off Gravelines, two leagues from Dunkirk, in full sight of Forbin, who 'observed them closely and made out that they were actually Men-of-War'. He again argued for the calling off of the expedition, and again he was not listened to.

In a few days James had recovered and insisted on embarking even though the wind did not permit the fleet to sail. Immediately a violent gale sprang up; James's staff and the military leaders were thoroughly seasick, to Forbin's unconcealed pleasure; three ships broke their cables and were nearly lost. James remained cool. Finally, on 8 March, with the wind now favourable, the battered fleet sailed. The convalescent James wrote (in French) to his mother on the 9th: 'Here I am at last on board. My body is very weak, but my courage is so high that it will make up for the weakness of my body. I hope that the next time I write you it will be from the palace of Edinburgh, where I expect to arrive on Saturday [the 13th].'

But James never saw the *palais d'Edimbourg*. The fleet sailed too far north, and first sighted land at Montrose. When they discovered where they were, they turned south, and anchored in the Firth of Forth. 'In vain,' wrote Forbin, 'we made signals, lit fires, and fired our cannon: nobody appeared.' At dawn the next day (Saturday the 13th) they sighted a large English fleet, under Sir George Byng, some four leagues away. Forbin cut his cables and turned hastily north. The Jacobite officers on board became alarmed for James's safety and wanted to put him ashore near a friendly castle (perhaps Slains Castle, seat of the Jacobite Earl of Errol), but Forbin successfully held out against this. They managed to shake off the English fleet, but not before one of their ships had been captured, with its load of troops. Forbin kept on sailing north, while Byng returned to watch and wait in the Firth of Forth, where he remained until he heard that the French fleet had returned to Dunkirk. An attempt by Forbin to land at Inverness was foiled by a change of wind, and with the risk of his ships scattering or running aground or falling into enemy hands, he decided to return home. After a difficult voyage, in which they encountered both adverse winds and frustrating calms, the depleted fleet arrived back in Dunkirk at the end of March.

> The King's Part was to hasten over to *Scotland* to bring Money, Arms and Ammunition for the Men he could raise, where, upon his Landing, to March strait to *Edinburgh*, there to Proclaim himself King of *Scotland*, declare the Union Void and Null, emit a Declaration or Manifesto, promising to Maintain and Govern his Subjects of both Kingdoms by the Established Laws thereof, Calling a New and Free Parliament, to whom should be referr'd the Determination of all religious Affairs, and further providing for the Security of both Civil and Religious Concerns; Lastly, requiring all his good Subjects to assist him on his Design of recovering his own and the Nations Rights and Privilidges, and as soon as the Parliament had adjusted Affairs, and form'd an Army, to March without Delay into *England*.

So wrote the ardent Scottish Jacobite Lockhart of Carnwath of James's intention in March 1708, and certainly that is what many people in Scotland expected him to do. 'It is too Melancholy a Subject to insist upon the Grief their disastrous Expedition raised in the Hearts of all true *Scots* Men', he wrote of the expedition's failure. But why did it fail? Would James, if he had landed on the shores of the Forth, have found welcome and support? And could Forbin have landed the troops there? The Duke of Berwick, illegitimate son of James II and VII by Arabella Churchill and one of the greatest military leaders of his day (he fought brilliantly on the French side in the War of the Spanish Succession), put the blame on the French – on inadequate preparation on their part as a result of bad feeling between Chamillart, Minister for War, and Pontchartrain, Minister of Marine. There is certainly some truth in this, as contemporary accounts by Forbin and others suggest. If a landing of troops had been effected a successful Jacobite rising might well have taken place. Scotland was waiting for James. English troops were engaged on the Continent. The Government was in a very nervous state. It has been suggested that Anne might have compromised and accepted her half-brother as her successor if James had actually appeared in Scotland at the head of an army.

The unfortunate James now sought service in the French army, where he served with distinction against the British at the battles of Oudenarde and Malplaquet. He behaved with particular gallantry in the latter battle (1710), charging twelve times with the *Maison du Roi* and receiving a wound in the arm. It is said that many in the British camp drank the health of their gallant enemy and that on several occasions he rode out beyond the French outposts in the direction of the British camp and was never fired on. Indeed, one sympathetic historian has suggested that if he had had the initiative to pay a surprise visit to that camp he might have been welcomed, and the whole course of events changed.

Malplaquet was probably James's finest hour. Three years later the Treaty of Utrecht, ending the War of the Spanish Succession, bound Louis to refuse to allow James to reside on French territory. So 'Jamie the Rover' left in February 1713 to take up residence with his little court-in-exile at Bar-le-Duc, in Lorraine. He took the opportunity afforded by his now being outside the jurisdiction of His Most Christian Majesty to allow free public worship for the Protestants among his entourage, something that would not have been possible in France.

On 1 August of the following year Queen Anne died. Contrary to what many people hoped and expected, there was no Jacobite *coup*. George I was proclaimed 'by the Grace of God King of Great Britain, France and Ireland' (the absurd inclusion of France as among the King's realms was a heritage of the Middle Ages) and the chance of a peaceful Stuart restoration was lost for ever. All James could do now, after a vain visit to France where he found Louis in no position to give him any assistance, was to return to Lorraine and issue a proclamation protesting his right to the throne.

The Whigs were now in the ascendant. Henry Saint-John, Viscount Bolingbroke, who had been Queen Anne's Secretary of State and who had been in communication with James in the hope of arranging for him to succeed Anne (many years later he denied this, but it does seem to be true), was dismissed from office on George's accession and turned his thoughts towards a Jacobite rising. So did the Duke of Ormonde, who had also held high office under Queen Anne. In April 1715 there were Jacobite demonstrations in London and Boston and in May there were rowdy demonstrations at Oxford.

In southern England, however, the Jacobite plans soon crashed. Bolingbroke, being led to believe that his life was in danger, succeeded in fleeing to France, in spite of having been recognized at Dover 'in disguise, having a black bob Wig on, with a laced Hat, and very ordinary Clothes'. He was impeached and attainted in his absence, and his name erased from the roll of peers: he became James's Secretary of State. Ormonde planned a rising in the south-west of England, to begin by taking control of Plymouth, Bristol and Exeter. But his plans became known to the Government, and he too fled to France on 21 July when he heard that Government troops were on their way to arrest him. Other Jacobite leaders in the south-west, planning to muster at Bath, were also discovered and arrested. The Government had been badly frightened, and there were plans for King George to flee to Holland if things became really bad.

One reason for the Government's success in obtaining advance intelligence was that on his fleeing to France in March 1715 Bolingbroke had taken up with an old mistress, the notorious ex-nun Claudine Alexandrine de Tencin, who was also the mistress of the Abbé Dubois. Dubois for his own reasons was strongly in favour of the Hanoverian Government in England and passed on what he gathered from his mistress to the second Earl of Stair,* who as the recently appointed British Ambassador in Paris had organized a most efficient intelligence system. Indeed, Stair nearly succeeded in effecting the capture and perhaps the murder of James and so ending the Jacobite threat once and for all: he was to be intercepted on his way to the French coast when he went there to be in readiness to join the rising; but James escaped, having been warned in time of the presence of suspicious strangers by a friendly village postmistress. James did not have the benefit of the kind of intelligence that his enemies were regularly receiving. As late as October 1715 he did not know what was going on, and, waiting to cross the Channel, sent Ormonde to land near Plymouth and find out what was happening. Ormonde moved westward along the coast and learned of the Government success and the arrest of those Jacobite leaders in the south who had not fled. He returned to St Malo and reported his discovery to James. Now once again Scotland seemed the only hope.

The original plan was for the centre of the rising to be in south-west England and for a rising in Scotland to play a subsidiary part. The flight of Bolingbroke and Ormonde and the Government's subsequent success in securing Bristol, Bath and (with more difficulty) the exuberantly Jacobite university and town of Oxford, put an end to James's intention of landing in Plymouth. In Scotland the Earl of Mar had been planning a Jacobite rising since early August. He was not the most obvious leader of such an enterprise. He had earlier been a member of

* Son of the Sir John Dalrymple, first Earl of Stair, who had carried so much responsibility for the Massacre of Glencoe.

the Court party, had supported the Union (for which he was one of the Commissioners) and had been Secretary of State for Scotland in the last year of Queen Anne's reign. But his dismissal from the secretary-ship at George's accession and his deliberate snubbing by King George after he had presented him with a loyal address turned him abruptly to Jacobitism. He had estates on Deeside, in Aberdeenshire, and just north of the Forth in Clackmannanshire, and he left London secretly by sea on 1 August 1715 to sail north in order to drum up support for a rising in his own country. When he got to Braemar he sent out invitations 'to all the Jacobites round the Country' (in the words of Peter Rae, whose detailed *History of the Late Rebellion Rais'd against His Majesty King George by the Friends of the Popish Pretender* appeared in 1718) inviting them to a *timchioll*, literally a 'circumference', a traditional Highland hunt where the beaters formed an enormous circle which they steadily narrowed until they were able to drive all the animals within the circle past the waiting huntsmen. A great hunt of this kind had long been a method of planning a military operation in the Highlands. Mar, who was a finer orator than soldier, addressed the gathering, and told them, according to Rae: 'That tho' he had been Instrumental in forwarding the *Union* of the two Kingdoms, in the reign of Queen Anne, yet now his Eyes were open'd and he could see his Error, and would therefore do what lay in his Power to make them again a Free People, and that they should enjoy their ancient Liberties, which were by that *cursed Union* (as he call'd it,) delivered up into the hands of the *English*, whose Power to enslave them further was too great, and their Design to do it daily visible, by the Measures that were taken, especially by the Prince of *Hanover*, ...' The only defence of 'their Liberties and Properties against the ... new Courtiers, and their Innovations' was to establish James 'upon the Throne of these Realms'. (Notice that an Anglophobe Scottish nationalism designed to present James as the saviour of Scottish national rights and dignity went side by side with a desire to see him King of all Great Britain: this confusion, which is historically understandable, runs right through the Jacobite movement in Scotland. Walter Scott understood this very well when he made the ultimate Jacobite, Redgauntlet, equate a Stuart restoration to the British throne with the restoration of Scotland's independence.)

Mar raised James's standard at Braemar on 6 September and proclaimed him King of Scotland, England, France (odd, considering their hope of French support – but this was one of the old traditional titles of the King of England) and Ireland. ''Tis reported,' says Rae, 'that when this Standard was first erected, the Ball on the Top fell off, which the superstitious *Highlanders* were very much concern'd at, taking it as an *Omen* of the bad success of the Cause . . .' According to James Hogg's *Jacobite Relics of Scotland*, the standard was blue, with the Scottish arms wrought in gold on one side and the Scottish thistle on the other: above the thistle was the ancient Scottish motto *Nemo me impune lacessit* ('No one injures me with impunity') and below were the words 'No Union'. A few days later Mar issued another declaration (he was magnificent at declarations) saying that 'our rightful and natural King', James VIII, had entrusted him with the direction of his affairs and the command of his forces in his ancient kingdom of Scotland and mentioning others of the King's 'faithful Subjects and Servants', including Lord Huntley, son of the Duke of Gordon and a Catholic, Lord Tullibardine, son of the Duke of Atholl (his father remained loyal to King George) and the Earl of Breadalbane, as agreeing that they should openly take up arms. James was proclaimed by different Jacobite officers at Perth, Aberdeen, Dundee, Montrose and Forres. Mar moved south, having collected an army of some 5,000 and marched over the Spittal of Glenshee to Kirkmichael where he had James proclaimed. Meanwhile, Perth was captured for the Jacobites by Colonel John Hay. It really looked as though the Jacobites were going to make it this time. Mar went to Perth, where he received letters from James promising massive French support. More clansmen rallied to his standard.

Meanwhile the Government had unintentionally helped Mar by passing an 'Act for Encouraging Loyalty in Scotland', 'which', says John, Master of Sinclair in his *Memoirs*, 'being put into execution speedilie after it past, fiftie of the most active or most considerable Lords and Gentlemen were cited, some to render themselves in fifteen days, and others in fortie, according to the distance they lived from Edinburgh, under pain of forfaulture of their liferent escheat [forfeiture of the profits of their estates accruing during their lifetime]. All those were buoy'd up to the last day of their citations by the great pains Mar and his emissaries took to make them expect the King daylie, or, at least the Duke of Berwick, with great secours from France; and no bodie, in that great ferment of spirits and great expectation, careing to give bad example by delivering up himself first, they were at last all caught in the same noose, their time being elapsed and no place left to repent.' But the immediate effect of this invitation to prominent Jacobites to come to Edinburgh and be put under arrest was to increase support for the cause. Only two of those cited turned up, and both were jailed.

Expectation of French support received a blow when news arrived of the death of Louis XIV, for the new Regent, the Duc d'Orléans, who ruled in the name of Louis's five-year-old grandson Louis XV, was not eager to support the Jacobites. Twelve ships loaded with men and ammunition lying at Le Havre and other French ports and ready to sail in support of the rising were unloaded, on the instructions of Orléans, who had been approached by the Earl of Stair, British Ambassador in Paris, and only a few small vessels managed to sneak away and reach Scotland. A further discouragement was the failure, under rather ludicrous circumstances, of a Jacobite plan to seize Edinburgh Castle. Nevertheless, Mar was sitting pretty. The Duke of Argyll was in command of a Government force of barely 3,000; by this time the Jacobite force under Mar, variously estimated by contemporaries at between 6,800 and 12,000, must have been well over 8,000. The Duke of Atholl wrote to his fellow non-Jacobite the Earl of Sutherland from Blair Castle on 9 October that 'the Earl of Marr is still att Perth, and master of all the countrys hereabouts benorth Forth, except this house, and my country about it'. He added that no one was 'wel affected to our King, on this side of Forth'. It was not only the Highlands; Fife and the east coast were also largely under Jacobite influence. In the words of Peter Rae, a hostile witness: 'The Rebels were now Masters of all the *Eastern* Coasts of *Scotland*, from *Brunt-Island* to *Murray-Firth*, ... and on the *West* side, the Isle of *Skye*, the *Lewise*, and all the *Hebrides* were their own; ... In a Word, they were possess'd of all that Part of the Kingdom of *Scotland*, which lies on the North-side of the River *Forth*; excepting the remote Counties of *Caithness*, *Strathnaver* and *Sutherland*; beyond *Inverness*: And that Part of *Argileshire*, which runs North-west, into *Lorn*, and up to *Loquhaber*, where *Fort-William* continued in the Possession of his Majesty's Troops.'

If the Jacobites in Scotland had now possessed a resolute and able commander they must have been successful. The obvious person would have been the Duke of Berwick. On 13 October James sent him a Commission as 'Captain-General and Commander-in-Chief of all our forces by land and sea in our ancient Kingdom of Scotland' and informed him that 'our will and pleasure is' that he should go at once to Scotland and take command (thus superseding Mar). But Berwick was now in the service of France, and could not give up his post there without permission of the Regent, who had no intention of giving permission. So the loquacious but irresolute Mar remained in command. He stayed in Perth. James did not arrive. Argyll was at Stirling, with his 3,000 men.

Finally, on 10 November, Mar marched south from Perth with the

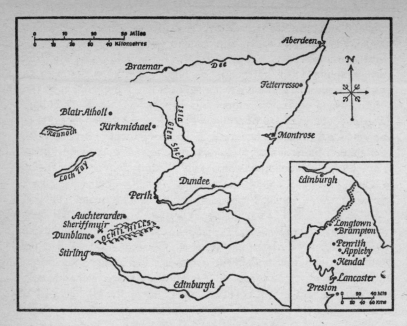

The campaign of the Fifteen

intention of pushing past Argyll and joining up with a Jacobite force in Lancashire headed by Thomas Forster, Member of Parliament for Northumberland, and joined by the young Earl of Derwentwater. When he heard that Mar was on the move, Argyll marched to Dunblane and encamped on Sheriffmuir, undulating moorland a few miles east of Dunblane, at the foot of the Ochil Hills. On 13 November Mar's army moved out of the village of Kinbuck, north of Dunblane, and formed into two lines on the high ground east of the village. He made a tremendous speech to 'all the Noblemen, Gentlemen, General Officers and Heads of the Clans', in Rae's phrase, which aroused great enthusiasm. His troops moved forward, up the slope.

It proved an odd sort of battle. The Highlanders on Mar's right charged Argyll's left wing when it was still moving into position and routed them. They fled as far as Stirling, and reported total defeat there on arrival. But on Argyll's right wing (commanded by the Duke personally) his cavalry attacked the Highland foot and, after heavy fighting, drove them back to Allan Water to the north-west. Thus each side almost simultaneously achieved a significant score. Mar had by far the larger forces; Argyll was the abler commander. Mar decided to call it a day and retired to Perth. There seems little doubt that Mar, with skill and determination, could have utterly defeated Argyll's much smaller army. Further, Argyll could afford a draw and Mar could not. Rae maintained that 'by this Battel, The Heart of the Rebellion was broke, the Earl of Mar was baulked of his Design; his Undertaking for a March to the South was laid aside, and never attempted afterwards'. This is to exaggerate; all was far from lost, and Mar indeed gave orders for a *Te Deum* to be sung in Perth giving thanks for victory. But the Battle of Sheriffmuir did mark the turn of the tide against the Jacobites in Scotland in the 1715 rising. The popular view is in the old song:

> *There's some say that we wan,*
> *And some say that they wan,*
> *And some say that nane wan at a' man;*
> *But, one thing, I'm sure,*
> *That at Sheriff-muir,*
> *A battle there was which I saw, man.*
> *And we ran, and they ran,*
> *And they ran, and we ran,*
> *And we ran, and they ran awa' man.*

The same day on which the drawn battle of Sheriffmuir was fought – 13 November 1715 – saw the surrender of Inverness by the Jacobites as a result of the initiative of that extraordinary and puzzling man Simon Fraser, who now appeared active on the Government side and rallied the Frasers away from the Jacobite cause to support King George (and recovered his estates as a result, together with recognition as Lord Lovat: later, in the hope of a dukedom if the Jacobites won, he joined their side again). The man who had been responsible for the capture of Inverness for the Jacobites at the beginning of the rising was Brigadier William Macintosh of Borlum, a tough old campaigner who in October, with Fife safely under Jacobite control, had realized the opportunity now presented for crossing to the southern shore of the Firth of Forth and had achieved the crossing in mid-October with a detachment of 2,000 men by a brilliant manoeuvre. Once across the Forth, Macintosh occupied Leith and then made for the Borders where on 20 October he joined up with the Jacobite force from Northumberland under Thomas Forster and a Scottish Border force under Lord Kenmure. There was now an Anglo-Scottish force poised for a march into England. But the whole thing was a mistake. In the first place, Mar's forces were now permanently split. Secondly, Macintosh's Highlanders and Forster's Englishmen did not get on at all. The Highlanders did not want to march into England and a fierce dispute arose 'Upon this Dispute,' wrote Rae, 'the Horse surrounded the Foot, in order to force them to March *South*; whereupon the *Highlanders* cock'd their Firelocks and said, *if they were to be made a sacrifice, they would choose to have it done in their own Country.* .... After this Debate, which lasted two Hours, They were at last brought to this, *That they keep together as long as they stay'd in* Scotland; *but upon any Motion of going for* England, *they would return back.*' Eventually 500 of Macintosh's Highlanders deserted, some with the intention of joining Mar at Perth and others going west perhaps to join the western clans. (The majority were in fact captured in Lanarkshire and sent as prisoners to Edinburgh and Glasgow.) Macintosh himself reluctantly agreed to join the march south with the rest of his men.

So southward they marched, proclaiming King James wherever they stopped, and hoping with unjustified optimism to pick up large numbers of supporters. Longtown, Brampton, Penrith, Appleby, Kendal, Lancaster, where they stayed twelve days, and finally, in the rain, to Preston on 11 November. But Government forces under General Carpenter were hard on their heels from the north-east, while to the south General Wills and his men arrived at the bridge over the Ribble on 12 November. Preston was now besieged. Forster gave up the following day, and met Government representatives to discuss surrender. The Highlanders were all for trying to fight their way out. After considerable confusion and argument the whole Jacobite force surrendered 'at discretion' (which meant unconditionally) on the 14th. Casualties among the Jacobites were light: under fifty killed and wounded. Nearly 1,500 were made prisoner: over 1,000 of these were Scots. The humiliating defeat at Preston took place at precisely the same time as the Battle of Sheriffmuir was being fought in the north.

So once again any hope there was for the Jacobites lay in Scotland. But things were getting worse there too. After Sheriffmuir the Highlanders started to trickle home. 'Amongst many good Qualities,' wrote Mar in his *Journal* 'the Highlanders have one unlucky Custom, not easy to be reform'd; which is, that generally after an Action they return Home'. Within a month Mar's forces has been reduced to 5,000, and they continued to shrink. Meanwhile, Argyll had been reinforced by two regiments sent north from Preston and, a few weeks later, by 6,000 Dutch troops. More sinister from the Jacobite point of view, as well as personally annoying to Argyll, was the arrival of General William Cadogan, who had been sent by the Government to make sure that Argyll did not pursue a policy of leniency towards the rebels: he eventually replaced Argyll as commander of the Government forces in Scotland. Mar grew increasingly pessimistic, and wrote a long letter to James on 24 November hinting at disaster and suggesting that it would be better to think of James's restoration 'at another time'. He even sent a messenger to Argyll asking if the Duke had power to treat with him, but Argyll replied that he had none, though he would 'write to Court upon the Subject'. The Government were in fact in no mood to treat, and suspected Argyll of being too kind-hearted towards his fellow Scots.

It was in the midst of this period of acute discouragement among the Jacobite forces that James finally landed in Scotland on 22 December. He had sailed from Dunkirk with five companions in a ship of 200 tons carrying eight guns. Abandoning the original intention to land at Montrose because of the sighting of a suspicious vessel, his ship had sailed further north and James went ashore at Peterhead. Disguised as 'Sea-Officers' James and his companions made their way to Fetterresso, principal seat of the Earl of Marischal, and there (in Rae's account) 'the Earl of *Mar*, *Marischal*, and *Hamilton* came up to wait on him. Having dress'd and discover'd himself, they all Kiss'd his Hand and own'd him as King; thereafter they caus'd Proclaim Him at the Gates of the House'.

But it was really all over. Whatever the cause of James's long delay in arriving – it was certainly not his fault, and the fact that he had travelled in unusually bitter winter weather under highly dangerous conditions is a tribute to his courage – he had come too late to be of any use. He was pursued by his usual ill-luck. He fell ill at Fetterresso and had to postpone his departure for Perth. He finally made a public entry into Perth on 9 January and stayed there three weeks. Some half-hearted preparations for a coronation ceremony seem to have been made, but they were soon abandoned. Realizing that Argyll's forces would soon attack, James was persuaded to order a 'scorched earth' policy (as it would now be called) between Dunblane and Perth to deny food and quarters to the advancing enemy. This order, 'to burn and destroy the village of Auchterarder and all the houses, corn and forage whatsoever within the said town, so as they may be rendered entirely useless to the enemy,' was carried out (although, according to Mar, 'the burning goes mightily against the King's mind') and provided excellent anti-Jacobite propaganda. On 29 January a strongly reinforced Argyll began his advance north from Stirling, and James with the Jacobite army retreated to Dundee, where they arrived on the same day that Argyll's army entered Perth. From Dundee they went north to Montrose, and on Saturday 4 February James, persuaded by

Mar and others that, in Mar's words, 'he had no course at present to take that was consistent with what he ow'd to his people in general, to those who had taken armes for him in particular, and to himself upon their account, but by retireing beyond the Sea, to preserve himself for a better occasion of asserting his own Right and restoreing them to their ancient libertys', embarked for France in the *Marie-Thérèse* of St Malo, a small ship of about 90 tons which 'happen'd very Providentially [to be] just ready in the Harbour'. Mar and a few other Jacobite leaders went with him, leaving the Jacobite forces under the command of General Alexander Gordon of Auchintoul. The day he left, James wrote a letter to Argyll (which, however, Argyll never received):

It was with the view of delivering this my Kingdom from the hardships it lies under and restoring it to its former happiness and independency that brought me into this country; and all the hopes of effectuating that at this time being taken from me I have been reduced much against my inclination, but by a cruel necessity, to leave the kingdom with as many of my faithful subjects who were desirous to follow me or I able to carry with me, that so at least I might secure them from the utter destruction that threatens them since that was the only way left me to show them the regard I had for them and the sense I had of their unparalleled loyalty.

The letter went on to express deep regret at having been 'forced to burn several villages' and left money to pay compensation to the victims. James asked Argyll to arrange this 'if not as an obedient subject, at least as a lover of your country', and Argyll would have been susceptible to this appeal on behalf of his countrymen. Indeed, now that the rebellion was virtually over he deliberately slowed down his advance so as to give the Jacobite forces time to disperse and so avoid unnecessary bloodshed. Argyll, chief of the Campbells who were themselves divided on the Jacobite issue, was an intelligent and generous-minded man (Sir Walter Scott gives a good portrait of him as the protector of Jeanie Deans in *The Heart of Midlothian*) who did not relish fighting in a civil war. When his dragoons were cutting down the Highlanders on the left flank of Mar's army at Sheriffmuir, he was heard to exclaim: 'Oh, spare the poor Bluebonnets!' This was not an attitude that commended itself to the Government, who replaced Argyll with the arrogant and less scrupulous Cadogan before depriving him (temporarily, as it turned out) of his other state offices.

Two peers captured at Preston, Viscount Kenmure and the Earl of Derwentwater, were executed in London after being found guilty of high treason. The official sentence – 'you must be hanged by the neck, but not until you be dead; for you must be cut down alive, then your bowels must be taken out, and burnt before your faces; then your heads must be severed from your bodies, and your bodies divided into four quarters' – was commuted to simple beheading in virtue of the victims' noble rank. Forster escaped from Newgate and reached France safely. Less exalted personages were hanged, drawn and quartered in the barbaric manner prescribed, and hundreds of common prisoners were deported to the American colonies to virtual slave labour for specified periods. Those involved in the rising in Scotland escaped with their lives. Many were imprisoned in Edinburgh and eventually released; 74 were sent for trial from Edinburgh to Carlisle (in gross violation of the terms of the Union). Many of these were later freed without trial; even those tried and found guilty were never sentenced, and were eventually released by the Act of Grace of 1717. Public opinion had been revolted by the executions in London and by 34 hangings, drawings and quarterings throughout Lancashire. Nineteen Scottish peerages, including those of Mar and Kenmure, were forfeited by attainder. Derwentwater is commemorated in a moving ballad, 'Farewell to pleasant Dilston Hall,' and Kenmure in a re-writing by Burns of an older song, 'O Kenmure's on and awa, Willie'. The people remembered.

'Nothing but an entire desolation from Stirling to Inverness. The Dutch have not left a chair or a stool, nor a barrel or a bottle, *enfin* nothing earthly undestroyed, and the English troops very little more merciful.' So wrote one Jacobite eye-witness after Cadogan's army had done its duty in Scotland: the people and their property suffered even if they were not hanged, drawn and quartered. And yet, though 'the Fifteen' was crushed so quickly, or rather destroyed itself through the hesitations and bad judgment of its leaders, it had posed a serious threat to the Government. Large numbers of people disliked or despised 'the wee German lairdie' and there was not the widespread feeling that there was to be in 1745 that it was wickedly irresponsible to disturb the peace of a country which had long settled down under the Hanoverians. The Fifteen was by far the most serious of all the Jacobite risings.

Back in France, James dismissed Bolingbroke, holding him ultimately responsible for the failure of the rising by failing to support the expedition with the necessary stores and arms from France. Bolingbroke eventually made his peace with the British Government and was pardoned, though not allowed to take his seat in the House of Lords. He was succeeded as James's Secretary of State by the Earl of Mar. But James now had more to think about than a change of secretary. On his return to Bar-le-Duc in February 1716 he found the Regent Orléans – who for his own political reasons needed England as an ally – positively hostile. Not only was James not allowed to live in France; he was now also forbidden Lorraine. So Jamie the Rover took to the road again, first to Avignon (which was in papal territory) then, after British protests to the Pope (for the Hanoverian Government for propaganda purposes wanted James to settle in Italy, visibly a Papist in a Papist country under Papal protection), to Turin and finally, after spending some time in Modena and in Rome, to Urbino. He lived at Urbino in an old palace provided by Pope Clement XI, from 11 June 1717 until the autumn of 1718, when he took up residence in Rome in the Palazzo Muti, rented for him from the Muti family by the Pope. The Pope also provided James with a summer palace in Albano, the beautiful and historic town in the Alban Hills near the lake of the same name.

The rising of 1715 in Scotland had not been actually defeated in the field, but had melted away in the weary indecisive weeks after Sheriff-muir, and therefore Jacobite hopes were not entirely crushed. James himself was now more convinced than ever that he could not win the crown without substantial foreign help. In the autumn of 1716 it looked as though Charles XII of Sweden, angry at the selling to George I by Denmark of the formerly Swedish duchies of Bremen and Verden, might prove the saviour. Baron Gortz, Swedish Envoy at The Hague, Count Gyllenborg, Swedish Minister in London, and Baron Spaar, Swedish Minister in Paris, corresponded with each other and with the Duke of Ormonde in France about a Jacobite plot. Charles XII was to invade Scotland with an army of 12,000 Swedish troops, while Philip V of Spain, anxious to overthrow the Regent Orléans and seeking to get at him through his ally George I, promised to provide a million livres: James in his turn unrealistically guaranteed a rising in England. But the plan never got beyond the drawing board. Gyllenborg's correspondence fell into the hands of the British Government, and all was revealed. Count Gyllenborg was arrested and the Swedish Legation successfully searched for further correspondence. And that was the end of the 'Swedish Plot'.

The 'Spanish Plot' of 1719 went further. It was the brain-child of Philip's brilliant chief minister Alberoni, who hoped to injure his enemy England by supporting a Jacobite invasion with arms, money and 5,000 troops. Alberoni invited Ormonde to Madrid for discussions, which duly took place in November and December 1718. In February 1719 James travelled to Spain secretly and with difficulty and eventually reached Madrid, where he was received with royal honours. The plan was for a large Spanish force to sail to England while a small diversionary force under the Earl of Marischal sailed to Scotland. But the main fleet was scattered by a violent storm on 29 March soon after starting out (the weather was invariably against the Jacobites) with the result that the main expedition, to England, was abandoned. But the smaller one, to Scotland, with 307 Spanish soldiers, had left San Sebastian on 8 March and it was too late now to recall it. So the Earl of Marischal and his little band of Spaniards held their course for Scotland. They landed in Stornoway, on the Island of Lewis, and there, after some confusion, they effected a rendezvous with a small party of Jacobites from France, brought in a small ship by the Earl of Marischal's brother, James Keith. The Marquis of Tullibardine (who had come over with Keith) disputed the leadership of the expedition with the Earl of Marischal, and the latter eventually allowed him command over the forces on land, though he himself remained in command of the ships. After various trials and misadventures the little fleet reached Loch Alsh and set up headquarters at Eilean Donan castle. But by now five Government ships were in nearby waters and an army under Major-General Wightman (who had fought against Mar at Sheriffmuir) was marching south-west from Inverness. Men from one of the Government ships captured the Spanish garrison of Eilean Donan and blew up the castle. A fair number of clansmen joined the Spanish troops, bringing the total strength of the Jacobite army to about 1,500. General Wightman had something like 1,100. The two sides met in Glenshiel on 10 June. Accurate mortar fire won the skirmish for the Government forces. The Highlanders disappeared. The Spaniards, after standing up bravely to the mortar fire, eventually surrendered; they were sent to Inverness and then to Edinburgh, where they were imprisoned under harsh conditions until their repatriation in October.

And that was the end of 'the Nineteen'. The Earl of Marischal and his brother managed to reach Peterhead whence they sailed for Holland. They eventually entered the service of Frederick the Great of Prussia, where both achieved great things. Tullibardine survived to fight in the Jacobite rising of 1745 and to die in the Tower after its failure. The capture of San Sebastian by the French put an end to Alberoni's schemes and he fell from power the following December. James left Spain for Italy in August and the following month met at last his fiancée Clementina Sobieska, granddaughter of King John Sobieski of Poland (the saviour of Europe from the Turks) and daughter of Prince James Sobieski, then living at Ohlau in Silesia. Having earlier that year decided on marriage, he had sent his Irish follower Charles Wogan to search for a suitable royal bride, and he had found Clementina. James Murray, second son of the fifth Viscount Stormont, had been sent to Ohlau to treat with Prince James for Clementina's hand, and the negotiations had been successful. In May Wogan had rescued Clementina from captivity in most romantic fashion after she had been arrested at Innsbruck on the orders of the Emperor Charles VI on her journey from Poland to Italy: the Emperor had been requested to do so by King George, who for obvious reasons had no desire to see James beget an heir. James and Clementina were married at Montefiascone on 1 September. She seems to have been frivolous in the early years of matrimony, in marked contrast to her husband's melancholy, and fanatically religious later. At no time was she any help to her husband or he to her. They were in fact quite incompatible and the marriage was far from happy. But it produced two sons, the elder of whom was born on 20 December 1720* and christened Charles Edward Louis John Sylvester Maria Casimir.

* This is the 'Old Style' date, which after 1700 was eleven days behind the 'New Style'. The difference, which is a constant plague to historians, resulted from Gregory XIII's reformed calendar of 1582. Until 1752, however, England stuck to the old calendar, while the Continent had long used the new. In this book the dates of events on the Continent will generally be New Style and those in Britain before 1752, Old Style. (The birth of Charles Edward, though it took place in Rome, is here regarded as a British event and is therefore dated Old Style; it was always celebrated in Scotland on 20 December; the New Style date would be 31 December.) Sometimes it is difficult to tell whether a contemporary narrative is using Old Style or New Style. The dating of the beginning of the new year on 25 March instead of 1 January, which is another feature of the old calendar, does not help matters.

CHAPTER FIVE

Early Years

EIGHT cardinals and a host of noble lords and ladies appeared with the Pope himself to do honour to the new-born infant in the Palazzo Muti. A salvo of guns sounded from the Castle of St Angelo. The Pope formally made over to James the Palazzo Muti, together with money for its furnishing. He had already provided 6,000 scudi worth of consecrated baby-linen for little Charles. Cash presents were also received from others of the dignitaries present. The day after the birth the Pope celebrated a Mass of thanksgiving. Silver and bronze medals were struck, with the busts of James and Clementina on one side and on the other a mother and child with the words *Spes Britanniae*, 'the hope of Britain'. Poets hailed the infant:

> *'Twas thus in early Bloom of Time,*
> *Beneath a Reverend Oak,*
> *In sacred and inspired Rhyme,*
> *An ancient* Druid *spoke.*
>
> *An hero from fair* Clementine
> *Long ages hence shall spring,*
> *And all the Gods their power shall join*
> *To bless the future King!*
>
> *Venus shall give him all her charms*
> *To win and conquer hearts.*
> *Rough Mars shall train the youth to arms,*
> *Minerva teach him Arts; ...*

Some Jacobites claimed that a new star had been seen in the heavens at the time of the birth, and that a fierce storm had simultaneously wrought havoc in Hanover. But the British agent in Rome, John Walton (whose real name was Baron Philip von Stosch and whom Sir

Compton Mackenzie has picturesquely described as 'an expatriated Prussian sodomite called Stosch'), anxious to please his Hanoverian master, wrote of the infant that his legs were so turned inward and deformed ('tellement tournées en dedans et estropiées') that it was extremely doubtful whether he would ever be able to walk. The level of truth in this statement was on a par with his subsequent assertions that Charles was daily showing such increasing physical imperfections that he could not live long, and that several female experts on babies ('plusieurs dames, connoisseuses dans le métier de faire les enfants') had said that his mother would be unable to bear another. The remarkable physical liveliness and endurance that little Charles showed from a very early age and the birth of his younger brother, Henry Benedict Maria Clement Thomas Francis Xavier, in March 1725, show the value of Walton's evidence. What he had to say later about the reasons for the estrangement between James and Clementina is clearly highly suspect.

Trouble between the parents began over the education of the young prince. James, aware that his chances of obtaining the throne that he regarded as his right depended on his willingness to tolerate Protestant established churches in England and Scotland, and on such willingness being publicly known, not only provided Protestant members of his court-in-exile with facilities for worship but also thought it politic to provide Charles with a Protestant tutor. Clementina, however, wanted only Catholics around her child. Charles's first governess was a Mrs Sheldon, a Catholic who came from the old Jacobite Court of St Germain (where there was still a Jacobite centre, which was in unfortunate rivalry with that at Rome) in April 1721. Writing to the Earl of Mar (or the Duke of Mar as the Jacobites now called him, since James had granted him that title in 1715) on 1 April, James said that he had sent for Mrs Sheldon. 'If I find her fitt to put about my son I am always master to do it, but whether she should be fitt or unfitt, it would be a satisfaction to me to have some persons in my view equall to such a trust. The qualities of a person for so important a charge are obvious. . . . what is above all requisite is prudence, a reasonable knowledge of the world, and a principle of obedience, attachment and submission to me, . . .' Mrs Sheldon seems to have lacked all these qualities, particularly 'obedience, attachment and submission' to James. But Clementina was devoted to her, and she became a source of trouble between husband and wife. Soon after the birth of his second child James gave orders for Mrs Sheldon's removal.

If James disliked Mrs Sheldon, Clementina disliked even more some of those whom James liked and trusted. Notable among these was John

Hay, who had been active in preparing for the Jacobite rising of 1715: he succeeded Mar as James's Secretary of State in 1724, after Mar had lost James's confidence. James created him titular Earl of Inverness in 1725. Hay and his wife Marjory were much with James, and gossip soon had it that Mrs Hay was James's mistress. Walton, naturally, reported such gossip as fact and with relish, and all over Europe news of Clementina's justified anger at her husband's adultery with Mrs Hay was assiduously spread, to the bitter chagrin of Jacobites, some of whom believed it and all of whom realized that such scandal did their cause no good. There is, however, no hard evidence at all of James's adultery. Walton's picturesque stories are obviously suspect. Clementina herself, though we know of her dislike of the Hays, never accused her husband of adultery with Mrs Hay or with anybody else. But that there were animosities and intrigues and recriminations we do know. Cardinal Alberoni, now banished from Spain to his native Italy, for political reasons of his own (he has been accused of being in the pay of the Hanoverian Court, but there is no proof of this), encouraged Clementina in her complaints and even forged letters from the Queen of Spain to James reproaching him for his behaviour to his wife.

Clementina was not the only one who disliked the Hays. The veteran Jacobite Lockhart of Carnwath blamed the estrangement between James and Clementina entirely on Hay, whom he described as 'a cunning, false, avaricious creature, of very ordinary parts, cultivated by no sort of literature, altogether void of experience in business; and his insolence prevailing often over his little stock of prudence he did and said many unadvised ridicolous things.' All parties in the affair publicized their views, and James was the sufferer. He was imprudent enough to circulate his own account of the causes of the breach between Clementina and himself together with letters of self-justification and reproach (written to Clementina), to the distress of many of his friends. 'I would not judge it very suitable to the King's dignity', wrote a Jacobite by the name of O'Rourke from Lunéville on 8 December 1725, 'to make much use of the two letters whereof you sent me copys. It will look odd to all people yt. such an affair should have been treated by letters betwixt the King and Queen within the precincts of his own house.' He adds that this is 'noe better than to justifie himself from being a very bad husband, a point noe body (I suppose) accuses him off, not even the Queen herself, at least as to her liberty and expenses, &c.'

By this time the breach between husband and wife had become physical: Clementina had retired to the Convent of St Cecilia in the Trastevere. The last straw had been the dismissal of Mrs Sheldon and the appointment of Protestant James Murray (who was Mrs Hay's brother, and was now created titular Earl of Dunbar by James) as Charles's tutor.* James, writing to her after she announced her intention of retiring to a convent, assured her he bore no resentment against her and attributed her decision to the intrigues of their common enemies. He simultaneously asserted his own rights ('je veux etre le maitre dans mes affaires et dans ma famille') and pleaded with her to return 'a la raison, au devoir, à vousmeme et à moy' – 'to reason, to duty, to yourself, and to me who only await your submission with open arms to give you all the peace and happiness I can'. Writing to Princess Constantine Sobieska on 1 December 1725 James complained that Clementina had 'listened to neither reason, duty nor interest' and had fallen into the trap laid by their enemies. 'Consulting neither her father, nor, I believe, any of her relations, she has entered a convent, following a lady Mrs Sheldon whom I had dismissed for good reasons.' But he talks of his 'tenderness' for his wife, which he wishes had been reciprocated.

With Clementina in the Convent of St Cecilia, James retired to Bologna. Church dignitaries intervened with both parties to the dispute to try and effect a reconciliation. The Pope himself went to see Clementina and argued with her. But in the end it was James who gave in: he dismissed Murray as Charles's tutor and sent away the Hays, though still professing his 'great and good opinion' of John Hay and hoping, as he put it, 'to have yet soon occasion to show in his person that I am incapable of abandoning my faithful servants.' Hay became converted to Roman Catholicism at the end of 1731, which is perhaps some tribute to his integrity, for if he had taken the step earlier it might have been of use to him.

The reconciliation effected, Clementina left the convent in order to join James at Bologna. But the death of George I in June 1727, when she was on her way from Rome to Bologna, sent James off for nearly a year of fruitless intrigue for a Jacobite rising in Scotland. 'As soon as I heard of the Elector of Hanover's death', he wrote to Lockhart of Carnwath from Nancy on 22 June, 'I thought it incumbent on me to put myself in a condition of profiting of what might be the consequence of so great ane event, which I was sensible I could never do at so great a distance as Italy; and that made me take the resolution of leaving that country out of hand and drawing nearer to England. . . .' He went first

* Walton gives the news of the appointment of Murray as Charles's 'governor' in November 1725 and specifically says that this was one of Clementina's major grievances. In fact, James's official order making the appointment is dated 4 July 1727. But he had announced his intention of appointing Murray governor eighteen months earlier.

to Lorraine, and stayed for some time in Nancy, but pressure from the British Government on the French Government led to the Duke of Lorraine's ordering him to leave. He went to Avignon, a Papal State, but British pressure on the Pope (a threat to bombard Civita Vecchia and a reminder of the vulnerable position of Catholics in England) led to his being advised by Benedict XIII to leave. So in January 1728 he returned to Italy, where he was at last re-united with Clementina after a separation of over two years.

The rest of Clementina's story is soon told. Clement XII succeeded Benedict XIII as Pope early in 1730. Clement, who believed firmly in a wife's obedience to her husband, advised Clementina not to maintain her hostility to the Hays and to agree to her husband's plans for her sons' education even if it meant that a Protestant might have some say in it. After some argument and some delay Clementina suddenly gave in completely and devoted the rest of her life to extreme piety, works of charity, and severe self-mortification. She died in January 1735, in her thirty-fourth year. She was buried in St Peter's but her heart was removed and placed in a green marble urn in the Church of the Holy Apostles, hard by the Palazzo Muti. It had been an unhappy marriage, and a deep incompatibility of temperament between husband and wife seems to have been the main cause of the unhappiness. This incompatibility was exacerbated by the frustrations, futilities and self-deceptions of a court-in-exile, with the continuous contrast between pretension and reality, between high ceremonial and the true facts of power, and humiliating financial dependence on doles from the Pope.

These were bad times for Jacobitism. The peaceful accession of George II 'with the favor of the populace', as Lockhart of Carnwath conceded (though he added 'whither more from that nationall genius which is constantly pleased with noveltys or out of odium to his father'), marked a low ebb in James's fortunes, which in 1728 appeared to Lockhart 'with a more dismall aspect than I ever knew them'. Lockhart attributed this largely to the removal of Mar from James's service; after this, 'great blunders were committed in the execution of affairs in Scotland (and the same was alledged and may be reasonably supposed elsewhere) so that people soon saw that they were not carryd on with the dexterity and secresie as formerlie; but that which struck the nail to the head was his allowing these his favorites (which seems to be a curse in a peculiar manner entaild on the royal race of Stewart) to rule under him in so absolute arbitrary a manner, that for their sake and on their account, the prerogatives of a soveraign and a husband are skrewed up to a pitch not tenable by the laws of God or man, or consistent with prudence; in so far as the royall consort, the mother of the royall issue, and subjects of the best quality and merit who had served the King with their blood and fortunes, are trampled upon and abused by a parcell of people who never were nor will be capable to do the King any materiall service and are contemptible in the sight of all that know them'. Lockhart considered that James had been seduced into wrong paths by the Hays, and this view was shared by other Jacobites, reflecting the divided counsels of the movement. The old Jacobite loyalties seemed to be fading. The last words in the Lockhart Papers, written in 1728, three years before their author's death, show him sunk in gloom. 'And thus while no party is acting for his [James's] interest, no projects formed, nothing done to keep up the spirits of the people, the old race drops off by degrees and a new one sprouts up, who ... enter on the stage with a perfect indifference, at least coolness, towards him and his cause, which consequently must daylie languish and in process of time be tottally forgot. In which melancholy situation of the King's affairs, I leave them in the year 1728.'

Meanwhile, Charles was growing into a handsome and lively boy. The Duke of Liria, son of James's elder (and illegitimate) brother the Duke of Berwick, greatly admired his young cousin, and we have a picture from his pen of little Charles at the age of six and a half, when the quarrel between his parents was at its height and his mother was in the convent of St Cecilia. The Duke described the Prince of Wales (as Charles was to all true Jacobites) as remarkable for his dexterity, grace and bearing, a fluent reader, skilful with a gun and on a horse, and surprisingly adept at killing birds with a crossbow. 'He speaks English, French and Italian perfectly' and is altogether the ideal Prince. This testimony, of course, is not altogether unbiassed, but later evidence suggests that it is not wildly exaggerated. A letter written probably by James Edgar, James's private secretary, on 22 March 1727, confirms the Duke of Liria's view of Charles. It speaks of the boy's daily improvement in mind and body. 'As to his studies he reads English now correctly, and has begun to learn to write. He speaks English perfectly well, and the French and Italian very little worse. He has a stable of little horses and every day diverts himself by riding.' His sports include 'shooting, the tennis, shuttlecock, &c.' and he is an excellent dancer. Charles's proficiency in tennis and shuttlecock is confirmed in letters from a Mr Stafford, who was appointed to look after Charles in October 1728; from him we learn also that Charles was very keen on 'the Golf'.

Charles's own first letter, written at the age of seven when he was with his mother at Bologna before his father's return from Avignon, obviously had its spelling corrected by his tutor, for his later letters show a total indifference to orthography:

> Dear Papa
>
> I thank you mightily for your kind letter. I shall strive to obey you in all things. I will be very Dutiful to Mamma, and not jump too near her. I shall be much obliged to the Cardinal for his animals. I long to see you soon and in good health. I am
>
> > Dear Papa
> > your most Dutiful and affectionate Son
> > Charles P

The promise not to jump too near Mamma tells its own eloquent story of a high-spirited boy and a nervous mother. Charles's handwriting in the letter is a clear if childish Italian hand, the characters well and evidently slowly formed, with some darker than others as a result of allowing too much ink on his pen.

We do not know very much about the kind of education Charles received. James Murray returned as a tutor in 1730 but does not seem to have got on well with his pupil. Walton actually reported that Charles was locked in his room for threatening to kill Murray. Two other tutors were more important. These were Andrew Michael Ramsay ('the Chevalier Ramsay': many Jacobites in exile on the Continent called themselves 'Chevalier'), scholar and writer and friend of Fénelon, under whose influence he had become a Catholic in 1710, and Thomas Sheridan, an Irishman and also a Catholic, who was to accompany Charles to Scotland in 1745, when the Prince knighted him. Ramsay and Sheridan seem to have stimulated Charles's imagination with stories of Scotland and Ireland and of his ancestral rights there. Dreams of glory evidently interfered with Charles's application to his studies. In 1733 the Earl of Marischal wrote from Rome that the boy 'had got out of the hands of his governors', so there may have been an element of truth in Walton's otherwise highly suspicious story. There is little doubt that from the age of at least thirteen Charles was dreaming excitedly of a Jacobite rising and a Stuart restoration. His father had by now pretty well given up any active hope of himself ascending the British throne, and remained melancholy and withdrawn.

Charles saw his first fighting in August 1734, when he was well into his fourteenth year. The dynastic ambitions of Spain in Italy had led to a Spanish army, supported by the French, invading Italy in order to drive the Emperor Charles VI from his joint kingdom of Naples and Sicily so that Don Carlos of Spain might obtain it. The Duke of Liria (who on his father's orders had become a naturalized Spaniard: his title was Spanish) fought with the Spaniards, and invited his cousin to join him outside Gaeta, in which fortified town a large part of the Austrian army was being closely invested. James, after some hesitation, gave his consent; he decided that Charles should go 'absolutely incognito, under my old name the Chevalier de St George'. (Here we have the first appearance of 'The Young Chevalier'.) Before leaving, he was received in cordial audience by the Pope, who gave him a generous cash present but, as James mournfully wrote, 'gave me no money on this occasion.' Charles set out on 27 July, accompanied by Murray, Sheridan, and a suite which included two friars and a surgeon. His younger brother Henry, recognized by the Jacobites as the Duke of York, kicked up a great fuss at not being allowed to go too, though he was only nine years old. James, who was especially fond of his younger son, wrote to Hay that he believed young Henry would have made as good an impression as Charles, adding that although the two brothers were devoted to each other he thought that the younger's 'affliction on his brother's journey proceeded as much from emulation as tenderness'.

The Duke of Liria – who had just succeeded to his father's title of Duke of Berwick on the latter's death at the siege of Philipsbourg – reported his admiration of his young cousin's behaviour in a letter of 7 August:

The Siege of *Gaeta* is now over, blessed be GOD; and though a very short one, I suffered more while it lasted than in any siege I have been heretofore present at.

You may easily imagine the Uneasiness I talk of, was my Anxiety and Concern for the Person of CHARLES Prince of *Wales*. The KING his Father, sent him hither under my Care, to witness the Siege, and laid his Commands on me, not only to direct him, but even to show him every Thing that merited his Attention; and, I must confess, that he made me pass some as uneasy Moments as ever I met with from the crossest Accidents of my bypast Life. Just on his Arrival, I conducted him to the Trenches, where he showed not the least Surprise at the Enemies Fire, even when the Balls were hissing about his Ears. I was relieved, the Day following, from the Trenches; and, as the House I lodged in, was very much exposed, the Enemy discharged, at once, Five Piece of Cannon against it; which made me move my Quarters. The PRINCE, arriving a Moment after, would, at any Rate, go into the House, tho I did all I could to disswade him from it, by representing to him the Danger he was exposing himself to, yet he staid in it a very considerable Time, with an undisturbed Countenance, tho' the Walls had been pierced through with the Cannon Ball. In a Word, this PRINCE discovers, *That in Great Princes, whom nature has mark'd out for Heroes, Valour does not wait the Number of Years.* I am now, blessed be GOD, rid of all my Uneasiness, and joyfully indulge myself in the Pleasure of seeing the PRINCE adored by Officers and Soldiers. His Manner and Conversation are really bewitching; and you may lay your Account, that were it otherwise, I would not have kept it a Secret from you. We set out for *Naples* in a Day or two, where I am pretty certain his ROYAL HIGHNESS will charm the *Neapolitans* as much as he has done our Troops. ... I wish to GOD, that some of the greatest *Sticklers* in *England* against the family of the *STEWARTS* had been Eye-Witnesses of this PRINCE's Resolution during the Siege, and I am firmly perswaded that they would soon change their Way of thinking. ...

But Charles himself wrote little. He did not write at all to his mother and annoyed his younger brother by not replying to his letters. James wrote him at length on 27 August, reproaching him with his 'omissions' which, he says, he realizes 'proceed from your too natural aversion to all application and constraint'. He advised him to 'endeavour to cultivate the Talents which Providence has given you' if he is not soon to 'lose that good character which your present behaviour is beginning to gain you'. James's gently querulous tone will be heard again in letters to his son, as it had been heard earlier in letters to his wife.

Don Carlos, who was now King of Naples, invited young Charles there, and he duly arrived by sea on 11 August. There is a story that his hat blew off while he was in the Bay of Naples and fell into the sea, and that, when it was proposed to lower a boat to recover it, Charles told the crew not to bother, for 'he should be obliged before long to fetch himself a hat in England [i.e., the Crown]'. Charles was much fêted in Naples, and continued to neglect his correspondence. His tutors tried in vain to get him to write longer and more frequent letters, and Sheridan asked James to speak to the boy on the subject. But throughout his life Charles remained a poor and infrequent letter writer.

Charles would have liked to accompany the Spanish army to Sicily, but James, who was getting worried about his son's behaviour and his health (the latter suffering, he believed, from intemperance in diet), would not hear of it, and the boy joined his father at his summer residence in Albano on 14 September. There James duly reprimanded him on the shortness and infrequency of his letters, and there seems to have been something of a scene. Nevertheless James did not doubt that his son's first military venture had been a personal triumph for him. As for Walton, waiting to convey to London any malicious gossip about the family in exile that he could pick up, he had to retract his earlier sneering at what he had considered Charles's empty bravado in setting out for the siege of Gaeta and admit the boy's courage, sense and popularity. 'Everybody says,' he added, 'that he will be in time a far more dangerous enemy to the present establishment of the Government of England than ever his father was.' It was in the January following Charles's return from Naples that Clementina died.

James continued to be uneasy about Charles. He thought him 'wonderfully thoughtless for one of his age' and considered his younger brother the more thoughtful. At the same time Charles was 'very innocent, and extreme backwards in some respects for his age'. Though he had something of his great-uncle's charm he had nothing of Charles II's ease and assurance in relation to members of the opposite sex. The ladies who swooned for Charles in Holyrood in 1745 were always the initiators and never the victims of the Prince's advances. Perhaps James considered Charles sexually backward for his age. At any rate, he thought that travel would help to wean him from 'little childish amusements' and to mature him generally, and early in 1737 he sent him on a tour of the chief cities of Italy under the title this time of Count of Albany. Charles left Rome on 22 April, together with Murray, Sheridan and a suite of twelve. At Bologna he declined a guard of honour on the grounds that he was travelling incognito. During his two-day stay there a public ball was given in his honour by the Marquis of Tibbia in his magnificent palazzo. In Parma, which he visited next, the Dowager Duchess Dorothea paid him the most flattering attentions and presented him with a gold snuff-box set with diamonds: she also made a ball for him, preceded by a state dinner. This time his incognito did not seem to bother Charles: he inspected troops before leaving for Piacenza. From Piacenza (after another ball in his honour) he went on to Genoa, where the Spanish envoy paid him particular attention and where once again he attended formal parties in his honour. There was the same story in Milan, except that there the officers of the Holy Roman Emperor had received special orders to ignore him. From Milan he went to Venice, where the pretence at incognito seems to have been completely abandoned, for there he was openly treated as royalty. After some days of feasting and high ceremony he went on through Padua, Ferrara and (once more) Bologna to Florence where he was accommodated at the Palazzo Corsini.

We know all this, because it was sourly reported home by Mr Fane, the British envoy at Florence. Fane, who had watched with increasing distress Charles's progress through other Italian cities, determined that in Florence he would find a change. Before Charles's entry into the city he called on the Grand Duke's secretary and expressed the view of his Government that no special celebrations should mark Charles's entry. The secretary agreed that no 'improper mark of distinction' should be paid to Charles, and Fane wrote happily home that, unlike the other Italian cities, Florence would distinguish herself by devotion to the House of Hanover. We can therefore judge of Fane's state of mind when he heard that on Charles's approach to Florence the coaches of the Grand Duke had been sent to meet him. He at once protested violently to the Duke's secretary, who blandly apologized and said that the Duke had never authorized the sending of his coaches, and that this must have been done by the Duke's Master of Ceremonies. Fane at once called on the said Master of Ceremonies, who denied that he had acted on his own responsibility: he had been ordered to do so by ministers of state. Fane protested strongly, and in the end the carriages were ordered to return. But it did not really make any difference. Charles was fêted in Florence as magnificently as elsewhere, and received all attentions paid him with the assured courtesy of someone who considered them his right. We should probably believe Walton for once when he reported having heard James Murray say to one of the Grand Duke's officials: 'It is not so much the attentions themselves which are shown to the Prince that displease the English Court, as the manner in which the Prince receives them.' Fane was however successful in preventing a meeting between Charles and the Grand Duke. He agreed at last that it would be in order for Charles to meet the Grand Duke privately, but the sudden illness and subsequent death of the Duke prevented this.

In addition to Fane's reports home, we have Murray's letters to James, waxing eloquent over 'noble dinners' and magnificent receptions and dances. There is a picture of Charles in morning curl-papers and a report that Charles requested the Irish officer who saw him in this state not to mention the fact in Dublin, as it might be misunderstood. In all public affairs Charles behaved admirably. However, 'I cannot but tell your Majesty' (Murray wrote) 'that in private we might make the same exceptions as formerly, and that he gives us rather more uneasiness when he travels. But this is only a trouble to his own people, and particularly to me who go in the chair with him.' Charles improved a bit as a correspondent, then fell off again, to be reproached once more by James, 'a father that loves you better than himself'.

From Florence Charles and his retinue proceeded to Lucca, Pisa and Leghorn, always with the same flattering reception, and so back to Rome. As reports reached London of Charles's triumphant progress, and especially of his royal reception in Venice, Government indignation rose. Businello, the Venetian resident in London, was ordered to leave the country within three days. And the Republic of Genoa was warned that it would be better for her if she treated the House of Hanover with more respect and the House of Stuart with less. But Charles was happy, for the moment at least. He returned to his father full of the attentions that had been paid him and the ceremonial with which he had been greeted. It all seemed, somehow, if not the fulfilment of his ambitions at least more like the real thing than the court-in-exile in Rome or Albano. To complete his sense of adult responsibility, on 3 August his hair was cut and he was fitted with a wig, and at the end of December, on his seventeenth birthday, he was shaved for the first time. All this did not make life at the Palazzo Muti any less tedious. Charles felt himself to be a man: he was anxious to be out in the world doing something for the Stuart claim to the British throne. 'Had I soldiers, I would not be here now, but wherever I could serve my friends,' he had remarked in the midst of the round of noble dinners and formal balls.

It was not to be long before events in Europe opened up a possibility for more active Jacobite activity than had existed since Charles was born. Meanwhile the young man hunted and shot and danced and wore brilliant uniforms glistening with jewels and orders, and dreamt of a Stuart restoration. He was fond of music, and played the 'cello. He was always courteous and graceful in public, and impressed visitors with his manner. In private he could be petulant and wilful. He seems to have had no particular interest in religion and wore his Catholicism lightly (though as a small boy he had impressed the Pope with his ability to repeat the Catechism by heart). In short, while he had ambition, energy and many external accomplishments, he was rather spoilt and self-indulgent, with little depth of character and no intellectual interests. He seems to have used other people as a way of fixing his own image of himself. Lady Mary Wortley Montagu, who observed him in Rome in 1741, thought him 'thoughtless enough'. But on the whole he lived up to the public image he had created with a skill that fascinated observers. The stage he trod so successfully he knew to be artificial, and he longed for real life.

CHAPTER SIX

An End of Waiting

THE first twenty years of Charles Edward's life was a period of lull for the Jacobite movement. After the failure of the attempt of 1719 a long period of peace and prosperity under the premiership of Sir Robert Walpole reduced Jacobitism in England to the merest sentiment, quite unable to prevail against the forces of growing wealth and indolent self-interest which Walpole knew so well how to use for his own purposes, while in Scotland Lowland merchants and landowners who had profited by the Union saw no reason to upset the *status quo* and those Highlanders and others who still looked to the King across the water realized the hopelesness of their cause without another European war which would bring them a foreign ally. Nevertheless, there was some Jacobite activity in England in the early part of this period. Francis Atterbury, Bishop of Rochester, who had offered to proclaim James III at the Royal Exchange on the death of Queen Anne but was dissuaded by Bolingbroke so that he actually took part in the coronation of George I, never gave up his Jacobite aspirations and was involved in a Jacobite plot in 1722. One of the leaders of this plot was Christopher Layer, a barrister of the Middle Temple, who planned to collect a force with which to seize the Tower of London, the Royal Exchange and St James's Palace. Layer was, however, betrayed by one of his many dubious lady friends, brought to trial in November 1722 and executed at Tyburn the following May. Another suspect was the non-juring clergyman George Kelly, who was arrested early in 1722 and sentenced to imprisonment in the Tower, from which he escaped after fourteen years of confinement. But Atterbury was more important than either Layer or Kelly, and Walpole, acting on his belief that 'every man has his price', tried to bribe the bishop on to the government side by the offer of the see of Winchester (when it became vacant) and a post at the Treasury for his son-in-law. Atterbury refused the deal, with the result that a Bill of Pains and Penalties against him was brought in at the House of Lords, and passed by a majority in spite of Atterbury's brilliant defence of himself in the House. This meant his banishment to the Continent (at exactly the same time as Bolingbroke, having made his peace with Walpole, was on his way back to England): he went abroad and entered the service of James Francis Edward. During Walpole's long premiership (1721–1742) there was also what might be called a constitutional Jacobitism, led by the Tory Member of Parliament William Shippen, 'honest Shippen' as Pope called him, who bitterly opposed Walpole in Parliament yet who remained a good personal friend of his. Shippen hoped to achieve a Jacobite restoration by parliamentary means, but by the time of his death in 1743 this had long been seen to be a wholly unrealistic ambition.

It was clear that no Jacobite attempt could succeed without French help. From October 1739, when popular opinion forced the peace-loving Walpole into war against Spain, the international situation began to look more favourable for a Jacobite rising made with foreign support. Walpole himself seems to have been communicating with James in 1739 through the historian Thomas Carte who had been secretary to Bishop Atterbury and who had fled to the Continent in 1722: he wanted to find out through Carte what James's intentions were with respect to the Church of England and to the persons of the House of Hanover, and received a reaffirmation of James's intention to protect the Church of England and a statement with respect to the Princes of the House of Hanover that if they fell into his power 'I shall certainly not touch a hair of their heads'. What the ageing and now politically thwarted Walpole was up to remains a matter of conjecture: perhaps this was his way of registering his belief that a changed European situation meant that Jacobitism was now once more to be taken seriously.

The European situation changed further with the death of the Emperor Charles VI in October 1740 five months after the death of King Frederick William I of Prussia and the succession to the Prussian throne of the brilliant and ambitious Frederick II. In the winter of 1740–1741 Frederick II marched into the Austrian province of Silesia thus undoing at a blow the Pragmatic Sanction, that family compact among European monarchs by which Charles VI had hoped to keep indivisible the lands belonging to the house of Austria and to secure to his young daughter Maria Theresa undisturbed succession to those lands. Frederick's action turned a war between Britain and Spain into a European war, the War of the Austrian Succession. Britain was concerned at Frederick's attack on Austria because she had guaranteed the Pragmatic Sanction in the Treaty of Vienna of 1731. Further, young Maria Theresa's call for help not only against Prussia but also against Britain's traditional enemies France and Spain (who followed Prussia's example in tearing up the Pragmatic Sanction) appealed immensely to the British popular imagination. So Britain was drawn into the war, at first indirectly by granting Maria Theresa a cash subsidy and sending a contingent of Danish and Hessian troops in British pay to fight for her. With Walpole gone and Britain's foreign affairs being run with great vigour by John Cartaret, British participation steadily increased, even before she was officially at war with France. A mixed army of Hanoverians, Hessians, Dutch, Austrians and Britons was sent into the field commanded by George II in person (he had succeeded his father in 1727) and his force met and defeated a larger French army under Noailles at Dettingen in 1743. This was the last occasion on which an English king personally took part in a battle.

At least as important for the Jacobite cause was the death in January 1743 of Cardinal Fleury, the French prime minister, and the consequent succession as director of French policy of Cardinal de Tencin. The Cardinal was the brother of the notorious Claudine de Tencin who had betrayed Bolingbroke's secrets to the Abbé Dubois, yet, oddly enough, he had been helped and patronized by James and as a result he was anxious to be of help to the Jacobites. Though Louis XV was not himself eager to give material assistance to the Jacobites, Cardinal de Tencin pressed James's claims very hard and eventually persuaded the French king to invite James's son, young Charles Edward, to Paris. The invitation came at the beginning of 1744, and met with an eager response from Charles, now just twenty-four years of age and impatient for action.

James and his little court-in-exile at Rome were of course aware of the improved prospects for Jacobitism since 1740. James had his agents in Paris and his contacts in Scotland. Among the former were Robert Sempill (or Sempil or Semple), who had been created a peer of Scotland by James in 1723, and William MacGregor (or Drummond) of Balhaldy, both of whom proved to be little more than ineffectual intriguers, and chief among the latter was John Murray of Broughton who was to play an important part in the Forty-five. James Edgar, James's secretary, corresponded regularly with Murray from April 1741. On 27 April Edgar wrote:

I had the honour to communicate to H.M. all your letters as I received them, and he now commands me to assure you that he is very sensible of your zeal and good heart towards him, of which you gave him so convincing a proof by your entering into this Correspondence. He makes no doubt but that you will give a general satisfaction by your discreet, prudent, and cautious conduct in it, and directs me, in making you a kind compliment in his name, to begin this correspondence on my part by the following Paragraph, as a mark of the particular confidence he places in you.

Edgar encloses a copy of that paragraph in James's own handwriting. It begins:

The King is informed, that his friends in England being apprehensive that some project might be forming in Scotland for his restoration, without an attempts being made in England, and by consequence without a sufficient prospect of success, his said English friends had advised those in Scotland not to proceed in any such project without heareing from the King. H. M^{ty} agrees entirely with his friends in England that no project should be excused in which both nations have not their share ...

James was clearly nervous about the rise in Jacobite enthusiasm which resulted from the outbreak of the War of the Austrian Succession. He did not want to risk another failure. But Charles was becoming increasingly impatient for action and never thought of possible failure.

On Cardinal Fleury's death in January 1743 Murray set out for Paris to see for himself what the prospects of French help now were. There he talked with Lord Sempill 'who took great pains' (Murray later wrote) 'to persuade me that things were in as much forwardness as could be wished'. Murray was sceptical, and when he said he would, like to have confirmation of this from Amelot de Chaillon, the French Foreign Minister, Sempill and Balhaldy confessed that they had exaggerated the strength of Jacobite support in Britain for political reasons and urged Murray to do the same in talking with Amelot. 'It was evident from this,' Murray commented in his later account of these proceedings, 'that they were not men of strict veracity, and had not represented the state of our Party fairly, but endeavoured to impose upon the French by augmenting their numbers'. Murray succeeded in being 'admitted for two minutes' to Cardinal de Tencin's antechamber, when the Cardinal 'said he would be extremely glad to have it in his power to serve the King my master, having a singular regard for him, as indeed he could not fail – Sa Majeste ayent la plus belle du monde'. What it was that was so *belle* Murray left out in his account, so we can only guess: but Murray took it as a shameful remark and was much shocked. He then (together with Sempill and Balhaldy) had an interview with Amelot, who made some encouraging noises but at the same time 'hoped the Gentlemen had well considered of what they were about; [saying] that it was an affair of the utmost consequence; and though the Scots were a brave undertaking people, yet such enterprises were dangerous and precarious'. Murray was 'startled not a little' by this remark, since Balhaldy had previously told him how enthusiastic the French were in the Jacobite cause. It was clear that there had been a lot of wishful thinking among the Jacobites in Paris. Murray suspected both Sempill and Balhaldy of worse than wishful thinking, and warned the Earl of Marischal against them. Mutual suspicion thus prevailed in the Jacobite camp. James in Rome, however, was unaware of this, and trusted Murray, Sempill and Balhaldy equally. It was Balhaldy who was chosen by James to go to Rome in December 1743 'to show the practicability of the road for another person', as he put it in a letter to Sempill. The 'other person' was, of course, Charles Edward, and the 'road' was the way from Rome to Paris.

Balhaldy made all the arrangements, and then returned to Paris. The plan was for Charles to leave Rome on the pretext of 'a party of *chasse*', go by devious ways incognito to Genoa, thence to Savona, thence by sea to Antibes, where he was to remain until he received a message from Louis XV that he should proceed to Paris. Secrecy was essential if the British Government was not to discover that Charles had left for France and thus become alerted to the possibility of a Jacobite rising. John Walton was still watching and reporting. 'The great precautions,' Walton had written to London as early as 8 July 1741, 'taken by the ministers of France and Spain in order to hide the most trifling steps of the Pretender's son are a certain argument that they intend to make him play an important *rôle* shortly upon the world's theatre.' Walton did in fact discover Charles's departure to France in January 1744, and he duly reported it. He also reported later, quite erroneously, that James had been strongly opposed to his son's leaving and had been persuaded to consent only by the Pope and Cardinal Acquaviva.

Charles acted his part in the dramatic journey with enthusiasm. Before dawn on 9 January he left his bed on the pretence of going boar-hunting at Cisterna. Though a chaise was provided, Charles told James Murray, his former tutor who was accompanying him, that he would rather ride than drive in a chaise, as he felt cold. He accordingly mounted a horse that a groom had been leading behind the chaise, and rode off towards Albano, Murray conveniently falling into a ditch in order to distract the attention of other members of the party. But Charles did not go to Albano. He swerved east and then north and, with passports and post-horses acquired en route from Cardinal Acquaviva, rode non-stop through heavy snow to Massa, in Tuscany. From Massa he got passage to Genoa on a Maltese bark. At Genoa he rested for a day and a night to recover from the fatigue of his strenuous journey, and then moved south-west along the coast of the Gulf of Genoa to Savona. He seems to have had some trouble at Savona, for his brother Henry, writing to him from Rome on 6 February to congratulate him on his safe arrival at Antibes, refers to it: 'I have already been upon thorns untill I heard you safely landed, and particularly whilst I heard you was locked up [shut up in quarantine?] at Savona, for certainly you was there in a very ugly situation, but now I thank God, that Providence has freed you from all these Dangers.' But eventually he found a Catalan felucca which took him right through the middle of the watching British fleet unnoticed to Antibes.

Henry, who had not been told in advance of the plan for his brother's journey, fully co-operated in a programme of deception once he did learn of it. He went to Cisterna and gave out that his brother was engaged in hunting there with him. He actually sent presents of wild geese from Albano to Rome, as though they had come from Charles. At this time the two brothers were on the most affectionate terms, as is clear from this further passage from Henry's letter of 6 February:

> I wish you cou'd see all the content and satisfaction my heart feels every time I hear anything that can redound to your honour and Glory, and that I am sure proceeds from the Respectuous love and tenderness I have for you, which, I can assure you, Dear Brother (were the King but to permit me) wou'd make me fly through fire and water to be with you.

Charles had ridden to the Tuscan border as a Neapolitan courier on his way to Spain, and wore the badge displayed by such persons. But once in Tuscany he removed the badge and showed the passport which Cardinal Acquaviva had obtained for him from the Grand Duke of Tuscany in which he figured as an officer in the Spanish service by the name of Don Biagio. He sailed from Savona to Antibes under the name of Graham. Once in Antibes he was safer. He did not wait there long, but proceeded via Lyons, where he rested for a short while, to Paris, without waiting for any royal summons from Louis. He reached Paris on 29 January.

There was always the chance that he might have been recognized and detained, by one expedient or another, between Rome and Savona. Walton discovered about Charles's plan long before he reached Paris.

Two days after Charles had left Rome Horace Mann wrote a description of him to the Duke of Newcastle, describing him as 'above the middle height and very thin'. He described his face as long and his complexion as clear but rather pale, and added: 'the forehead very broad, the eyes fairly large, blue, but without sparkle, the mouth large with the lips slightly curled; and the chin more sharp than rounded'. This description might have helped to save Charles from detection, for his eyes were in fact brown, not blue.

There is conflicting evidence about Charles's welcome in Paris. He himself wrote to his father: 'I have met with all that could be expected from the King of France, who expresses great tenderness, and will be careful of all my concerns'. Yet Aeneas Macdonald, the young Jacobite Scottish banker of Paris, brother of Donald Macdonald of Kinlochmoidart, who invested money in the rising of 1745 and was to accompany Charles to Scotland, said at his examination in September 1746 that neither the French King nor any of his ministers nor any persons os distinction took the slightest notice of Charles when he was in France. Certainly James was sceptical of Louis's intentions. 'The promises of France are not to be reconciled with her negligent and indifferent behaviour to the Prince,' he wrote to Sempill on 13 February 1744. James asserted that his son had never seen the King of France and that he was obliged to remain incognito. But at this stage Charles was determined to put the best construction on everything. He kept writing to his father that everything was going well. Marshal Saxe was preparing for an invasion of England, at which Charles would be present. After only about two weeks in Paris Charles went secretly to the little coastal town of Gravelines (about twelve miles west of Dunkirk), under the name of Chevalier Douglas. He had decided that this was to be his headquarters until the expedition set off. His only companion at Gravelines was Balhaldy, who acted as his secretary.

Preparations for a French invasion of England were indeed under way. Troops were concentrated at Aires, Saint-Omer and Bergues, in readiness to proceed to Dunkirk for embarkation. The British Government, which had already protested to the French Foreign Minister about Charles's presence in France as constituting a breach of treaty, was perfectly aware of what was going on and assembled a fleet in the Straits of Dover under Sir John Norris. (This had taken time, because much of the British fleet had been in the Mediterranean, but French delays in their preparations enabled the British to complete theirs.) Admiral Roquefeuille was in command of the French fleet. Unable to find the British fleet off Spithead, where he had been informed it had anchored, he wrongly assumed that it had taken refuge in Portsmouth, and therefore ordered the expedition, commanded by Marshal Saxe and accompanied by Charles, to set sail from Dunkirk. Seven thousand troops embarked on French transports and made ready for imminent departure for England. Meanwhile Admiral Roquefeuille, sailing up the English Channel, had literally nearly run into Sir John Norris's fleet almost at nightfall and, seeing it vastly exceed his own, prudently decided to slip away before dawn, when battle would have commenced. But Hanoverian weather once again prevailed. A mighty storm arose, blowing straight on to the French coast, and did severe damage to Roquefeuille's retreating squadron. Worst of all, it struck the laden transports in Dunkirk harbour. Some of the ships were dashed to pieces and all on board lost. Others were thrown against the shore and the men rescued with difficulty. Most of those ships which had already put out from Dunkirk were sunk with all hands, although that which contained Marshal Saxe and Charles succeeded in returning safely to port.

This disaster happened at the end of February. Charles returned to Gravelines and refused to despair. But many Jacobites now gave up hope, and the French turned their attention elsewhere. Marshal Saxe was sent to command the French army in Flanders. French forces were withdrawn from Dunkirk. Charles Edward was on his own. He thought of sailing to Scotland alone, in a chartered fishing smack, but was dissuaded by the Earl of Marischal. He wrote cheerfully to his father from Gravelines on 6 March:

The little difficulties and small dangirs I may have run, are nothing, when for the service and Glory of a Father who is so tender and kind for me, and for the service of a countrey who is so dire to him. Thank God I am in perfect good health, and every thing goes well, as to particulars as I have no sifer (cipher), Lord Sempil will enform you. . . .

The letter has a rather touching P.S.: 'Tho it was fore a clock before I could get my dinner by being busy yet I could not resist writing to my Brother reflecting that it was his Birthday'.

King Louis wanted Charles to return to Paris, but he could not bring himself to leave Gravelines and abandon the hopes of a successful expedition which it stood for. In fact French official opinion had now changed with respect to the Jacobites, for Cardinal de Tencin had lost influence and the French Government was concentrating wholly on the campaign in Flanders under Marshal Saxe. Nobody seems to have told

Charles just how hopeless the situation was, and he stayed on in the dreary little French coastal town alternating between hope and despair. He wrote to his father on 3 April:

> The situation I am in is very particular, for nobody nose where I am or what has become of me, so that I am entirely burried as to the publick, and cant but say but that it is a very great constrent upon me, for I am obliged very often not to star out of my room for fier of some bodys noing my face. I very often think that you would laugh very hartelly if you sau me goin about with a single servant bying fish and other things and squabling for a peney more or less. I hope your Majesty will be thouroughly persuaded, that no constrent or trouble what soever either of minds or body will ever stope me in going on with my duty, in doing anything that I think can tend to your service and Glory. . . .

Charles kept forming wild plans. He offered to serve with the French army in Flanders but the Earl of Marischal said that was impossible; he suggested that he go to Scotland with the Scots and Irish soldiers serving in the French army, but received no reply. James advised him to 'avoid precipitate and dangerous measures, some rash or ill-conceived project, which would end in your ruin, and that of all of those who would joyn with you in it'. In May he was in Paris, as we know from a letter he wrote his father from that city on 11 May:

> I have received yours of April ye 1st ye 7th and 15th at my arrival here where I am come at the desire of the King of France, whose directions I exactly follow according to your orders. Before going down to the Army in Flanders, he sent one word by Lord Semple to come here in the privitest manner, and to continue so until he sent me word, otherwise; and what I was to do; he sed also that as soon as he would be arrived at the Army, he would discorce with Marrischall de Noaille about me and the ordering of my Equipage which he would take kere of himself. The K. of France always expressed great tenderness for me, but it is much incresed by my conduct at Gravelin, and a letter which I, writ to Lord Semple for to be shewn him. The K. of France kindness for me is very remarcable, by his speking very often about me, and saying that he regretted mitely that sircumstances had not permitted him to see me hitherto.

The letter goes on to complain about the Earl of Marischal, who has prevented his serving in the army in Flanders: 'He tels them that serving in the Army in flanders, it would disgust entirely the English, by serving in the same Army, that it is to fite against them and so forth'. The Earl is also culpable for having discouraged everybody 'to the last degree' after the storm broke up the expedition from Dunkirk and for having 'pleaged' him with letters 'which were reather Books'. As for 'the K. of France kindness' for him, it existed entirely in Charles's imagination. Louis seems to have found Charles nothing but an embarrassment and to have avoided an interview with him.

Nothing is drearier than the recriminations of frustrated plotters in exile, and Charles's bitter months of waiting incognito in Paris, surrounded by bickering Jacobites giving him conflicting information and contradictory advice, were both dull, exasperating and humiliating. Murray of Broughton thought that Sempill and Balhaldy were misinforming Charles and in July 1744 himself set out for France to find out what was really going on. When he reached Paris, he went to the house of Aeneas Macdonald, where Charles was at the time, and the following day was presented to Charles by Sempill and Balhaldy 'at the great stables in the Tuilleries'. Murray, who was to turn king's evidence on his capture after Culloden, reported in his examination in 1746 that at this interview 'the Pretender assured him that the French had been serious in the Invasion, which had been disappointed by the Weather and other accidents; that he, the Pretender, had the strongest assurances from the French King and his Ministers that it would be put into execution that Harvest'. He added, however, that when he saw Charles alone the following day he 'represented to him that his Friends in Scotland were dissatisfied with the Letters sent from Drummond [of Balhaldy] and Sempil, and doubted whether the French were in earnest in support of him'. Murray gives a fuller account of these conversations – but after a longer lapse of time and therefore perhaps less wholly dependable – in the *Memorials* he wrote much later both as a vindication of himself and as a history of the Jacobite campaign of 1745–1746. In this account he reports that Charles would not believe that Sempill and Balhaldy were to blame 'except in some particulars' and he added a footnote about Charles's conduct in the difficult circumstances in which he found himself:

I believe it will be very difficult, if possible, to find an instance in history, where a young Prince acted with so much moderation and temper upon discovering that he had been ill used, imposed upon, and (if I may say so) treated like a boy incapable of advising in or directing his own affairs. Most would have flown out into a passionate and high resentment, without regard to anything but their grandeur, and the indignity thrown upon it: whereas, here is one of 23 or 24 years of age, never accustomed to controul, acting with as much coolness, caution and circumspection, as the most experienced

Statesman. Whoever seriously considers this affair from first to last must be astonished to hear that his Highness had so much command of temper, as not only never to upbraid them, but even to receive them civilly.

Murray took pains to explode the ill-founded optimism of Sempill and Balhaldy concerning expectations of French help to the Jacobite cause, explaining how fully committed the French now were elsewhere. 'His Royal Highness seemed to think what I advanced was not void of reason; and said, that at all events he was determined to come the following summer to Scotland, though with a single footman.' At further conversations between Murray and Charles there was talk of a possible landing in Scotland by the Earl of Marischal with 3,000 men, together with a simultaneous descent on England, and both men expressed their confidence that if this happened there would be total support for the Jacobite cause in Scotland and considerable support in England. But of course there was no prospect of this happening. The Earl of Marischal had no prospect of getting 3,000 troops and further he was not really inclined to take any risks for Charles, being more of a republican Scottish nationalist on the pattern of Fletcher of Saltoun than a committed supporter of the claims of the Stuarts. Meanwhile, Murray continued to stir up Charles's suspicions of Balhaldy, and other Jacobites in Paris, including George Kelly and Sir Thomas Sheridan, played their part in the exchange of hopes and fears and dreams and complaints on which the exiles so largely lived.

Murray returned to Scotland, with messages and instructions for the Jacobite leaders. The Earl of Traquair was asked to go to London and find out whether the English Jacobites would rise when the Scots did, or wait until the Scots marched to their assistance. But the cautious Traquair was one of those Jacobites who refused to do anything without absolute assurance of French help, and declined point blank to go, much to Murray's disgust. He had more success with Donald Cameron of Lochiel, who put in writing 'that having maturely considered his Royal Highness's resolution, he was of opinion that to land in Scotland without assistance from abroad might prove an unsuccessful attempt: but as he was entirely devoted to the interest of the Royal Family, if he should land, he would join him at the head of his Clan'. Murray also busied himself with getting promises of financial support from Jacobite sympathizers, and managed to get such promises from the Duke of Hamilton, the Duke of Perth, Colonel Francis Charteris of Amisfield, Nisbet of Dirleton and James Murray of Abercairny. The Earl of Traquair was finally prevailed upon to go to London to sound out the

English Jacobites so that 'the Scots might be at no loss to know what they were to depend upon, and the manner after which they were to act, if once Masters of their own Country'. Traquair then thought it would be better to go on to France and let Charles know exactly how his friends in England and Scotland were situated: he said he was determined to see the Prince, 'though in a bawdy house'.

Talk of a Jacobite landing in Scotland, with hope of support in England, was thus in the air throughout the latter part of 1744 and the early part of 1745, but nobody seemed to know how serious it was or what the prospects really were. Charles was eating his heart out in Paris, increasingly disillusioned with Louis XV and the prospects of French support. On 14 July he had written to Louis – spelling his French rather better than he ever spelt his English – mentioning 'the wise precautions which Your Majesty has taken in keeping me hidden since my arrival in your Kingdom' as having completely fooled the British Government and saying that in spite of the arrival in England of Dutch troops and of other preparations made by the British Government to compensate for the virtual denuding of the country of British troops, his faithful friends, both English and Scots, had advised him that it was possible, even with the superiority of the British fleet, to transport a body of troops to join those which His Majesty had embarked at Dunkirk and that with this assistance he would have the honour of re-establishing the King his father on the throne without exposing the nation to the evils of a civil war. The Scots, however, 'plus ardents et entreprenants,' were not at all afraid of the idea of civil war, and only asked from Louis arms and 'the little help [le peu de secours] which they need in order to begin the campaign'. Louis made no response.

In a letter to his father written at the end of September Charles talks of his 'fiers of his [Louis's] sincerity'. James wrote to his 'Dearest Carluccio' (as he always called him in his letters) on 23 October throwing light on Charles's problems with respect to the French Court:

I am indeed persuaded that the Court of France will not allow you to go entirely out of this Incognito, but I can never think it can be their intention, that you should absolutely see nobody, and much less that you should be in the straits you represent; tho' if they have given you a competency, and that ill management has been the cause of your being now pinched, they are not so much to blame in that particular, but then, indeed, you must take care to manage well for the future. As to what relates to you personally, the Court of France is certainly obliged in honor to have all sort of regard and consideration for you (tho' in greater matters I own I don't think that to be the case) and therefore I cannot really doubt but that, if right application is made, will make you as easy as they can in what relates to your own person, and this makes me less uneasy than I would otherwise be at your present situation.

They are bound to behave properly towards you, especially if you ask nicely, is what James is telling Charles. But it didn't sound very convincing even to James himself and could not be expected to cheer Charles up much.

On 16 November Charles wrote to his father that his debts amounted to 30,000 crowns. 'You may well imagine how out of Youmer I am: when for comfort I am plagued out of my life with tracasyrs (mischiefmakers) from ower own People, who as it would seem would rether Sechrifise me and my Affairs, than fail in any private view.' He concludes: 'The more I dwell on these matters, the more it makes me melancholy, for which I end.'

A French Foreign Office minute of 30 December notes that the Prince of Wales had made representations that it was about eight months since he was recalled from Gravelines to Paris and required to live there incognito and that he had submitted to that unpleasant condition only because he had been given to understand that it would not last more than six months at most. Charles went on to say that he had been paid 3,000 crowns (écus) per month [by Louis] and had been given to understand that this modest sum would soon be augmented, but this promise remained unfulfilled and he had been unable to live without contracting debts which amounted to 30,000 or 35,000 and which were increasing monthly. He was about to withdraw, with the King's permission, to the château of Fitzjames in Picardy (the seat of the Duke of Berwick's younger brother, the Duke of Fitzjames) and could not leave Paris without paying his debts. Argenson, the French Minister of War, added in his own hand a note that Charles's debts should be paid to the amount of 30,000 crowns and it should be arranged with the Controller General that that was to be absolutely all ('et arranger avec M. le Controleur General déclarer qu'on ne les payera plus').

At Fitzjames Charles surrounded himself with Irish officers, some of them sons of veterans of the Boyne, others exiles of 1715 or of later vintage, some apparently just hopeful adventurers. These encouraged Charles in his dreams of glory and advocated immediate action. Charles no longer trusted Sempill or Balhaldy, both of whom he had caught out in lying to him. In April 1745 he was writing to his father complaining of untrustworthy and even dangerous followers, in one letter adding pathetically and uncharacteristically: 'I am very young, and it is very hard for me to forsee many things, for which all I aim at is at leste not to do harm, not being able to do good'. He was thinking of action, all the same, as events were shortly to prove.

Meanwhile in Scotland Murray of Broughton was drumming up support and keeping in touch with Charles through various go-be-tweens. The defeat by the French Army (or rather the Irish Brigade in the French service) under Marshal Saxe on 11 May 1745 of a combined British, Dutch, Hanoverian and Austrian force under the Duke of Cumberland raised Jacobite hopes and strengthened Charles's resolve. At the end of May Murray received 'a letter from his Royal Highness, saying he was to set out from France in a short time with some money and arms, and expected to be in Scotland in the month of July; that he proposed to come to the island of Ouist, and would make such and such signals'. On 12 June Charles wrote to King Louis:

After having tried in vain all methods of reaching Your Majesty in the hope of obtaining from your generosity the help necessary to enable me to play a role worthy of my birth, I have resolved to make myself known by my actions and to undertake alone a project to which even a small amount of help would guarantee success. I am bold enough to flatter myself that Your Majesty will not deny it me. I would never have come to France if the expedition planned more than a year ago had not made me aware of Your Majesty's good intentions towards me and I hope that the unforeseen accidents which rendered that expedition impracticable for the time being have not changed anything. May I not flatter myself at the same time that the Signal Victory which Your Majesty has just won over his enemies and mine (for they are the same) will have brought about some change in the situation and that I can reap some advantage from this new blaze of Glory that surrounds you ('ce nouvel éclat de Gloire qui vous Environne'). I beg Your Majesty most urgently to consider that in upholding the justice of my rights he will be putting himself in a position to achieve a solid and durable Peace, the sole object of the War in which he is now engaged. . . .

The letter was as much a reproach as an appeal. It was not delivered to the King until Charles had set out.

In Scotland, there was much plotting and planning, as well as considerable apprehension when the news of Charles's intention be-became known. Murray of Broughton found an armourer in Edinburgh who 'had got betwixt three and four hundred blades' and he 'bargained with him to mount them at half a guinea'. He adds (in his *Memorials*): 'I was even so minute as to provide several sets of brass moulds, and employed a gunsmith to pick up all the muskets he could find, and by his means procured a number: all which was conducted with so much secresy, that there never was the least whisper or suspicion of it to this day, though several boxes of them were carried to my house in the Country, and a part conveyed to Mr Buchannan's of Arnprior for the Duke of Perth's people.' Murray met Sir Hector Maclean in Edinburgh; he had come with messages from Charles of considerable importance. But, 'having appeared too publickly' in the city, Sir Hector was arrested and imprisoned in Edinburgh Castle. This was a great blow to the Jacobite cause, for the Clan Maclean depended on their Chief for leadership if they were to join a Jacobite rising. As Murray later reflected: 'I can safely say it was one of the greatest misfortunes that could have befallen the Prince at that time, as it might easily be made manifest that had he gone to the Highlands and joined His Royal Highness his army would have been much more numerous than it ever was: and if Macleod* was capable of speaking truth, he would acknowledge that had Sir Hector seen him, which he was resolved to do, he would have had but one of two choices, either to turn out, as he had not only engaged to do to him when at Boulogne but made him assure the King in his name, or be put to death, an alternative which Sir Hector resolved, and I fancy the other would not have chosen.'

On the same day that Charles wrote to Louis XV – 12 June – he wrote to his father, both letters being dated from the Château de Navarre, where he was staying with the Duc de Bouillon, but not dispatched until the eve of his departure. The letter, he tells him at the outset, will come as a great surprise. 'I have been six months ago invited by our Friends to go to Scotland, and to carry what money and arms I could conveniently get; this being they are fully persuaded, the only way of restoring you to the crown, and them to their liberties.' He complains of the 'scandalous usage' he has received from the French Court and asserts that he is prepared to die with his friends rather than live miserably in France or be obliged to return to Rome. 'Your Majesty cannot disapprove a son's following the example of his father.' And again: 'I have taken a firm resolution to conquer or to dye, and stand my ground as long as I have a man remaining with me.' He owes 60,000 livres to 'old Waters' and 120,000 to 'the young one'. (Waters and Son were Paris bankers from whom Charles had borrowed money to purchase arms: James repaid this, but he did not pawn Charles's jewels in Rome, as

* Norman Macleod of Macleod, who had expressed scepticism about the success of a Jacobite attempt without foreign aid but who promised to join the Prince nevertheless at the head of his clan if he came to Scotland, and who later went back on his word.

Charles asked him to do in this same letter.) Charles had also been financially helped by Aeneas Macdonald, who put him in touch with an Irish ship-owner in Nantes named Anthony Walsh.

Macdonald had preceded Charles to Nantes, and Charles followed him after writing (but not yet dispatching) his letters to Louis and James. It was agreed that the seven men who were to accompany him to Scotland would make their way to Nantes separately. Once there, they lodged in different parts of the town and pretended not to recognize each other. Charles dressed like a student of the Scots College at Paris, and went under the name of Douglas. He let his beard grow. Two ships had been provided, the *Du Teillay* (commonly written *Doutelle* by contemporary and later historians) by Walsh and the *Elisabeth* by Walter Rutledge, an Irish merchant of Dunkirk. Rutledge had obtained 'letters of marque' (a licence to fit out an armed vessel and employ it in the capture of an enemy's subjects without incurring the charge of piracy) from the French Ministry of Marine which allowed him to use the 68-gun frigate *Elisabeth* off the Scottish coast. The military stores to be carried included 1,500 muskets, 1,800 mounted broadswords, 20 small field pieces, ammunition and 'a good quantity of powder, ball, flints, dirks, brandy, etc.' These were the purchases Charles had made with the money borrowed from Waters and Son, as he explained in a letter to James Edgar. The *Elisabeth* also had 700 men aboard, according to Charles's last letter to his father before setting out, written on 12 July.

This letter was written from Belle-Île, whither Charles and his companions had sailed on the *Du Teillay* from Bonne Anse on the Loire estuary. 'After having waited a week here,' Charles wrote, 'not without a little anxiety, we have at last got the escort I expected, which is just arrived.' He is well, but has been a little sea-sick and expects to be more so. On 16 July (New Style; 5 July Old Style: we shall be using Old Style now in discussing Charles's campaign in Britain) the two ships set out from Belle-Île for Scotland. With Charles on the *Du Teillay* were the seven companions who were later to become known in Jacobite folklore as the 'Seven Men of Moidart'. They were the elderly and rather unwell William Murray, Marquis of Tullibardine, recognized by the Jacobites as the second Duke of Atholl though he had been attainted for his part in the 1715 rising and as a result it was his brother James whom the British Government recognized as succeeding the first Duke in 1724; Colonel Francis Strickland, the only Englishman in the group, a member of an old Westmorland Jacobite family; Aeneas Macdonald, the expedition's banker, who had been intending to go to

Scotland on his own business affairs and was with some difficulty persuaded to accompany Charles in order to win over his brother Donald of Kinlochmoidart and his many relatives; and four Irishmen – Sir Thomas Sheridan, a veteran of the Battle of the Boyne and now over seventy; George Kelly; Sir John Macdonald, an elderly man, fond of the bottle, who had served in the French cavalry in Spain; and Colonel John William O'Sullivan, who had fought in the French army and was the only one of the group who would play an important part in the campaign they were setting out to conduct.*

It was a desperate enterprise. 'It is doubtful whether any man ever set out to conquer a kingdom with so little backing,' Sir Charles Petrie has remarked, adding that 'to find a parallel in English history for so desperate a venture it is necessary to go back as far as the landing of Edward IV at Ravenspur in 1471, though even in that case the royal exile was at any rate personally acquainted with the country which he proposed to subdue'. And the chances of the expedition's success were to be further diminished almost immediately. For a few days after setting sail, en route for the Hebrides by the west coast of Ireland, the two ships sighted a British man-of-war, H.M.S. *Lion*, off the Lizard, and it was decided that the *Elisabeth* should attack. In the action that ensued the *Elisabeth* was badly damaged and Captain Douaud, who commanded her, mortally wounded. Walsh refused Charles's repeated urgings that the *Du Teillay* should go to the help of the *Elisabeth*, and threatened to confine him below if he persisted: Walsh's main concern was to protect his Prince. The *Elisabeth* had to put back to Brest to refit. Aeneas Macdonald strongly advised that the *Du Teillay* return to Nantes and that the expedition should be postponed to a more favourable occasion, and in this he was supported by Strickland and Macdonald, but Charles was absolutely adamant that they should go on alone. Most of the military stores and all the 700 men were gone. This expedition to gain a kingdom now consisted of just over a dozen men on board a single frigate of 44 guns. But at least the ship and its occupants were unharmed, for the engagement had been solely between the *Elisabeth* and the *Lion*. Taking advantage of his ship's smaller size and superior speed, Walsh slipped away, crowded all sail and made straight for the west coast of Scotland.

* In addition to the 'Seven Men of Moidart', Charles himself and Walsh, there were Duncan Buchanan, a clerk in the house of Aeneas Macdonald, the Abbé Butler, related to the Duke of Ormonde, who acted as chaplain to the group during the voyage, an Italian follower of both James and Charles named Michele Vezzosi, and a former servant of Lochiel's called Duncan Cameron, a native of Barra who knew that coast and so was able to act as pilot.

CHAPTER SEVEN

Tearlach Mac Sheumais

THE *Du Teillay* sailed steadily northward and eventually sighted the island of Barra, at the southern end of the Outer Hebrides. As they approached Barra, Tullibardine saw an eagle hovering over the ship, and took it as a good omen. He pointed it out to Charles, saying: 'The king of birds is come to welcome your royal highness upon your arrival in Scotland'. Charles sent off a boat to the house of MacNeil of Barra with George Kelly and Aeneas Macdonald (whose sister had married MacNeil), but MacNeil was not at home. As they waited, they caught sight of a suspicious-looking vessel outside the bay where the *Du Teillay* lay, and Charles thought it best that they should find a place to land. Duncan Cameron was sent out in the long boat to find a pilot, and by a happy coincidence he met MacNeil of Barra's piper, an old friend. He brought the piper on board and he guided them safely to an anchorage on the west side of the little island of Eriskay that lies between Barrà and South Uist. On this island, on 23 July, at a spot still known in Gaelic as Cladach a' Phrionnsa, the Prince's Shore, Charles first set foot on Scottish soil. A rose-pink convolvulus, said to have grown from seeds gathered by Charles while he was waiting on the French coast and which now dropped from his jacket pocket, grows here, and is not found elsewhere either in Eriskay or on any other Hebridean island.

Charles was still incognito, dressed like an abbé. A strong wind was blowing and there was what O'Sullivan described in the account of these events which he later wrote as 'a cruel rain'. Charles knew he was in Macdonald country, and he was confident of Macdonald support. But the first job of the party was to find shelter for the night. They were taken to a cottage of a Macdonald tacksman (tenant) called Angus Macdonald, and, as Duncan Cameron later told the story, 'they catched some flounders which they roasted upon the bare coals. The Prince sat at the cheek of a little ingle, upon a fail sunk [a seat made of peats], and laughed heartily at Duncan's cookery, for he himself owned he played his part awkwardly enough.' Angus Macdonald had no idea who Charles was, and, as Aeneas Macdonald later told the story, when the Prince was almost choked by the smoke coming from the fire in the middle of the room ('there being no other chimney than a hole in the roof') so that he had to go frequently to the door for fresh air, his host called out: 'What a plague is the matter with that fellow, that he can neither sit nor stand still, and neither keep within nor without doors?'

Charles's original intention had been to go straight to the house of Alexander Macdonald of Boisdale in South Uist, and he now sent him a message across the two-mile stretch of water which separates Eriskay from South Uist. Boisdale (it prevents confusion if we employ the Scottish custom of calling each Macdonald by his territorial title) arrived the next morning and Charles received him on board the *Du Teillay*. Boisdale had already heard from Sir Alexander Macdonald of Sleat and Norman MacLeod of MacLeod that both intended to go back on their earlier pledge to join Charles, and he told Charles that he had been told by them to say (in the words of O'Sullivan, who was present at the interview) 'that there was nothing to be expected from the contry, that not a soul wou'd joyn with him, & that their advise was that he shou'd go back & wait for a more favorable occasion'. O'Sullivan continues:

> Every body was strock as with a thunder boult, as you may believe, to hear that sentence, & those dispositions in the Contry, especially from MccCloud [MacLeod], who was one of those that said, he'd be one of the first that wou'd joyn the Prince, in case even he came alone; every body was for his going back except H.R.Hs., Welsh [Walsh], & Sullivan. . . .

Sir John Macdonald, who also wrote an account of these events (in French), confirms that 'the majority of the counsel, then held, was in favour of returning'. He adds: 'I was in favour of returning, H.R.H. wished to disembark and supported his opinion with admirable reasoning and greatness worthy of a Prince capable of great and perilous enterprises. Welch was on his side, and H.R.H. having decided, every one followed him.' It was during this debate, after Boisdale had strongly advised Charles to return home, that the Prince is said to have replied: 'I am come home, sir, and I will entertain no notion at all of returning to that place from whence I came, for that I am persuaded my faithful Highlanders will stand by me.'

Charles's passionate determination to count on Highland support for a rising in spite of the bitter discouragement he received on first reaching Scotland was the single decisive factor in making the campaign possible. In the light of the cold facts available to him it was an extraordinary, even a lunatic decision. Yet, as Sir Charles Petrie has effectively summed up, 'within five months Scotland was lost to the Union, a victorious Jacobite army stood in the very heart of England, and George II was thinking that the time was at hand which he should have to return to Hanover'.

Charles decided to sail at once for the mainland of Scotland and establish further contacts. His decision was hastened by the presence of a man-of-war on the horizon that appeared to be tacking in an endeavour to approach. So on the night of 24 July the *Du Teillay* put to sea again and sailed the sixty or so miles to the mainland, arriving the following day between twelve and one o'clock at Loch nan Uamh, a sea loch running into the Sound of Arisaig between Arisaig and Moidart. There they anchored. Aeneas Macdonald went off in a small boat to fetch his brother Macdonald of Kinlochmoidart. He also brought the important chief Macdonald of Clanranald, elder brother of Boisdale, and some other Macdonalds. The following day Clanranald's son, known simply as young Clanranald, arrived. One of the Macdonalds present, who internal evidence suggests may well have been the great Gaelic poet Alexander Macdonald, later gave an account of the rising which includes this description of the meeting:

We called for the ships boat and were immediately carryed on board, and our hearts were overjoyed to find ourselves so near our long wished for P——ce. We found a large tent erected with poles on the ships deck, covered and well furnished with variety of wines and spirits. As we enter'd this pavilion we were most chearfully welcom'd by the Duke of Athole to whom some of us had been known in the year 1715. [This was Tullibardine, whom the Jacobites still recognized as the legitimate Duke of Atholl.] While the Duke was talking with us, Clanronald was a-missing and had, as we understood, been called into the P——ce's cabin, nor did we look for the honour of seeing His R.H. at least for that night. After being 3 hours with the P., Clanronald returned to us, and in about half ane hour after there entered the tent a tall youth of a most agreeable aspect in a plain black coat with a plain shirt not very clean and a cambrick stock fixed with a plain silver buckle, a fair round wig out of the buckle, a plain hatt with a canvas string haveing one end fixed to one of his coat buttons; he had black stockins and brass buckles in his shoes; at his first appearance I found my heart swell to my very throat. . . .

When this youth entered, . . . he saluted none of us, and we only made a low bow at a distance. I chanced to be one of those who were standing when he came in, and he took his seat near me, but immediately started up again and caused me to sitt down by him upon a chest. I at this time taking him to be only a passenger or some clergyman, presumed to speak to him with too much familiarity, yet still retained some suspicion he might be one of more note than he was said to be. He asked me if I was not cold in that habite (viz. the highland garb) I answered I was so habituated to it that I should rather be so if I was to change my dress for any other. . . . Severall such questions he put to me; then rising quickly from his seat he calls for a dram, when the same person whisper'd me a second time, to pledge the stranger but not to drink to him, by which seasonable hint I was confirm'd in my suspicion who he was. Having taken a glass of wine in his hand, he drank to us all round, and soon after left us.

Charles sent young Clanranald to Skye with messages for Sir Alexander Macdonald of Sleat and MacLeod of MacLeod, but he brought back discouraging replies. Kinlochmoidart was sent with messages to the Duke of Perth, Murray of Broughton and Donald Cameron of Lochiel. Lochiel sent his brother Dr Archibald Cameron to dissuade Charles, then came himself to advise him that as he had come over without the expected French aid there was no prospect of a successful rising and he had better return to France. Once again Charles refused to take this advice. 'In a few days,' he is said to have replied, 'with the few friends that I have, I will erect the royal standard, and proclaim to the people of Britain, that Charles Stuart is come over to claim the crown of his ancestors, to win it, or to perish in the attempt: Lochiel, who, my father has often told me, was our firmest friend, may stay at home, and learn from the newspapers the fate of his prince.' This was too much for Lochiel, who declared: 'No, I'll share the fate of my prince; and so shall every man over whom nature or furtune hath given me any power.' Another sign of encouragement came from the younger brother of Macdonald of Kinlochmoidart. On hearing the discouraging news from Macdonald of Sleat and MacLeod of MacLeod, Charles turned impulsively to this young man, who was standing on the deck of the ship. 'Will *you* not assist me?' he asked. 'I will! I will!' the young man is said to have replied excitedly, 'though not another man in the Highlands should draw a sword. I am ready to die for you!' This had its effect on the reluctant chiefs who were present, and there was no more talk of Charles's returning to France. Lochiel's support was particularly important: he was an influential Highland chief, and knowledge that he would bring his clan out in support of the Prince had considerable effect throughout the Highlands. Alexander Macdonald of Keppoch now also added his support and influence, impressed by Charles's resolution.

Murray of Broughton gives an account of the effect of the Prince's determination:

> And here I must be allowed to observe that nothing has so great an effect upon brave and generous minds as when a person appears to despise their own private safety when in competition with the good of their country. Had the Chevalier seemed in the least daunted by the apparent caution of his friends, or agreed to their not raising in arms for some time and keep'd the ship hovering on the coast for retreat, it is more than probable that the interest of L[ord] Lovat, S[r] A[lexander] M[c]Donald with M[c]C[leod] had with the others, together with the many dangers that would have occurred to them every day would have obliged him att last to return after a fruitless attempt and if not rendered him despicable in the Eyes of foreigners would att least have enduced them to believe that he had no freinds and had been foolish enough to undertake a thing of such vast consequence to himself and country without any proper encouragement, so ready are menkind to judge and conjecture of the actions of others tho entirely ignorant of their motives.

On 6 August Charles wrote a brief letter to Louis XV announcing his arrival in Scotland and appealing for French help, only a moderate amount of which, he said, would soon put him in a position to enter England. On the 11 James wrote to Louis that he had heard only a few days before 'à mon grand étonnement' of his son's actually having left France for Scotland, having formed and executed his resolution to do this without having consulted his father. 'I knew absolutely nothing about it, but now that it has happened, I frankly admit that I cannot help admiring him.' As for himself, James continued, Louis had known for some time that he wished to renounce his rights in favour of his son.

Charles's decision to send away the *Du Teillay* meant that the die was now cast, and strengthened the resolution of his companions. Walsh bore a letter from the Prince to his father, saying that if he could not get help from France he was ready to die at the head of his brave Highlanders. He and his companions spent some time at a farmhouse at Borrodale on the north shore of Loch nan Uamh. Alexander Macdonald (assuming that it really was the poet who left the first-hand account from which we have already quoted) described the scene:

> We there did our best to give him a most hearty welcome to our country, the P. and all his company with a guard of about 100 men being all entertaind in the house &c of Angus McDonald of Borradel in Arisaig in as hospitable a manner as the place could aford. H.R.H. being seated in a proper place had a full view of all our company, the whole neighbourhood without distinction of age or sex crouding in upon us to see the P. After we had all eaten plentifully and drunk chearfully, H.R.H. drunk the grace drink in English which most of us understood; when it came to my turn I presumed to distinguish myself by saying audibly in Erse (or highland language), *Deoch slainte an Righ* ['a Drink: the King's health'] H.R.H. understanding that I had drunk the Kings health made me speak the words again in Erse and said he could drink the Kings health likewise in that language, repeating my words; and the company mentioning my skill in the highland language, H.R.H. said I should be his master for that language. . . .

How much Gaelic Macdonald managed to teach his Prince we do not know. There is a tradition that when the standard was unfurled at Glenfinnan on 19 August the poet recited *Tearlach Mac Sheumais* ('Charles son of James') one of the many Jacobite songs he wrote, which opens:

> *O Theàrlaich mhic Sheumais, mhic Sheumais, mhic Theàrlaich,*
> *Leat shiubhlainn gu h-eutrom 'n am éighlich bhith màrsal, . . .*
> (O Charles son of James, son of James, son of Charles,
> With you I'd go gladly when the call sounds for marching, . . .)

If Charles could not understand Macdonald's Gaelic, he must at least have soon come to realize that the form of his name which rapidly grew popular, 'Charlie', was simply the Gaelic for Charles, *Tearlach*, as it sounded to the ears of English-speakers (the initial 'te' being pronounced 'tch'). When we talk, therefore, of Prince Charlie, we are giving him the name by which he was called by his beloved Highlanders, not using an English diminutive.

While Charles was at Borrodale, most of his company stayed at Kinlochmoidart, six miles to the south, between Loch Moidart and Loch Shiel. There they had their scanty provisions increased unexpectedly: Walsh, as he started on his return journey to France in the *Du Teillay*, met two sloops laden with barley and oatmeal, which he captured, only to ransom them on condition that they proceeded to

Kinlochmoidart and sold their grain there. This they did, to the relief not only of Charles's men but of the whole neighbourhood, 'there having been a scarcity for five months past', as Sir John Macdonald tells us in his account. When Clanranald had gathered about a hundred of his men, Charles joined the others at Kinlochmoidart. Meanwhile Lochiel was also gathering his men, and so was Alexander Macdonald of Keppoch, a devoted Jacobite who had been created a baronet by James in 1743 and was to fall at Culloden.

It was at Kinlochmoidart that Murray of Broughton joined Charles, after having spent some days in devious schemes to blind the representatives of the Government as to what was really going on. He found a great deal of activity in the Prince's quarters. 'The Chevalier had been all this time busied in incitting his freinds to gett their people together, and to have his arms and amunition, &c., convey'd from the place where they were landed to his own quarters, which notwithstanding his own continual care and industry, was a great whille of being accomplished, so superiorly indolent and Idle are the people of that part of the Country.' He gave Charles 'a list of such persons as he thought ought to be wrote to, either to persuade them to join who had already previously engaged themselves, or to such who had not, for prudential reasons, been lett into the secret, but might possibly join, or give money, with some others as a polite perswasive to act a neutral part'. He also advised that someone should be sent over to Holland, 'not only to sound some of the Dutch officers of the Scotts Brigade, but in case they was found inclinable to serve the Chevalier, to have proper Authority to make such agreement with them as should be thought necessary'. Murray was appointed Charles's secretary.

Two days before Murray's arrival, the first fighting of the 1745 rising had taken place. It was a tiny skirmish, but the Jacobites won it without any losses and considered this a good omen. What happened was that two additional companies of the first Royal Scots regiment of foot had been sent from Fort Augustus to reinforce the garrison at Fort William, as a result of the Government's nervousness about Jacobite intentions. Captain John Scott, commanding the two companies, was ambushed at High Bridge, about eight miles from Fort William, by eleven men and a piper under Macdonald of Tirnadrish, a near relative of Macdonald of Keppoch who had received intelligence of Captain Scott's movements and had devised the trap. The Macdonalds rushed out from behind an inn, with the piper playing for all he was worth and the men yelling, so that the Government 'troops were struck with such an accountable panick as with one consent to run of without so much as taking time to observe the number or quality of their enemy' (in Murray's words). After five or six miles the Highlanders, now increased in number to between 45 and 50, caught up with the retreating soldiers, who were now quite exhausted, and exchanged fire with them. Keppoch himself now appeared on the scene, and with drawn sword ran up to Captain Scott and told him that his men would be cut to pieces if they did not surrender instantly. Scott's men then laid down their arms. Scott himself was wounded in the shoulder, four or five of his men were killed, and about a dozen wounded. None of the Highlanders received a scratch.

On 18 August Charles with his followers left Kinlochmoidart and went half way up Loch Shiel to Glenaladale. Here he was met by John Gordon of Glenbucket – 'Old Glenbucket' as he was generally called, a veteran of the rising of 1715 – who brought with him Captain Swettenham, an English army engineer who had been captured by Keppoch's men on his way to Fort William to assist in the repair of the fortifications there and who was then released on parole not to serve again. On the morning of the 19th they moved north-east up to the head of Loch Shiel to Glenfinnan.

Glenfinnan, at the head of Loch Shiel, is a narrow valley flanked by mountains between which the River Finnan flows into the loch from the north. It is a place of great beauty and serenity, and as the visitor stands today by the monument to Prince Charlie which rises simple and solitary not far from the loch shore and looks southwest across the water he may recapture something of Charles's feelings when he arrived there to find it quiet and unpeopled and set himself to wait anxiously for the promised arrival of Lochiel and Keppoch with their men. He waited about two hours before the two chiefs arrived, each at the head of his men. 'Never', wrote Sir John Macdonald later, 'have I seen anything so quaintly pleasing as the march of this troop of Highlanders as they descended a steep mountain by a zigzag path.' He says that Lochiel brought about 900 men and Keppoch 500; O'Sullivan gives the numbers as 700 ('good men, but ill armed') and about 350 ('clivor fellows') respectively. Murray of Broughton gives the number of Lochiel's Camerons as 750 and Keppoch's as about 300. Murray's account continues:

In less than an hour after the whole were drawn up, and the Royal Standard display'd by the D. of A[thole]* when the Chevalier made

* 'Athole' is the regular spelling in the eighteenth century. The modern spelling is 'Atholl'.

them a short but very Pathetick speech. Importing that it would be no purpose to declaim upon the justice of his Father's tittle to the Throne to people who, had they not been convinced of it, would not have appeared in his behalf, but that he esteemed it as much his duty to endeavour to procure their welfare and happyness as they did to assert his right, that it was cheifly with that view that he had landed in a part of the Island where he knew he should find a number of brave gentlemen filled with the 'noble example of their predecessors, and jealous of their own and their Country's honour, to join with him in so glorious an enterprise, with whose assistance and the protection of a just God who never fails to avenge the cause of the injured, he did not doubt of bringing the affair to a happy issue'.

After this ceremony was over, he retired to his quarters, which he had taken up in a little barn att the head of the Loch.

According to O'Sullivan, the unfurling of the royal standard and the proclamation of James as King (and of Charles as his Regent) on 19 August 'was followed by a general Housaw, & a great deal of Allacrety'. Charles ordered casks of brandy to be delivered to the men so that they might drink the King's health. Then he waited two days, to give time for Clanranald to raise all his men and to determine on details of policy. He also sent messages to a variety of clans and their chiefs between Glencoe and Glen Garry asking them to join him in marching to Fort Augustus. On 21 August he marched eastwards with his supporters to the head of Loch Eil, where he halted for a few days. They were short of horses to carry their baggage and ammunition; they had had to bury twelve 'large swevel guns' (Murray) or 'pieces of smale Cannans' (O'Sullivan) at Glenfinnan and now had to leave some of their ammunition and equipment, which they were unable to carry, at Loch Eil. On 23 August they were at the house of Lochiel's brother, John Cameron of Fassifern, only a few miles from Fort William, and though Fassifern himself remained loyal to the House of Hanover and retired to Fort William for protection from the Jacobites, his wife received and entertained the Prince hospitably.

They had to keep to the north side of the River Lochy to be out of range of the cannon at Fort William, so they went north-east along the river to Moy, only two miles from the head of Loch Lochy. The road built by General Wade in the 1730's (as part of the Government's campaign to make the Highlands more accessible and thus more easily controlled) ran from Fort William to Inverness on the south side of the string of lochs that mark the Great Glen, so the Prince and his men had to make their way with difficulty over mountainous country on the north side until they finally crossed the River Lochy near Moy and joined the Wade road on the other side. They pushed on to High Bridge, Wade's remarkable bridge across the River Spean.

The inscription on High Bridge read: 'In the ninth year of His Majesty King George II, this bridge was erected under the care of Lt. General Wade, Commander in Chief of all the forces in North Britain – 1736'. It was thus peculiarly fitting that it was here that Charles learned that the present 'Commander in Chief of all the forces in North Britain', Lieutenant-General Sir John Cope, was marching towards him from Stirling.

Cope had heard of Charles's landing, somewhat belatedly, and prepared to march north and engage the rebels. The total force under his command in Scotland was about 3,800 troops, of whom about 3,100 were infantry. The troops were inexperienced and ill-armed. On first hearing rumours of the rising, Cope had consulted the civil authorities in Scotland, notably Duncan Forbes of Culloden, Lord President of the Court of Session and prominent supporter of the Government who played a large part in keeping important sections of the Highlands from joining the Jacobite side in 1745, Andrew Fletcher of Milton, the Lord Justice-Clerk (nephew of Andrew Fletcher of Saltoun), and Robert Craigie of Glendoick, the Lord Advocate. These men did not take the Jacobite threat seriously. They doubted whether Charles, that 'crazy young adventurer', could get any substantial support from the clans and thought it would be a question of dispersing a small number of 'loose lawless Men of Desperate Fortunes' by a mere show of force. In view of this advice, Cope decided that his best plan would be to march north as quickly as possible and put an end to the rising once and for all. He was assured that he would find on the way large numbers of friendly Highlanders who would act as local guides and as guards of his flank as he marched through defiles and mountain passes.

The Highlands had been disarmed by Act of Parliament after the rising of 1715. It was illegal for a clansman to carry firearms. Of course the law was widely evaded. Nevertheless, there was a problem here for Cope: the more loyal to the Government a Highlander was, the more likely he was to have observed the law and to have no arms. Cope had, therefore, to get arms to Highland loyalists if they were to be of any use to him. The Government had turned down an earlier suggestion he had made that, in anticipation of a rising, arms should be lodged in the Highland forts which had been built along the Great Glen to help pacify the Highlands – Fort William, originally built by General Monk in 1655 and enlarged and renamed after William III by General

Hugh Mackay in 1690; Fort Augustus, built in 1716 as Kilchumin or Kilcumein and enlarged and renamed by General Wade in 1730 (Augustus was George II); and Fort George, built by Wade on the Castle Hill of Inverness on a site which had held a fortified building since the twelfth century. If these forts were not made secure, all the Highlands north of the Great Glen and a large area south of it could easily come under Jacobite control. So Cope felt that it was his duty to go north and bring arms to the Government's many friends in the Highlands, who he was assured really existed. Otherwise he might have done what Argyll had done in 1715 and waited at Stirling for the Jacobite army to come south.

Cope concentrated his forces on Stirling in preparation for the march north, but as the days went by he became less and less confident that his ill-equipped and inexperienced troops would be able to cope with the difficult Highland terrain in country which intelligence now suggested was much more likely to be hostile than friendly. He therefore changed his plan, and decided to take a small column of 300 men to Fort Augustus, 'to support the Garrisons in the North', as he explained in a letter to the Marquis of Tweeddale, Secretary of State for Scotland. 'This resolution I took not thinking it safe to leave the Capital of this Part of the Country exposed to a second landing.' But his civilian masters would have none of this. Cope was curtly ordered to carry out his original plan, and march north with his army. So, against his better judgment, he set out for Fort Augustus from Stirling with about 2,000 men. His plan was to march by Crieff, Aberfeldy, Dalnacardoch and Dalwhinnie over the Corrieyairack Pass to Fort Augustus. He reached Crieff on 21 August, and there he was met by the Duke of Atholl (the Hanoverian one, not the elder brother, Tullibardine, whom the Jacobites recognized as the Duke) and Lord Glenorchy, who reported, to Cope's astonishment, that they had been unable to raise a single man for the Government cause. So there was nobody to whom Cope could give the arms he had brought with him. He sent some of these back to Stirling – for they were hampering his progress – and, urged by a dispatch from Tweeddale, pushed on north. As he marched he received no significant additions to his forces, but met with frequent sabotage in the form of stolen stores and horses, ripped grain sacks, and desertions from the Highland companies among his men. He also learned from Captain Swettenham (on his way south after having been released on parole) that a formidable Jacobite army was in possession of the difficult and dangerous Pass of Corrieyairack. And he received a letter from Forbes of Culloden carefully explaining

. the great danger of his (Cope's) position. He was in a dilemma.

Though Charles had sent further messages to Macdonald of Sleat and MacLeod of MacLeod after the unfurling of the standard at Glenfinnan, pleading with them in vain to join him, he had been gathering more support. Charles Stewart of Ardshiel brought 250 Stewarts of Appin, Macdonald of Glencoe 150, young Glengarry – at whose father's house Charles stayed the night after he reached High Bridge – and the Grants of Glenmoriston had provided clansmen. On 27 August he donned Highland dress, which he had previously worn only at a ball in Rome, and as he laced his brogues he announced that he would be 'up with Mr Cope before they were unloosed'. His aim was to reach the Pass of Corrieyairack before Sir John Cope and his army.

On 4 August it had been announced in the *London Gazette* that the Government would give a reward of £30,000 to anyone who captured Charles on his landing. News of this reached Charles when he was at the head of Loch Eil, and he at once countered with a proclamation issued in the name of the 'Regent of the Kingdoms of Scotland, England, France, and Ireland', signed by Murray as his secretary. This referred to 'a certain scandalous and malicious paper' which offered a reward of £30,000 'to those who shall deliver us into the hands of our enemies'. It went on: 'We could not but be moved with a just indignation at so insolent an attempt. And though from our nature and principle we abhor and detest a practice so unusual among Christian Princes, we cannot but out of a just regard for the dignity of our person promise the like reward of £30,000 sterling to him or them who shall seize and secure till our further orders the person of the Elector of Hanover, ...' There is a tradition that Charles at first wanted to offer only £30 for the capture of George II and that he was with difficulty persuaded to raise the sum to equal what was offered for his own capture. We know from a letter that Charles wrote to his father from Perth on 10 September that it was his 'faithful Highlanders' who insisted against his own inclination on his following what he considered the 'mean, barbarous principle' of replying to the Hanoverian offer of a sum for his capture with an equivalent offer for the capture of George.

Charles had from the beginning believed that audacity rather than delay and caution would win the day – this remained his view throughout the whole campaign – and was keen to confront Sir John Cope's troops. But Cope now had second thoughts about pushing on through the Corrieyairack Pass to Fort Augustus. The approach to the pass from the south was a series of steep zig-zags, while the approach from the north, from which direction the Jacobite force would come, was long and gradual; a very small number of men at the top of the pass could prevent its ascent by even a very large number from the south. And Cope's men had as yet seen no active service even on less difficult terrain. What was Cope to do? He could have stayed at Dalwhinnie, and waited there for the approach of the clans. 'Had he [Cope] encamped upon the plain about two miles south of Dalwhinny,' wrote Murray of Broughton, 'he would have difficulted the Chevalier very much, for by this means it would have been impossible to bring him to an action, which was what the Chevalier wished for, except upon very advantageous terms, and he had Athole in his rear from whence to draw provisions, whereas the Chevalier had no bread for his people, nor was it in his power to procure any'. It seems to have been lack of stores together with a steady stream of desertions that decided Cope against awaiting battle at Dalwhinnie; and in any case the Highlanders, if they had wished to avoid battle, could have outflanked Cope's army by ways through the mountains that only they knew or had skill to negotiate and so got into the Lowlands leaving Cope and his men to the north of them. Another course now open to Cope was to fall back through Blair Atholl to Stirling. But the men of the Atholl country, through which he would have had to retreat, were becoming increasingly hostile, in spite of the loyalty to the Government of the (Hanoverian) Duke of Atholl; they had robbed his stores and harassed his men on his way north, and would be likely to do so to an even greater degree if they saw him in retreat.

In the event Cope decided to take the road that runs north-east from Dalwhinnie to Inverness instead of pushing up due north and then north-west, along the other fork of the Wade road, that led over the Corrieyairack Pass to Fort Augustus. He had been informed that the Highlanders already occupied the Corrieyairack. Later Cluny MacPherson, chief of the MacPhersons, who was playing a double game in the campaign, first raising a company ostensibly intended for service on the Government side and later taking it over to the Jacobites, informed Forbes of Culloden that on 28 August he had got reliable secret information 'that the Highlanders had altered their route of Corrieyarick and designed to march down the side of Lochnes and intercept the General before he crossed the Water of Nairn'. He added that this plan was well known in the Highlands. Now crossing the Water of Nairn involved negotiating the precipitous ravine of Slochd Mor, between Carrbridge and Tomatin on the Dalwhinnie–Inverness road. If therefore Cope believed that Highlanders were already in possession of Corrieyairack and others were about to occupy Slochd Mor (which could not possibly be traversed in safety if even a very small enemy force were already there), it becomes understandable why he decided to proceed by forced marches to Inverness in order to cross Slochd Mor before the Highlanders got there. At Inverness he would be at Fort George, the most north-easterly of the chain of forts to which he had been instructed in general terms to march. So if he could get to Inverness quickly he would both be extricating his forces from two traps that had been or were being prepared and fulfil the letter of his instructions.

Charles and his men passed the Corrieyairack 'like lightning, but in good order,' as O'Sullivan put it, '& finding by other accounts that Cope was to camp that night at Garvamore, the Prince marched directly to him, with a design to attack him wherever he met him'. Garvamore is about seven miles along General Wade's road from the Corrieyairack, by the River Spey. Charles reached there on 28 August, and found that Cope had been expected there that night but, having received a report that the Prince was marching against him, had turned off on the Inverness Road to Ruthven, where there were Government barracks. He had already left Ruthven, pushing on 'in the greatest hurry & disorder to Invernesse, so that he left the Prince paisseble possessor of the Camp of Garvamore & nothing to oppose him from thence to Edinburgh'.

The next day, the 29th, was hot and sunny, the first really good weather Charles had seen since his arrival in Scotland. The heat seems to have worn the tempers of some of the clansmen, who were bitterly disappointed to hear that Cope had escaped them and clamoured to be allowed to pursue him to Inverness and engage him there. Charles and the chiefs had great difficulty in dissuading them from this course. About sixty Camerons, against Charles's advice but on the urging of the chiefs, set off to raid Ruthven barracks, but the raid was beaten off by an Irish sergeant called Molloy who held the post with sixteen men.

Cope was at Inverness by the 29th. The road to Edinburgh was open. On the 30th Charles pushed on towards Blair Castle, through the Atholl country, and, as Murray of Broughton reports, 'on the road was extreamly pleased with the sight of the people of the Country; men, women and children who came running from their houses, kissing and caressing their master [the Duke of Atholl], whom they had not seen for thirty years before [he had been in exile since his part in the 1715 rising], an instance of the strongest affection, and which could not fail to move every generous mind with a mixture of greif and joy'. On 1 September Charles was at Blair Castle. The Hanoverian Duke of

Atholl had fled and his elder brother, the Jacobite Duke, took possession. At Blair, the following day, the Prince reviewed his troops and found that many Highlanders, annoyed at not having been allowed to pursue Cope, had left. 'Officers were sent to the Contry, & brought the most part of them back.' On 3 September Charles left for Dunkeld by the Pass of Killiecrankie, and on 4 September he reached Nairne House, between Dunkeld and Perth, and dined there with Lord Nairne* (who with his father had fought in 1715) and the Dowager Lady Nairne, while Lochiel led a body of men to occupy Perth where James was proclaimed as King and Charles as his Regent. That evening Charles made a triumphal entry into the city on horseback at the head of his troops.

This was the first time that Charles really savoured his role as Bonnie Prince Charlie, the dazzling young charmer whose very presence seemed to announce victory for his cause. He rode on a horse that had been given him by Macdonald of Tirnadrish, and he was attended by the Duke of Perth (son of the Duke of Perth who had served James Edward), Oliphant of Gask and Robert Mercer of Aldie, who had joined him as he passed through their estates. He wore a handsome suit of tartan trimmed with gold lace. The Jacobites in the crowd cheered enthusiastically as he rode by on his way to the lodging prepared for him in the house of the Jacobite Viscount Stormont. If the magistrates and merchants of the city were less enthusiastic they could hardly be blamed: Charles seized £500 of the city's public money having, as he said, but one guinea left in the world when he entered Perth. At Perth too he received considerable reinforcements, including Lord Ogilvy, son of the Earl of Airlie, who promised to bring in a whole regiment of his clan, and did so, and Lord George Murray, younger brother of the two rival Dukes of Atholl. The Duke of Perth (whose title, it will be remembered, was a Jacobite one, not recognized by the Government) and Lord George were appointed by Charles joint lieutenant-generals: he retained supreme command himself.

Charles spent a week in Perth, where Lord George gave his army some much needed drilling; from Perth he sent Murray of Broughton to collect local taxes in Dundee (where James was proclaimed on 5 September), Montrose and other Lowland towns north of the Tay. On Sunday the 8th he attended a religious service conducted by a Mr

* Lord Nairne was a cousin of Lord George Murray and his brothers the Hanoverian Duke of Atholl and the Marquis of Tullibardine (the Jacobite Duke of Atholl). His mother, the Dowager, was a redoubtable Jacobite who exercised great influence on her nephews Tullibardine and Lord George.

Armstrong of the Scottish Episcopal Church, thus publicly demonstrating his religious tolerance. (This is believed to be the first time the Prince had attended a Protestant place of worship.) Mr Armstrong's text was Isaiah, 14: 1-2. 'For the Lord will have mercy on Jacob, and yet choose Israel, and set them in their own land: and the strangers shall be joined with them, and they shall cleave to the house of Jacob. And the people shall take them and bring them to their place: and the house of Israel shall possess them in the land of the Lord for servants and handmaids: and they shall take them captives, whose captives they were; and they shall rule over their oppressors.'

On 11 September Charles turned south on the road to Stirling, no longer a lone adventurer pleading passionately for support in an apparently hopeless cause, but a brilliant Prince on a triumphal progress.

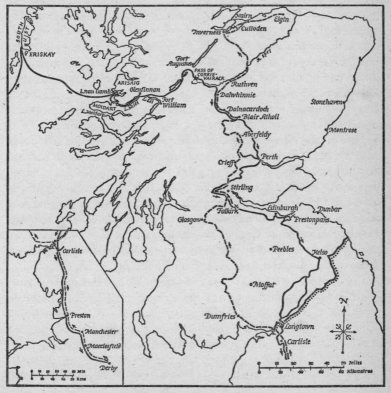

The campaign of the Forty-five

CHAPTER EIGHT

From Perth to Edinburgh

BY THE TIME they left Perth, the Jacobite forces had increased from about 1,300 to about 2,400 men. The army's two lieutenant-generals Lord George Murray and the Duke of Perth, were very different characters. James Johnstone, known as the Chevalier de Johnstone, who joined Charles at Perth and served successively as aide-de-camp to Lord George and to the Prince himself, has left interesting accounts of both in his *Memoirs* (originally written in French). He recorded his surprise at the smallness of the Prince's army, whose size, he said, had been exaggerated in Edinburgh – no more than 1,000 men, he estimated, before they were joined by the Duke of Perth and Lord George with the former's 'vassals' and some of the 'vassals' of the latter's brother, the Jacobite Duke of Atholl. Lord George Murray, who 'had charge of the whole detail of our army, and who conducted it entirely, had a natural genius for war, which, culti-vated by the study of the military art, had rendered him truly one of the greatest generals in Europe'. He was 'tall, robust and brave'. When he led the Highlanders to the charge, he used to say: 'My boys, I don't ask you to advance before me, but only to follow me'. He was 'vigilant, active, and diligent. The execution of his plans were prompt, and his combinations always correct'. But the Chevalier de Johnstone admitted that Lord George was 'fierce, haughty, blunt, and proud,' and 'he desired always to dictate everything by himself, and knowing none his equal, he did not wish to receive his advice'. The Duke of Perth, on the other hand, 'although brave even to intrepidity, a perfectly upright man, endowed with a great deal of sweetness of character, was of a feeble genius, and intermeddled with nothing'. Murray of Broughton gives a fuller account of the Duke of Perth:

James D. of Perth was about 34 years of age, six foot high, of a slender make, fair complection, and weakly constitution, had a good genius for emprovement in w^h he spent much of his time, and fired with an extraordinary love for his Country, gave great encouragement upon all occasions to manufactors of several kinds, but his unparaleld affection for the Exiled family of Stuart made him bend most of his thoughts towards their interest, and to accomplish that end he laboured with unwearied zeal, ... as he was bred in France till the age of 19, he never attain to the perfect knowledge of the English language, and what prevented it in a great measure was his overfondness to speak broad Scotts. His judgement of things was very just and good, but his Ideas were so various, and crowded so fast upon him, which, together with his want of the Language, made him a little prolix and rather over tedious in his discourse. He was very affable and of easy access, being void of all ceremony, tho' no man knew better when any one faild in the respect due to his birth. He was Roman Catholick, but far from being bigotted, never introducing the subject, and if introduced rather choosing to shunn it; full of disinterestedness, of undaunted courage, the most examplary, humanely, and universally beloved.

The two lieutenant-generals were not really compatible. Murray's parents had been Whig and Calvinist and he himself, though, like his brother William, much influenced by his strong-minded Jacobite aunt Lady Nairne, had come to accept the Union and in 1739 had reluctantly taken the oath of allegiance to George II, in spite of his intense dislike of the Whig administration. He was in many respects a progressive, interested in agricultural and industrial improvement in Scotland and prepared to co-operate in improving measures with like-minded Whig lairds. Duncan Forbes of Culloden, the most understanding and compassionate of the anti-Jacobite Scots leaders, shared many of his intellectual interests. All this made him suspect in the eyes of those unwavering Jacobites who looked to the past rather than to the future to justify their conduct. But once Charles was in Atholl and the men of Atholl whom his brother James (the Hanoverian Duke of Atholl) had sent to join General Cope had deserted and his brother William (the Jacobite Duke) was being hailed by the men of Atholl, on his return from exile, as the true Duke who would lead them against Cope, Lord George returned to his Jacobite allegiance from which he never again swerved.

It had not been an easy decision. As he wrote to his brother James, explaining the motives for his action, on 3 September: 'My Life, my Fortune, my expectations, the Happyness of my wife & children, are all at stake (& the chances are against me), & yet a principle of (what seems to me) Honour, & my Duty to King & Country, outweighs evry thing'. The fact, however, that he had at different times in his life professed loyalty to both sides in the conflict left permanent suspicion in the minds of many Jacobites, and the genuine sacrifice he made for the cause was little appreciated. Accusations of preparing treachery were constantly being made against him, generally by means of rumour only, and this, combined with his proud bearing and high self-esteem, lessened the confidence in him as a commander – not on the part of the main body of Highlanders, who were devoted to him, but on the part of certain chiefs, of Murray of Broughton, and, largely through Broughton, of Prince Charles himself.

Charles was aware from the beginning of a certain coolness between Lord George and the Duke of Perth, and tried to solve the problem of a clash of temperament between his two lieutenant-generals by allotting each the same number of men in battle and giving them alternate command of the right and left wings and supreme command on alternate days. This was symptomatic of the effect of personal rivalries and jealousies on the efficiency of the Prince's army which was to manifest itself in various ways again and again and prove in the end to be a significant factor in the final outcome of the rising.

One of Charles's favourite characters was the Irishman O'Sullivan, whom he appointed quartermaster-general of the army. Lord George despised O'Sullivan, and the Scots in general were suspicious of the Irish 'men of Moidart' – especially Sir Thomas Sheridan, Sir John Macdonald and John William O'Sullivan – resenting their intimacy with the Prince and suspecting them of poisoning his mind against his Scottish advisers. Macdonald and O'Sullivan in turn spread rumours against Lord George among the men and accused him of planning to take the Atholl Brigade (of whose first battalion he was colonel) over to the enemy when opportunity arose. But Lord George was extremely popular with the men of Atholl, who knew him as *duine firinneach* (the true or righteous man).

Meanwhile Sir John Cope, at Inverness, in spite of the support of Duncan Forbes of Culloden, found to his great disappointment only one clan, the Munroes, willing to give him immediate support. Then, on 31 August, he learned that the Jacobite army was on its way south, and determined to try and reach Edinburgh by sea before Charles and his army could reach it by land. He left Inverness on 4 September for Aberdeen and sent orders to the 85-year-old Lieutenant-General Guest, stationed in Edinburgh and commanding two dragoon regiments in the Lowlands, to send him shipping to enable him to move his men to the Firth of Forth and defend the capital. The Jacobite army, learning of Cope's intentions, hastened to Edinburgh in order to put themselves in possession of the city before Cope's forces could land at Leith.

Charles and his men marched south-west from Perth 'in very good order', as Lord George recorded: they crossed Streathearn and moved west of Auchterarder to Tullibardine, Lord George's home, 'where the armie was to halt & refresh & the Prince to dine'. It was on the way to Tullibardine that the first brush between an Irish and a Scottish officer occurred. Sir John Macdonald, probably as a result of having drunk too much, was highly offensive to Lord George Murray in the presence of Macdonald of Keppoch. The always courteous and sensible Keppoch persuaded Lord George not to take offence by saying 'he believ'd Sir John must either be drunk or mad, if not both, & it was best taking no notice of him'. This was followed shortly afterwards by another incident, this time involving O'Sullivan. When they reached Tullibardine it was found that O'Sullivan had (again in Lord George's words) 'brought with him the old Provost of Perth, and another Burgar, prisoner, under pretence that the Post Master's wife (for the man himself was not in town) had not pay'd twenty pounds sterling to which she was taxt'. Such treatment of decent Perth citizens horrified Lord George, who was always anxious to show that the Prince and his followers treated everybody, and especially civic dignitaries, with courtesy and respect. Sheridan, like O'Sullivan used to military situations in Europe where respect for the susceptibilities of civilians encountered in the course of campaigning was not regarded as necessary or even desirable, supported O'Sullivan's action, saying: 'We must show these kind of people our power or they will spit upon us'. Lord George complained to the Prince and eventually 'with abundance of difficulty got the provost Liberat'. That evening the Prince reached Dunblane, though Lord George and most of the army did not get there until the following morning. After a day's halt at Dunblane they pushed on, crossing the Forth unopposed at the Fords of Frew and spending the night of the 13th at Touch, just over two miles west of Stirling.

Of the two dragoon regiments that had been left by Cope in the Lowlands when he marched north, one, in command of Colonel James Gardiner, was stationed at Stirling, and the other, Hamilton's, was at Edinburgh. Gardiner, who had spent a gay not to say dissolute youth but had later undergone a religious conversion which had left him melancholy and fatalistic, made no attempt to stop Charles's army from crossing the Forth but retreated with his regiment to Falkirk. The

Jacobite army followed. As they passed through St Ninians, a town immediately south of Stirling, 'some few shott was fired from Stirling Castle, but' (Murray of Broughton continues) 'tho the balls fell very nigh him [the Prince] they hurt nobody'. They halted for a while at Bannockburn, and doubtless meditated on Robert the Bruce's glorious victory there in 1314, and there they learned that Gardiner's dragoons had retired from Falkirk to Linlithgow. The army then continued towards Falkirk, where Charles stayed at Callendar House with the Earl of Kilmarnock, who had actually dined with Gardiner and his officers that same day and had left them at six o'clock. When he learned that Gardiner's dragoons were at Linlithgow and intended to defend Linlithgow Bridge Charles determined to make a surprise attack on them there. He sent Lord George with 1,000 men to surprise the dragoons in their camp ('the Prince wou'd go himself,' O'Sullivan recorded, 'but the rest of the men declaired they'd all march if he did, so was obliged to stay, to contain the rest'.) But when they got there they found the camp empty: the dragoons had retreated towards Edinburgh.

Charles entered Linlithgow on the morning of 15 September. 'It happening to be of a Sunday,' wrote Murray of Broughton, 'the Chevalier ever careful to show the world how much he was determined to keep up to the engagements in his Manifesto, encamped his army to the eastward of The Town, and discharged any of the men from entering save a very small guard he keept with himself in the Palace, ordered the bells to be rung, the church doors to be open'd, and gave orders to assure the magistrates in his name that they should not be disturbed in their worship, notwithstanding of which the Minister either left the Town, or declined preaching, to enduce the ignorant vulgar to believe that if he had, he would have been insulted and persecuted'. Meanwhile Gardiner had reached Corstorphine, three miles west of Edinburgh, where he was joined by Hamilton's dragoons and by a few hundred men from the hastily formed Edinburgh regiment and from the Town Guard. Then they retired eastward towards the city, encamping in a field near Coltbridge.

Coltbridge, once a little village on the Water of Leith with two bridges, an old and a new, is now completely absorbed in the western New Town of Edinburgh and its name, unknown to most modern Edinburgh citizens, is remembered by historians only because of what happened there. The incident became known as the 'Coltbrig Canter', and what happened was this:

On the evening of the 15th Brigadier Thomas Fowke arrived in

Edinburgh from England to take command of the two regiments of dragoons and he reviewed them in their camp the next morning. He found everything in an appalling condition. He reported that he found 'many of the Men's and some of the Officer's Legs so swell'd, that they could not wear Boots; and those who really were to be depended upon, in a manner overcome for want of Sleep'. The horses, having been at grass, were quite unfit for combat and often their backs were 'not fit to receive their riders'. Colonel Gardiner complained that his regiment was in a thoroughly bad condition, having been 'harass'd and fatigued for eleven Days and eleven Nights, little or no Provision for the Men, or Forage for the Horses'. If they stayed another night on that ground, he said, 'it was to be feared his Majesty would lose two Regiments of Dragoons'. He added that Brigadier Fowke might do as he pleased, for he himself had not long to live.

In the light of this state of affairs, it was decided, on the recommendation of Lieutenant-Colonel Guest, to withdraw the men to Leith Links so that they could join up with Sir John Cope's forces who were expected to arrive at Leith at any moment. But before this could be done, reports arrived that the Jacobite army was advancing. These reports came from a small rearguard that had been left at Corstorphine. The traditional account (based on John Home's contemporary report) is best given in the elegant early nineteenth-century language of Robert Chambers:

> The insurgents, observing them [the rear-guard] on their approach to Corstorphine, sent forward one or two of their number on horseback to take a view of them, and bring a report of their number. These gentlemen, riding up pretty near, thought proper to fire their pistols *towards* the party; and the poor dragoons immediately, in the greatest alarm, wheeled about, without returning a shot, and retired upon the main body at Colt Bridge, to whom they communicated all their fears. The whole party immediately broke up, and commenced a retreat, not to Edinburgh, with the design of still defending it within the walls, but to the open country beyond it. In the movement, afterwards styled the *Canter of Coltbrigg*, the men rode over the ground now occupied by the New Town, where they were exposed to the view of the citizens. The Jacobites beheld the spectacle with ill-concealed pleasure, and the Whigs were proportionately discouraged.

Brigadier Fowke later maintained that it was an orderly withdrawal, as planned, but the tradition of the canter became speedily entrenched in the folk memory and there must have been something behind it.

Certainly Colonel Gardiner himself complained to General Lord Mark Kerr, when the latter arrived at Dunbar some days later, of 'the retreat, I may say run a way, of the two Reg^{ts}. of Dragoons'. What is indisputable is that the withdrawal of the Government forces, whether in terror or with deliberation, left Edinburgh in a state of panic. The dragoons did not even stay at Leith, but withdrew first to Musselburgh and then, on Gardiner's suggestion, to Prestonpans, near his own estate of Bankton, where, on the grounds of illness, he was given permission to spend the night in his own house.

Meanwhile the Jacobite army had encamped at Gray's Mill, near Slateford, two miles to the south-west of Edinburgh, and from there Charles sent the following summons to the Provost and Magistrates of the city:

Being now in a condition to make our way into this capital of his Majesty's ancient kingdom of Scotland, we hereby summon you to receive us, as you are in duty bound to do. And in order to it we hereby require you upon receipt of this to summon the Town Council and take proper measure in it for securing the peace and quiet of the city, which we are very desirous to protect. But if you suffer any of the Usurper's troops to enter the town, or any of the canon, arms, or ammunition now in it, whether belonging to the publick or to private persons, to be carried off, we shall take it as a breach of your duty and a heinous offence against the king and us, and shall resent it accordingly. We promise to preserve all the rights and liberties of the city, and the particular property of every one of his Majesty's subjects. But if any opposition be made to us we cannot answer for the consequences, being firmly resolved at any rate to enter the city, and in that case, if any of the inhabitants are found in arms against us, they must not expect to be treated as prisoners of war.

(Signed) CHARLES, PRINCE REGENT

From our Camp, 16th September 1745

On reading this summons, Provost Stewart and the city magistrates decided to send a deputation to the Prince partly to gain time and partly to find out what his terms were. Charles asked Murray of Broughton to see them. They asked Murray exactly what was expected of them, and Murray replied simply opening their gates to the Jacobite army, delivering up the arms of the town and garrison with the ammunition and military stores in the town. They replied that they could take no responsibility for delivery of arms, but 'desired time to return and consult with their brethren'.

They were given two or three hours. Meanwhile, news that Sir John Cope's army was in the Forth suggested to the Provost and magistrates that they might stall for more time, but Charles realized their purpose in proposing further delays and consideration, and on the 16th sent by Murray a fairly curt note demanding 'a positive answer, before two o'clock in the morning, otherwise he will think himself obliged to take measures to conform'. A final deputation then set out, to ask for a suspension of hostilities until nine o'clock the next morning, but their plea was unsuccessful and they were told to 'get them gone'. Murray of Broughton takes up the tale:

The deputies had no sooner liberty to return, than the Chevalier sensible that they meditated to gain time and tire him out by a trifling treaty, and exasperated to think that they should have the inpudence to pretend terms for the surrendery of a Town quite defenceless, proposed to send a Detachment to render themselves Masters of it by force, in case the deputies did not return at the time appointed with a resolution to surrender. With this view he ordered Locheil to putt his people under arms to be ready to march upon a minutes warning, and ordered Mr M[urray] to be their guide, as he was well acquainted with all the avenues to the place, giving strickt orders to behave with all moderation to the Inhabitants, and that the sogers should not be allowed to taste spirits, and to pay for wtever they got, promising them two shillings each so soon as they rendered themselves Masters of the place. The detachment ... passed without being observed by the garrison of the Castle, tho so near as to hear them distinctly call their rounds, and arrived at the nether bow Port without meetting any body on their way, and found the wall of the Town which flanks the Pleasants and St. Marys wynd mounted with cannon, but no person appeared. [They demanded admission at the Netherbow Port, but this was refused, so] it now being clear daylight Mr M. proposed to retire to a place called St Leonards hills [i.e. Arthur's Seat], and after securing themselves from the cannon of the Castle, to waite for orders from the Chevalier where to attack the town, ... This retreat being thus agreed to Mr M. went to the rear of the detachment to make them march and guide them to the place proposed, but before they had time to get so far, the Coach which had returned with the deputies came down the High Street and oblidged the Guard to open the Port, upon which Locheil took the advantage and rushed in, the guard immediately dispersing. Thus did the Chevalier render himself master of the Capital without shedding a drop of Blood, notwithstanding all the mighty preparations and associations entered into for its defence.

The opening of the city gate to admit the coach of the returning deputies, thus allowing Lochiel and his men to rush in, was the first piece of absolute good fortune the Jacobite cause had had for a long time. It enabled Charles to make himself quickly master of Edinburgh, though the Castle remained in the control of the Government garrison of 600 men under the aged General Guest. In the early morning, immediately after the rushing of the gate, in the words of a Highland participant, 'our people with drawn sword and target, with a hideous yell* and their particular manner of making ane attack (they not knowing what resistance they might meet with in the town), marched quickly up street, no one leaving their rank or order, and forced their way into the city guard-house, and took possession. The main body drew up in the Parliament closs, and guards were immediately placed at every gate of the city; and the inhabitants cannot in justice but acknowledge that the behaviour of our Highlanders was civil and innocent beyond what even their best friends could have expected'.

A lively picture of feeling in Edinburgh at this time has been left us in the autobiography of Dr Alexander ('Jupiter') Carlyle, then a young man of 23:

> The city was in great ferment and bustle at this time; for besides the two parties of Whigs and Jacobites – of which a well-informed citizen told me there were two-thirds of the men in the city of the first description, or friends to Government; and of the second, or enemies of Government, two-thirds of the ladies, – besides this division, there was another between those who were keen for preparing with zeal and activity to defend the city, and those who were averse to that measure [among whom he numbered Provost Stewart and his friends] ...
>
> On Sunday morning the 15th ... news had arrived in town that the rebel army had been at Linlithgow the night before, and were on full march towards Edinburgh. This ... made thinking people fear that they might be in possession of Edinburgh before Cope arrived. The Volunteers rendezvoused in the College Yards before ten o'clock, to the number of about 400. Captain Drummond appeared at ten, and ... addressed us in a speech of some length, the purport of which was, that it had been agreed by the General, and the Officers of the Crown, that the military force should oppose the rebels on their march to Edinburgh, consisting of the Town Guard, that part

* Another account by a participant says that 'eight or nine hundred Highlanders under the command of Keppoch, young Lochiel, and O'Sullivan marched in between the Long Dykes [where Princes Street now is] without a hush of noise' and when the gate was opened for the coach 'the lurking Highlanders rushed in (it being then peep of day) and made themselves masters of the city without any opposition, or the smallest noise'. It is strange that one account should emphasize the noise and the other the silence.

of the new regiment who had got arms, with the Volunteers from the country. What he had to propose to us was that we should join this force, and expose our lives in defence of the capital of Scotland and the security of our country's laws and liberties. ...

We were marched immediately up to the Lawnmarket, where we halted till the other companies should follow. They were late in making their appearance, and some of their officers, coming up to us while in the street, told us that most of the privates were unwilling to march. During this halt, Hamilton's dragoons, who had been at Leith, marched past our corps, on their route to join Gardiner's regiment, who were at Colt Bridge. We cheered them, in passing, with a huzzah; and the spectators began to think at last that some serious fighting was likely to ensue, though before this moment many of them had laughed at and ridiculed the Volunteers ...

While we remained [in the Lawnmarket] ... the mob in the street and the ladies in the windows treated us very variously, many with lamentation, and even with tears, and some with apparent scorn and derision. In one house on the south side of the street there was a row of windows, full of ladies, who appeared to enjoy our march to danger with much levity and mirth. ... In marching down the Bow, a narrow winding street, the scene was different, for all the spectators were in tears, and uttering loud lamentations.

[They halted in the Grassmarket, where several clergymen came to harangue them.] Dr William Wishart, Principal of the College, was their prolocutor, and called upon us in a most pathetic speech to desist from this rash enterprise, which he said was exposing the flower of the youth of Edinburgh, and the hope of the next generation, to the danger of being cut off, or made prisoners and maltreated, without any just or adequate object; that our number added so very little to the force that was intended against the rebels, that with-drawing us would make little difference, while our loss would be irreparable, ...

But the Coltbrig Canter led to a clamour among the Volunteers 'that it would be madness to think of defending the town, as the dragoons had fled'. In the midst of the confusion, 'a man on horse-back, whom nobody knew, came up from the Bow, and, riding at a quick pace along the line of Volunteers, called out that the Highlanders were at hand, and that they were 16,000 strong. This fellow did not stop to be examined, but rode off at the gallop'. This was the end of any serious thought of defending the city.

The lawyers, clergymen and tradesmen of Edinburgh were on the whole in favour of the Government, if only for the sake of peace and quiet, though there were some who had Jacobite sympathies without being willing to put themselves to any risk for their sake. The poet Allan Ramsay, who had written Scottish nationalist poetry showing strong Jacobite feeling, cannily went off to Penicuik where a convenient sudden illness forced him to stay for some weeks (thus leaving his house near the Castle, the well-known 'Goose Pie', as a vantage point from which the Highlanders could fire on the Castle sentries). There was a considerable amount of anti-Union feeling in Edinburgh still, especially among ordinary folk and 'the mob', as the Porteous Riots of 1736 had grimly shown, and there was considerable confusion between outraged Scottish national sentiment and Jacobite feeling. A profession of Jacobitism was often the only way open for frustrated nationalism, even for someone with no love for the house of Stuart. Charles had some sense of this, but neither he nor any of his advisers had the skill in public relations to exploit this confusion as fully as they might have done.

In Edinburgh, Charles was joined by Lord Elcho, whom he had known in Rome and who was to become commander of the Prince's life-guards. He and the Duke of Perth flanked the Prince when on 17 September he rode to the ancient royal palace of Holyrood House in Edinburgh after the proclamation at the Market Cross of his father as King and himself as Prince Regent. They had marched by Duddingston and the King's Park, below Arthur's Seat, to avoid fire from the castle cannon. John Home, later the author of the tragedy *Douglas* and then, like Carlyle, a young man of 23, observed the scene as a volunteer on the Government side and later gave an account of it in his *History of the Rebellion in the Year 1745*:

> The Park was full of people (amongst whom was the Author of this history), all of them impatient to see this extraordinary person. The figure and presence of Charles Stuart were not ill suited to his lofty pretensions. He was in the prime of youth, tall and handsome, of a fair complexion; he had a light-coloured periwig with his own hair combed over in front; he wore the Highland dress, that is, a tartan short coat without the plaid, a blue bonnet on his head, and on his breast the star of the order of St. Andrew. Charles stood some time in the park to shew himself to the people; and then, though he was very near the palace, mounted his horse, either to render himself more conspicuous, or because he rode well, and looked graceful on horseback.

The proclamation read at the Market Cross promised a full pardon for all 'Treasons, Rebellions and Offences' committed at any time against Charles's grandfather and father and against himself, promised to maintain the Church of England and the Protestant Churches of Scotland and Ireland as by law established, guaranteed to individuals and institutions 'the full Enjoyment and Possession of all their Rights, Privileges, and Immunities' and denounced the Act of Union for having reduced Scotland 'to being no more than an English province'. It also denounced the disarmament of the Highlands, the malt tax, and other unpopular measures introduced under the Hanoverians. It was a bid to capitalize on a wide variety of discontents, and it deliberately avoided any suggestion of returning to the policies which had lost his grandfather his throne.

But it was the Scottish nationalist argument that was most conspicuously effective. As Charles was about to enter the palace, Home recorded, 'a gentleman stepped out of the crowd, drew his sword, and raising his arm aloft, walked up stairs before Charles. The person who enlisted himself in this manner, was James Hepburn of Keith'. Hepburn was a veteran opponent of the Union, and a man respected by all for his openness and integrity. The theatrical gesture of this silver-haired old patriot made a great impression on the crowd. It was a fitting prelude to Charles's occupation of the palace of his ancestors, itself a deliberately histrionic act.

CHAPTER NINE

Victory

'JUPITER' CARLYLE, whose father was minister of the parish of Preston-pans, which lies on the Firth of Forth 9½ miles east of Edinburgh, set out for his father's house there on 16 September, rightly believing that the surrender of Edinburgh to the Jacobites was imminent. At Lucky Vint's Courtyard, an inn near Prestonpans, they met Lord Drummore, a judge of the Court of Session, who, on learning that Carlyle had come from Edinburgh, anxiously inquired if the town had surrendered. '"No! but it was expected to fall into the hands of the rebels early to-morrow." "Were there any Highlanders on their march this way?" "Not a soul;" I could answer for it, as I had left Edinburgh past eight o'clock, and had walked out deliberately, and seen not a creature but [a] horseman in the sands.' Lord Drummore repeated this information to officers of the two dragoon regiments who were at the inn, but they refused to believe it; they insisted that the Highlanders were at hand 'It was in vain to tell them that they had neither wings nor horses, nor were invisible – away they went, as fast as they could, to their respective corps, who, on marching from Leith, where they had thought themselves not safe, had halted in an open field, above the west end of Prestonpans, between Prestongrange and the enclosures of Mr. Nisbet lying west from the village of Preston.' The next day Carlyle heard that Cope's transports had been seen off Dunbar, and in fact by the evening of that day Cope had already disembarked his infantry and most of his artillery. 'But', Carlyle recollected, 'it was not this news, for it was not then come, that made the dragoons scamper from their ground on the preceding night. It was an unlucky dragoon, who, slipping a little aside for a pea-sheaf to his horse, for there were some on the ground not led off, fell into a coal-pit, not filled up, when his side-arms and ac-coutrements made such a noise, as alarmed a body of men, who, for two days, had been completely panic-struck.'

Carlyle went on to Dunbar, to make certain of Sir John Cope's arrival, and there he visited Colonel Gardiner, who was staying with the local minister. 'He looked pale and dejected,' and described the hasty retreat of the dragoons as 'a foul flight'. He did not believe that he could count on his men. 'I'll tell you in confidence,' he told Carlyle, 'that I have not above ten men in my regiment whom I am certain will follow me. But we must give them battle now, and God's will be done!' John Home had already arrived and reported that the Highlanders numbered about 1,900, 'but that they were ill armed, though that defect was now supplied at Edinburgh'. Home later estimated that the Prince's total force numbered about 2,400. Cope's total forces numbered about 2,200 men, but he and his officers believed that his army was greatly outnumbered by the Highlanders whom they believed to be at least 5,000 strong. On the morning of 19 September Cope's army began its advance to Haddington, intended as the first stage on the way towards Edinburgh.

When Charles heard that Cope had disembarked his army at Dunbar he remarked laconically, 'Has he, by God?' A Jacobite proclamation demanding the surrender of arms in Edinburgh brought in some 1,200 muskets but nothing else of great significance. Only about 1,500 of Charles's men had both swords and muskets. About a hundred had nothing but scythes fastened on poles. The clans engaged were summed up by Andrew Lang as 'Macdonalds of all septs, Camerons, Atholl men, Stewarts of Appin, Macgregors, Perth's regiment, MacLachlans, Nairne's band, and a few Lowland gentry and servants' and he considered 2,500 as the highest possible estimate of their numbers. Some volunteers were recruited in Edinburgh, particularly for the Duke of Perth's regiment. The army was encamped in the King's Park, and on the morning of the 19th moved eastward under the shadow of Arthur's Seat to the village of Duddingston.

At Duddingston, in the words of Murray of Broughton, 'the Chevalier putt himself att the head of his small army, [and] drawing his sword, said with a very determined Countenance, Gentlemen, I have flung away the scabbard, with Gods assistance I dont doubt of making you a free and happy people, Mr Cope shall not escape us as he did in the Highlands'. The Jacobite army proceeded eastward through Musselburgh, where they learned that Cope, having spent the preceding night in a field on the west side of Haddington, was approaching Tranent. From this it was inferred that he intended to engage the Jacobite army on the moorland west of Tranent, and this led to a speeding up of Charles's march in order to reach the top of Carberry Hill before Cope. But soon it was learned that Cope and his army had turned north to occupy low ground between the villages of Preston and Seton. Carlyle, with other Government volunteers, was now with Cope's army, and was greatly surprised at this move. At nine o'clock in the morning of the 20th, he reported, 'to my great surprise, instead of keeping the post-road through Tranent Muir, which was high ground and commanded the country south for several miles, as it did that to the north for two or three miles towards the sea, they turned to the right by Elviston and the village of Trabroun, till they past Longniddry on the north, and St. Germains on the south, when, on entering the defile made by the enclosures there, they halted for near an hour, and then marched into an open field of two miles in length and one and a half in breadth, extending from Seaton to Preston, and from Tranent to the sea'. Cope evidently intended to push on to the River Esk, between Musselburgh and Dalkeith, to obtain protection from the river and provisions from the two towns. 'But', continues Carlyle, 'they were too late in marching; for when they came to St. Germains, their scouts . . . brought them intelligence that the rebel army were on their march, on which, after an hour's halt, when, by turning to the left [southwards], they might have reached the high ground at Tranent before the rebels, they marched on to that plain before described, now called the field of battle. This field was entirely clear of the crop, the last sheaves having been carried in the night before.'

When Charles realized where Cope had posted his army, he took this to mean that Cope wished to avoid an action, and this, according to Murray of Broughton, 'made him determine, if possible, to attack him the same day'. In fact, Cope had chosen the stubble field as an ideal battle-ground. 'There is not', he afterwards wrote, 'in the whole of the Ground between Edinburgh and Dunbar a better spot for both Horse and Foot to act upon'. To the north was the sea, and on the south, parallel to the road between Preston and Seton, was a ditch, with a morass behind it. The Chevalier de Johnstone records that Cope's position was recognized by the Jacobite army as a strong one. 'We proceeded after mid-day to reconnoitre his position, and our anxiety and chagrin tended only to augment at every moment by our discoveries of the locality, seeing no means of attacking him without visibly exposing ourselves to be hewn in pieces with dishonour.'

Further, the Jacobite army was troubled with the kind of dissension that was to plague it continually. There was dispute among the clans as to which should have the position of greatest honour, and this, in Murray of Broughton's words, 'might, upon the Eve of a battle, prove detrimental to the Common interest'. Charles had proposed at Perth that the matter should be settled by the drawing of lots, and this was agreed. The Macdonalds of Glen Garry, Clanranald and Keppoch, choosing to fight together, drew the lot that placed them on the left, and the Camerons and Stewarts of Appin, also fighting together, drew the lot for the more honourable position on the right. The Macdonald clansmen, however, having been informed of the result of the drawing of lots when the army was at Duddingston, refused to accept the less honourable position on the left. The dispute was settled by the good sense of Cameron of Lochiel, who, in Murray's words, 'generously offered that in case no action happened that day [the 20th] which did not seem probable he would willingly quite his post the next to the Mcdonalds nothwithstanding the agreement, in persueance of which the Mcdonalds marchd from the left next morning and formed the right of the whole'.

Another unhappy incident took place after Charles, fearing that Cope and his army might try to slip away westward to Edinburgh along the road from Preston to Musselburgh, ordered O'Sullivan to post the Atholl Brigade west of Preston to cover this route. According to O'Sullivan's narrative (and it must be remembered that he disliked Lord George) this infuriated Lord George Murray, who 'asked the Prince in a very high tone, what was become of the Athol Brigade & the Prince told him, upon wch Ld George threw his gun on the Ground in a great passion, & Swore God, he'd never draw his sword for the cause, if the Bregade was not brought back. The Prince with his ordinary prudence, tho' senseble of the disrespect, & too senseble of the consequence it may be of, gave orders that the brigade shou'd come back, but Ld George who was brought to himself, as it is said, prayed the Prince to send the brigade to their first destination' but it seems that yet another order was given countermanding this and reaffirming the order to send the brigade back. Murray of Broughton simply says that Charles was informed 'that the detachment of five hundred Atholl men which he had posted upon the west side of the Village of Preston had rejoined the army; this made him very uneasy lest the Enemy had filed off during the night by that road and taken possession of the Citty of Edin^r, to prevent which and to intercept the runaways had enduced him to make that disposition'. At first he thought of ordering them to return, but then, still according to Murray, 'he judged it safer and better to put up with the disappointment and continue the rest of his plan, tho he could not help complaining that his orders had been neglected in so material a point'. Still, says Murray, Charles 'kept in very high Spirits the rest of the night'.

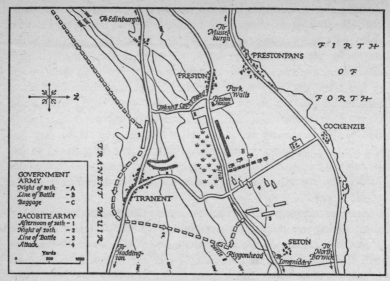

The battle of Prestonpans

The Jacobite army was now approaching Cope's position from the south-west, and on the afternoon of the 20th they were drawn up immediately west of the village of Tranent. What happened then is best told in the words of the Chevalier de Johnstone;

At sunset our army crossed the village of Tranent, which was on our right, taking up a new position opposite the morass. General Cope at the sametime placed his army in four divisions, supporting his right against the ditch of the enclosure, his left to the sea, and having his front to the pond. Mr. Henderson [actually Robert Anderson of Whitburgh in East Lothian], the proprietor of the morass, came to the Prince about night-fall, very opportunely to relieve us of a terrible embarrassment. He assured the Prince that there was a passage through the morass where we could pass, and that he had crossed it daily in shooting. The Prince having sent at once to reconnoitre the passage, found his report correct, and that General Cope, believing it impracticable, had neglected to place a guard on it. During the night he made his army to pass over it. The Highlanders defiling one after another without encountering any opposition on the part of the enemy, formed their ranks according as they got out from the morass, and the column extended itself along the seashore.

General Cope at daybreak mistook for bushes our first line, which was in battle array, about two hundred paces in front of his army. It consisted of about twelve hundred men, and our second line of six hundred was composed of those who were badly armed, many as we have said above, having only sticks in their hands. Mr. Macgregor, Captain in the regiment of the Duke of Perth, in default of other arms, took scythes, well sharpened, which he attached to the ends of sticks from seven to eight feet long, the points in height like the lance of a spontoon, with which he armed his company, and which, was a most murderous weapon.

When the first line had passed the morass, Lord George Murray sent me to watch for the purpose of seeing that the second line, which the Prince conducted himself, should also pass it without noise or confusion. Having surveyed the spot and not finding anything in disorder, in returning to rejoin Lord George, I found the Prince at the head of this column with Lord Nairn; at the moment he entered the morass, and that I had crossed it with him for the second time, we were not again beyond it when the enemy fired his alarm gun on perceiving at the break of day our first line in battle array.

Close to the edge, on leaving the morass, there was a deep ditch, three or four feet broad, which it was necessary to leap, and the Prince in jumping it, fell on his knees on the other side, and I seized him by the arms immediately, and raised him up. On examining his countenance, he appeared to me to be struck by this accident as an evil omen.

Lord George, at the head of the first line, did not leave the English any time to recover from their surprise. He advanced at quick time and so precipitately, that General Cope could with difficulty put his army in battle array; and the Highlanders threw themselves upon them, head foremost, sword in hand. They had been often recommended to deal their sword strokes upon the noses of the horses without attacking the horsemen, explaining to them that the natural movement of the wounded horse in front, would be to make him bolt round; and that a few wounded horses at the head would be sufficient to throw a whole squadron into disorder, and without their being able to remedy it. They followed this advice with exactitude, and the English cavalry were immediately in disorder.

The result was a rout, which can be best described from the point of view of the other side. The author of the so-called Woodhouselee MS. was a fiercely anti-Jacobite Presbyterian Whig in Cope's army. He describes with great picturesqueness what happened next:

They [the Highlanders] came on with furiows precipitation. This disconcerted all the poor generals [Cope's] fyne disposition and he was in surprize and confusion, the canon was turnd and gave 2 or three discharges but they wheeled and formed. The Highland troups battell came on so furiowsly that in a moment they were in sword in hand. The dragowns run off at the first fyer. Some of Gardener's men advanced abowt 15 or 16 but that was the most. The foot stood after the horse were gon, but there was no orders from the generall what to doe, and all went soon to confusion. The trowpes of horse behind to gwarde the artilery never advanced to defend them, and the Highlander came up and seased them and the pultrown Irish [the dragoons, which this writer had earlier called 'the two dastardly Irish regiments of dragowns'] fled. The rebells turned the Kings cannon upon us but were slow in charging and not good marksmen with great guns. Cope had the gunners of the *Fox* man of war ... but he lost artillery, amonition and all, and it may be fittly called the Chase of Cockenie or Tranent reither than the battell, for never deers run faster befor hownds than these poor betrayed men run befor a rabbell. Disiplined they were, but had no head and no confidence in there leaders. They were surprised in the twelight by men came on with a resolut rage.

Murray of Broughton gave his version:

In a few minutes the rout was total; the Dragoons on the right run of by the high road through the Town of Preston, and those on the left by the Shore towards the east; the few of the foot that saved themselves escaped by Preston Park, the wall of which had been broke down the day before by G[ll]. Copes orders. All the baggage of the army was placed in a yard upon the left of their army, guarded by two Companys of L. Lowdons Regiment, where so soon as the action was over Cap[t] Bazil Cochran of Coll. Lees [Lee's regiment, the 44th; later the Essex Regiment] was sent by L. G. M. to tell them that if they would immediatly surrender as prisoners of war they should be used as such, if not, they would be immediately attack'd and no quarter given, upon which they readily gave up their arms.

'In this action on the side of the Chevalier,' Murray wrote, 'there were not above three or four officers killed, and these people of no distinction, with about thirty private men and seventy or eighty officers and Solgers wounded; whereas of G[ll]. Copes, according to the best Computation that could than be made, there were seven or eight officers [including Colonel Gardiner] and about three hundred private men killed, and betwixt four or five hundred wounded, with almost the whole taken prisoners, of whom there were eighty three officers.'

The whole action lasted less than ten minutes. The Battle of Prestonpans (or the Battle of Gladsmuir* as it is sometimes called, though the village of that name is some four miles south-east of Prestonpans) was fought in the early morning of Saturday, 21 September. It was more than a signal victory for the Jacobite army: it was a shameful defeat for the Government forces. The reason for the speed and completeness of the defeat of Cope's army was partly the night-time crossing of the morass by the Jacobites, to attack at daybreak from the east when they were expected from the south, so that Cope had suddenly to swing his whole army round at right angles, which caused a certain amount of confusion; partly the inexperience of the bulk of Cope's troops, and partly the Highland method of attack: they 'knew no other manoeuvre but to rush upon the enemy sword in hand', said the Chevalier de Johnstone. According to John Home, the Highlanders first fired on the dragoons, causing them to reel and fall into confusion, then 'threw down their musquets, drew their swords and ran on.' The impetuosity and fierceness of this kind of attack represented a kind of warfare which Cope's men were not trained for and did not expect: they found it demoralizing. Not the least demoralized was Cope himself, who arrived the next day at Berwick, where tradition says that Lord Mark Kerr sardonically congratulated him on being the first general to bring the news of his own defeat. (Actually, Brigadier Fowke had got to Berwick before Cope, and news of the defeat was known there before Cope's arrival.) Throughout the nation Jacobites exulted in the victory of Prestonpans and gloated over the unfortunate Cope. There are several versions of a triumphantly mocking Jacobite song about him, set to the lively tune of the old song 'Will you go to the coals in the morning'. One is by Burns:

> Sir John Cope trod the north right far,
> Yet ne'er a rebel he cam naur,
> Until he landed at Dunbar
> Right early in a morning.
> (Chorus) Hey Johnie Cope are ye wauking yet,
> Or are ye sleeping I would wit;
> O haste ye get up for the drums do beat,
> O fye Cope rise in the morning. . . .

* According to the *Memoirs* of Sir John Clerk of Penicuik (1676–1755) the Jacobites 'affected to call' the battle Gladsmuir rather than Prestonpans 'to make it quadrat with a foolish old prophecy of Thomas the Rhymer, "In Gladesmoor shall the battle be"'.

It was upon an afternoon,
Sir Johnie march'd to Preston town;
He says, my lads come lean you down,
And we'll fight the boys in the morning.
  Hey Johnie Cope &c.

But when he saw the Highland lads,
Wi tartan trews and white cockauds,
Wi' swords and guns and rungs and gauds, [cudgels and iron bars]
O Johnie he took wing in the morning. . . .

Sir Johnie into Berwick rade,
Just as the devil had been his guide;
Gien him the warld he would na stay'd
To foughten the boys in the morning. . . .

Says Lord Mark Car, ye are no blate, [you are not backward]
To bring us the news o' your ain defeat;
I think you deserve the back o' the gate,
Get out o' my sight this morning. . . .

Though the Highlanders had attacked with savagery – the scythes mounted on sticks inflicted terrible damage on both men and horses – there is ample testimony that Charles and his officers behaved with conspicuous humanity. The Duke of Perth was particularly assiduous in procuring proper attention for enemy wounded. 'So soon as the action was over,' says Murray of Broughton, 'the Chevalier gave orders to have the wounded dressed and carriages provided to take them of the field, which was executed by his Surgeons w^t all the care and expedition imaginable, to the great loss of the wounded of his own army, who from being neglected till most of the troops were taken care of, their wounds festered, being all gun Shott and mostly in the legs and thighs.' Murray may have exaggerated, but even the strongly anti-Jacobite Whig historian Andrew Henderson reported that he 'went to the Road-Side where the Chevalier, who by Advice of Perth, &c. had sent to Edinburgh for Surgeons, was standing. He was clad as an ordinary Captain, in a coarse Plaid and blue Bonnet, his Boots and Knees were much dirtied: he seemed to have fallen into a Ditch, which I was told by one of his Lifeguards he had'. Colonel Gardiner's Bankton House was turned into a hospital, though this did not prevent clansmen from looting it.

1 A contemporary anti-Jacobite print highlights episodes in the 1715 rising. Around the centre-piece, which depicts Argyll's march to Perth, are vignettes showing the main events, from the plotting by Mar and his friends (top left) to James's flight (bottom right)

2 When, contrary to King George's hopes, James fathered a son and heir, the Pope himself baptized the infant Charles Edward (painting by Pier-Leone Ghezzi)

3 Clementina Sobieska, descendant of the Sobieski kings of Poland, wife of James and mother of Charles Edward. The marriage was not happy, but it produced two sons

4 The Palazzo Muti, Rome, where Prince Charles Edward was born and where, sixty-eight years later, he died in his daughter's arms. It was a gift from the Pope to James

5 Thanksgiving medals were struck hailing the babe as 'Spes Britanniae', the hope of Britain, and defiantly entitling him Prince of Wales

6 A miniature of Charles, resplendent with ribbon and star of the Garter, and his brother Henry, the future cardinal

7 Prince Charles's monument at Glenfinnan, at the head of Loch Shiel. Here the Royal Standard was unfurled by the Duke of Atholl and James was proclaimed King, with the Prince as his Regent, on 19th August 1745

8 *right* This portrait of Charles in tartan dress, by the Swedish painter Hans Hysing, must have been painted about the time when the young prince, then aged fourteen, saw his first battle, at Gaeta, between Rome and Naples

9 The Duke of Cumberland, 'Butcher' Cumberland, third son of George II

10 A contemporary broadsheet shows General Cope fleeing to Berwick after the battle of Prestonpans, 'the first general that ever was the messenger of his own defeat'

11 Prince Charles in Highland dress

12 The titular Duke of Perth, joint Lieutenant-General of Charles's army

13 Lord George Murray, joint Lieutenant-General under the Prince's command with the Duke of Perth

14 One of the cannon that defended Carlisle against the invading Highlanders in 1745

'Some hours after the action,' to quote Murray again, 'the Chevalier quitted the feild and went to Pinkey house [Pinkie House, on the southern outskirts of Musselburgh], having given the Strictest orders to have the [captured] officers used with all imaginable Civility. The dead to be buried and all the arms secured. The whole baggage of the army was taken,' including 'betwixt two and three thousand' pounds, found among General Cope's papers. The next day – the 22nd – Charles returned to Holyrood, 'and being told that rejoicings and bone fires were intended for the victory, he gave possitive orders against it saying that he was far from rejoicing att the death of any of his fathers Subjects, tho never so much his enemies yet he pittied their unhappy way of thinking, which had drawn so many misfortunes upon the Country, and ended in their own fall, and that he should think it unnatural in his followers to make publick rejoices upon the deaths of their own Country men'. (In reporting this – and the report paraphrases Charles's proclamation of 23 September, which Murray himself drew up and signed – Murray contrasts the behaviour of the Government after the Jacobite defeat at Culloden the following year: public rejoicings were ordered and those who would not illuminate their houses had their windows smashed.)

Charles sent messages to the Presbyterian ministers in Edinburgh that they should preach as usual on Sunday the 22nd, and when the ministers sent a deputation to Sir Thomas Sheridan asking if they could pray for King George, 'the Chevalier resolved to give them no grounds for Complaints, was pleased to direct Sr Tho: to tell them as from himself, their deputation being to him, that he could not pretend to give them that Liberty, which in its self would be a flatt Contradiction, but that he would venture to assure them that no notice should be taken of any thing they said, which tho it must, by every impartial person, be allowed to have been an unheard of instance of humanity and good nature, yett they, nevertheless, refused to comply, pretending fear of insults or the like'.

The Jacobite army was now partly encamped at Duddingston and partly quartered in Edinburgh and adjacent villages, but care was taken not to burden citizens with compulsory billeting of men in their houses (a practice for which the Hanoverian army was to be bitterly blamed the following spring). Many of the men lay on straw in the Tron Church and in the lobby of Parliament House. 'The Burgesses and people of fashion were not harrassed with common fellows for their guests,' says Murray of Broughton, although 'publick houses and people of low rank were burdened with them'. Many were quite happy to have

Jacobite officers as lodgers, especially now that things seemed to be going Charles's way. The ladies in particular fell for Bonnie Prince Charlie, and demonstrated their enthusiasm by wearing white cockades and tartan sashes.

Charles was now, in the words of the Chevalier de Johnstone, 'entirely master of the kingdom of Scotland,' where there were now no Government troops except the garrisons of Stirling, Edinburgh and Dumbarton Castles, and in the Highland forts and barracks. The Prince had compelled his acknowledgment by all the important towns of Scotland as Regent of the kingdom for his father. Edinburgh Castle was still a thorn in Jacobite flesh, but there was nothing that Charles could do to remove it. Hearing that its garrison was short of provisions, he tried to force its surrender by cutting off supplies, but this provoked General Guest to order the Castle guns to fire on the city, with resulting civilian casualties among those living in areas exposed to the bombardment. Realizing that such casualties were doing his cause no good, Charles called off the blockade, and Castle and city continued to face each other, one under Hanoverian control and the other under Jacobite, without further incident. The blockade lasted from 29 September to 5 October.

The officers taken prisoner by the Jacobite army were eventually released on parole, each giving his word not to take up arms again against Prince Charles before 1 January 1747, but later the Duke of Cumberland, commanding the Hanoverian army, ordered the officers to break parole, which nearly all of them did, though Lieutenant-Colonel Peter Halkett of Lee's Regiment honourably refused, saying, 'His Grace commands my commission, but not my honour.' Carlyle saw the captured officers 'walking on the sea-shore, at the east end of Prestonpans' and reported that 'almost every aspect bore in it shame, and dejection, and despair. They were deeply mortified with what had happened, and timidly anxious about the future, ...' Most of them had regarded the clansmen opposing them as little more than banditti (as Horace Walpole called them) and they could not reconcile themselves to their defeat at such hands.

Charles wrote briefly to his father from Edinburgh on 7 October:

Tis impossible for me to give you a distinct gurnal of my procydings becose of my being so much hurried with business, which allows me no time; but notwithstanding I cannot let slip this occasion of giving a Short accoun of the Batle of Gledsmuire, fought on the 21 of September, which was one of the Most Surprising action that ever was; we gained a complete Victory over General Cope who commanded 3000 fut and to Regiments of the Best Dragoons in the island, he being advantajiosly posted with also Baterys of Cannon, and Morters, wee having neither hors or Artillery with us, and being to attack them in their position, and obliged to pas before their noses in a defile and Bog. Only our first line had occasion to engaje, for actually in five minutes the field was clired of the Enemy, all the fut killed wounded or taken prisoner, and of the horse only to undred escaped like rabets, one by one, on our side wee only losed a hundred men between killed and wounded, and the Army afterwards had a fine plunder.

The Prince's legendary charm was not epistolary. His fine bearing, his boyish impulsiveness, his romantic sense of his own destiny, his genuine feeling for Scotland and for his Highlanders, all contributed to the air of picturesque glamour which surrounded him and helped to build up the tradition embodied in innumerable folk-songs about him, such as the one which Burns re-worked, with the chorus:

> An' Charlie he's my darling, my darling, my darling,
> Charlie he's my darling, the young Chevalier.

But though he excited the ladies, they do not seem to have particularly excited him. He was not a philanderer, and was happier on horseback acknowledging the blown kisses of the ladies at their windows than in situations of more intimate gallantry. That there were women in his life, later chapters will make plain. But he seems to have been a sexually shy person. There were certainly no scandals at Holyrood.

The tradition of the splendour and gaiety of Charles's court at Holyrood during his stay in Edinburgh is well established, and Sir Walter Scott drew on it in describing the ball at Holyrood on the eve of the Battle of Prestonpans, where Waverley was 'dazzled at the liveliness and elegance of the scene now exhibited in the long-deserted halls of the Scottish palace' and the Prince danced with Flora MacIvor before talking to the various guests with a seductive mixture of authority, tact and charm. But the evidence of what really went on at Holyrood during the Prince's stay there is conflicting. 'The court at the Abbey was dull and sombre,' reported Carlyle, who was in Edinburgh at the time, ' – the Prince was melancholy; he seemed to have no confidence in anybody, not even in the ladies, who were much his friends.' James Maxwell of Kirkconnel, who took part in the rising and later wrote an account of it, recorded that the Prince never danced at Holyrood. The anti-Jacobite Andrew Henderson, in his History of the Rebellion, reported that he disobliged the ladies by declining to give even one ball, saying that he would give one on his return in safety. But John Home quotes the memoirs of a Jacobite officer who recorded that when Charles returned to Holyrood House in the evening he 'received the ladies who came to his drawing room; he then supped in public, and generally there was music at supper and a ball afterwards'. An Englishman sent from York in the middle of October to spy on Charles's behaviour gave this account of him:

> The young chevalier is about five feet eleven inches high, very proportionably made; wears his own hair, has a full forehead, a small but lively eye, a round brown-complexioned face; nose and mouth pretty small; full under the chin; not a long neck; under his jaw a pretty many pimples. He is always in a Highland habit, as are all about him. When I saw him, he had a short Highland plaid waistcoat; breeches of the same, a blue garter on, and a St. Andrew's cross, hanging by a green ribbon, at his button-hole, but no star. He had his boots on, *as he always has*. He dines every day in public. All sorts of people are admitted to see him, then. He constantly practises all the arts of condescension and popularity – talks familiarly to the meanest Highlanders, and makes them very fair promises.

Maxwell of Kirkconnel agrees that Charles, even if he did not dance, was immensely popular and was regularly visited by 'a vast affluence of well dressed people' who came 'either out of curiosity or affection, or the desire of seeing the Prince'. 'Everybody,' he went on, 'was mightily taken with the Prince's figure and personal behaviour. There was but one voice about them .... Sundry things had concurred to raise his character to the highest pitch, besides the greatness of the enterprise, and the conduct that had hitherto appeared in the execution of it. There were several instances of good nature and humanity that had made a great impression on people's minds.'

There is no doubt that Charles acted with generosity and magnanimity after Prestonpans. The proclamations he issued in Edinburgh on the 23rd were kindly in tone; one of them expressed his anxiety that nobody should be prevented from passing to and from the city on business and granted formal protection to all the inhabitants and to those living in the surrounding countryside 'from all insults, seizures, injuries, and abuses of our army against them respectively'.

He could afford to be magnanimous. When the Camerons entered Edinburgh barely three hours after the battle, exhibiting the colours captured from Cope's dragoons, with the bagpipes playing lustily the old cavalier air, 'The king shall enjoy his own again,' the tide of Jacobite fortunes seemed to have turned at last. Prince Charles Edward was master of Scotland. His Highlanders had showed themselves invincible. He himself had been proved right in all his decisions so far and was thus encouraged to rely on his own judgment rather than on that of his advisers. Yet he was but a youngster of twenty-four, whose only military experience had been ten days at the Siege of Gaeta at the age of thirteen. Further he was, in Lord Elcho's words, 'very badly educated; he knew nothing of geography or history' and he had an unrealistically optimistic view of the support he could count on in England; he knew little of conditions in Britain and really believed his Irish supporters' view of King George 'as a hated Usurper who would be deserted by everybody upon the Prince's appearing'. Whatever happened, it was clear that he was going to need a great deal of luck if this initial victory was to mark the first blow in a successful campaign.

CHAPTER TEN

Into England

THERE was some suggestion that Charles might follow up his decisive victory at Prestonpans by marching with his army immediately to Berwick, whither Cope had fled. According to Murray of Broughton, Charles not only proposed this course himself, 'but for some hours Considered Sereously of it'. Eventually, however, he decided against it, for three reasons: his army was too small ('not above 2700 men' says Murray) to allow him both to occupy Berwick and to keep communications open with Edinburgh; Government troops, reinforced by 700 Dutch who had landed at Berwick and others who were about to disembark at Newcastle, 'would have taken possession of Ed^r and Newcastle, thereby putting him betwixt two fires' as well as making it difficult for new supporters to join him from the north; and 'it is well known how difficult it is to assemple an irregular army after an action, that his was a good deal dispersed, . . . and I am of opinion, that had he determined to march to Berwick he would not have had above 1500 men to follow him, by which means the others would have had an opportunity to run home, to which they are too much given, even when Victorious, . . .' This last point is one that crops up again and again in contemporary Jacobite accounts of the campaign. Charles's army, although, according to Murray, 'kept in better order than ever any highland army was before', was largely a volunteer force of clansmen serving under their own chiefs, totally unused to the sustained discipline required for a long campaign and feeling perfectly free to return home at any time stow away their booty or visit their wives or help in the harvest. Certainly as long as they were in Scotland there were always some of them missing for one reason or another; they knew their way about the country and were liable to desert temporarily or permanently for purely personal reasons. Charles needed to stay in Edinburgh for some time in order to consolidate and give further training to his army and, if possible, to gain new recruits.

The Orderly Book of Lord Ogilvy's Regiment contains passages which reveal the position very clearly. For example:

Parole. James and Montrose.
Lord George Murray. Lieut.-General of the Day.

H.R.H.'s intention is that the Major, or an Officer in his place, from each Regiment should assemble every day at Eleven o'clock at his R.H.'s quarters to receive the orders. That every Captain should give immediately to the Major of his Regiment a List, as well of the Officers, Serjeants, and Private men of their Companies, as of those that are absent or sick; that the Major should make a general controul to present it to H.R.H.; that wherever the Regiment be either encamped or in Quarters, that the Major or Adjutant, or some other Officer to act for them, should be always present to execute the orders that they may receive. That an officer of each Company should give every morning an account to his Major, or he that acts for him, of any Disorder, Desertion, etc., that happens in his Company; that the Major may make his report when he comes to receive orders; that the Major should publicly intimate if any Private man is taken half a mile from the Camp or Quarters where they are in, shall be treated as a Deserter and punished according to the law of war, unless they have a permission in writing from their Captain.

It is clear that the Highlanders did not always behave in as gentlemanly a manner as some of the Jacobites who wrote accounts of the campaign would have us believe. At worst, however, they went in for looting rather than for slaughter outside the actual field of battle: it was the Duke of Cumberland's Hanoverian army who were to prove themselves past masters of the latter art. The Whigs, of course, exaggerated the plundering habits of the clansmen. 'They robed some butchers on owr Linton rod,' complained the author of the Woodhouselee MS in his atrocious spelling, 'and last night came to Bread Howse and took all they cowld lay hands upon from Mrs Brown, and October 12, came this rod and did all disorders of plunder and robry that lawless wandring wasters (such as they ar) cowld doe.' Pillaging, however, was strictly forbidden by a proclamation of Lord George Murray on 23 September: 'if any soldier or officer, in his royal highness's army, shall be guilty of any abuse in taking, pillaging, or disturbing any of the good people of Edinburgh or in the country, by forcibly taking away their goods, without making a fair Bargain, and Payment made, [he] shall be punished, whenever taken up, and found guilty of the above offenses, by a court martial and shall suffer death, or whatever other punishment the court-martial think fit to inflict upon them.' Murray of Broughton believed that as a result of this proclamation 'there is no instance in the history of any times in whatever Country where the Soldiery either regular or irregular behaved themselves with so much discretion, never any riots in the Streets, nor so much as a Drunk man to be seen.'

Charles levied taxes and customs in Edinburgh, collected rents from forfeited estates, sent a party to Glasgow which raised £5,000 in cash and £500 in goods (making it clear, according to Murray of Broughton, 'that he did not intend to have it by force but in freindship, with ample Security for pay^t when affairs were Settled'), and got shoes for his Highlanders from the shoemakers of Selkirk. But he needed men as well as money. A messenger dispatched to Skye to assure Sir Alexander Macdonald of Sleat and MacLeod of MacLeod that in spite of their inactivity so far the Prince was ready to welcome them and their powerful clans as the most favoured of his father's loyal subjects brought the news that they had committed themselves definitely to the Government side. Duncan Forbes of Culloden had already used his great influence on these two, as he had on others. It was Forbes who had the idea of obtaining from the Government twenty commissions to enable him to form twenty 'independent companies', as they were called, of a hundred men each, of Highlanders loyal to the Government cause. This attracted some. Simon Fraser Lord Lovat, influenced by the victory at Prestonpans and playing both ends against the middle as always, finally ordered his eldest son, the Master of Lovat, to bring out the Frasers. The Mackenzies, the Mackintoshes, the Gordons and the Grants were divided. In the far north the Mackays, the Sutherlands and the Munroes were for the Government. But some clansmen did rally to the Prince. John Gordon of Glenbucket brought three hundred men from Aberdeenshire and Lord Ogilvy brought the same number from Angus. Mackinnon of Mackinnon brought 120 from Skye. Cluny MacPherson, who had originally held a Government commission in Lord Loudoun's regiment, came over to the Jacobites with three hundred men. Lord Elcho was put in command of a newly formed troop of Life Guards, Lord Pitsligo commanded another newly-raised body of horse, William Boyd, fourth Earl of Kilmarnock, one of the few Lowland noblemen to join, commanded a small troop, and Lord Balmerino commanded one originally intended for Lord Kenmure (who remembered 1715 and his father's fate and stayed at home), while Murray of Broughton had his own picturesquely attired 'Hussars': all these provided a welcome addition to Charles's scanty cavalry. Gradually the Jacobite army was built up to about 5,000 foot and 500 horse.

The Marquis of Tullibardine (the Jacobite Duke of Atholl), 'Governor of Atholl and Commander of the King's forces benorth the Forth,' had a hard time collecting more Atholl men and reassembling those who had gone home, as the increasingly anxious letters to him from his brother Lord George Murray indicate: 'For God's sake send up what men of your own people you can, and don't let them wait for any body else' (2 October); 'The Prince is waiting here with the greatest impatience for his friends joining him, not being able to proceed into England without a greater force' (another letter of the same date); and again on 4 October;

Dr Brother, – I wrote to you this morning, & I now send this express to let you know that it is resolved in a Council of Ware to march Southwards Thursday the 10th. I believe we will not make quick marches for some days after that; but I conjure you let your Atholl men be with us at or before that time, that I may see every thing got right for them as far as it is in my power. ...

Lord George wrote again on the 9th:

Dr Brother, – I am vastly impatient for your coming up, at least the men and the officers. Once more, for God's sake, cause make all the heast in your power, for the success of our cause depends upon your expedition. I have no more time but to tell you his R.H. depends much upon your diligence upon this occasion, ...

But still the Atholl men delayed. 'I write once more by his Royall Highness special commands, who desires you to come in person, and all the men possible, with the utmost expedition and join him,' Lord George wrote to his brother on the 11th (Charles actually remained in Edinburgh until 1 November). And again on the 14th: 'The Prince Regent is in the utmost concern for the presious time which is lost by your not comming up. I have wrote to you so often, by his orders, upon that subject, that I can add nothing to what I have already said, only that it seems the opinion of every body if you delay any longer it will be the uter ruine of the Cause'. And on the 19th: '... his R.H. ... desires me to write to you ... that he insists you should come up with all your Force with the utmost expedition, for all depends upon our marching into England, & nothing will hinder a moment after you join'. They came at last on 30 October, about a thousand men.

Meanwhile, Charles had, in Lord Elcho's words, 'formed a council which met regularly every morning in his drawing-room. The Gentlemen who he called to it were the Duke of Perth, Lord Lewis Gordon, Lord George Murray, Lord Elcho, Lord Ogilvie, Lord

Pitsligo, Lord Nairne, Lochiel, Keppoch, Clanranald, Glencoe, Lochgarry, Ardshiel, Sir Thomas Sheridan, Colonel O'Sullivan, Glenbucket, and Secretary Murray'. The Council met in the evening of 30 October to plan the march into England. It was of course open to Charles to stay in Scotland and consolidate his position there, regarding it as an independent country after denouncing the Union. The Chevalier de Johnstone says that this was the advice given the Prince by most people, 'and if he had followed it, perhaps he would have been still in possession of the kingdom'. Johnstone wanted Charles to make the campaign into a 'national' Scottish war, in which case he believed that France would have given substantial aid. But Charles would have none of this: in spite of his love of Scotland and his affection for his Highlanders, he 'had his mind occupied only by England, and appeared little flattered by the possession of the kingdom to which, nevertheless, the race of the Stewarts owed their birth and royalty'.

Expected French aid did not materialize in any significant degree, though three French ships did come to Montrose and Stonehaven bringing arms, including six Swedish field-guns and ten French gunners with whom was Lieutenant-Colonel James Grant, 'an able mathematician,' who was appointed commander of the Prince's artillery. Moral support came with the arrival on board one of the French ships of the Marquis d'Eguilles as envoy from the French King: Charles received him as a regular ambassador, though in fact he was not sent in exactly that capacity. On the Government side, massive forces were building up, many of them (including three battalions of the Guards, eighteen line regiments, nine squadrons of cavalry and four artillery companies) withdrawn specially from Flanders. Six thousand Dutch troops had also landed. Troops from Ireland disembarked at southern ports. When all these were added to the regular Government forces already in the country, it totalled a massive army, which, divided into three groups, was on the move before the end of October: one, under Field-Marshal Wade (now an old man of 72), marching to Newcastle, another, under Lieutenant-General Sir John Ligonier, to Lancashire, and a third to the south-east coast to prevent a French landing there.

Charles, with his usual desire to force a confrontation, was all for marching to Newcastle and engaging with Wade's forces there. If they were to march into England at all, Lord George Murray strongly favoured approaching it from the west, thus by-passing Wade's army. This plan would also have the advantage of attracting the English Jacobites who were supposed to exist in large numbers in the north-west of England. 'After a very long debate on both sides' (wrote Murray of Broughton) 'the Council was adjourned till next morning at nine aClock to consider further of what had been offerd on both Sides, but when the Chevalier had retired to his own apartment he begun to reflect that as the most, if not all the Cheifs were for marching to Carlile, his forcing them the other road contrary to their inclinations, might be of bad Consequences, . . . Accordingly, next day how soon the Council had mett, he told them in a very obliging manner that he had Seriously Considered of their arguments the night before, and was now, upon reflection, given to think they was in the right, and that he was ready to follow their advice, . . . This condescention on his part, made in so oblidging a manner, and as if proceeding from the Superior strength of their arguments seemd to give great contentment.'

During his stay in Edinburgh Charles had taken steps to assert the legality of his position. On learning that Parliament had been summoned to meet at Westminster on 17 October he issued a proclamation warning and commanding 'all his Majesty's Liege Subjects, whether Peers or Commoners, to pay no Obedience to any such Summons' as this would now be 'an ouvert Act of Treason and Rebellion' not covered by 'his Majesty's gracious Pardon offered for all that is past'. He had a special warning for the Scots: 'And for those of his Majesty's Subjects of this his ancient Kingdom of *Scotland*, whether Peers or Commoners, who shall, contrary to these our express Commands, presume to sit or vote as aforesaid, as soon as the same shall be verified unto us, the Transgressors shall be proceeded against as Traitors and Rebels to their King and Country, . . .' He followed this up with a Proclamation explaining and justifying his policy and insisting that his main aim, far from being to enslave a free people, was 'to redress and remove the encroachments made upon them'. He attacked the grievous burden of the National Debt, which he proposed to remove in any way advised by Parliament. He denounced 'the pretended union of the two nations,' saying that 'the King cannot possibly ratify it, since he has had repeated remonstrances against it from each kingdom; and since it is incontestable that the principal point then in view was the exclusion of the Royal Family from their undoubted right to the Crown'. He pours scorn on the 'dreadful threats of popery, slavery, tyranny, and arbitrary power, which' (according to certain clergymen and weekly papers) 'are now ready to be imposed upon you by the formidable powers of France and Spain'. 'My expedition was undertaken unsupported by either: but, indeed, when I see a foreign force brought by my enemies against me, and when I hear of Dutch, Danes, and Hessians, and Swiss, the Elector of Hanover's allies, being called over to protect his government against the King's subjects, is it not high time for the King my father to accept also of the assistance of those who are able and who have engaged to support him?' He insists that the House of Hanover have brought to the people of Great Britain nothing but a load of debts, placemen, venality, penal laws, and misery at home and abroad.

Charles and his army left Edinburgh on 1 November for Dalkeith. There he divided it into two columns, the first commanded by Tullibardine and the Duke of Perth, and the second commanded by himself and Lord George Murray. The second column moved south-east through Lauder to Kelso, with the deliberate intention of misleading Wade into believing that the Jacobite army was going to march into England through Northumberland and thus causing him to remain at Newcastle, which in fact he did. The first column, with the cannon and the heavy baggage, went by Peebles and Moffat. The Prince spent the night of the 3rd at Lauder Castle and went on the next day to Kelso, where he spent two nights; then on the 6th he crossed the Tweed and moved westward to Jedburgh, where he spent the night. He then marched through Liddesdale, spent the night at Haggiehaugh (now called Larriston) and on Friday the 8th crossed the River Esk and was in England. 'It was remarkable,' says Murray of Broughton, 'that this being the first time they entered England, the Highlanders without any orders given, all drew their Swords with one Consent upon entering the River, and every man as he landed on tother side wheeld about to the left and faced Scotland again.' This was a symbol of their reluctance to leave Scotland to enter a country of whose geography and people most of them were wholly ignorant. There were, in fact, a considerable number of deserters on the way to the Border.

On the 9th, Charles's column was joined by the first column which had come by Moffat and Lockerbie and the Prince assembled them, as Johnstone reports, 'upon a waste heathery common in England, distant about a quarter of a league from Carlisle'. 'There was such a fog [the next day],' O'Sullivan remembered, 'that a man cou'd hardly see his Horses Ears.' In spite of the fact that, in the words of Murray of Broughton, 'the fog was so great that there was Scarcely a possibility of reconnoitring,' the Duke of Perth and O'Sullivan, with some men of the Atholl Brigade, 'went within pistole Shot of the walls ... and into the Suburbs opposite to Penrith port' to reconnoitre, and on their returning and reporting it was decided to undertake a regular siege of the city. The Duke of Perth was put in charge of the siege, with his own regiment of 750 men and some Lowlanders; they began by digging trenches opposite the Penrith gate. Meanwhile Charles, having received a report that Wade was marching westward from Newcastle, had set off with the rest of the army for Brampton, seven miles east of Carlisle, 'being determined to give him battle there, as being the best ground in that part of the Country'. But the report proved to be untrue, and after two days Lord George and half the army returned to the siege of Carlisle, though Lord George admitted he 'understood nothing of sieges'.

During the wars between Scotland and England Carlisle had been an important frontier garrison, but in 1745 its defences had long been neglected. The garrison of its Castle consisted of 80 infirm elderly men, four gunners (one of whom was quite ancient) and a master-gunner, reinforced by 500 foot and 70 horse of the Cumberland and Westmorland Militia; Lieutenant-Colonel Durand was in command, and he suffered badly from gout.

Before going to Brampton Charles had already sent a message to the Mayor of Carlisle asserting his own authority in the name of the King his father and asking him to open the city's gates 'to avoid the effusion of blood'. If he was refused entrance, there would follow 'the dreadful consequences which usually attend a town's being taken by assault'. The acting Mayor, Alderman Thomas Pattison, made no reply, and, having seen Charles and his men depart for Brampton, thought he had scared them off. 'I told your Lordship,' he wrote with great complacency to Lord Lonsdale, 'that we would defend this city; its proving true gives me pleasure, and more so since we have outdone Edinburgh, nay, all Scotland.' But the garrison had no stomach for a fight, nor had the citizens for a siege. Murray of Broughton tells what happened:

The Trenches being opened under a very Smart fire from the walls of Cannon and small arms, the Cannon were brought up to batter the Town, more to intimidate than from any hopes that they could peep upon the walls, but the dread the inhabitants had of a Seige, together with the Cowardice of the militia, made them hang out a white flag the 14th in the Evening, which being carried to the Chevalier at Brampton whilst sitting at Supper, he immediatly ordered Mr Murray to go to the Duke of Perth's quarters, and together with him to treat with the deputies from the Town.

Pattison and other town representatives came accordingly to discuss surrender terms, and 'after a good deal of reasoning on both Sides,' it was agreed that both town and Castle with all cannon and other arms should be given up, with everybody's 'liberties and effects' safeguarded and Colonel Durand and the garrison being allowed to go to their homes. Alexander Macdonald's report shows his usual pride in Highland discipline: 'The militia that served in Carlisle, and all the inhabitants of the city and neighbourhood can testify the exact disipline of our army who payed for every thing they got, and all were protected in their libertys and propertys'.

The rapid surrender of the city was largely the result of an exaggerated notion of the strength of the Highland army (13,000 said Pattison in his letter to Lonsdale) and fantastic ideas about the habits of the Highlanders. Both Murray of Broughton and Colonel O'Sullivan independently report a significant incident which illustrates the latter. Here is Broughton's version:

> To show how incredibly ignorant the Country people of England are, and industrious the freinds of the government were to impose upon their ignorance and credulity, in the little house where the Chevalier was quartered after he had been for above an hour in the Room, some of the gentlemen who attended him heard a ruseling below the bed, and upon Searching they found a little girl of five or six years old. The mother comeing into the room to fetch something, seeing the Child discovered, called out for God's sake to Spare her Child, for She was the only remaining one of Seven she had bore. Upon which some of the gentlemen being curious to know what She meant, followed to the door and enquired what made her express herself in that manner. To which she answered that indeed She had been assured from Creditable people that the highlanders were a Savage Sett of people and eat all the young Children.

It was at Carlisle that an unfortunate quarrel developed between the Prince and Lord George Murray which was to cast a shadow over the whole subsequent campaign. There had been a coolness between the two for some time, partly because of Lord George's proud bearing, partly because Charles knew that Lord George had more relevant knowledge and experience than he had; Lord George was also disliked by Charles's Irish advisers who circulated unpleasant rumours about him. It seems that on this occasion Lord George was offended that the Duke of Perth and Murray of Broughton were put in charge of arranging the surrender terms and he himself was ignored in the matter. He also (if we are to believe Broughton) was provoked that Broughton had more influence with the Prince than he himself had. Whatever the precise causes of his resentment, Lord George wrote to Charles on 14 November resigning his commission. 'I cannot but observe,' his letter began, 'how little my advice as a General officer has any weight with your Royal Highness . . . I therefore take leave to give up my commission.' He reaffirmed his 'firm attachment to the Royal Family, and in particular to the King, my master,' and offered to continue serving in the army as a volunteer. Instead of trying to calm the ruffled feelings of his Lieutenant-General, the Prince coldly accepted his resignation the same day:

> I think yr advice ever since you join'd me at Perth has had another guess weight with me than what any General Officer cou'd claim as such. I am therefore extremely surprized you shou'd throw up yr commission for a reason which I beleeve was never heard of before.
>
> I am glad of yr particular attachment to the King, but I am very sure he will never take anything as a proof of it but yr deference to me. I accept of yr demission as Lieutenant General, and yr future services as Volunteer.

Lord George wrote to his brother the Marquis of Tullibardine, the Jacobite Duke of Atholl, on the 15th, showing how much he was taken aback by Charles's acceptance of his resignation, and wrote again on the 16th saying that he had explained to Sir Thomas Sheridan that in not specifically mentioning the Prince as the object of his particular attachment he had inadvertently offended: 'for, having mentioned the King and Royal family (and designing my letter to be short), I thought it needless to be more particular'.

The Duke of Perth had now sole command of the Jacobite army, under the Prince; but this was not to last long. Voices were raised in the army objecting to the Duke of Perth's command on the political grounds that his being a Catholic would be injurious to the Prince's interests in England. The Duke, though personally popular, was not highly esteemed as a military man. When he heard the objections to his command, 'as he had nothing at heart but the Chevaliers interest' (as his admirer Broughton put it), he resigned, and this 'compleated the dryness that had almost from the beginning Subsisted betwixt them [i.e., Lord George and the Duke of Perth].' Under pressure from his army, Charles asked Lord George to resume his commission, which he did, replacing Perth as sole commander under Charles. But the damage was done: henceforth the Prince and his Lieutenant General were never on really good terms; on the Prince's side there was always a latent mistrust, fed by malicious rumours questioning Lord George's loyalty, ready to spring to the surface, and on Lord George's there was a tendency to irritation and anger.

When Charles was still in Brampton he learned that Lord John Drummond (brother of the Duke of Perth) had arrived from France at

Montrose with what were at first reported to be 3,000 men but which in fact turned out to be 800 (his own regiment of Royal Scots and 50 men from each of the six Irish regiments in French service). Charles sent Maclachlan of Castle Lachlan to Viscount Strathallan at Perth, where he had been gathering a force of Frasers, Mackintoshes, Mackenzies and others, asking him to bring his force south and to confirm the news about Lord John Drummond. But, as O'Sullivan reports, Strathallan 'wou'd not suffer the highlanders to come, & said they were necessary there to protect the Contry'. So Drummond's men, as well as those collected by Strathallan, stayed in the north. Charles did not know the true facts about Lord John Drummond's force until 5 December. On 18 November he held a Council to decide on future action.

The situation was complicated. About a thousand Highlanders had deserted between Edinburgh and Carlisle, and the Prince's army was probably now no more than 4,500 men. Behind him, in Scotland, the Whigs were raising their heads again. Legal and social luminaries who had fled from Edinburgh when the Jacobite army threatened had now returned, and Edinburgh, Glasgow and Stirling had raised volunteers to fight on the Government side. Hanoverians were also active in Perth. Lieutenant-General Handasyde reached Edinburgh on 14 November with a force of infantry and cavalry and went on to Stirling. Gardiner's and Hamilton's Dragoons returned to Edinburgh. Lieutenant-General Sir John Ligonier was on his way north from London to confront Charles if he continued his march south: the Duke of Cumberland, who had been appointed Captain-General of British land forces at home and in the field, was soon to take command of Ligonier's army and concentrate his forces in the neighbourhood of Stafford. Marshal Wade and his army, having moved westward as far as Hexham and been forced back by bad weather, were now about to move south from Newcastle.

What should Charles do? Some proposed that he should march to Newcastle and there engage Wade's army; others that he should retreat to Scotland, since there was no sign of a French invasion or of a Jacobite rising in England. Charles, characteristically, argued for marching on London, whatever the risks, and Lord George Murray, though aware of the dangers, said that if that was what Charles wanted, the army would follow him. So the decision was to proceed south. 'To have laid there any longer,' commented Murray of Broughton, 'would have been both idle and dangerous; idle, having no prospect of a junction from his freinds in those parts, and from the disposition that at that time seem'd to be formed by the Enemy, he must have been cooped up in that Corner by the Dukes army from the South, Mr Wade at Newcastle, and the 2 Regiments with the foot detached to Scotland on his left, so to prevent a junction of the D. and Mr Wades armies, his only proper methode was to march forward, that in case he came to action he might have only one army to deal with, . . .'

Leaving a garrison of between 100 and 200 men at Carlisle Castle, the Jacobite army marched out of Carlisle in two divisions on 20 and 21 November. The first division, commanded by Lord George Murray, consisted of 'two companies of life-guards, composed of young gentlemen', as the Chevalier de Johnstone describes them, one under the command of Lord Elcho and the other commanded by Lord Balmerino, and in addition 'a body of one hundred and fifty gentlemen on horseback, commanded by Lord Pitsligo'. The Prince followed on the 21st, commanding the infantry. They marched by Shap, Kendal, Lancaster and Garstang to Preston, where the two divisions joined on the 27th. The weather was awful, 'the roads being so full of Snow and Ice,' reports Murray of Broughton, 'that it was necessary to give all possible rest to the horses'. Remembering the disaster that Preston had been for the Jacobite army in 1715 as well as to a Scottish army in 1648, Lord George – 'than whom nobody knew the humours and dispositions of the Highlanders better' – marched the army through the town to the south side of the Ribble, 'to convince them' (again in Broughton's words) 'that the Town Should not be their *ne plus ultra* for a third time, which seemed to give them a good deal of Satisfaction'. A Catholic gentleman named Townley and two Welsh gentlemen named Morgan and Vaughan 'and some few common people' joined them in Preston, 'but no numbers as was expected'. At every town they passed through, King James was proclaimed, with Charles as his Regent. At Preston there was some cheering at the reading of the proclamation.

On the 28th the whole army went on to Wigan and the following day they entered Manchester, the Prince taking up his quarters in a handsome house in Market Street. On the 29th, according to a local Manchester historian,

the public crier was sent round the town to require that all persons who had any duties to pay, or any public money in their hands, should pay the amount into the hands of Secretary Murray, at the palace [as the house in Market Street came to be called], . . . As evening approached, the bellman was again despatched to announce that there would that night be an illumination in honour of the Prince. The illumination accordingly took place; bonfires were made, and the bells rung joyfully; but the treasury was not much replenished till peremptory demand was made upon the inhabitants. ... The borough-reeve, James Waller, of Ridgefield, Esq., was made the reluctant organ for communicating the proclamation of the rebel army to the people; but the Rev. Mr Clayton celebrated, in strains of eloquence, the arrival of the Prince in the collegiate church, for which act of disaffection to the reigning sovereign he was afterwards degraded. A young clergyman, of the name of Coppoch, lately from the university, received the appointment of chaplain to the Prince.

Manchester was at that time a centre of Jacobite feeling, and here at last Charles had some success in recruiting new adherents. 'The recruiting service went on briskly, and from 200 to 300 young men, chiefly of the lower class, were dignified with the name of the Manchester Regiment, of which Francis Townley, Esq. was appointed commander.' But this addition of strength was a trifle compared to what Charles had expected in England, and there was further talk of retreating among his officers. Lord George Murray had always considered the possibility of retreating if there was neither an insurrection in England nor a landing from France. But he agreed to postpone a decision until they reached Derby.

The Jacobite army had not yet encountered any real opposition in England. Local militias disappeared on their approach, and the only attempt to frustrate their advance was the destruction of bridges. But sooner or later an encounter was inevitable. Wade was now at Catterick, but the Duke of Cumberland, now in command of Ligonier's army, was due south of them in Staffordshire. On 1 December the Jacobite army left Manchester in two divisions, one under the Prince and one under Lord George, but they joined at Macclesfield that evening. Leaving the Prince's division at Macclesfield, Lord George took his division south-west to Congleton, where Kingston's Light Horse had posted an advance guard which withdrew on his approach. He was anxious to find out where and how numerous was Cumberland's army, and for this purpose sent a party of horse towards Newcastle-under-Lyme; on the way to Newcastle this party accidentally discovered and captured the noted Government spy John Weir or Vere, whom Charles refused to allow to be shot, much to the disgust of Sir John Macdonald, who deplored 'this fatal principle of tenderness for the enemy' and attributed this lenity to the advice of Lord George Murray against the Prince's opinion though Murray of Broughton specifically says that it was Charles's own decision. From Weir they obtained important details of Cumberland's army, including a list which gave its numbers as 2,200 horse and 8,250 foot. Cumberland himself, expecting the Jacobite army to move westward, perhaps to Wales, concentrated his forces on Stone, some seven miles north of Stafford. This meant that by going on to Derby the Jacobite army could outflank him to the east. A Council of War was held at Leek, where the main body of the army arrived on 3 December, and it was decided that they should proceed at once to Derby.

The Prince entered Derby on the evening of 4 December, and there, according to O'Sullivan, 'was parfectly well recd.' O'Sullivan continues: 'Bon-fires on the roads, the Belles ringing; we arrived a little leat, it was really a fine sight to see the Illuminations of the Town. The Princes raison for stricking to the left towards Darby was, that he expected by that to gain two days march on Cumberland, & of consequence to arrive at London before him.' The rejoicing was premature. Let O'Sullivan again tell the story:

> The accts we had from all sides were, that Comberland marched with the greatest dilligence to get before us, & that each trooper carryed a foot souldier behind him; that Wade was in March on the other side, & 6000 men that marched from London, or at least all the forces they cou'd spare; that the three armys cou'd joyn together & that we cou'd not possibly make our way, nor pretend to conquer them, for they wou'd be four again one. Ld George comes very early the next morning to H.R.Hs, represents him the Scituation he was in, & that it was every body's opinion that the only party that was to be taken was to retire; the Prince was astonished at this proposition, & repeated, 'to retire Ld George, to retire, why the Clans kept me quite another Language & assured me they were all resolved to pierce or to dye.'

A full debate followed, opened by Lord George, who pointed out that Cumberland, having realized that the Jacobite army had not turned west, was pushing on by forced marches to London and at the same time Wade was pushing south by forced marches. A third army, said to number 30,000 men, was said to be assembling in London. When these three armies joined up they would constitute an enormous force, overwhelmingly superior in numbers to the Prince's army of under 5,000. If the clans were defeated there would be no possibility of any one of them escaping. In the absence of a French landing or an English insurrection they had no alternative but to retire to Scotland where they could join with Lord John Drummond's troops and other forces there. One by one other members of the Council spoke up in support of this view. 'The Prince' (Lord Elcho later reported) 'heard all these arguments with the greatest impatience, fell into a passion and gave most of the Gentlemen that had Spoke very Abusive Language, and said they had a mind to betray him.' The discussion went on and on. In vain Charles stormed and pleaded and cajoled. His courage and determination were admired, but his judgment doubted. After a second meeting in the evening the Council maintained its view that there was no alternative to a retreat to Scotland, and Charles, reluctantly and with a very bad grace, gave way. Sunk in gloom and chagrin, he now left everything to Lord George Murray.

Many must have realized then that it was the beginning of the end, though few would have admitted it, even to themselves. The courage, determination, gaiety and cheerful resolution that had marked Charles's behaviour from the beginning of the expedition seemed now to be over-whelmed by the bitterness of his disappointment. Before this, his behaviour had struck his followers with incredulous admiration. Here is one of O'Sullivan's many tributes:

'Tis not credible the movemt that Prince gave himself, to get tember, carryed to repair those bridges, as well as to reconnoitre the foards, tho' he had people, that he cou'd depend upon for those things. As well on this occasion as on all others, I cant imagine, how he resisted, in those great marches we made. He went alwaise a foot, only when he was to come into a Town, & nothwithstanding the rigor of the season we were in, he never come to his lodgings until he saw the guards posted, & the men quarter'd, & to cause no jeallousy, marched allternatively at the head of each Regimt; every man had acces to him, especially those that had the least detail, so that he enter'd into the State of every thing, & continued this all the time. He was never heard to say a rash word to any man, prais'd most graciously those that served well, & treated very mildly those that did not; no Prince can have a greater tallent to gain the hearts of mankind, nor keeps his temper better.

But he did not keep his temper at that fateful Council meeting, nor in the days immediately following it.

CHAPTER ELEVEN

The Retreat from Derby

THE southernmost point reached by the Jacobite invasion in England in 1745 was Swarkstone Bridge, six miles beyond Derby, on the road to London, where an advance guard was posted and kept until retreat had been definitely decided on. 'No former host from Scotland,' reflected Robert Chambers, 'penetrated beyond the Tees, or overran more than the frontier counties; but this last, and, it may be added, *least*, of all the armies Scotland ever sent against the Southron, had thus reached the Trent, traversed five counties in succession, and insulted the very centre of England.' It was indeed essentially a Scottish invasion of England, though Charles insisted on seeing it as aimed at the liberating restoration of the legitimate monarch of England and Scotland alike. The Londoners thought of the Jacobite army as barbarian Highlanders who were simultaneously ridiculous and terrifying. Horace Walpole, writing to Sir Horace Mann on 22 November, put their number at 13,000. Writing again on 9 December he expresses immense relief at the news that the rebels were retreating from Derby. 'They must either go to North Wales, where they will probably all perish, or to Scotland, with great loss. We dread them no longer.' Londoners had certainly been in a panic, even though at Cambridge the poet Thomas Gray wrote that they 'had no more sense of danger than if it were the battle of Cannae' and reported talk of 'three sensible middle-aged men' hiring a chaise to go to Caxton to watch the Highlanders on their way from Derby to London, as though it were a kind of circus. The Chevalier de Johnstone describes the terror of the Londoners:

They heard in London on the 5th of December of our arrival at Derby, and the next day, which the English call Shrove Tuesday, this news immediately published through the whole city caused there a terror and consternation inconceivable to all the inhabitants, the greater part of whom retired to the country with whatsoever effects they deemed most precious, and all the merchants shut their shops. Every one ran to the bank for payment of their notes, and bankruptcy was only avoided by a stratagem. ... Having learnt ... that our army was only within the distance of a league from that of the Duke of Cumberland, they looked every moment for the news of a battle, of which they tremblingly anticipated the issue, and expected to see our army, in two or three days, enter London in triumph. King George made all his yachts come with speed to the quay at the tower, causing them to embark on board all that he had most precious, and ordered them to hold themselves in readiness to depart at a moment's notice. They assured me in London, when I was there after this occurrence, that the Duke of Newcastle, Minister and Secretary of State for War, kept himself shut up in his house the whole day of the 6th, deliberating upon the course he should take, and in uncertainty if he should not declare himself all at once for the Prince. They even pretended at London that there were fifty thousand men collected in that city to go out and meet the Prince, and join themselves to his army; and nobody in that capital actually doubted that if we had beaten the army of the Duke of Cumberland, we should not have found another English army at Finchley Common, which would have even dispersed of themselves; and that in advancing immediately to London, we would have taken possession of the city without finding there the least opposition on the part of the inhabitants, nor a shot of the gun on the part of the troops. The King having taken the resolution of embarking without delay, in case the issue of the battle at Derby, with his son the Duke of Cumberland, should not prove favourable, and to set sail immediately for Holland, – thus we should have seen, without comprehending it, a revolution take place in England, equally surprising and glorious for the small number of Scots who had accomplished it, and which posterity could scarcely believe.

Was Lord George Murray right in insisting that the only course open to Charles and his army was to retreat to Scotland? In some respects the situation at Derby was more hopeful than it had ever been. English and particularly Welsh Jacobites, impressed at last by Charles's achievement in penetrating so far south, seem to have been preparing to join in some numbers, but of course changed their minds when they heard of the retreat. But in any case, if he could have reached London before Cumberland he would have found opposing him in the capital only the hastily formed army at Finchley, which would certainly not have stood up to a Highland charge even if it had remained to wait for it. There was a considerable Jacobite party in London, led by Alderman

Heathcote, who would have given their support. Further, Charles's brother Henry was at last completing preparations to embark 10,000 French troops at Dunkirk and land them on the south coast of England – a plan which was abandoned on the news of the retreat. Though speculation of the 'if's' of history is a barren occupation, there is reason to believe that if Charles had had his way and pushed on by forced marches to London he might well have succeeded in bringing about a Stuart restoration.

'How far [a retreat to Scotland] was the properest course,' reflected Alexander Macdonald in his account of the expedition, 'has been much canvassd; ... One thing is certain, never was our Highlanders in higher spirits notwithstanding their long and fatiguing march; they had indeed got good quarters and plenty of provisions in their march and were well paid; so that we judged we were able to fight double our numbers of any troops that could oppose us; and would to God we had pushed on tho' we had been all cutt to pieces, when we were in a condition for fighting and doing honour to our noble P. and the glorious cause we had taken in hand, rather than to have survived and seen that fatall day of Culloden when in want of provisions money and rest &c. we were oblidged to turn our backs and lose all our glory.'

Though the Highlanders had been reluctant to enter England in the first place, now that they were within 127 miles of London they were excited at the prospect of entering the capital and most reluctant to turn back. In fact, it was necessary to leave Derby before daybreak on the 6th in order that the clansmen should not realize at first in which direction they were marching. Johnstone gives a vivid account of what happened: 'The Highlanders, believing at first that they were in march forward to attack the army of the Duke of Cumberland, testified great joy and alacrity; but as soon as the day began to clear in the distance, and that they perceived we were retracing our steps, we heard nothing but howlings, groans, and lamentations throughout the whole army to such a degree as if they had suffered a defeat.'

Lord George Murray commanded the reauguard, at his own wish, though he stipulated that the 'cannon and carriages' (with ammunition) should go in front 'and so early that it might not stop the marches'. The Prince sulked, and gave Lord George no co-operation. Lord George himself recorded the difference between Charles before and after Derby: 'His Royal Highness, in marching forwards, had always been first up in the morning, and had the men in motion before break of day, and commonly marched himself afoot; but in the retreat he was much longer of leaving his quarters, so that, though the rest of the army were all on their march, the rear could not move till he went, and then he rode straight on, and got to the quarters with the van.' They went by Leek and Macclesfield to Manchester, where they arrived on 9 December and where they found a very different reception from the one which had greeted them on their first arrival: the army was threatened by a mob. Against Lord George's advice, Charles insisted on spending a night there. O'Sullivan was fired on 'out of a windor or door, as he retired his last poast' from the city. People in the countryside were now also unfriendly. 'They were quite prepared'. wrote Lord Elcho, 'in case the army had been beat to have knocked on the head all that would have escaped from the battle. Whenever any of the men straggled or strayed behind they either murdered them or sent them to the Duke,' and any sick men left behind were either killed or 'after being very much abused' confined to prison. The Highlanders in their turn relaxed their discipline and plundered when they could.

The Duke of Cumberland, hearing of Charles's retreat, sent an express to Wade who was at Doncaster. 'We are here at Coventry,' he wrote on the 6th, 'the rebels at Ashbourne [some 12 miles north-west of Derby], and you at Doncaster. It seems to me much to be feared that if you can't move westward into Lancashire these villains may escape back unpunished into the Highlands, to our eternal shame.' It was as a result of this that Wade decided to send a detachment of cavalry under Major-General Oglethorpe in pursuit of the Jacobites while his main army marched to Newcastle. It was while Charles and his army were at Manchester that they received intelligence that General Oglethorpe with his cavalry were expected there daily. Lord George Murray was anxious to press on. 'The Prince,' says Lord Elcho in his Journal,' 'who loved to contradict Lord George Murray, wished to stay some days at Manchester, knowing nothing at all of the country roads. If he had followed his own opinion, he could have been caught between two fires, and would never have got back to Scotland.' Charles, who would not allow the use of the word 'retreat', was anxious not to give the impression of a hasty flight, and this was one reason for his desire to make frequent stops. But Manchester was now hostile, Oglethorpe was approaching, and the Jacobite army left on the 10th for Wigan which they entered late at night after a hard march over bad roads. On the 11th they were back at Preston. There the Duke of Perth was despatched to Lord Strathallan at Perth to urge the sending of reinforcements, but the Duke, who was now a very sick man, had to travel in his coach, which with its cavalry escort was attacked by militia at Kendal so that the party had to retire to Penrith and re-join the army.

At Preston Charles announced that he would stay there to await the reinforcements from Scotland and then march on London, but he was persuaded to move on from that town, so ill-omened for Jacobites, to Lancaster. It was just as well: General Oglethorpe took possession of Preston an hour after the rear of the Jacobite army had left, and at the same time the Duke of Cumberland, without his exhausted infantry but with cavalry and 1,000 mounted foot, entered Wigan. At Lancaster the Prince again called a halt, to 'show the world he was retiring and not flying,' in Johnstone's words, and on the morning of the 14th, the day after their arrival, ordered Lord George and O'Sullivan to reconnoitre a field of battle. This was done, and in the process some of Oglethorpe's men were captured. But in spite of Charles's having, as Johnstone put it, 'taken a fanciful taste for battles from the ease with which he had gained the victory at Gladmuir or Prestonpans, with small loss', he changed his mind, even after Lord George reported 'that, if our number would answer, I could not wish a better field for Highlanders' and ordered the army to march to Kendal the next day.

There was trouble with the ammunition carts. The four-wheeled waggons the army had been using proved too cumbersome to negotiate the difficult roads in the Lake District, and on the evening of their arrival at Kendal Lord George asked O'Sullivan to provide two-wheeled carts. He found O'Sullivan supping with the Prince, drinking 'mountain Malaga, which he seemed very fond of' and not very co-operative (apart from offering him some of the Malaga). The next morning – the 16th – it rained heavily; when the main body of the army had reached Shap 'the rear guard were oblidged to stop at a farm four miles from Kendal', in Alexander Macdonald's words, 'by reason that a great many of the carriages and particularly the fourwheeld waggons, in which was part of the ammunition, could not be got forward because of the steepness of the hill and badness of the road'. Eventually smaller two-wheeled carts were procured. Officers of the Manchester regiment together with Glengarry's Macdonalds were particularly helpful in trying to get the waggons moving, some of the former going 'into the water up to the middle to push the wheels,' as Lord George reported, while the latter 'are reckoned not the most patient, but I never was better pleased with men in my life; they did all that was possible'. Charles, hearing of the difficulty with the ammunition waggons, sent an aide to Lord George from near Penrith where he now was 'to tell that he must by no means leave anything behind, and that he would rather return than that one cannon-ball should be left'. Lord George replied that when he had undertaken at Derby to be always in the rear in order to organize the retreat effectively he had expressly said that 'he could not be answerable for any of the carriages and baggage', but nevertheless 'he would do all that man could do'. This exchange was characteristic of the Prince's worsened temper and Lord George's stiffly correct response. Matters were not made any better by continual harassment by local militia and the overt hostility of the country people.

Heavy rain, bad roads, bad temper, accidents such as the overturning and falling into the water of a cannon and an ammunition cart when crossing a bridge, complicated Lord George's task, but he kept his promise to 'do all that man could do', even to the point of getting the men to carry to Shap over two hundred cannon balls that had been in the overturned cart, for a reward of sixpence a head. Charles, too, despite his ill humour, never flagged in his physical exertions, as O'Sullivan was at pains to point out: '. . . we had the cruellest rain that day, that ever I saw, we had several torrents to passe; the Prince was alwaise a foot, & foarded those torrents as the men did, never wou'd he get a' horse-back, & if it was not for the way he acted that day, I verilly believe we cou'd not keep half our men together'. Charles and the bulk of the army reached Shap late on the night of the 16th and spent the night there, but Lord George with the Atholl men and Cluny Macpherson's and Glengarry's regiments did not arrive until 'about twelve or one the next day'. By this time Charles had left for Penrith, leaving a message for Lord George with O'Sullivan asking him to proceed the same day to Penrith, but Lord George sent back an answer that his men were too tired and they would spend the night at the village of Clifton, a few miles south of Penrith. The Prince, with the main body of the army, was at Penrith on the evening of the 17th, and there he awaited Lord George and the rearguard.

On the way to Penrith from Shap Lord George and the rearguard became aware of enemy activity. They noticed (in Johnstone's words) 'a great number of the enemy's light horse continually hovering about us' and at one stage, discovering 'cavalry, marching two and two abreast on the top of [a] hill' and hearing 'at the same time a prodigious number of trumpets and kettle-drums', Glengarry's men and some others, without consulting Lord George, 'threw their plaids and ran forward to attack them'. 'We were', says Johnstone, 'agreeably surprised when we reached the top to find, instead of the English army, only three hundred light horse and chasseurs, who immediately fled in disorder.' Had they not been so timid, the Glengarry men's uphill charge might have proved disastrous, and Lord George was annoyed at their having taken this unauthorized and unnecessary risk. He continued to advance to Clifton, from where he sent the artillery ahead to Penrith, and then with Glengarry's men he reconnoitred nearby Lowther Hall, seat of Lord Lonsdale, where he conjectured the light horse they had encountered might be quartered. They found the park gates closed, but some Highlanders climbed over the wall and apprehended a footman who had rushed out of the house together with 'another person cloathed in green who appeared to be an officer', as Alexander Macdonald described him. The footman proved to be a servant of the Duke of Cumberland who had been sent to give notice that his master intended to sleep that night at Lowther Hall. From these two they learned 'that the Duke of Cumberland was within a mile with about 4000 horse and dragoons besides light horse and militia'.

Lord George, remaining at Clifton, sent Colonel John Roy Stewart to Charles at Penrith to ask for urgent assistance. But Charles sent back a message that he intended to proceed at once to Carlisle and ordered Lord George to retire to Penrith. While awaiting this reply Lord George was joined at Clifton by the Duke of Perth, ill though he was, and it was he who first saw on Clifton Moor 'not above cannon-shot from us, the enemy appear and draw up in two lines, in different divisions and squadrons. His Grace said he would immediately ride back [to Penrith], and see to get out the rest of the army' (Lord George Murray's Journal). The story is taken up from the Penrith side by Captain John MacPherson of Strathmashie, in a letter to Bishop Forbes:

... there came ane Huzar up with us at the gallop, who told that if those of the escort lately mentioned were not immediatly supported they would infallibly be cut to pieces. To prevent which (if it could be) our colonel [Cluny Macpherson] instantly ordered his regiment to front from the rear and march directly towards Clifton. To which place I cannot say we marched, but run like hounds; but on our arrival, to our great contentment, found the Glengary regiment safe, at the same time that we observed the main army of the enemy all drawn up in form on a small eminence about cannon shot of us. ... thinking as it was soe late that there would be noe play till the morning, and that the whole army join'd, we begun a march towards Penrith again, the Glengarry regiment then taking the front, Stewarts of Appin the center, and ours the rear. But this march was not much more than begun when there came express orders to us from Lord George to return to Clifton immediately, he himself haveing remain'd there all the time. But the position we were then in, in marching back towards to Clifton our regiment had the front, the Stewarts, commanded by Ardsheal, the centre as formerly, and

Glengary the rear, and thus we marched till we joined his lordship at Clifton, when we found that the enemy continued in the same order as when we had the first view of them; only my Lord, it seems, judged they meaned to advance towards Clifton. Upon which he, on foot, together with the colonel at the head of our regiment, marched from Clifton towards the enemy a little to the left until he planted us at the back of ane hedge not quite a gunshot, I think, from Clifton, the Appin battalion in the center betwixt us and Glengarrie's, who lined a stone dyke to the right of Appin's. In this posture we continued for some minutes, prepared to receave the enemy, and by this time it was quite night upon us; and the General, finding it proper that we should break our then situation by penetrating through our hedge ... through the hedge we made our way with the help of our durks, the prictes being very uneasy, I assure you, to our loos'd tail'd lads. [Lord George tells Cluny Macpherson that he will attack on the right and Cluny should do the same on the left.] The disposition thus made, when with great rapidity we were make-ing our way towards the other hedge, the advanced parties of the enemy, being dismounted dragoons, met us full in the teeth, .. The General ... ordered us to draw our broad-swords, which was readily done, and then we indeed fell to pell-mell with them. [They broke 14 of their broadswords on the dragoons' skull caps, but took no less than 50 swords from dead dragoons.] What the number of their slain might have been I cannot really say that any of our side can with any exactness account for ... but ... we saw them in great plenty flat as dead in our return, ... and at the time we believed the carnage to have been pretty considerable.

The dragoons, in fact, lost 40 killed and wounded and the Jacobites 13. The engagement took place on a cloudy night, with intermittent moonlight which showed up the dragoons more clearly than the High-landers. Lord George had about a thousand men in all. The dismounted dragoons that Cumberland ordered to advance on the Highlanders consisted of detachments of three regiments, but, except that the official Government report (in a letter from Robert Dundas, Solicitor General, to the Lord President) mentions 'about 400 of Bland [Bland's (3rd) dragoon regiment] and L. M. Kerr's Dragoons, & part of Ligonier's Horse', it is not clear just how many were involved on the Government side. The Government report claimed that the dismounted dragoons attacked the Highlanders ' & put them fairly to flight', but it is clear that the dragoons withdrew after the skirmish to rejoin their main body on Clifton Moor, receiving flanking fire from Glengarry's regiment as they went. 'We had now done what we proposed,' said

Lord George in his report of the affair; 'and being sure of no more trouble from the enemy, I ordered the retreat: ... it was half an hour after the skirmish before we went off.'

The Skirmish of Clifton, as the engagement is generally called, checked Cumberland's pursuit and enabled the Jacobite army to move forward safely to Carlisle. It was, however, fought against Charles's orders, for by the time Colonel John Roy Stewart had returned with Charles's order to Lord George to retire to Penrith it was too late. As Lord George himself reports:

> Colonel Roy Stewart ... told me His Highness resolved to march for Carlisle immediately, and had sent off the cannon before, and desired me to retreat to Penrith. I showed Colonel Stewart my situation, with that of the enemy. They were, by this time, shooting popping shots among us. I told him, if I retreated, being within musket shot of the enemy, they would follow up the lane, and I must lose a number of men, besides discouraging the rest; that from Clifton it was a narrow road, with very high walls, so that I could not line them to secure my retreat; and that probably my men would fall into confusion in the dark, and that the enemy, by regular platoons in our rear, being encouraged by our retreat, must destroy a great many; and by taking any wounded man prisoner, they would know our numbers; ...'

Writing of the skirmish some four years after it had taken place, Lord George admitted that he had 'disobeyed orders', adding 'but what I did was the only safe and honourable measure I could take, and it succeeded'. In spite of his disobedience, when Lord George finally did retire to Penrith to find Charles and the rest of the army ready to leave for Carlisle, the Prince, in Lord George's words, 'seemed very well pleased with what had happened'.

Lord George and the regiments with him stayed some hours at Penrith for rest and refreshment, of which they had much need, before following Charles and the main army to Carlisle. It may have been partly because of Lord George's fatigue after two days of difficult hill marching with heavy equipment and a night battle that he did not press harder his objections to the Prince's resolve to leave a garrison at Carlisle. 'I had been so much fatigued for some days before that I was little at the Prince's quarters that day [the 19th, when they were at Carlisle], but I found he was determined on the thing,' he later wrote. It seems to have been Colonel O'Sullivan and other of Charles's Irish advisers who insisted on leaving a garrison – O'Sullivan defends the decision strongly in his account of the expedition – but most other officers agreed that the city was not capable of defence. The Chevalier de Johnstone stated that Carlisle 'could not hold out for more than four hours against a cannonade from a few field-pieces'. The Duke of Perth was 'very unwilling to leave any of his men' and asked in Charles's presence why so many of the Atholl men were not asked to stay. Lord George then offered to stay with the Atholl Brigade, 'though I knew my fate; for so soon as they could bring cannon from Whitehaven I was sure it was not tenable'. He was right: heavy guns brought by Cumberland from Whitehaven forced the garrison's surrender within ten days of the departure of the Jacobite army. The garrison numbered about 400 and included the recently formed Manchester Regiment together with men from the Duke of Perth's, Lord Ogilvy's, Gordon of Glenbucket's and Colonel Roy Stewart's regiments. 'I wish I could have blooded the soldiers with these villains,' wrote Cumberland to the Duke of Newcastle on the garrison's surrender on 30 December, 'but it would have cost us many a brave fellow, and it comes to the same end, as they have no sort of claim to the King's mercy, and I sincerely hope will meet with none.' His hope was fulfilled. George II, Cumberland's father, was to confirm sentence of death – which meant hanging, drawing and quartering – on nine of the eighteen English and Scottish officers captured at Carlisle: the other captured officers and men were sentenced to virtual slavery in the Plantations.

Charles, of course, fully expected to be able to return and relieve the garrison at Carlisle and expected the garrison to be able to hold out until that undefined time should come. His intention was to join Lord John Drummond's French troops and Lord Strathallan's Highland contingents in Scotland and then return in triumph, but by this time he must surely have wondered whether the expedition, however reinforced, could return to England again. The Jacobite army left Carlisle on the 20th, leaving behind in the charge of the garrison most of the guns of which Charles had been so proud and which he had so peremptorily ordered Lord George Murray to make sure of bringing along intact. This was a decision of a Council of War held at Carlisle, and the Prince agreed provided that he could keep three of his Swedish field-guns that had come from France. When the army were about to cross into Scotland at the River Esk at Longtown they found the river much swollen. 'The men,' says O'Sullivan, 'seeing the horses go over tho' with a great deal of difficulty, cryed out that they wou'd passe it, as they did, wch was one of the most extraordinary passages of a river that cou'd be seen. The Prince stoped them, & went in himself with all the horse we had, to break the stream, that it shou'd not be so rapid for the foot; this of his own motion. The foot marched in, six in a brest, in as good order, as if they were marching in a field, holding one another by the collars, every body, & every thing past, without any losse but two women, that belonged only to the publick, that were drownded. . . . It is very particular it was the Princes birth day.' O'Sullivan noted that the Prince was both in England and in Scotland on his birthday, and hoped that this was a good omen.

So they were in Scotland again, and in good spirits in spite of everything. Charles was no longer sulking, though he could have bad moods. The men danced themselves dry with reels. It was hardly a triumphant return, yet their achievement had been unprecedented and their situation was still far from desperate. They had entered England on 8 November and re-entered Scotland on 20 December: Robert Chambers, in his elegant early nineteenth-century rhetoric, has summed up their achievement very well:

An expedition was thus completed which, for boldness and address, is entitled to rank high amongst the most celebrated in ancient and modern times. It lasted six weeks, and was directed through a country decidedly hostile to the adventurers; it was done in the face of two armies, each capable of utterly annihilating it; and the weather was such as to add a thousand personal miseries to the general evils of the campaign. Yet such was the success which will sometimes attend the most desperate case, if conducted with resolution, that from the moment the inimical country was entered, to that in which it was abandoned, only forty men were lost, out of nearly 5000, by sickness, marauding, or the sword of the enemy. A magnanimity was preserved even in retreat beyond that of ordinary soldiers; and instead of flying in wild disorder, a prey to their pursuers, these desultory bands had turned again and smitten the superior army of their enemy, with a vigour which effectually checked it. They had carried the standard of Glenfinnan a hundred and fifty miles into a country full of foes; and now they brought it back unscathed, through the accumulated dangers of storm and war.

It was indeed a remarkable achievement. The question they had to ask themselves now was, quite literally, 'Where do we go from here?'

CHAPTER TWELVE

The Battle of Falkirk

'No CONCERT had been taken what route we were next to follow,' wrote Lord George Murray. Charles asked Lord George's opinion and he advised that the army should split into two, with himself marching at once with six battalions to Ecclefechan, thence the next day to Moffat and then, having made a feint towards Edinburgh, proceeding by Douglas and Hamilton to Glasgow. Charles would lead the other division and go by Annan and Dumfries. This was agreed. Lord Nairne and Lord Ogilvy went with Lord George; with the Prince went the Duke of Perth, Lord Elcho, Lord Pitsligo, Lochiel, Clanranald, Glengarry and Macdonald of Keppoch. Dumfries was a centre of Whiggish and indeed Cameronian sentiment, and on their march south the Jacobite army had had some baggage looted by Covenanting anti-Jacobites from the town. Nevertheless, Charles found comfortable quarters in the house of a well-disposed gentleman who avoided the risk involved in receiving the Prince personally by getting so drunk that he was not able to be present, so that his wife did the honours. But, mindful of the looting of his baggage, Charles fined Dumfries £2,000 and 1,000 pairs of shoes. From Moffat Lord George sent an express to Lord John Drummond in Perth asking him to march south immediately to join the main Jacobite army near Stirling: the Duke of Perth went north himself to give urgency to the instructions. Lord George and his division of the army reached Glasgow on Christmas Day. Charles, who stayed at Drumlanrig Castle on the 22nd and spent the 23rd at Douglas Castle, seat of the Duke of Douglas, where he passed a day shooting on the estate and bagged two pheasant, two partridges and a deer, arrived with his division in Glasgow on the 26th. Though the Prince was generally scrupulous in paying for his food and lodging, it seems that both at Drumlanrig and at Douglas, whose proprietors were known opponents of the Jacobite cause, he paid nothing. He did make some payment at Hamilton, where he stayed in the palace of the Duke of Hamilton immediately before moving on to Glasgow, the Duke being considered well-disposed to the cause. But there is a tradition that the usual tips to the servants were omitted.

The reason for Charles's and Lord George's decision to occupy Glasgow, then an attractive small town but rapidly growing in wealth through its trade in sugar and tobacco with the West Indies and the American colonies, was partly to obtain clothes and shoes for the now ragged army and partly to punish its citizens for their persistent Hanoverian principles and behaviour. 'The Prince,' wrote O'Sullivan, 'was resolved to punish the Town of Glascow, who shew'd a little too much Zelle to the Govermt, in raissing their millitia, & entertaining 'um at their own expence, but all that cou'd be done, there was little or no mony to be had, but obligded them to furnish the vallu of five or six thousand pounds, of Cloaths, linnin and leather as much as cou'd be had, to Cloath the men, wch they wanted very much.' Charles's demand for '6000 cloth short coats, 12000 linnen shirts, 6000 pair of shoes, 6000 bonnetts, and as many tartan hose, besides a sum of money' (£15,000 later reduced to £5,500) did nothing to endear him to the hostile citizens of Glasgow, who had already raised a militia regiment for the Government, which, commanded by Lord Home, was now in Edinburgh with Price's and Ligonier's regiments and two regiments of dragoons. It is said that only the remonstrations of 'the gentle Lochiel' prevented some of the Highlanders from sacking and burning the town. Nowhere, said Charles bitterly, had he found so few friends as in Glasgow. He made a special effort to dress elegantly on his public appearances, and though he aroused the devotion of a few Jacobite ladies he could do nothing to diminish the stern Whig hostility of the Glaswegians. He reviewed his army on Glasgow Green on 2 January, and only sixty new men joined up. Five hundred had already deserted since the army's return to Scotland.

On 3 January the Jacobite army set out for Stirling, Lord George going with his six battalions by Cumbernauld and Charles with the rest of the army by Kilsyth. The Prince spent the night of the 3rd at Kilsyth and the next day went on to Bannockburn House, where he was entertained by his loyal supporter Sir Hugh Paterson: his troops occupied the villages of Bannockburn, Denny and St Ninians, immediately south of Stirling, while Lord George occupied Falkirk. Stirling, summoned to capitulate, could not hold out long, its crumbling defensive wall being defended only by a small body of militia and townsmen. The Jacobites took possession of the town at three o'clock on the afternoon of the 8th. Stirling Castle, however, defended by

General Blakeney, a courageous and determined old soldier of seventy-four who had fought under Marlborough, proved a very different matter.

Meanwhile, there were disputes within the Jacobite camp. Charles and Lord George had quarrelled over the distribution of clothing to the army in Glasgow, but now there was a more serious difference between them. Ever since the decision to retreat from Derby had been arrived at, Charles had refused to hold a Council of War, relying for advice on Murray of Broughton and Sir Thomas Sheridan, much to the annoyance of Lord Elcho and some others. On 6 January Lord George sent Charles a memorandum arguing for the regular calling of a Council of War and also advising that a committee of five or seven, making decisions by a majority in the Prince's presence, should be entrusted with all future military planning. He also asked that in any battle emergency, power should be allowed to those in command, which 'is the method of all armys'. 'If this plan is not followed', he added, 'the most Dismall consequences cannot but ensue. Had not a Council Determined the Retreat from Derby, what a catastrophy must have followed in two or three days!'

Charles was deeply offended at Lord George's memorandum and replied on the 7th with studied coldness:

When I came into Scotland, I knew well enough what I was to expect from my Ennemies, but I Little foresaw what I meet with from my Friends. I came vested with all the Authority the King could give me, one chief part of which is the Command of his Armies, and now I am required to give this up to fifteen persons, who may afterwards depute five or seven of their own number to exercise it, for fear, if they were six or eight, that I might myself pretend to the casting vote.

He goes on to deny that this is the method of all armies, or indeed of any army in the world, then continues:

I am often hit in the teeth that this is an Army of Volontiers, consisting of Gentlemen of Rank and fortune, and who came into it meerly upon motives of Duty and Honour; what one wou'd expect from such an Army is more zeal, more resolution, and more good manners than in those that fight meerly for pay; but it can be no army at all where there is no General, or, which is the same thing, no obedience or deference paid to him.

Every one knew before he engaged in the cause what he was to expect in case it miscarried, and shou'd have staid at home if he cou'd not face death in any shape. but can I myself hope for better usage? at least I am the only Person upon whose head a price has already been set, and therefore I cannot indeed threaten at every other word to throw down my arms and make my Peace with the Government.

He adds that he does take advice, especially Lord George's, and will continue to do so, and ends by telling Lord George 'that my Authority may be taken from me by violence, but I shall never resign it like an Ideot'.

With Lord George discouraged and the Prince petulant the prospects for Jacobite morale did not look bright. Lord George was further worried by the desertion of many of his Atholl men, about which he wrote to his brother William, the Jacobite Duke of Atholl, on the 11th, urging him to go himself to Blair Castle and do everything possible to send the men back. Valuable reinforcements came, however, with the arrival from Perth of Lord Strathallan, with Frasers, Mackenzies, Farquarsons and 400 Mackintoshes raised by Lady Mackintosh whose husband, the clan chief Mackintosh of Mackintosh, was on the Government side. These had already been joined by the troops from France that had landed at Montrose, Stonehaven and Peterhead with Lord John Drummond (these included detachments from the Irish Brigade generally described in contemporary accounts as the 'Irish picquets'). Together the new forces now joining Charles's army amounted to between 3,000 and 4,000 men: 'by this reinforcement,' commented the Chevalier de Johnstone, 'our army amounted to eight thousand men, and found itself all of a sudden double the number which we had in England.'

Lord John Drummond's French forces brought with them a train of artillery, consisting of what O'Sullivan described as 'two pieces of sixteen, two of twelve and two eight pounders', which they had difficulty in getting across the Forth for use in the siege of Stirling Castle. The French cannon were in charge of 'one Monsieur Gourdon (alias le Marquis de Mirabelle, *nome de guere*) a French engenier', together with 'anothere young man that had apply'd himself to that business (a volentire never in commission) and ten or twelve French gunners (which was all of that kind that came from France'. (This description is from an anonymous journal among the Lockhart Papers.) Johnstone calls the French engineer 'M. Mirabelle de Gordon' and says that at first great hopes were held that he would be able to reduce the Castle, 'which would annoy the Highlanders much in preventing their going and returning to their own country, believing that an engineer of France of a certain age, and decorated with an order, behoved necessarily to have experience, talents, and capacity, but they discovered, unfortunately too late, that these requisites of his genius were very limited, and that he had not the shadow of judgment, discernment, or good sense; his figure being as ridiculous as his spirits – the Highlanders changed his name of Mirabelle, and called him always M. Admirable'. Neither the French guns nor those in charge of them proved adequate to achieve the surrender of Stirling Castle, and its siege turned out to be a dangerous waste of time and effort.

The Government had not allowed Charles's army to return to Scotland without appropriate action on their own part. Lieutenant-General Roger Handasyde occupied Edinburgh with Price's and Ligonier's regiments and what was left of Hamilton's and Gardiner's dragoons soon after Charles had crossed back into Scotland. They were joined there early in January by the forces of Lieutenant-General Hawley, who had succeeded Wade, the Duke of Cumberland having been recalled south to take command of a force designed to repel a French invasion on the south coast. Under Hawley were a total of twelve battalions from ten regiments: the Royals, Howard's, Barrel's, Wolfe's, Pulteney's, Blakeney's, Cholmondeley's, Fleming's, Munro's and Battereau's. (At this time regiments were known by the names of their colonels, not by numbers. The numbers and names by which these regiments were later known are respectively: 1st, the Royal Scots; 3rd, The Buffs, Royal East Kents; 4th, King's Own Royal Regiment; 8th, King's Liverpool Regiment; 13th, Somerset Light Infantry; 27th, Royal Iniskilling Fusiliers; 34th, the Border Regiment; 36th, Worcesters; 37th, the Hampshire Regiment; 62nd. Price's was later the 14th, West Yorks Regiment and Ligonier's the 59th.) The total force under Hawley's command was about 8,000 men. Hawley, popularly known as the 'chief-justice', had a reputation as a savage disciplinarian. His brigade-major James Wolfe wrote of him: 'The troops dread his severity, hate the man and hold his military knowledge in contempt'. It was rumoured that he enjoyed the favour of both George II and of the Duke of Cumberland because he was a natural son of the King (and thus a half-brother of the Duke). He had served at the Battle of Sheriffmuir, where his being on the victorious right wing had left him with some dangerous illusions about the lack of courage and resolution of Highlanders in battle. 'I do and allwayes shall despise these Rascalls' was his verdict on the clansmen.

On 13 January Hawley's second-in-command, Major-General John Huske, advanced from Edinburgh towards Linlithgow with five battalions together with the Glasgow Militia and Hamilton's and

Ligonier's Dragoons, and Hawley followed with the rest of the army on the 15th and 16th. (By this time he had been joined by Cobham's Dragoons, who had fought at Clifton.) On the 13th Lord George Murray, having heard of Huske's advance, moved forward with five battalions to Linlithgow and then sent forward Elcho's horse on the road to Edinburgh to find out what was happening. Elcho returned with the report that he had made contact with English dragoons, who had fallen back on a larger body of both horse and foot. Lord George waited by the bridge across the River Avon for the enemy to cross, with the intention of attacking them after half of them had done so, but none of them came up to the bridge. Then, learning of the advance of the rest of Hawley's army, he withdrew to Falkirk and the next day rejoined Charles at Bannockburn, billeting his troops in the villages around Stirling. On the evening of the 16th Hawley's army were encamped in a field immediately to the north-west of Falkirk, and there he was joined the next morning by Lieutenant-Colonel John Campbell, who had come from Glasgow with three companies of Lord Loudoun's regiment and part of Lord John Murray's regiment (the Black Watch – so-called because they wore a dark tartan instead of the scarlet uniform worn by the 'Red Soldiers' – which had been formed in 1739 in an attempt to enlist Highland military energy on the Government side) and the Argyll Militia.

The Jacobite army was drawn up in battle order on Plean Muir. south-east of Bannockburn, on the 15th, awaiting news of the enemy, On the 16th Charles assembled the army again, according to O'Sullivan drawing it up 'two days running, that every one may know their Ground'. On the 17th, having drawn them up for the third day, Charles reviewed his troops and, in the words of the anonymous journal already quoted, when he 'saw the good appearance his men made, it was resolved to march directly and attack General Hally ... and accordingly the march was begun with a great deal of chearfulness towards Dunnypace, where they cross'd the water'. Their objective was the rough upland of Falkirk Muir, two miles south-west of the enemy camp, in order to gain the rising ground known as the Hill of Falkirk before the enemy. The Highlanders were impatient to attack.

General Hawley never dreamed that the Highlanders would take the initiative. He was staying at Callander House, on the east side of Falkirk, guest of the unwilling Lady Kilmarnock, whose sympathies were with her husband, on the other side; but she realized that she could do her bit for the cause by making the General as post-prandially relaxed as possible while the Jacobite army was advancing. On its being reported

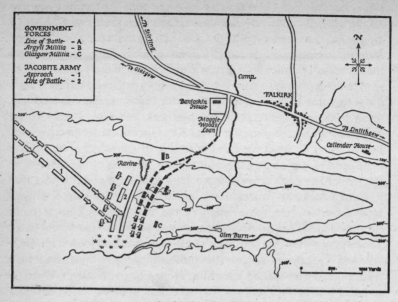

The battle of Falkirk

to him that the Highlanders were in motion, he remained calm and ordered his men to put on their accoutrements but not to get under arms. The troops then proceeded to take their dinner, and the General to enjoy a lavish meal tête-à-tête with his hostess, washed down with abundant wine. When a final desperate message reached him General Hawley at last realized the situation and, in Chambers' elegant language, 'he now came galloping up to his troops, with his head uncovered, and the appearance of one who has abruptly left an hospitable table.'

The Government forces moved south from their camp immediately to the north-west of Falkirk, led by the dragoon regiments, past the east side of Bantaskin House, along the lane known as 'Maggie Wood's Loan' and then in a south-westerly direction up the slope to draw up towards the top in lines that ran roughly north and south. In front, on the left, were the three dragoon regiments. The other regiments were drawn up behind them in two lines, with (from left to right) Wolfe's, Cholmondeley's, Pulteney's, Price's, Ligonier's and the Royal regiments in front and Blakeney's, Munro's, Fleming's, Battereau's and Barrel's regiments behind. In the rear, behind Battereau's, was Howard's, and also in the rear, fairly far out on the left, was the Glasgow Militia. The Highlanders, approaching from the north-west up the other side of the slope, formed with the Macdonalds on the right (the three regiments respectively of Keppoch, Clanranald and Glengarry), the Stewarts of Appin and the Camerons on the left, and the Farquharsons, Mackintoshes, Macphersons and Frasers in the centre. The Atholl Brigade were on the right of the second line; then came Lord Ogilvy's and Lord Lewis Gordon's regiments. Behind them, in reserve, was Lord John Drummond with the Irish picquets, part of his own regiment and the cavalry with whom he had earlier made a conspicuous feint march on the road from Bannockburn to Falkirk to mislead the enemy about the Jacobite army's intentions. The Prince was with them, in command. It was now raining hard, with a strong wind blowing from the northwest – right into the faces of the Government troops, and on the backs of the Highlanders. The ground between Hawley's camp and their present position was marshy, and Hawley's cannon stuck in a bog just to the south of Maggie Wood's Loan, and could not be moved.

The light was fading fast on this wet, windy afternoon of 17 January when General Hawley ordered the three dragoon regiments to begin the attack. For some extraordinary reason he believed implicitly that Highlanders could not stand up to cavalry – and this in spite of Prestonpans! Lord George Murray waited until they were ten yards away, and then gave the command to fire (he himself fought on foot, at the head of the army). Dragoons, variously estimated by eye-witnesses at between 24 and 80 in number, fell dead on the spot. In the growing dark and the driving rain it was difficult for anybody to see exactly what happened, and accounts of the battle by those who participated in it vary considerably in details. Here is part of the Chevalier de Johnstone's account of what occurred next:

[The enemy] cavalry closing up immediately their ranks and files, opened by our discharge, formed a buttress to their horses, and rushed upon the Highlanders at a grand trot piercing into their ranks, driving all before them and trampling the Highlanders under their horses' feet. Then ensued a combat the most remarkable and surprising. The Highlanders extended on the earth, pitched their poinards into the horses' bellies; others seizing the cavalry men by their dresses, and pulling them down, slew them with strokes of their poinards; many used their pistols, but there were few that had elbow room to be able to wield their swords. M. Macdonald, of Clan Ranald, chief of one of the Clans of that name, told me that being extended on the ground, below a dead horse, which had fallen upon him, without his being able to disengage himself, he saw a dismounted horseman in shackles with a Highlander, who held one another round the middle, when, for his good luck, the Highlander being by far the stronger, threw the horseman to the ground, and having killed him with his dirk, he then came to his assistance and tore him with difficulty, from below the horse. In short, the resistance of the Highlanders was so incredibly obstinate, that the English cavalry, after having been for some time in their ranks, pell mell with them, were in the end repulsed, and forced to retreat. But the Highlanders not slacking the fight, pursued them vigorously with sabre strokes, running after them as quick as their horses, and leaving them not a moment's respite to be able to recover from their fright; in so much, that the English cavalry rushed through their own infantry in the battlefield behind them; there it immediately fell into disorder, and dragged their army with them in their rout.

Alexander Macdonald takes up the story:

As the enemys dragoons rode off to their right betwixt the lines, our men ran eagerly in pursuit of them, but were much surprised to find themselves stopt by our generals and officers who with difficulty restrained them with their drawn swords and cocked pistols conjuring them to return to their ground or they would be undone. As the dragoons in their flight betwixt the lines past by our left wing they could not forbear giveing them part of their fire likewise. Our left had not been fully formed when the attack begun on the right; a considerable body of the enemys horse came up also to attack them but receiving part of the fire of our left they broke and run off; their infantry comeing in upon that side were opposed by some of our battalions who receiving the enemys fire went in amongst them sword in hand and drove them down the gill with great impetuosity and slaughter, but not being in sight of our right (by reason of the uneaveness of the ground) they made a halt till such time as the two wings should join in the center and the second line come up. His R.H., whose attention was turned to all quarters, observing that our left wing was outlined by the enemy, sent Brigadeer Stapleton with the pickets of the Irish Brigade and some other battallions from the second line, which extended our first line and recovered the disorder we were like to be put into. Then our whole army marched down towards the enemy who were retreating on all sides in great disorder but by reason of the uneaveness of the ground and night comeing on with a storm of wind and rain they could not overtake them, as they were positively ordered to keep their ranks.

Alexander Macdonald was with the Macdonalds, and it was these regiments – Glengarry's and Clanranald's men – whom Lord George Murray ordered to stay but whom it proved impossible to restrain from dashing after the fleeing dragoons. 'Some pursued the dragoons,' wrote James Maxwell of Kirkconnel, 'others fell a plundering the dead; a considerable body that kept a just direction in their march, fell in with the Glasgow militia, and were employed in dispersing them.' Lord George complained that 'there was no posebility of making the Macdonalds keep their ranks'.

Colonel John Roy Stewart, aware that the men of Ligonier's, Price's and Barrel's regiments on their left were standing firm and firing into the flank of the pursuing Highlanders, suspected a trap and called on the clansmen to stop. 'It is very often more dangerous,' commented Johnstone, 'to check the flight and impetuosity of soldiers, the best of whom are but machines, and still more of undisciplined masses who do not pay attention to orders, than to leave them to run all hazards to extricate themselves.' As a result of Colonel Stewart's call, the order to stop 'flew immediately from rank to rank' and considerable disorder resulted. Some men stayed where they were, some returned to the place where they had been drawn up, others again went back to Bannockburn and Stirling. They had no clear picture of the result of the battle, and some believed that they had lost. In fact, the unexpected rallying of Cobham's Dragoons, who came up the hill in the rear of the Jacobite army's position, put the Prince himself briefly in jeopardy, but the advance of the Irish picquets put an end to this danger and caused the dragoons to retreat.

Some indication of the confusion during the battle is suggested by the unhappy experience of Macdonald of Tirnadrish who, mistaking men of Barrel's Regiment for Lord John Drummond's men, went up to them and asked, 'Why don't ye follow after the dogs and pursue them?' He was right in the midst of them before he realized who they were. A cry went up: 'Here is a rebel! Here is a rebel!' and he was taken prisoner: General Huske was dissuaded from shooting him on the spot, but it was a doubtful deliverance, since he was later hanged. Macdonald of Tirnadrish was the only prisoner that General Hawley carried back with him to Falkirk.

Some of Charles's officers wanted 'to retreat towards Dunipace & the places adjacent, where the men might be cover'd, it being a prodigious rain,' as Lord George later wrote. But Lord George himself wanted to march at once into Falkirk, where Hawley had retreated, while his army was still in confusion there. He ended his argument 'with Count Mercy's expression at Parma, "that he would either ly in town or in Paradice"'. He soon heard that Hawley had ordered his tents to be burned before marching eastward in the direction of Linlithgow.

Lord George with the men of Atholl, Lord John Drummond with the French troops, together with Lochiel, Keppoch and a portion of the Highland army – 1,500 men in all – spent that night in Falkirk. There they obtained possession of the large quantity of military stores – not only tents and baggage, but seven pieces of cannon, three mortars, 600 muskets, a large number of hand grenades, and a great quantity of powder, among other things – that Hawley had not been able to remove and which the people of Falkirk had not already made free with.

The Battle of Falkirk had not lasted longer than twenty minutes. Though not realized by everyone on the Jacobite side at the time, it was a clear Jacobite victory: General Hawley and his forces fled the field – though some regiments briefly rallied and then retreated in good order – and that was that. Only the dark and the rain prevented the Highlanders from pursuing the defeated Hanoverian army and wreaking further destruction. Hawley lost an unusually high proportion of his senior officers; his official return of 55 men killed and 280 'killed, wounded, and missing' is certainly an underestimate: the total of men killed was more like 400. Sir Robert Munro, commanding Munro's Regiment, was the most distinguished of the officers killed. Colonel François Ligonier, who commanded the dragoon regiments, was ill with a quinsy before the battle; the soaking he got during it exacerbated his condition and he died a few days later. On the Jacobite side there were about 50 killed and between 60 and 80 wounded. A sad accidental casualty was the death the following day of Colonel Aeneas Macdonald, Glengarry's second son, 'shot by the accident of a Highlandmans cleaning his piece,' as Alexander Macdonald put it. 'This poor gentleman satisfyed of the unhappy fellows innocence, beggd with his dying breath that he might not suffer; but nothing could restrain the grief and fury of his people, and good luck it was that he was a McDonald (tho not of his own tribe but of Keppochs) and after all they began to desert daily upon this accident, which had a bad effect upon others also and lessend our numbers considerably, . . .'

General Hawley wrote a letter to Cumberland on his arrival at Linlithgow: it began, 'Sir, My heart is broke'. He admitted that he had had enough men to beat the enemy – he put his forces as 2,000 more than the enemy's. 'But suche scandalous Cowardice I never saw before. The whole second line of Foot ran away without firing a shot.' The next day he returned with his army to Edinburgh, and soothed himself by hanging numbers of his own men for desertion on the gallows he had had erected before leaving the city for the hanging of the Jacobite rebels he expected to capture. Others were shot for cowardice and many were flogged. Five officers were put under arrest and some were later cashiered with ceremonious degradation. These were the usual practices of the British army.

All this was evidence enough that on the Government side at least it was recognized that the Prince's army had won a resounding victory. Yet somehow it did not seem as satisfactory to the Jacobites as it might have. This was partly because the night and the rain had prevented their immediate pursuit of the defeated enemy, partly because there was still the irritatingly unfinished business of the siege of Stirling Castle, and partly because of the recriminations that went on in the Jacobite camp. There was the usual disagreement over what to do next. In the end, instead of marching on the demoralized enemy at Edinburgh, Charles (according to Johnstone it was his own decision) resolved to stay and continue the siege of Stirling Castle – an objective which any knowledgeable military engineer could have told him was impossible with the means at his disposal. The Chevalier de Johnstone wrote bitterly about this decision: 'The possession of this pretty fort was of no essential importance to us; on the contrary it was of more advantage to us that it should remain in the hands of the enemy, in order to restrain the Highlanders, and prevent them from returning, when they pleased, to their own country, . . .' As it was, Lord George Murray stayed with his division in Falkirk and the Prince returned on the 19th with the rest of the army to Bannockburn. There he stayed again at Bannockburn House with Sir Hugh Paterson and his ardently Jacobite niece Clementina Walkinshaw.

Clementina's father, of an old Scottish family, had fought on the Jacobite side at Sheriffmuir, where he was taken prisoner, but escaped to go to the Continent and serve Charles's father. Clementina, who was born perhaps in Rome and probably in 1721, was called after Charles's mother, who was her godmother. She was now on a visit to her uncle Sir Hugh Paterson, who had married her father's sister. She is said to have nursed Charles at Bannockburn House when he developed a bad cold, but there is no evidence whatever that there was anything like a romantic attachment on his side at this stage. Charles attracted the enthusiastic attentions of Jacobite women throughout the campaign of 1745–46, but he himself showed no inclination to take sexual advantage of this, remaining generally cool and shy with the admiring ladies. The story that Charles fell desperately in love with his nurse at Bannockburn House and exacted from her a promise to follow him wherever he might have to go if he failed in his present campaign is pure legend, deriving by a process of romantic hindsight from the fact that several years later she did join him and became his mistress.

At the end of January the Duke of Cumberland arrived in Edinburgh to take over command of the Government forces, which had now been reinforced by artillery from Newcastle and by Campbell's Regiment (the Royal Scots Fusiliers), Sempill's Regiment (the King's Own Scottish Borderers), and three squadrons of Lord Mark Kerr's Dragoons (11th Hussars). The Glasgow Militia was 'honourably dismissed', and Hamilton's and Ligonier's dragoons were sent off. On 31 January Cumberland and most of his army were at Linlithgow. The officers of the Jacobite army had already decided on a retreat northwards.

'On the 29th Janr,' wrote Lord George Murray in his account of the retreat from Stirling, 'when the Officers who were at Falkirk (which were all the Clans) had certain advice that the Duke of Cumberland was to march that day, or nixt, from Edr, & had strenthen'd his Armie with three new Regements, besides those that had been at the last Batle, & that they allso were inform'd that the sege of Stirling Castle was so far from advancing, that the Batrie, which had been mounted with great trouble & loss of time, was so far from doing hurt to the Castle, that two of the cannon of the Batrie were dismounted that morning by superior fire from the Castle; they being met togither, & taking in to their serious consideration their situation, they drew up a paper, with the humble opinion to H:R:H:, which was subscribed by them all, & by Ld Geo: Murray, who was with them. This representation was immediatly sent to [the Prince at] Banukburn; in it they gave their reasons for retreating over the Forth.' The memorial sent to the Prince argued that since so many of the Highland soldiers had gone home since the Battle of Falkirk and were continuing to do so, and since it was proving more difficult than expected to take Stirling Castle, 'we can foresee nothing but utter destruction to the few that will remain, considering the inequality of our numbers to that of the enemy.' It was therefore recommended

that there is no way to extricate your Royal Highness and those who remain with you out of the most imminent danger, but by retiring immediately to the Highlands, where we can be usefully employed the remainder of the winter, by taking and mastering the forts of the north; and we are morally sure we can keep as many men together as will answer that end, and hinder the enemy from following us in the mountains at this season of the year; and in spring, we doubt not but an army of 10,000 effective Highlanders can be brought together, and follow your Royal Highness wherever you think proper.

Lord George sent the memorial to John Hay of Restalrig, asking him to lay it before the Prince immediately. 'We are sensible that it will be very unpleasant,' he wrote to Hay, 'but in the name of God what can we do?' Murray of Broughton brought the document to O'Sullivan at Bannockburn House, coming into his room at eleven at night and showing it to him without a word. Broughton was apprehensive of what the Prince would say and do. 'The Prince', O'Sullivan reports him as saying, 'went to bed very cheerfully, but this will set him mad, for he'l see plainly, that it is a Caballe & that Ld George has blinded all those people.' O'Sullivan asked Broughton not to wake the Prince and when he spoke to him to persuade him to stay and fight at Bannockburn where Robert the Bruce had gained such a great victory over the English. Charles was in fact shown the document the next morning. According to Hay, 'when Charles read this paper he struck his head against the wall till he staggered, and exclaimed most violently against Lord George Murray. His words were: "Good God! have I lived to see this?"' He sent Sir Thomas Sheridan to Lord George at Falkirk with a strongly worded remonstrance against the policy of retreating northwards. That evening Lord George himself arrived. 'The Prince recd him very couldly,' wrote O'Sullivan, 'but after some time, began to enter on matters with him, but nothing cou'd persuade Ld George; he must retire & recd very cavallier-like all the Prince said to him, but the Prince kept his temper, & never said a hard word to him, tho' he gave him provocation enough.' O'Sullivan told Lord George 'that there was nothing regulated for the march', and 'Ld George answer'd that he'd make the retraite himself, after a mocking way & went off, with a parsel of gents that follow'd him'. Charles then wrote a second letter to the signatories of the memorial, reluctantly agreeing to their proposal but disclaiming all responsibility for the consequences. The fact of the matter is that by not pursuing Hawley's army to Edinburgh the day after the Battle of Falkirk the Jacobite army had lost the initiative and with it their last chance of a really meaningful victory.

On the evening of 31 January Lord George Murray with the clan regiments marched to Bannockburn. That night, in the Prince's presence, they agreed on a place of rendezvous with the rest of the army, to the east of the village of St Ninians, at nine the next morning. The Duke of Perth, Lord John Drummond, and many other officers and men were at Stirling. A message was sent to the Duke and Lord John to be ready to leave the next morning, but not to evacuate Stirling until they received further orders. Lord George was to take a body of selected clansmen to cover the retreat. Patrols were sent out to watch for the enemy's movements. Confusion developed, however, over the message about evacuating Stirling. 'It seems an order was sent from Banukburn, contrary to what had been reslov'd upon, to Stirling to evacuat it by break of day,' wrote Lord George, and instead of waiting for further orders the troops marched out from Stirling, as well as from the various neighbouring villages where many had been quartered, in complete disorder. No guard was placed at the town gate through which the troops left Stirling, 'so that the very town's people shut the gait & keept in severalls of the army who had not been apris'd of the retreat in time'. Neither was a guard placed at the Forth below Stirling where several boats were kept 'for a free passage', so some prisoners were taken there too. 'In short,' Lord George summed up, 'it was by no means a retreat, but a flight, & the men were going off like so many sheep scatred upon the side of the Hill, or like a broken and flying armie after a defeat & hott pursuit.'

Lord George himself went that morning from his quarters at Easter Green Yards to Wester Green Yards where the shoes and clothing obtained at Glasgow were stored ('which by some reason not to be accounted for had never been distrebute', he drily noted) to see about getting them loaded, but he found far too few horses, so he decided to distribute the clothing 'to any man that would carry it' for otherwise 'most of them things would be lost, as there were not horse to carry them off'. While he was seeing about this he heard a loud explosion and at first believed that this was firing from Stirling Castle on the retreating troops. But he discovered, on reaching the place of rendez-vous, that the explosion had been caused by the accidental blowing up of St Ninians Church, where gunpowder had been stored and was in the process of being carried out. Some of the civilians carrying the barrels had opened them in order to take some of the powder for their own use, so that a train of powder ran from the bulk of the barrels in the church to the place outside where they were being taken: when a sentinel fired to frighten a pilferer he unwittingly set the train alight and the church blew up.

Lord George and the officers with him found nobody at the place of rendezvous, only some country people gaping at the ruined church an hour and a half after it had been blown up. Then 'they observed at a distance the scatr'd men all runing off as iff an enemy were in pursuite of them, which they well knew was not the case.' Lord George was enraged: all his plans for an orderly withdrawal had come to nothing. He blamed O'Sullivan for not having informed him of the change of plan, and O'Sullivan blamed him for having decided on the retreat in the first place, against the Prince's advice. Lord George went after the retreating troops in a very bad temper.

Lord George found Prince Charles at Leckie House, just over a mile south of the Fords of Frew, mounting his horse after having dined, and immediately 'expressed great concern at the manner of the Army's goeing off, so contrary to what had been agreed upon, & so dishonourable to them'. He asked Charles to name the man who had given such pernicious advice, for he feared it was deliberate betrayal, but the Prince who believed the adviser to have meant well and not to have acted 'out of any senistrious views', declined to name anybody and took the responsibility himself, 'so' – as Lord George concludes his account of the incident – 'there was no more to be said'. O'Sullivan, in his account, says that Lord George addressed the Prince in a most disrespectful and impertinent manner, 'teling him before all the Compagny, that it was a most shamefull & courdly flight, that they were a persel of Villans that advis'd him to it; as if he had never consented, nor had any share in it'.

The Highland army crossed the Forth at the Fords of Frew on 1 February, Charles having previously eaten his last meal in the Lowlands at the farm of Boquhan, owned by a Jacobite farmer. They reached Dunblane that evening, and Charles went on some ten miles further north to Drummond Castle, seat of the Duke of Perth, where he spent the night. On the evening of the 2nd the army reached Crieff, and the Prince slept at Lord John Drummond's house of Fairnton (now Ferntower, about a mile north-east of the town). A review of the army at Crieff showed that only 1,000 Highlanders had deserted, not 3,000 as had been supposed. At Crieff Charles also held a Council of War. According to O'Sullivan, Lord George Murray proposed to divide the army, with himself taking the low road to Inverness by the coast 'with the regular troops the horse and the low Contry peoples' and the Prince going by the mountains with the clans and artillery, while the Prince wanted the whole army to go by the coast, by Montrose and other east coast ports where he expected daily assistance fom France. The discussion was long and acrimonious, but in the end Lord George's plan was agreed. Most of the army spent two days at Crieff and on 4 February they set off in two divisions by their separate routes to the north. That day Cumberland's army left Stirling in pursuit of the Jacobites. One by one the alternatives left open to Charles were falling away, and his squabbling officers gave notice by their ill-temper of their sense that they were no longer masters of their own strategy but were an army on the run.

CHAPTER THIRTEEN

Culloden

THE incompetence with which the Government dealt with the early stages of the Jacobite rising of 1745 was bound up with their improvisatory manner of governing Scotland. Since the Union of 1707, and indeed earlier, Scotland had been governed by the Cabinet in London, but not in any consistent way or through any permanently organized machinery. Sometimes (1707–25; 1742–46) there was a Secretary of State for Scotland and sometimes there was not. When there was not, influence on Scottish affairs might be exerted by whatever minister was most interested. But since Scotland retained its own legal system after the Union, the Scottish law officers, especially the Lord Justice-Clerk and the Lord President of the Court of Session, were also instruments of Government policy which they nevertheless sometimes questioned or modified. The correspondence between the Marquis of Tweeddale, Secretary of State for Scotland, and Lord Milton, Lord Justice-Clerk, in the summer of 1745 (it is printed in John Home's *History of the Rebellion*) shows the significant but undefined position the Scottish law officers had in the administration of Scotland. Writing to Lord Milton from Whitehall on 20 July about information that had come to him from the Lords Justices that Charles had landed in Scotland, Tweeddale says: 'Your Lordship will easily judge how necessary it is for all His Majesty's servants to keep a strict look out; and it has been recommended to me by the Lords Justices, that I should give you an account of this intelligence, that you may consult with the rest of His Majesty's servants, and concert what is proper to be done, in case of such an attempt taking place.' Lord Milton replies on 4 August that he is on his way to the Highlands to get intelligence of what is going on, adding: 'But it is too obvious that we civil officers can do little on such occasions, when superior force is on the other side'. On 29 August Tweeddale replies to a letter of Milton's which, he says, 'I this day laid before the Lords Justices' and on 3 September he writes

15 This detail from a painting by David Morier shows that the English infantry had learnt the lesson of previous battles. First the musket, then the thrust of the bayonet when the Scots had only the claymore left

16 'The Highland Chace' is the title of this rather fanciful print, showing Cumberland in his coach pursuing the fleeing 'rebels'

17 Gravestone of the Camerons on the battlefield

18 This print of the battle of Culloden shows the Government forces drawn up in three lines on the right, Highlanders 'furiously attempting with Swords & Targets to break in upon the left of the Duke's front line' in the centre. An officer in the foreground points to the breach in the wall through which Lord Mark Kerr's dragoons are riding to turn the Jacobite right wing

Prince Charles's flight. Framed in elegant scrolls, these vignettes from a 1747 print illustrate some episodes in the Prince's escape

19 With Sheridan and O'Sullivan he rides from the battlefield, making for Fort Augustus

20 The 'stout eight-oar'd boat' in which the Prince was taken across to Benbecula

21 The meeting with Flora Macdonald on South Uist

22 The Prince disguised as Flora's Irish maid, Betty Burke

23 The French privateer *L'Heureux* takes the Prince aboard in Loch nan Uamh

24 Flora Macdonald, after a portrait by
Allan Ramsay

25 *below* Loch nan Uamh today. The
cairn marks the spot where the Prince
embarked, almost the same place where
he landed fourteen months earlier

26 The no longer young Chevalier: flabby, unloved, often fuddled with drink – but still, in his own eyes, the King

27 Henry, Cardinal York: Charles's often censorious younger brother

28 Louise de Stolberg, at twenty the bride of the fifty-two-year-old exile

29 Charlotte, Charles's daughter by Clementina Walkinshaw. At the end of his life he legitimized her and created her Duchess of Albany

30 Canova's monument to James Francis Edward and his two sons, 'last of the royal house of Stuart'

again saying that he had put Milton's express of the 29th before the King. The law officers in Scotland were clearly expected to serve the Government in London as advisers, intelligence officers and indeed general dogsbodies in Scottish affairs. Duncan Forbes of Culloden, Lord President of the Court of Session, did more than any other single man to prevent many of the clans from joining the rising. (He got no gratitude whatever from the Government for his loyal services once the crisis was over.)

But over and above these official channels was the massive patronage exercised by the Duke of Argyll, who 'managed' Scotland for the Westminster Government and was responsible for most of the important appointments in that country. It is significant that Duncan Forbes of Culloden was the estate adviser and agent for the second Duke of Argyll as Lord Milton was for the third Duke. Matters of estate policy and matters of high Government policy were closely related, for reasons which will appear below. Further, the system agreed on in the Treaty of Union that the Scottish peers should elect only sixteen of their number to sit in the House of Lords made it easy to keep together and control a consistent band of Government-oriented elected peers, to whom patronage was extended. As for the Highlanders, there was not enough patronage available in Scotland to extend to clan chiefs who might have been tempted into support of the Government by the offer of important political positions. There were virtually no important political positions in the Highlands.

Another reason for the confusion of government in Scotland at the time of the rising was that Argyll and Tweeddale were political opponents. Argyll worked well enough with the law officers, most of whom owed their appointment to him, but Tweeddale was the representative of a different element in the coalition which came in after the fall of Walpole in 1742. He knew nothing of the Highlands and tended to put off action until he was overtaken by events. By contrast, the Duke (who succeeded to the title in 1743) had a definite policy for combating Jacobitism: he worked hard at appeasing Jacobite chiefs under his superiority and at the same time he insisted on all his tenants taking the oath of allegiance to the Government. But Tweeddale's lack of practical energy did not prevent him from wanting to run Scotland himself, and his jealousy of Argyll and the law officers produced a lack of co-operation and frequent complaints and bickering on the part of both sides. After the defeat of Cope at Prestonpans Tweeddale was accused by the Earl of Marchmont of neglecting 'the common and necessary precautions to defend the Kingdom out of resentment to the Duke of Argyll'; Marchmont said that Scotland 'was undone in the dispute between two men who should be viceroy'. If there was to be a Viceroy of Scotland, Argyll was certainly the better qualified candidate.

The house of Argyll, the senior branch of Clan Campbell, stood alone among the Scottish clans. From the late fifteenth century it had pursued a calculated policy of extending its lands and its power. By the early seventeenth century it had effectively destroyed the *imperium in imperio* of the Macdonalds, which had so troubled earlier Scottish kings, and in the process acquired much of the Macdonald possessions on the mainland. Later in the century, by adroit use of feudal law and financial manoeuvring, the Earl of Argyll had been able to take advantage of the financial difficulties of the Macleans in order to acquire their territory also. By representing feudalism, as opposed to the traditional clan system, in the Highlands for well over a century the house of Argyll had, by the end of the seventeenth century, aroused the enmity of many other clans but had also achieved a unique position in Scotland. The Earl of Argyll was not only landlord of over 500 square miles; he was now also feudal superior of chiefs and holders of land in about 3,000 square miles of territory in Argyllshire and western Inverness-shire. Further, as hereditary Sheriff of Argyll he administered justice throughout a large part of the West Highlands, while as lord lieutenant of the county he was in command of its armed forces. Archibald Campbell, tenth Earl and first Duke of Argyll, had joined William of Orange in Holland and accompanied him to England: he administered the Scottish coronation oath to William and Mary and got his dukedom in 1701 for his loyalty to the principles of the Whig revolution of 1688. His son, the second Duke, was an active supporter of the Union of 1707, while his younger son, the third Duke, who had fought for the Government at Sheriffmuir as Earl of Islay, is the Duke referred to in the previous paragraph. By dissociating themselves from the Stuarts and associating themselves firmly with the new Hanoverian order, the house of Argyll had broken that older alliance with the Scottish crown to which it owed its original rise to power and made itself instead the prime agent of the central government in Scotland. In doing so, it made it inevitable that the western clans at whose expense it had grown, and whose lands it had acquired would be sympathetic to Jacobitism. Thus the Camerons, Macleans, Macdonalds and Appin Stewarts supported the Jacobite cause. Hatred of the Campbells, sympathy for the claims of a dispossessed prince in the light of their own feeling for patriarchal and hereditary power, and also sometimes Roman Catholic and Episcopalian discontent with the religious establishment in Scotland, were all operative factors. In the north-east, where the Scottish Episcopal tradition was strong and where the demand for a Scottish Episcopal Church was refused, the religious element in Jacobitism tended to be dominant. Though the Church of England had of course been episcopalian from the beginning, the Government had viewed Scottish episcopalianism with suspicion ever since 1688, and, with some reason, regarded a supporter of the Scottish Episcopal Church as automatically a Jacobite.

The Dukes of Argyll were men of great ability, and in their pursuit of power and influence had a genuine ideal of social and economic improvement. But it was an ideal deeply at variance with the traditional Highland social structure and way of life. For them, economics rather than kinship determined the system of land-tenure, and tenants who wanted to retain their land had to show their ability to pay an economic rent with regularity and to carry out specified improvements. When, therefore, the Campbells faced the Macdonalds, Camerons and others in a conflict about the rightful succession to the throne, they were also representatives of a new and more impersonal order confronting representatives of the old familial system of the clans. History was on the side of the former, quite apart from the dynastic issue.

At the same time the leaders of the house of Argyll were very conscious of being Scotsmen and Highlanders, and did not relish the task of pursuing their fellow Highlanders with the cruelty often demanded by the English officers of Government forces. On more than one occasion a Campbell officer fighting for the Government intervened to prevent the cruel treatment of defeated Highlanders.

In spite of all that has been said, it must be remembered that less than half of the total number of clansmen in the Highlands fought for the Prince in 1745-46, and many of those who did were virtually conscripted by their chiefs against their own will or at least without any passionate desire to fight. The Mackenzies, Mackintoshes, Gordons and Grants were clans divided among themselves. In the far north, where the Campbells had not made enemies, the Mackays, Sutherlands and Munroes supported the Government. A modern historian has remarked that the Highlanders did not fully realize the extent to which their traditional institutions and customs were in jeopardy until after Culloden; if they had, support for the Jacobite cause might well have been universal among them.

It is perhaps worth mentioning once again that the Highland army was a volunteer army, at least as far as the chiefs were concerned. The chiefs themselves felt free to come and go as they wished, and even those of their humble clansmen whom they had forced from their routine labours to join them had no scruple in slipping away when they had some booty to take home or some domestic problem to attend to. It is difficult for the modern mind to comprehend the precise mixture of unquestioned loyalty to the chief, deep sense of blood kinship with other members of the clan, and individual feelings of pride and independence that co-existed in the mind of the ordinary clansman. Charles discovered that the loyalty of those Highlanders who had pledged themselves to him was both passionate and devoted and at the same time hedged around with a touchy sense of their own dignity. He learned by experience to take from the chiefs what he would never have taken from any subject elsewhere. He found himself involved in concepts of honour that had long been lost in the rest of civilized Europe, and he had to play it by ear. The paradoxes – the apparent mixtures of impertinence and devotion, of obstinacy and high courtesy, of absolutism and individualism, of graspingness and generosity, even of prudent timidity and extravagant courage – fascinated Lowlanders throughout the eighteenth century, a fascination that culminates in Walter Scott's gallery of Highland characters in *Waverley*. Scott saw – what Charles discovered fully in his wanderings and had partly discovered in his first days in Scotland – that the chiefs had sometimes been corrupted by economic and other temptations from the outside world or by a desire for power unrelated to the traditional pattern of their society, and that the humble clansman often displayed the traditional virtues of the Gael with more simple-minded dependability.

It is worth reminding ourselves of these points before returning to the Highland army as they made their way north again with the Prince in the cold of a Highland February. They moved up from Crieff through the Sma' Glen by Amulree and Milton, through Glen Cochill to cross the River Tay by the bridge at Aberfeldy on 4 February. Meanwhile, Lord George Murray with the rest of the army had gone to Perth before turning north-east to the coast. Charles had wanted him to send the cannon ahead to Blair Castle, which was on his own route north, but it did not prove possible to take them all and eventually, having spiked them, Lord George threw fourteen into the bed of the Tay, from which they were fished out by the Duke of Cumberland's men a few days later.

Charles arrived at Blair Castle on 6 February and stayed there until the 9th. He then pushed on by Dalnacardoch to Dalwhinnie 'by the

cruellest snow that cou'd be seen' (in O'Sullivan's words) and so to
Ruthven and the Government barracks there. He had sent on before
him such cannon as he had left ('three Swedish pieces, & the Cannon he
took at Falkirk,' says O'Sullivan) and with these it was easy to force the
small garrison at Ruthven into surrender. He ordered the barracks to be
burned and gave the bedding and other useful equipment in it to Cluny
Macpherson's men, as this was their territory. From Ruthven they took
the road by Aviemore, where they crossed the Spey, towards Inverness.
On Sunday 16 February Charles reached Moy Hall, some eight miles
south-west of Inverness, seat of the Laird of Mackintosh, who was
himself absent on Government service, but his wife, 'la belle Rebelle'
as she was nicknamed, entertained him and his immediate attendants
most hospitably. The men encamped in the neighbourhood.

Inverness was held for the Government by an army of about 1,700
men which Lord Loudoun had collected in the north while Charles
and his army were marching into England: they included his own 'New
Highland Regiment' and the independent companies that had been
raised by Duncan Forbes of Culloden. Learning that Charles was
sleeping at Moy, with only a few attendants, Lord Loudoun decided to
attack at night and capture him. Fortunately, Lady Mackintosh [the
wives of clan chiefs always enjoyed the title 'Lady', even when the
chief was not a knight] was nervous about the Prince's safety and
privately ordered one Donald Fraser, a blacksmith, and four of her
own servants to sneak out beyond the guards and sentries to see if they
could see anything. Captain Malcolm Macleod later told the story to
Bishop Forbes:

> The blacksmith and his faithful four accordingly went pretty far
> beyond all the sentries, and walked up and down upon a muir, at the
> distance, Captain MacLeod said he believed, of two miles from Mac-
> Intosh's house. At last they spied betwixt them and the sky a great
> body of men moving towards them, and not at a great distance. The
> blacksmith fired his musket and killed one of Loudon's men, some
> say, the piper; ... The four servants followed the blacksmith's
> example, and it is thought they too did some execution. Upon this
> the blacksmith huzzaed and cried aloud, 'Advance, Advance, my
> lads, Advance! (naming some particular regiments) I think we have
> the dogs now.' This so struck Lord Loudon's men with horrour
> that instantly they wheel'd about, after firing some shots, and in
> great confusion ran back with speed to Inverness. ... An express
> had been sent off privately to Lady MacIntosh by some friend in
> Inverness to warn her of the danger. [This in fact, as we know from
> another source, was a boy of twelve or fourteen years old called

Lachlan Mackintosh.] He came to the house much about the time that the trusty five discovered the body of men advancing towards them. Lady MacIntosh ran directly to the room where the Prince was fast asleep and gave him notice of Lord Loudon's design. Instantly he jumped out of bed and would have been going down stairs directly, but Lady MacIntosh importuned him to stay in the room till she should get him further notice and try what could be done. They were soon put out of any apprehension of danger. ...

Another eye-witness account points out that Charles did not in fact stay in his room. 'For upon getting the alarm he run hastily out of bed to call up his men, and as it was a keen frost contracted thereby such a cold as stuck to him very long, and I may ev'n say endanger'd his life, which was one great reason of his staying so much at Inverness afterwards, to the great detriment of his affairs in other places.' Charles had never fully recovered from the severe cold he had developed at Bannockburn House, and this time he became really ill.

Charles, who was not yet suffering the full effects of his exposure to the frosty night air on the occasion of what became known as the 'Rout of Moy', marched on to Inverness on the 18th. Loudoun did not defend the town, but retreated in a hurry across the ferry at Kessock to Easter Ross, taking all available boats with him to prevent pursuit. The Castle however – called Fort George after its rebuilding by Wade in the 1720's – held out for two days, garrisoned by a company of Grants under Major Grant of Rothiemurchus, a company of Macleods and eighty regular troops. On its surrender, it was blown up, to the delight of the Highlanders, who had a special detestation of the Government forts. Sixteen pieces of cannon and a hundred barrels of beef fell into the hands of the Jacobite army. The garrison were made prisoners. Brigadier Stapleton, with Lochiel's, Keppoch's and Lord John Drummond's regiments and the Irish picquets, marched south-west to Fort Augustus, which also surrendered after a two-day siege. Part of this force then went on to Fort William, but after a siege which lasted from 7 March to 4 April they were obliged to retire unsuccessful, rejoining the main army at Inverness.

Lord George Murray's division, after marching in blinding snow-storms from Aberdeen (their route there had been via Perth, Coupar-Angus, Glamis, Forfar and Montrose), had joined the rest of the army at Inverness on 21 February. Loudoun and his men were still in Ross-shire and the Earl of Cromarty had been sent with a strong force in early March to pursue him, but could achieve nothing. Lord George and the Duke of Perth joined the hunt. Loudoun kept moving about in Easter Ross and Sutherland. 'Lord George,' in the report of Colonel Ker of Graden, 'having given the necessary orders to Lord Cromarty, (who continued to command in that country), returned to Inverness, where it was resolved the Duke of Perth should be sent to take upon him the command [Cromarty being apparently quite ineffectual] and if possible to get as many boats together as would ferry over his men [across the Dornoch Firth], and to drive Lord Loudon out of Sutherland if he would not stay to fight. The boats were got together, and the Duke of Perth with his men passed over without being perceived and surprized [some of] Lord Loudon's people, obliged them to capitulate and made them prisoners.' Loudoun, however, and Duncan Forbes of Culloden who was with him, together with the Macleod and Macdonald independent companies, escaped, and managed to make their way to Skye by Kyle of Lochalsh, to sit the war out there until after the Battle of Culloden. Among the prisoners taken at what was called the Battle of Embo, fought on 20 March, was the Laird of Mackintosh. The Prince sent him back to his wife at Moy, telling him that he could not receive safer or more honourable treatment anywhere else.

In the middle of March Lord George Murray decided to move south again to his own Atholl country and dislodge such Government forces as had established themselves there: many houses in Atholl had been occupied and fortified by Government forces, and by re-occupying them Lord George apparently thought he could tempt Cumberland from Aberdeen, where he now was, to the rescue of his men in Perthshire. He went first to Rothiemurchus, in Strathspey, taking with him about 700 men. Lord Nairne was in Speyside with a small body of troops to keep an eye on the Grants many of whom were unsympathetic to the Jacobite cause. Nairne and Lord George joined forces to take Castle Grant. Ludovic Grant, the son of the owner who was with Cumberland's army, reported to his father on 24 March with panicky exaggeration that Nairne and Lord George had approached the Castle with about 1,600 men and two nine-pounder cannons, and 'when our people saw that force, they agreed to give access to the house immediatlie; so Lord Nairn was sent to Castle Grant, and Lord George Murray proceeded to Atholl to attack some forcess were in Blair Castle'. The siege of Blair Castle, which was the seat of the Dukes of Atholl, caused some bad feeling between Lord George and his brother the Jacobite Duke. 'If we get the Castle, I hope you will excuse our demolishing it,' Lord George wrote to the Duke, and the Duke's reply was understandably cool. But in fact the siege of Blair Castle, which lasted from 17 March to 2 April, had to be abandoned almost at the moment of success, for on the 2nd Lord George received expresses from Sir Thomas Sheridan asking him to return to Inverness as the Duke of Cumberland was expected there in a day or two. Charles had been unhappy about Lord George's Atholl venture from the beginning. It at least gave the Highlanders a chance to vent some of their anger at the wanton depredation wreaked by Government troops in Jacobite houses which they had occupied.

The Duke of Cumberland had arrived in Perth on 6 February and spent some time there before proceeding to Aberdeen, and from there he sent out parties to plunder and harass the lands of Perthshire Jacobites. The Duchess of Perth and the Viscountess of Strathallan were both seized in their houses and carried prisoners to Edinburgh Castle, where they remained until the following November. It was from Perth that he sent a detachment of 500 men to take Blair Castle and another detachment of 200 to Castle Menzies. Then he learned that his brother-in-law the Prince of Hesse had arrived in the Firth of Forth on the 8th with about 5,000 men and had landed at Leith the same evening, so on the 15th he went to Edinburgh to consult with Hesse about future operations. All the Government generals seemed to think that with the withdrawal of the Jacobite army to the north the war was virtually over and all they needed to do now was to wait until the weather got better and then march into the Highlands to ferret the rebels out of the mountain fastnesses. But Lord Milton, at whose house the Council of War was held, insisted that the rebellion was not at an end and that the Highlanders, secure from Government forces during the Highland winter, would re-unite and risk a battle again before thinking of giving up. Cumberland returned to Perth the next day, convinced by Lord Milton's arguments, and soon afterwards set out with his army for Aberdeen. He went by Dundee and Montrose, and arrived at Aberdeen on the 25th. 'It was unfortunate,' Robert Chambers has cogently remarked, 'that the commander of the royal army should have marched on this occasion through Angus and Aberdeenshire, because the symptoms of disaffection which he saw in these districts must have given him an extremely unfavourable impression of the kingdom in general, and had a strong effect in disposing him to treat it, after his victory, as a conquered country. Most of the gentlemen, throughout Angus at least, he found absent with the insurgent army; others paid him so little respect, as to recruit almost before his eyes.' This perhaps partly explains the notorious severity with which he treated the Jacobites after Culloden, and also the less appalling but still distressing confiscatory activities which he and his officers indulged in when quartering themselves in private houses in Aberdeen and elsewhere.

Cumberland decided to stay in Aberdeen and await the approach of spring before advancing further, and meanwhile, as Chambers elegantly put it, 'he marked his sense of the disaffection of this part of the country by subjecting it to the terrors of military law'. Aberdeen was the centre of Scottish episcopalianism, which, as we have seen, was regarded by the Government as a guarantee of Jacobitism, and among the other punitive destruction which was deliberately wrought by Cumberland in Aberdeenshire and Angus, there was a burning of episcopal meeting-houses and even of Bibles and prayer-books. This fat young third son of George II – he was four months younger than Charles – had of course a personal interest in the destruction of Jacobitism, for his father's throne was at stake. He was not an incompetent soldier. He had served in Germany in 1743 and was wounded at the Battle of Dettingen. In 1745 he was made captain-general of the British land forces at home and in the field and fought courageously at Fontenoy. He enjoyed a rough popularity with his men, who remembered his courage in Flanders, and the floggings and hangings with which he administered army discipline were not unusual in the British army at the time. The calculated cruelty of his treatment of Jacobite Highlanders was something quite different, and flouted the laws of war then generally recognized.

This fact is well illustrated by the difference between Prince Frederick of Hesse and the Duke of Cumberland in the treatment of their opponents. There were four battalions of Hessians encamped in the neighbourhood of Dunkeld when Lord George Murray was besieging Blair Castle, and the besiegers took a Hessian hussar prisoner during a skirmish. Lord George and the hussar conversed in Latin, their only common language, before the latter was sent back by the former to Prince Frederick with a letter, which began:

> Sir, – As our men have taken one of your Serene Highness' people prisoner, I return him to your Serene Highness.
>
> I shall be very glad to know upon what footing Your Highness proposes making war in these Kingdomes, and with you would incline (as we do), to have a Cartel [i.e., an agreement about the exchange of prisoners] setled.

Lord George went on to say that prisoners 'of the Elector of Hanover's army' which they had previously taken 'and us'd with the greatest tenderness' had broken their solemn word of honour not to serve against the Jacobite army any more. This being so, 'His Royal Highness the Prince Regent is much difficulted, how to use the other Prisoners who have lately been taken, for tho' He desires to show the greatest lenity to His Father's subjects, that even opposed him upon his first coming to these kingdoms and Setting up the Royal Standard, yet those who have the Honour to serve Him, cannot but resent the unpresidented behaviour of their Ennemies, who I have some reason to believe have orders to give no Quarters.' When the Prince of Hesse sent this letter to Cumberland at Aberdeen, asking how he should answer it, the Duke replied (in French) that he was sure the Prince would not think of answering a letter from a rebel, adding: 'I admire the insolence of these rebels, who dare to propose a cartel, having themselves the rope round their necks'. Prince Frederick took a poor view of this reply, and in consequence did not move with his troops north of Pitlochry, asserting that he was 'not enough interested in the quarrel between the Houses of Stuart and Hanover' to sacrifice his men's lives in 'combatting men driven to despair'. Thus Cumberland lost the services of 6,000 Hessians at Culloden.

Cumberland remained at Aberdeen from 25 February until 8 April. There was some activity in March, when a division of his army under Major-General Bland moved north-west into Strathbogie and surprised a Jacobite force of about 1,000 men under Colonel John Roy Stewart, forcing them to retreat to Keith; but at Keith Stewart was able to turn the tables by surprising and capturing Bland's advance guard of men from the Argyll Militia and Kingston's Horse. Cumberland with the rest of his army left Aberdeen on the 8th and joined up with Bland and his men at Cullen on the 11th.

The previous November, the Government sloop of war *Hazard*, carrying sixty guns, twenty-four swivel guns and about eighty men had entered Montrose harbour and fired on the town for the next three days and nights. A party of Jacobites from Angus with the help of guns from a French frigate which arrived two days later with French officers, men from Lord John Drummond's regiment and the Irish picquets, captured the *Hazard*, which was re-named *Le Prince Charles* and sent to France, whence she returned in March with £12,000 in English guineas for the empty Jacobite coffers. But by this time the eastern coastal ports of Scotland, Montrose, Aberdeen and Peterhead, were in Cumberland's hands, and *Le Prince Charles* tried to come in to the small tidal harbour of Portsoy on the Moray Firth under cover of darkness. But Commodore Thomas Smith was patrolling from Buchan Ness to the Firth of Forth with a squadron of Government ships of much greater gun-power, and when Captain Talbot of *Le Prince Charles* caught sight of four of these ahead of him in the Moray Firth he fled northwards, pursued by the twenty-four-gun *Sheerness*. Round into the Pentland Firth they went, and Talbot sought refuge in the shallow waters of the Kyle of Tongue by Melness hoping that the *Sheerness*, with her larger draught, would be unable to follow. But Captain Lucius O'Brien of the *Sheerness* (it is interesting that the captains of both ships were Irishmen) risked running aground to anchor within range of *Le Prince Charles*. In the ensuing cannonade Talbot and his men were overcome and the survivors took refuge on shore where they were eventually captured by men of one of the Mackay Independent Companies. So the Jacobite army never got the desperately needed and anxiously awaited money, and Captain O'Brien brought the *Hazard*, as she had now once more become, back in triumph to Aberdeen harbour.

It was on 25 March that the treasure was lost. On 14 March Murray of Broughton had written from Fort Augustus to Lochiel, who was engaged in the siege of Fort William, asking him to hasten the siege and then to march through Argyllshire with his own and the Macdonald regiments, not only to 'correct' the Argyll men but to give an opportunity for their 'few friends' to join, while the Prince with the rest of the army returned to Perth. 'This our scarcity of money renders absolutely necessary, as we have no prospect of getting any unless in possession of the Low-country; and as Cumberland must of necessity follow us, the coast will be left clear for our friends to land.' This was desperate advice, which was never taken (nor was Fort William), but it shows the financial straits of the Jacobite leaders, who were now reduced to paying their men in meal, to their considerable annoyance.

Charles remained at Inverness from 18 February to 14 April, except for a stay in Elgin from 11 to 20 March. It was in Elgin that his cold developed into pneumonia and for two days his condition caused grave anxiety, but 'a timely bleeding' helped or at least coincided with his recovery. (O'Sullivan says that Charles's illness was 'a spotted favor', which was kept an absolute secret, and that he was in bed for nine or ten days and got up against the doctor's orders with the remark that people were only sick when they thought themselves so.) At Elgin Murray of Broughton also fell sick, and his place as secretary was taken by Hay of Restalrig, who proved quite incompetent and was largely responsible for the failure of provisions. At Inverness Charles seems to have played little part in military deliberations, but led an active social life, shooting, fishing, and, if we are to believe Maxwell of Kirkconnel, giving 'frequent balls to the ladies of Inverness, and danc[ing] himself which he had declined doing at Edinburgh in the midst of his grandeur and prosperity'. We sense an undercurrent of desperation in the air of deliberate gaiety which the Prince now assumed. It was towards the end of his stay in Inverness that he received news that he was definitely not to expect any military aid from France, as an expedition designed to have embarked at Boulogne and then one later contemplated from Dunkirk had both been given up.

It was known that the Duke of Cumberland was now advancing from Aberdeen, and an attempt was made to re-unite the scattered Jacobite forces. The Earl of Cromarty was in Sutherland with a force of Mackenzies, Macgregors and Macdonalds to try and raise men and money; they took Dunrobin Castle, seat of the Earl of Sutherland who escaped them, but his wife remained and professed zeal for the Jacobite cause: however, while Cromarty and some of his officers were taking their leave of her to thank her for her kindness to them, a force of Lord Sutherland's and Lord Reay's men surrounded the castle and took them prisoners. The Macdonalds, under Col. Macdonald of Barrisdale (who was later suspected of treachery by the Jacobites and taken to France by some of them as a prisoner), arrived too late for the coming battle. Others in the Highland army had returned temporarily to their crofts for the spring sowing; these included the Macphersons, who also got back too late. But Lochiel and Keppoch with the troops at Fort William together with the Irish picquets at Fort Augustus were summoned back to Inverness in time. Charles's army was about 2,000 under strength.

Jacobite intelligence was poor, and Cumberland's exact movements were unknown; it was not until 13 April that Charles learned that Cumberland had already crossed the River Spey with surprising ease the day before. The Duke of Perth and Lord John Drummond, with the 'Army of the Spey' assigned to cover the Spey crossings, had to withdraw hastily and rejoin the main army. On Sunday 14 April Charles 'ordered the drums to beat and the pipes to play to arms. The men in the town assembled as fast as they could, the canon was ordered to march, and the Prince mounted on horseback and went out at their head to Culloden House [seat of Duncan Forbes, who was away], the place of rendezvous; and Lord George Murray was left in the town to bring up those that were quartered in the neighbourhood of Inverness, which made it pretty late before he joined the Prince at Culloden.' (Colonel's Ker's account.) The next day, 15 April, Lord John Drummond joined them with his men. On that day, Tuesday, 'the whole army marched up to the muir, about a mile to the eastward of Culloden

House, where they were all drawn up in order of battle to wait the Duke of Cumberland's coming'. That day was the Duke of Cumberland's 25th birthday, and he and his army lay encamped at Nairn.

At Culloden Moor (which is at the north-western edge of the much larger stretch of rough upland country known as Drummossie Moor or Muir, between the River Nairn and the Moray Firth) the army was drawn up in battle order 'and the whole was reviewed by the Prince,' reports Colonel Ker, 'who was very well pleased to see them in such good spirits, tho' they had eaten nothing that day but one bisket a man, provisions being very scarce, and money too'. The choice of the Moor as a battle ground was O'Sullivan's; Charles agreed that they should await Cumberland's attack there, but Lord George Murray, who does not seem to have been consulted at all before the choice was made, strongly disapproved. 'I did not like the ground,' he later wrote: 'It was certainly not proper for Highlanders. I proposed that Colonel Ker and Brigadier Stapleton should view the ground on the other side of the water of Nairn, which they did. It was found to be hilly and boggy; so that the enemy's cannon and horse could be of no use to them there.' This stretch of open moorland, a mile to the south-east of Culloden House, was calculated to be of maximum assistance to the enemy, he believed. 'Not one single souldier but would have been against such a ffeeld had their advice been askt. A plain moor where regular troops had ... full use of their Cannon so as to annoy the Highlanders prodigously before they could make an attack.'

But, in spite of Lord George's serious misgivings, there they were on the morning of the 15th on this stretch of open moorland, awaiting the enemy's attack which, however, did not come. Cumberland stayed at Nairn, celebrating his birthday with a special issue of brandy to his soldiers. By noon it was clear that the Duke had no intention of moving that day. Charles told his men that they could refresh themselves by sleep 'or otherwise' – which was somewhat ironical since, thanks to Hay's incompetence, such food as there was was still in Inverness. Learning that nothing was stirring in the enemy's camp, Lord George now decided that the best way to retrieve the situation was to make a surprise night attack on Cumberland's army. Charles agreed with alacrity. It was likely that the celebrating Government troops would be, as Lord George put it, 'drunk as beggars'. Nairn was about twelve miles away.

It was eight o'clock in the evening before the move eastwards to Nairn got under way. They marched in two columns, Lord George with the Atholl men, Camerons and Appin Stewarts in front, the Prince

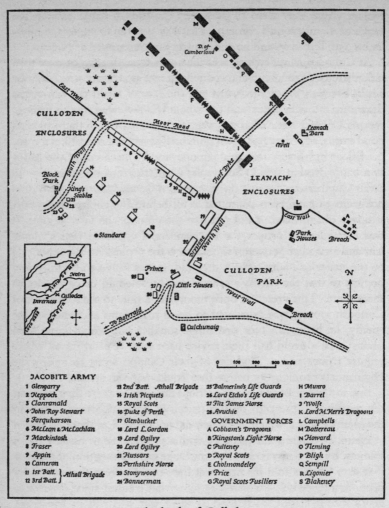

The battle of Culloden

and the Duke of Perth with the rest of the army behind. Charles was in a highly excited state. 'When Ld George was in march,' says O'Sullivan, 'the Prince joyns him, takes one of his hands, & sets another hand about his neck, holding him thus, tels him, 'Ld George, yu cant imagine, nor I cant express to yu how acknowledging I am of all the services yu have rendred me, but this will Crown all. You'l restore the King by it, you'l deliver our poor Contry from Slevery, you'l have all the honr & glory of it, it is your own work, it is yu imagined it, & be assured, Dr Ld George, that the King nor I, will never forget it'. ... Ld George never dained to answer one word ... [He] took of his Bonnet made a stif bow, & the Prince went off, ...'

The plan was for the first column to go round Nairn and attack the Duke of Cumberland's camp from the east and north, while the second was to attack simultaneously from the south and west. The night was dark and foggy, and in the darkness some men slipped away, as others had done before the march began, to seek food in Inverness. The men were cold and hungry. The bulk of the army in the second column moved more and more slowly. Colonel Ker tells what happened:

The night being dark occasioned several halts to be made for bringing up the rear. When about half way Lord George Murray ordered Colonel Ker, one of the Prince's aid-de-camps, to go from front to rear and give orders to the respective officers to order the men to make the attack sword in hand, which was thought better, as it would not alarm the enemy soon, and that their fire-arms would be of use to them afterwards. When he returned to the front to acquaint Lord George Murray of his having executed his orders, he found they were halted a little to the eastward of Kilravock House, deliberating whether or not they should proceed (having then but four miles to march to Nairn, where the enemy was encamped) or return to Culloden, as they had not an hour at most, or thereabout, to daylight; and if they could not be there before that time the surprize would be rendered unpracticable, and the more so as it was not to be doubted that the enemy would be under arms before daylight, as they were to march that morning to give the Prince battle. The Duke of Perth and his brother, Lord John [Drummond], who had been sent to advise the Prince, returned to Lord George. Lochiel and others, who were in the front, hearing that there was a great interval between the two lines, which would take up most of the time to daylight to join, resolved to return to Culloden, which was accordingly done; which, some say, was contrary to the Prince's instructions.

Another report from one who was present says that they were almost at Kildrummie, just over two miles from Nairn, when they were suddenly ordered to wheel about and return to Culloden. It appears to have been Lochiel who first realized that with daylight almost upon them an attack by tired troops on a much superior force would be suicidal, and he communicated his view to Lord George, who agreed. This account continues:

Be that as it will, certain it is that the Prince was not consulted, and tho' master of his temper beyond thousands, 'tis impossible to express the concern he was in upon meeting the Duke of Perth's regiment in their way back. Some positively say that he cry'd out, 'I am betray'd. What need I give orders when my orders are disobey'd?' He call'd for the Duke of Perth, who came soon up to him and inform'd him that the other column had retreated, and that Lord George had sent orders to him, viz. the Duke of Perth, to return to Culloden. He was very keen for sending orders to Lord George to return; but being told that Lord George was already so far on his way back that it would be impossible to bring up the army time enough to execute the intended plan, he said with an audible voice ''Tis no matter then. We shall meet them and behave like brave fellows.' So back they march'd, and arriv'd at Culloden about sev'n o'clock in the morning. The fatigue of this night's march, join'd to the want of sleep for several nights before and the want of food, occasion'd a prodigious murmuring among the private men, many of them exclaiming bitterly ev'n in the Prince's hearing, which affected him very much. Many of them fell asleep in the parks of Culloden [House] and other places near the road, and never waken'd till they found the enemy cutting their throats.

Others, both officers and men, went to Inverness in search of food, which', Colonel Ker drily remarks in his account, 'was very much wanted'. He adds: 'The Prince, with great difficulty having got some bread and whiskie at Culloden, where, reposing himself a little after having marched all that night on foot, had intelligence brought that the enemy was in sight, whereupon those about Culloden were ordered to arms, and several officers sent to Inverness and places adjacent to bring up what men they could meet with.' The abortive attempt to raid Cumberland's camp at Nairn had meant a night march of nearly twenty miles by tired and hungry men who for two days had subsisted on a biscuit and water. In addition they were seriously under strength and outnumbered by the enemy by several thousand. And they were preparing to fight on ground that favoured the enemy and put themselves at a disadvantage. No one could have blamed Charles and Lord George if they had ordered an immediate retreat and refused to face the enemy until their own forces were enlarged, rested, and fed. This is what d'Eguilles, the French 'Ambassador', entreated Charles to do. But they stayed on Culloden Moor, and at eleven o'clock some Mackintoshes and Camerons, posted in advance of the Jacobite army, got their first glimpse of the advancing redcoats. If they got back from their night march at seven – another report says six and yet another says nine – it meant that they had had a maximum of four hours' rest before facing the enemy in the decisive battle of the campaign.

Colonel Ker, sent out to reconnoitre, reported that the enemy's foot were approaching in three columns with their cavalry on their left, so that they could form their line of battle 'in an instant'. 'The Prince ordered his men to be drawn up in two lines, and the few horse he had in the rear towards the wings, and the cannon to be disperst in the front, which were brought up with great difficulty for want of horses.' There had been the usual quarrels about who was to have the place of honour on the right wing. The Macdonalds claimed it, having occupied it in the two previous battles and, they insisted, enjoying this position as a hereditary right since Robert the Bruce gave it to a Macdonald ancestor. Lord George argued that his Atholl men were entitled to it, and, according to Maxwell of Kirkconnel, Charles 'found it easier to prevail with the commanders of the M'Donalds to waive their pretensions for this once, than with Lord George to drop his claim'. Alexander Macdonald concludes his account of the expedition of 1745–6 with a report of this disagreement and the reluctant conceding of the right wing to Lord George's Atholl men, 'which we of the Clan McDonalds thought ominous'. The trouble was, he said, that 'our sweet natured P. was prevailed on by L. and his faction to assign this honour to another on his fatall day, which right they will not refuse to yeild us back again next fighting day'.

The clearest of many accounts given by those who participated of what happened next is probably that of Colonel Ker:

As there was not time to march to the ground they were on the day before, they were drawn up a mile westward, with a stone inclosure on the right of the first line, and the second at a proper distance behind; after having reconnoitred the inclosure, which ran down to the Water of Nairn on the right, so that no body of men could pass without throwing down the wall. And to guard further against any attempts that might be made on that side, there were two battalions placed facing outwards, which covered the right of the two lines, and to observe the motion of the enemy, if they should make any attempt that way.

The Duke of Cumberland formed his line at a great distance, and marched in battle-order till he came within canon shot, where he halted and placed his canon in different places, at some distance in his front, which outwinged the Prince's both to the right and left without his cavalry, which were mostly on the left, some few excepted that were sent to cover the right. As soon as the Duke's canon were placed, he began canonading, which was answered by the Prince's, who rode along the lines to encourage his men, and posted himself in the most convenient place (here one of his servants was killed by his side) to see what pass'd, not doubting but the Duke would begin the attack, as he had both the wind and weather on his back, snow and hail falling very thick at the same time.

The front line of the Jacobite army, with the Atholl men on the right, the Macdonalds on the left and Camerons, Stewarts of Appin, Frasers, Mackintoshes, Macleans and MacLachlans (these two forming on this occasion a single regiment), Farquharsons and John Roy Stewart's Edinburgh Regiment between them, from right to left, were drawn up in a line that ran roughly from south-east to north-west and were thus at an oblique angle to Cumberland's front line, so that their right (which was flanked by the wall that Ker mentions) was no more than 500 yards at most from the enemy while their left was at least 800 yards away. A hundred yards behind the Jacobite front line were, from right to left, Lord Ogilvy's Angus Regiment (two battalions, guarding the wall), Lord Lewis Gordon's and John Gordon of Glenbucket's regiments, the Duke of Perth's Regiment, Lord John Drummond's troops from France known as the Royal Scots (but generally known by modern historians as the Scots Royals to distinguish them from the Royal Scots or Royals on the Government side) and the Irish picquets. Behind them were what was euphemistically called the reserve, with the Prince and the standard. These were some of Kilmarnock's Foot Guards, Strathallan's Horse and Pitsligo's Horse, none of whom had a horse left, and the equally horseless Bagot's Hussars. FitzJames's Horse (which had arrived in Scotland from France in February) and the forty that were left of the Prince's Life Guards still had horses: the latter served as Charles's bodyguard. Lord George Murray commanded the front line, on the right. The Duke of Perth commanded the left wing. Brigadier Stapleton, commander of the Irish picquets, was the commander of the second line. Lord George estimated that the Jacobite army at Culloden consisted of 'not above

3,000 in the field, and those not in the best order'. The Jacobite Muster-Master Patullo estimated under 5,000 men.

Cumberland's final battle order was this: in the front line were six regiments under the command of the Earl of Albemarle: they were, from right to left, Pulteney's, the Royals, Cholmondeley's, Price's, Campbell's (Royal Scots Fusiliers), Munro's and Barrel's, with Wolfe's at right angles to Barrel's, in front. In the second line, commanded by Major-General Huske, were Battereau's, Howard's, Fleming's, Conway's, Bligh's and Sempill's. In the rear, under Brigadier-General John Mordaunt, were Pulteney's (after they were moved up to the front) and Blakeney's. The cavalry – Cobham's Dragoons, Lord Mark Kerr's Dragoons and Kingston's Horse – were divided between the right and the left of the front line. In all, Cumberland's army consisted of 6,400 foot and 2,400 horse.

The opening cannonade by Cumberland's army went on and on, perhaps for as long as half an hour. The Jacobite army stood firm, ready to repel an enemy advance. But while his artillery was effectively thinning the Jacobite ranks at no risk to himself, there was no reason why Cumberland should attack. The weather cleared, but the inadequate Jacobite gunners had their view obscured now by smoke, which the wind blew into their faces. Brevet-Colonel William Belford, who commanded Cumberland's Train of Artillery, knew exactly what he was doing. It did not take him long to put most of the Jacobite guns out of action, though Lord George urged the guns on the right wing to keep on firing as long as possible and a late arriving French engineer succeeded in bringing up a gun that had been left behind; it was hauled into the enclosure on the army's right, from where it could not have done much damage. Belford's deadly round-shot went on.

This was not the kind of warfare the Highlanders were used to, and as their comrades dropped around them they grew more and more impatient for a charge. Meanwhile, four companies of Campbells of the Argyll Militia came up behind the wall on the Jacobite right, pulled it down and, followed by hundreds of dragoons, attacked the Jacobite right flank. Although there was a deep and muddy ditch with steep sides between them and the Jacobites, so that neither side was able to attack across it, the Campbells and the following cavalry were able to pour carbine fire and pistol shots into the Jacobite flank and rear. The Chevalier de Johnstone clearly exaggerated when he wrote that 'the English having accomplished the breaking down the wall of this enclosure, there entered it two regiments of their cavalry, with four pieces of cannon, which they got to play upon our right with grape shot, close to the muzzles, producing a fire so terrible that they mowed down our right wing, like as they cut down a field of corn, and swept away whole ranks'. The 'grape shot' was in fact coming from Belford's guns, but Johnstone's account is significant in indicating the confusion and sense of destruction that now prevailed at least on the right flank of the Jacobite army. The wall should have been pulled down by Charles's men as soon as they realized it was there: it never seemed to occur to anybody that the enemy could use it as cover in outflanking them and then pull it down themselves: a Scottish 'dry-stane dyke' is not difficult to pull down. O'Sullivan has been blamed, for this was his responsibility: he had in fact an impracticable plan to garrison the enclosure formed by the wall.

Belford's guns then turned from round-shot to grape-shot which raked the Highland lines and 'very much galled' the Highlanders. But now at last the order to charge was given to the impatient clansmen. The Mackintoshes in the centre could no longer be restrained. And Lochiel had been standing among his dying Camerons sword and pistol in hand, in anguish and anger. He sent a message to Lord George saying he could not hold his men. Lord George then (as Colonel Ker reports):

sent Colonel Ker to the Prince to know if he should begin the attack, which the Prince accordingly ordered. As the right was further advanced than the left, Colonel Ker went to the left and ordered the Duke of Perth, who commanded there, to begin the attack, and rode along the line till he came to the right, where Lord George was, who attacked at the head of the Athol men (who had the right of the army that day) with all the bravery imaginable, as did indeed the whole line, breaking the Duke's line in several places, and making themselves master of two pieces of the enemy's canon.

Charles had sent his aide, young Lachlan MacLachlan, to pass the message to attack down the line, but he was killed by a cannon ball on the way. He then sent Brigadier Stapleton to Lord George, repeating the order to attack. But on the left, though Colonel Ker delivered his message to the Duke of Perth, the Macdonalds, still angry that they had not been given the place of honour on the right, refused to advance. They bore the heavy enemy fire without flinching, but they would not move. The Duke of Perth, according to O'Sullivan who was now with him and Lord John Drummond, 'runs to Clenranolds Regimt takes their Collors & tels them from that day forth he'l call himself MccDonel [Macdonald] if they gain the day'. There were three Macdonald Regiments, Glengarry's, Keppoch's and Clanranald's, and they were all in a sulky mood. At last, with the other clans already off on their charge, Macdonald of Keppoch called out '*Mo Dhia, an do threig Clann mo chinnidhmi?*' ('My God, have the children of my clan abandoned me?'), rushed forward, pistol in one hand and drawn sword in the other, and met his death from two musket shots. That brought the Macdonalds on at last, but even then they did not charge, but moved forward and halted, in the face of withering fire, on three separate occasions, 'firing their pistols and brandishing their swords,' as Cumberland later reported, evidently trying to provoke the enemy to charge. Cumberland's officers merely laughed at this suicidal behaviour. Some of the gentlemen of the three regiments followed Keppoch's example and charged headlong at the enemy: Keppoch's brother Donald did so and was killed; Clanranald received a severe wound in the head but was able to escape; the Chevalier de Johnstone, charging with his friend Macdonald of Scotus, reported that they came 'not more than twenty paces from the enemy, who let fly their discharge at the moment when the right began to be on the retreat, and which communicated itself from the right to the left of our army with the quickness of a flash of lightning.'

Among the rest of the clans the Mackintoshes and their associated clans, MacBeans, MacGillivrays and others who together called themselves by the ancient name of Clan Chattan, were the first to charge, followed by the other clans in the centre and then by the whole of the right wing. They had been told to hold their fire until they were near enough to be sure that it was effective, and on no account to fling away their muskets. But in fact their charge was too headlong to allow them to use their muskets at all, and many did throw them away. The Frasers, Appin Stewarts, Camerons and Atholl men, whose attack Lord George Murray was leading, found themselves pressed between their own centre and the wall on their right, so that they could hardly draw their swords. At the same time they suffered the fire of the Campbells on their right and even fiercer fire from Wolfe's regiment which was also on their right but immediately ahead of them.

Cumberland's soldiers had been carefully trained in Aberdeen in ways of meeting a Highland charge: they knew exactly how and when to use the musket and then the bayonet. With grape-shot from Belford's guns continuing to cause heavy destruction among their ranks, the clansmen advanced over the dead bodies of their fellows to face disciplined musket fire from soldiers firing one rank after another in ordered continuity. Colonel MacGillivray of Dunmaglas, who led the Clan Chattan regiments, charged through the front rank of the enemy only to meet the fatal fire of the men of Bligh's and Sempill's.

He was killed, with masses of his men and nearly all his officers, while the survivors, having thrown away their muskets, stood in front of the firing enemy lines, unable to counter the deadly fire, falling where they stood in impotent rage. Dunmaglas's standard-bearer was one of the first killed in the charge, but the standard was rescued by a clansman who held it aloft until the inevitable withdrawal began.

Lord George and the men from the right wing, in spite of being constricted by the wall and by the murderous effect of the heavy flanking fire they received, which kept progressively thinning their ranks, moved towards the right as they advanced towards Barrel's and Munro's regiments and, like the Mackintoshes on their left climbing over their own dead, Lochiel's men succeeded in denting the centre of Barrel's. (Lochiel himself had both his ankles broken by grape-shot and was eventually carried off the field by his men.) The Highlanders wrought considerable havoc with their swords and dirks. Barrel's centre fell back on Sempill's regiment behind. The Camerons followed. But Sempill's men (they were Lowland Scots), says John Home, 'allowed them to come very near, and then gave them a terrible fire, that brought a great many of them to the ground, and made most of those who did not fall turn back. A few, and but a few, still pressed on, desperate and furious to break into Sempill's regiment, which not a man of them ever did, the foremost falling at the end of the soldier's bayonets'. Sempill's men remembered the new bayonet drill they had received at Aberdeen and made effective use of it.

It is thought that 500 men, mostly Camerons and Stewarts of Appin, penetrated the enemy lines and engaged with Sempill's regiment. But they were virtually trapped between the two lines. For the enemy front line formed again, and turned round to bayonet the Highlanders in the back while Sempill's men, as an eye-witness account put it, 'discharged with the muzzles of their guns at the rebels breasts'. The casualties were considerable on both sides, but by far the greater among the Highlanders. The surviving clansmen, many of them wounded and all of them exhausted, began to fall back, first individually, then in groups. Lord George Murray, who had been ahead of his men in the charge and had had his wig and hat blown off and his sword broken, went back for reinforcements when he saw how things were going, but when he returned with men of Glenbucket's and Lord Lewis Gordon's regiments, it was too late: the Camerons and the Stewarts were in full retreat, and they bore Lord George and his reinforcements back with them. At this point the Argyll men behind the wall fired into the flank of the retreating Highlanders and then, drawing their swords, climbed over the wall and attacked. Some sharp fighting followed, and the Campbells did not have it all their own way. But by now the battle was really over, and soon the whole Jacobite army was in flight, leaving the battlefield littered with their dead and dying.

On the Jacobite left, Kingston's Horse came up in a sweeping movement to outflank the Macdonalds, then moved left to attack the Royal Scots in the Highland army's second line while Cobham's Dragoons came round from the other side to attack from the rear. Everywhere the clansmen were fleeing. The enemy cavalry came right round to the east, in an encircling movement, and Lord George made some attempt to draw up the Life Guards and Fitzjames's Horse opposite the dragoons, on the other side of a steep hollow, but they were a hopelessly inadequate force. Yet they did succeed in holding up the dragoons' attack for long enough to allow the Jacobite right wing to escape. Kingston's Horse went after the Macdonalds and the regiments from the centre, who were in full flight along the road to Inverness.

At some stage in the progressive worsening of Jacobite fortunes during the battle (it is not clear exactly when, because his account telescopes a great deal into a few sentences) O'Sullivan 'runs to Shea [Colonel Robert O'Shea, in command of Fitzjames's Horse] ... & tels him, "yu see all is going to pot. Yu can be a great succor, so before a general deroute wch will soon be, Seize upon the Prince & take him off" '. All had indeed gone to pot by the time Cumberland's cavalry was on the scene. But at least Lord George and the right wing of the Jacobite army was able to retreat in some order, with pipes playing, across the River Nairn at Faillie. Charles had gone about a mile and a half south-east of the battlefield, to Balvaid, with Glenbucket's and John Roy Stewart's regiments, the shattered remnants of his army. There, halting under a tree, he heard the cheering of Cumberland's victorious soldiers. Charles's last battle had been fought and lost and, though he did not yet realize it, the Jacobite cause was in ruins.

Cumberland, professing to believe that the Jacobites themselves had given orders that no quarter should be given to their enemies (he produced a forged Jacobite order to this effect), ordered that no quarter should be given to the defeated clansmen. Except for troops in the service of King Louis of France, who were regarded as foreign enemies rather than rebels, all who supported the Jacobite rising in any way were regarded as rebels and therefore subject to the rigours of the laws of treason. Immediately after Culloden they were regarded as outside the law altogether. The numerous wounded lying on the field were systematically bayoneted or shot or clubbed to death. The dragoons pursued the fleeing clansmen on the road to Inverness and sabred pretty well everyone they saw during the pursuit, whether they were innocent bystanders or Jacobite soldiers. Stories of the atrocities after Culloden – for which 'Butcher' Cumberland, as he now came to be called in Scotland, was responsible yet which the brutal Hawley probably indulged in more actively – are legion, and though no doubt some of those collected by Bishop Forbes in the years following Culloden are exaggerated, there can unfortunately be no doubt that there was systematic killing of men, women and children, the men being both soldiers and civilians, as well as punitive looting and burning and a variety of acts of deliberate *Schrecklichkeit*. At the same time a policy of calculated de-Gaelicizing was embarked on by the Government even to the proscribing of the kilt. The clansmen had shown themselves to be the only significant reservoir for a Jacobite army: their way of life, already threatened by the movement of history, had therefore to be destroyed once and for all. The Government would see to that. The Battle of Culloden marked the beginning of the end of Highland society. When tartan and the kilt and the romance of the clans revived again in British esteem, it was to be in a mood of literary nostalgia and romance.

But all that is another story; so is the fate of the prisoners – there are three bulky volumes of the Scottish History Society devoted to 'The Prisoners of the '45'. But we may take a brief look forward at the fate of those Jacobites who were captured or surrendered. Four peers, because of their rank, were given the privilege of being beheaded rather than hanged: they were Lords Balmerino and Kilmarnock whose trial and execution are described in memorable letters by Horace Walpole, the Earl of Derwentwater, brother of the executed 3rd Earl, who had escaped from Newgate after the '15 and was captured at sea in November 1745 on board a French vessel taking arms to the Jacobites in Scotland, and the seventy-eight-year-old Lord Lovat, who, after a lifetime of continually changing sides, finally found himself on the losing one, in spite of his device to make it appear that his son had led out his men against his will. Dr Archibald Cameron, Lochiel's brother, was hanged at Tyburn in 1753. A total of 120 people were executed. About 936 were transported and banished to America and 121 others banished 'outside our Dominions'. Altogether, 3,471 men, women and children were taken prisoner. It is probable that over 600 died in prison. Many Jacobites escaped to the Continent, to live in exile. Murray of Broughton, who voluntarily remained in Scotland, when he could have got away, in order to look after Jacobite gold from France which had been buried at Loch Arkaig (where some of it probably still is), was betrayed by a cowherd and taken prisoner. He saved his life by turning King's evidence, and testified at Lovat's trial. But, as Compton Mackenzie has said, 'his evidence brought no man to the block, not even old Simon Lovat himself. Murray was a Peter, but he was no Judas'. He earned the contempt of most Scotsmen, even of loyal Whigs (like Walter Scott's father), but Charles himself, to whom he remained personally loyal, forgave him.

The Government and middle classes had been thoroughly frightened by the rising of 1745–46, and heaved an enormous sigh of relief after Culloden (or Drumossie Moor, as the battle was sometimes called). There is no doubt that the majority of people in Britain shared this relief – not out of any love for George II but because they were terrified of violence and the breakdown of order. Most of them thought of Prince Charlie and his Highlanders as a desperate adventurer leading a horde of savages. Yet, in Scotland at least, even among those who were glad to see the Jacobite threat removed, there remained a strong feeling of sympathy with the unfortunate Prince and his cause. And once the cause was well and truly lost, and Jacobite sentiment no longer posed a threat to the established order, that feeling grew, to express itself in folk song and a variety of cultural gestures. Robert Burns picked up one of these folk songs and sent it, perhaps with some polishing of his own, to James Johnson for inclusion in his collection of Scottish songs:

> The luvely Lass o' Inverness
>   Nae joy nor pleasure can she see;
> For e'en and morn she cries, Alas!
>   And ay the saut tear blins her e'e:
> Drumossie moor, Drumossie day,
>   A waeful' day it was to me;
> For there I lost my father dear,
>   My father dear and brethren three!
>
> Their winding-sheet the bludy clay,
>   Their graves are growing green to see;
> And by them lies the dearest lad
>   That ever blest a woman's e'e!
> Now wae to thee, thou cruel lord,
>   A bludy man I trow thou be;
> For mony a heart thou has made sair
>   That ne'er did wrong to thine or thee!

But it was the Gaelic poets who composed most of the laments for Culloden, many of them written by men who had fought in it. John

Roy Stewart, an able officer with the Jacobite army, was also an accomplished poet in Gaelic. He wrote many Jacobite poems, including two laments for Culloden. One of them begins 'O, gúr mor mo chùis mhulaid,' ('Great is the cause of my sorrow'), speaks of the tyranny of Cumberland, and goes on to mourn the fate of 'handsome red-haired Charlie' and the dead clansmen lying unburied on the battlefield:

> Mo chreach, armailt nam breacan
>   Bhith air sgaoileadh 's air sgapadh 's gach àit', . . .
> [Woe is me for the host of the tartan,
>   Scattered and spread everywhere, . . .]

CHAPTER FOURTEEN

The Fugitive Prince

THERE has been considerable controversy over Charles's immediate actions and intentions after the battle of Culloden. The Irish officer Captain Felix O'Neil, who was personally devoted to the Prince, gives in his Journal a picture of Charles attempting vainly to rally his troops: 'The Prince gallop'd to the right, and endeavouring to rally them had his horse shot under him. The left followed the example of the right, which drew on an entire deroute in spite of all the Prince could do to animate or rally them.' But we know that one item in this account is inaccurate: the Prince's horse was not shot under him, at least not seriously. James Gib, who was 'Master-Household and provisor for the Prince's own table', later assured Bishop Forbes that 'he himself was near the Prince all the time of the action, viz., in the Prince's rear, and that it was not true that the Prince had a horse shot under him'. O'Sullivan reports that 'the Prince was at this time rallying the right, his horse is shot in the Shoulder kicks & cappors, he's oblidged to change horses'. The 'Account of the Young Pretender's Escape' in the Lockhart Papers ('written by a Highland Officer in his army') says that his horse was wounded but survived and 'is now in the possession of a Scots gentleman'. This is a minor matter, but it illustrates that even eye-witnesses did not always see the same thing. O'Neil's report continues:

Previous to the battle the Prince had ordered the chieftains that (in case of a defeat) as the Highlanders could not retreat as regular troops, they should assemble their men near Fort Augustus. In consequence of this, immediately after the battle the Prince dispatched me to Inverness to repeat his orders to such of his troops as were there. That night the Prince retir'd six miles from the field of battle and went next day as far, and in three days more arrived at Fort Augustus, where he remained a whole day in expectation his troops would have join'd him. But seeing no appearance of it, he went to the house of

Invergary and ordered me to remain there to direct such as pass'd that way the road he took. I remained there two days and announc'd the Prince's orders to such as I met, but to no effect, every one taking his own road.

O'Sullivan says that Charles refused to retire in spite of 'all that could be told him' of his danger, and that he said, 'Well, they won't take me alive' on seeing a regiment advance to cut off his retreat. But eventually, according to O'Sullivan, Charles saw that it was time to retire. He himself, he says, 'parted some time after the Prince & joyned him at the river Nairn' – which is in contrast to an eye-witness report that it was O'Sullivan who 'laid hold of the bridle of the Prince's horse and turned him about'. Charles himself wrote in 1750 that he was 'led off the field by those about him'. In 1829 Sir James Stuart Denham, nephew of Lord Elcho, told Sir Walter Scott that in his uncle's unpublished memoirs there was a story that Elcho had ridden up to Charles and begged him to lead a charge to retrieve the battle or die sword in hand, and that Charles refused, on which Elcho called him 'a damned cowardly Italian'. But there is in fact no word of this in Elcho's *Memoirs* and the story is thus suspect; in any case, Elcho's continuous bitterness against Charles makes him a dubious witness. O'Sullivan, between whom and Lord George Murray there was no love lost, says quite erroneously that Lord George and his men 'were of the first that retired off the field', and this presumably deliberate error is indicative of the ill-feeling between the Prince's Scottish and Irish followers which helps to explain some of the discrepancies in the various accounts.

There seems little doubt that Charles did attempt to rally certain regiments on the left wing, though he was already a mile from the enemy front line when he did so. It seems clear, too, that the Irish about Charles, especially his old tutor Sir Thomas Sheridan, pleaded with him strongly to save himself. The Chevalier de Johnstone's account shows very clearly how some at least of the Scots felt about the Irish:

The Prince, when he saw the rout commence, saved himself with some cavalry of the piquet of Fitz James. Lord Elcho found him some hours after the battle, in a hut near the river Nairn, surrounded by Irishmen not a single Scotchman being with him. He was in total prostration, lost to all hope of being able to retrieve his affairs, having his mind completely imbued with the evil counsels of Sherridan and other Irishmen, who governed him at their will, and giving up every design but that of saving himself in France as soon as he possibly could. Lord Elcho represented to him that this defeat was nothing in reality, and his Lordship did all in his power to persuade him to dream of nothing but to rally the army, put himself at their head, and try once more his fortune. This disaster, he said, could very easily be repaired; but the Prince was insensible to all his lordship could say, and would not hear him.

Charles in fact seems to have been in a state of shock. He had believed his Highlanders invincible ever since Prestonpans, and the vivid evidence provided by Culloden that this was a delusion must have been shattering. Elcho's account confirms this, describing the Prince as 'in a deplorable state' and adding that he seemed more concerned with the Irish than with the Scots. He seemed to think that the Scots intended to betray him. But it was Lord George Murray and his right wing that vindicated the courage and prowess of the Scots and it was he who rallied such men as he could before retiring in an orderly and disciplined manner to Ruthven in Badenoch (not the same Ruthven where the barracks were, which was south of Kingussie) to await Charles's further instructions. There was apparently the impression among many of the officers of the Jacobite army that Charles had named both Fort Augustus and Ruthven as places of rendezvous. Johnstone gives a perhaps somewhat romanticized account of what happened at Ruthven:

I found there the Duke of Athole, Lord George Murray, his brother; the Duke of Perth, Lord John Drummond, his brother; Lord Ogilvie, and a great many other Chiefs of Clans, with about four or five thousand Highlanders, all in the best disposition possible for renewing the contest, and having their revenge. . . . Lord George Murray sent at once a force to defend [the defiles around Ruthven]; at the same time he despatched an aide-de-camp to inform the Prince that a great part of his army was collected together at Ruthven; that the Highlanders were armed, full of ardour, and breathing with impatience for the moment to be led back to the enemy; that the Clan Grant, and other Clans of Highlanders who had until then remained neuter, were disposed to declare themselves for him, seeing the destruction of their country inevitable by the proximity of the victorious Duke of Cumberland; that all the absent clans would return thither in a few days, and that in place of five or six thousand men who were present at the Battle of Culloden, as well by the absence of these into their own country on leave, as by those who had dispersed themselves on arriving at Culloden on the morning of the 16th for the purpose of going to sleep, he could reckon at least on eight or nine thousand men, even more than he had ever had in his army. Every one beseeched the Prince most earnestly to come thither quickly to put himself at their head.

But the Prince did not come. Instead, according to Johnstone, he sent back the aide-de-camp with the answer 'that every one should look out for the means of saving himself as best he could' – an answer that Johnstone understandably describes as 'not a little dispiriting and heart-rending to those brave men who had sacrificed themselves for him'. Johnstone was convinced that, since Lord George was master 'of the defiles between Ruthven and Inverness' and Cluny MacPherson's 500 men had joined them, they could have re-established their army within eight days and avenged 'the horrors and barbarities of the Duke of Cumberland'. 'But the Prince was unalterable, and immovable in his resolution to abandon the enterprise, and terminate most ingloriously his expedition, the rapid progress of which had attracted the attention of all Europe.' He blamed 'the Chevalier Sherridan and other Irishmen, who were altogether ignorant of the situation of the country and the character of the Highlanders, ...' Whatever we think of the advice given to Charles by his Irish followers, there can be no doubt of the devotion of those of them who followed him in his subsequent wanderings. Further, it is clear from what Lord George himself later wrote – 'Besides our defeat, there was neither money nor provisions to give: so no hopes were left' – that it was his own view that the situation was hopeless, so that it was wrong to blame Charles as the sole source of the decision to abandon further action.

This was the end of the Jacobite army. 'The breaking up of the entire force at Ruthven produced a most touching and affecting scene,' Johnstone goes on. 'There were eternal adieus when they took leave of one another, no one being able to foresee his fate, or that his days might not be ended on the scaffold. The Highlanders sent forth screams and howlings, groaning and weeping with bitter tears at seeing their country at the mercy of the Duke of Cumberland, on the point of being ravaged, and themselves and their families reduced to bondage, and plunged in misery without remedy.' Those Irish and Scottish soldiers who had come from France and were technically in the service of King Louis had more to hope for, since under international law as it then was their lives were safe. These men fell back from Culloden to Inverness and surrendered on terms. But the great bulk of the Jacobite army, now in total disintegration, were liable on capture to treatment of the most savage kind at the hands of a vindictive enemy.

From Ruthven Lord George Murray wrote Charles a reproachful letter protesting 'that nixt to the safety of your R.H. person, the loss of the cause, with the present unhappy situation of my countrymen, is the only thing that greivs me, for I thank God I have a resolution to bear with my own and familie's ruine without a grudg' and criticizing Charles's judgment in having raised his standard in the first instance without positive assurance of substantial French aid. 'I hope your R.H. will now accept of my dimission,' he concludes, 'and whatever commands you have for me in any other station you will please honour me with them'.

Charles probably did not send the message reported by Johnstone in exactly those words, but his aim now seems to have been to escape to France from the west coast as quickly as possible and return with a French force; at the same time he had not yet given up all hope of his Highlanders gathering again and fighting. But as the weeks went by and it became clear that his position as a hunted fugitive was going to last indefinitely, his immediate aim became mere survival, and that was achieved with difficulty amid hair-breadth escapes and fantastic adventures. The story of his hardships, dangers, disguises, concealments, stratagems, and almost incredible endurance over a period of five months before he finally boarded a ship for France has long taken its place as one of the great romantic episodes of history. The more one studies it, the more one reads the contemporary accounts and the reports of friends and companions, the more astonishing it becomes. Research confirms rather than debunks the almost incredible nature of the Prince's adventures after Culloden, which are given an added dimension by the fact that throughout the whole period he had a price of £30,000 on his head and was not betrayed even by the most distressed and impoverished clansman among the many such that he met. 'All the world,' says Andrew Lang, 'has regretted that the Prince did not fall as Keppoch fell, leaving an unblemished fame, that he did not ride back, if it were alone, like d'Argentine at Bannockburn, and die with glory'. Certainly when we think of those terrible years of decline and disintegration after his return to the Continent we might well wish that Bonnie Prince Charlie had died a hero's death on the field of Culloden. At the same time his courage, stamina, optimism and even gaiety during those desperate months as a fugitive wiped away the memory of the moods of petulance and self-will which he had indulged in all too frequently especially after Derby and established a living legend of Highland loyalty to a wandering prince and a remarkable folk tradition associated both with that loyalty and with the slow-dying hope of Charles's eventual return that has enriched Scottish song and Scottish sensibility. It was his months as a wanderer in the Scottish Highlands that established him as a figure in Scottish rather than general British history.

The anonymous account of the Prince's wanderings collected from the mouths of eye-witnesses and published at London in 1765 recounts how, after exchanging his wounded horse for another, he retreated across the River Nairn and went by Tordarroch, Aberarder and Farraline to Gortuleg (now Gorthlick) accompanied by Sir Thomas Sheridan, Sir David Murray, Alexander MacLeod, O'Sullivan, O'Neil, John Hay of Restalrig, Edward (Ned) Burke, a servant of MacLeod's, who was their guide, 'a servant of Mr Hay's and one Allan Macdonald'. (Burke's own account includes Lord Elcho in the company.) Gortuleg was the house of Lord Lovat's steward. 'Here he found Lord Lovat; who exhorted him most pathetically to keep up his courage, and remember his ancestor Robert the Bruce, who after eleven battles lost, (he said) by winning the twelfth restored the kingdom. On the other hand, O Sullivan and O Neille, taking their master aside, begged him to consider the imminent danger, and to listen to no insinuations of another rising.'

We are not told how Charles answered his advisers. After (according to another anonymous contemporary account) taking 'some refreshment and two hours rest' he and his party pushed on towards Fort Augustus 'where' (says O'Sullivan) 'he expected to make a head, & that the most part of those of that contry wou'd joyn or assemble. But having waited near Forte Augustus till about two hours of day, & not finding a soul, nor meeting any mortel that cou'd give him any accts, went to Glengary's house that is about three mils from yt'. They reached the house of Macdonell of Glengarry between five and six o'clock on the morning of the 17th. 'Tho' this castle was not yet burnt' (to quote the 1765 account again), 'nor its owner made prisoner; yet, the family being absent, it could afford no entertainment. Edward Burk, however, by break of day catched two salmons, which furnished an ample repast. A little wine had been provided for the P——'s use; but this, nor any other good would he ever share in preference to the sharers of his fortune.'

It was now judged safer for Charles to travel with fewer companions, and he retained only O'Sullivan, Allan Macdonald and Edward Burke. He actually changed his outer clothes with Burke, which indicated an increasing fear of pursuit and discovery. 'At 3 o'clock afternoon,' as Burke reports, 'the Prince, O'Sullivan, another private gentleman, and the guide set out and came to the house of one Cameron of Glenpean, and stayed there all night. In this road we had got ourselves all nastied, and when we were come to our quarters, the guide [Burke] happening to be untying the Prince's spatterdashes, there fell out seven guineas.

They being alone together, the Prince said to the guide, "Thou art a trusty friend and shall continue to be my servant".

Where was Charles going, and what was his intention? How serious had been his expectation of a new gathering of the clans at Fort Augustus? It is clear enough where he was now going: on the Road to the Isles. It was on the west coast that he expected to pick up a ship from France and it was also among the Highlanders of the north-west (especially the Macdonalds) that he felt safest. It is reasonably clear, too, that he was in a pretty confused state of mind at the beginning of his journey and may well have had some unclear notions of an agreed rendezvous at Fort Augustus when he waited near there on the way to Invergary.

Donald Cameron of Glenpean lived at the end of Loch Arkaig, and Charles reached his house about midnight on the 18th after a difficult journey through rugged country, first south-west down the shore of Loch Lochy 'with terrible mountains on his right', as O'Sullivan remarked, so that he had to go on foot most of the time, and then striking west along the north shore of Loch Arkaig. At Cameron's house the Prince got the first night's sleep he had had for five or six nights. The next morning Cameron conducted him through Glen Pean to Loch Morar 'by the cruelest road that cou'd be seen'. At the eastern end of Loch Morar he waited in vain for a boat that had been sent for. As dark was coming on and no boat had arrived he 'past one of the highest & wildest mountains of the highlands' to a cottage of a Macdonald, who gave him milk, curds and butter, and shelter for the night. On the 20th he arrived at the house of Alexander Macdonald, brother of the Macdonald with whom he had stayed when he first landed, in Arisaig. He stayed here until he embarked for Uist on the 26th. 'He was pritty well here; he had a little meal, lamb, butter & straw to ly upon, he wanted it for he had not eat a bit of bread since he supt at Ld Lovets the night of the battle.'

While Charles was at Arisaig, Hay of Restalrig arrived, with accounts of Government troops at Fort Augustus and a strong detachment in Fort William. 'Ah!' says the Prince (in O'Sullivan's report), 'there is all communication cut wth Badenoch, by the troops that are at Forte Augustus, & since that detachemt is gone to Forte William without being attacked in a Contry where they cou'd be cut to pieces, there is nothing to be expected.' Shortly afterwards they heard that Lord Loudoun, who was commanding a Government force in Skye, had received orders to leave the island and proceed to Fort William by Arisaig and Moidart, ravaging all that country as he went. News also came in of clans preparing to give themselves up and of Glengarry's men delivering up their arms at Fort Augustus. It was not clear how accurate the news was, but it was disturbing. On 23 April Charles sent a letter to Sir Thomas Sheridan enclosing a post-dated letter for the chiefs to be handed to them after he had sailed for France. To Sheridan he wrote: 'I . . . have nothing further or more to add to what I have wrote formerly, being still of the same opinion that we have traitors among us which has made me take my party and which at the same time is the best in the whole world for the good of the cause, altho' risking in it self . . .' (The handwriting, and so the uncharacteristically good spelling, is John Hay's.) His letter to the chiefs (also in Hay's handwriting) began: 'When I came into this Country, it was my only view to do all in my power for your good and safety. This I will allways do as long as life is in me. But alas! I see with grief, I can at present do little for you on this side the water, for the only thing that now can be done, is to defend your selves till the French assist you. If not, to be able to make better terms.' He says that he will be of little use in Scotland, but if he goes to France, however dangerous the journey may be, he will 'certainly engage the French Court either to assist us effectually and powerfully, or at least to procure you such terms as you would not obtain otherways'. He suggests that the policy of the French Court is not to restore King James but to keep Britain in a continual state of civil war, to France's advantage, and that his own leaving the country will put a stop to this policy. 'Before leaving off, I must recommend to you that all things should be decided by a Council of all your Chiefs, or, in any of your absence, the next Commander of your several corps, with the assistance of the Duke of Perth and Lord George Murray, who, I am persuaded, will stick to you to the very last.' But in fact the Duke of Perth, now very ill, together with Lord John Drummond, Lord Elcho, Sir Thomas Sheridan, Hay of Restalrig, Lockhart of Carnwath the younger, and some others, embarked on 3 May on the French privateer the *Mars*, which was fiercely engaged in Loch nan Uamh by the twenty-four gun *Greyhound* commanded by Captain Thomas Noel, the senior Government naval officer in those waters, and the sloop *Baltimore*, and though badly crippled was able to get away to France. The Duke of Perth died on the voyage. (If the *Mars* had not been crippled, Captain Rouillée, who commanded her, would have searched for Charles in the Western Isles and taken him on board. If Charles had not taken the decision to cross to Uist he would probably have been picked up by either the *Mars* or the *Bellone*, which arrived in Loch nan Uamh on 30 April, in spite of the presence of the

Government ships, the *Greyhound*, the *Baltimore* and the *Terror*. The Prince also missed the 40,000 *louis d'or* brought by the French ships: the money was buried at Loch Arkaig, and was the cause of later suspicions and dissensions among Jacobite leaders. On 3 May the *Hardi Mendiant*, a French cutter from Dunkirk, entered the Minch with volunteers and cargo for the Jacobites: on learning of the disaster of Culloden, it was decided to land two officers only, Lieutenant John M'Donell and Captain Lynch, with money and despatches for the Prince from his brother and then to return with everybody else. The *Hardi Mendiant* evaded the Government ships and sailed back to Flanders. Thus another chance for Charles's rescue was lost.

Meanwhile Aeneas Macdonald had been to the island of Barra to collect a sum of money from France which had been disembarked there, having hired the elderly Donald MacLeod as pilot. The voyage was made in a small boat, and they reached Barra 'though the sea was swarming with sloops of war, boats and yawls full of militia, viz., the Campbells, the MacLeods, and MacDonalds of Skye, etc.' (in the words of Donald MacLeod's own lively account of his adventures as given to Bishop Forbes). They finally got back to Kinlochmoidart, where Aeneas Macdonald received a letter from Charles giving him the news of Culloden and asking him to meet him at Borrodale. It was then arranged that Donald MacLeod should be asked to pilot the Prince to Uist. As Donald was going to meet the Prince at Borrodale he ran into him walking alone in a wood. Here is Donald's account:

The Prince, making towards Donald, asked, 'Are you Donald Mac-Leod of Guatergill in Sky?' 'Yes,' said Donald, 'I am the same man, may it please your Majesty, at your service. What is your pleasure wi' me?' 'Then,' said the Prince, 'You see, Donald, I am in distress. I therefore throw myself into your bosom, and let you do with me what you like. I hear you are an honest man, and fit to be trusted.'

Charles then asked Donald to take letters from him to Sir Alexander Macdonald and MacLeod of MacLeod, but Donald flatly refused, telling the Prince that both these men 'were then, with forces along with them, in search of him not above the distance of ten or twelve miles by sea from him, but a much greater distance by land; and therefore the sooner he left that place the better'. Charles then said to Donald: 'I hear, Donald, you are a good pilot; that you know all this coast well, and therefore I hope you can carry me safely through the islands where I may look for more safety than I can do here.' Donald replied that he would do anything in the world for the Prince. He 'procured a stout eight-oar'd boat, the property of John MacDonald, son of Aeneas or

Angus MacDonald' of Borrodale, and on 26 April they went on board 'in the twilight of the evening' at 'the very spot of ground where the Prince landed at first upon the continent [mainland]'. 'There were in the boat the Prince, Captain O'Sullivan, Captain O'Neil, Allan MacDonald, commonly called Captain MacDonald (of the family of Clanranald), and a clergyman of the Church of Rome; and Donald MacLeod for pilot managing the helm, and betwixt whose feet the Prince took his seat.' There were also eight boatmen, one of whom was Donald MacLeod's son Murdoch and another was Ned Burke, whom Donald described as having been 'a common chairman in Edinburgh'. (Burke was of Irish extraction but had been born in North Uist. Most 'chairmen' in Edinburgh were Highlanders.) Murdoch MacLeod was a schoolboy of fifteen, attending the Grammar School of Inverness. When he had heard of the imminence of a battle he provided himself with a claymore, dirk and pistol and ran away from school to Culloden. 'After the defeat he found means to trace out the road the Prince had taken, and followed him from place to place; "and that was the way," said Donald, "that I met wi' my poor boy." '

A storm was brewing, and Donald MacLeod urged the Prince not to set out that night. But Charles, 'anxious to be out of the continent where the parties were then dispersed in search of him,' insisted on setting out at once. The storm broke violently soon after they left shore, with thunder and lightning and torrential rain. Their only hope of safety lay in making for the open sea, for to try and land anywhere on the lochside would have meant being dashed on the rocks. Even so, with neither pump nor compass nor lantern on the boat and the night pitch dark, they were in great danger. 'But,' as Donald told Bishop Forbes, 'as God would have it, by peep of day we discovered ourselves to be on the coast of the Long Isle [i.e., the long string of Hebridean islands including Lewis, North and South Uist and Barra, among others, which from a distance looks like a single long island], and we made directly to the nearest land, which was Rushness [Rossinish] in the Island Benbecula. With great difficulty we got on shore, and saved the boat, hawling her up to dry land, in the morning of April 27th.' At Rossinish they found an uninhabited hut, where they made a fire to dry their clothes, and then the Prince went to sleep on an old sail spread on the ground.

'There were Cows about the house,' O'Sullivan tells us, 'he [Charles] orders the men to shoot one that he'l pay for it.' So they killed and ate the cow, while the storm (which lasted two days) raged outside. They sent a man to Clanranald's house, several miles away, and he found Clanranald's second son, who had left the Jacobite army before Culloden; he came to pay his respects to the Prince bringing some biscuits, meal and butter. Charles's plan now was to go to Stornoway and there hire a ship to go first to Orkney and then to Norway, and thence 'to make the best of his way to France, to see if he cou'd engage the King of France to sent troops with him to Scotland'. The weather improved, and on 29 April the party set out again, in the same eight-oared boat, for the island of Scalpa, over thirty miles to the north-east, 'the Prince and O'Sullivan going under the name of Sinclair,' as Donald reports, 'the latter passing for the father and the former for the son'. On Scalpa Donald brought the party early in the morning of the 30th to the house of his friend Donald Campbell. Donald MacLeod was sent by the Prince to Stornoway the next day 'in order to hire a vessel under a pretence of sailing to the Orkneys to take in meal for the Isle of Sky, as Donald used to deal in that way formerly,' while the Prince stayed at Campbell's house for four days. Campbell's young son Kenneth went fishing with the Prince, who he had been told was a shipwrecked foreigner, and there was an embarrassing moment when Kenneth, who had served some time at sea, asked about the tonnage of the wrecked ship and caught Charles out in an inconsistency.

In a few days Charles received a message from Donald MacLeod in Stornoway that he had managed to hire a ship. So on 4 May the Prince, with O'Sullivan, O'Neil and Ned Burke, set out to join him. Donald Campbell sent his son and his servant 'with a little boat' to take them to Loch Seaforth, from the head of which they intended to go on foot to Stornoway. A guide sent to show them the way got lost, and they found themselves, in O'Sullivan's words, 'in the wildest contry in the universe, nothing but moors & lochs, not a house in sight, nor the least marque of a road and path, walking all night with a continual heavy rain'. They finally reached the vicinity of Stornoway at eleven o'clock at night, after walking since daybreak, and Charles sent Donald MacLeod a message saying where they were and asking for him to send them a bottle of brandy and some bread and cheese. (This is the first mention of Charles's consumption of brandy in his wander-ings. Mention of both brandy and whisky becomes more and more frequent in eye-witness accounts of subsequent months: it was clearly his increasing use of spirits to combat the hardships he encountered in his wanderings that developed the abuse of alcohol which was to have such a sad effect on his later life.) Donald brought the desired refresh-ment and arranged for the exhausted and soaking wet Prince to stay at the house of Mrs Mackenzie of Kildun, near Stornoway. 'The Prince was in a terrible condition,' wrote O'Sullivan, 'setting aside cold & hunger without even complaining, he had not a Shoe to his feet, all tore to pieces, they held only with coards that they tyed up with, his toes were quit stript.' At Mrs Mackenzie's he found a good fire, warm milk, eggs, butter, biscuits and whisky, as well as clean straw and blankets, which enabled him to have a good sleep.

But something went wrong with the plan to get a ship at Stornoway. When Donald MacLeod returned from visiting Charles at Mrs Mackenzie's he found the town in an uproar and he himself was violently abused by a group of gentlemen who accused him of having brought 'the plague' on them – that is, the Prince, whom they had discovered to be near Stornoway and believed to have five hundred men with him. The news had come from John Macaulay, a clergyman in South Uist who had passed it to his father in Harris and he in turn had passed it to Mr Colin Mackenzie, a Presbyterian teacher in Lewis. The Mackenzies of Lewis were terrified of losing both their cattle and their lives, and wanted Charles to leave at once 'and go to the continent, or anywhere else he should think convenient'. They did not wish to harm him, but they desperately wanted to be spared the embarrassment and danger of his presence. They would not even let Donald have a pilot. He returned with the bad news to the Prince. It was necessary to leave. Mrs Mackenzie, who remained loyal and friendly, supplied a cow to be killed and only accepted payment for it on Charles's absolute insistence. She also provided meal and butter, while Donald provided brandy, sugar, tobacco and several pairs of shoes. With these provisions they set off on 6 May in Donald Campbell's boat with six boatmen, two of the original eight having 'run away from Stornoway, being frighted out of their wits at the rising of the men in arms', as Donald reported.

Charles first thought of going to Orkney, then he decided to sail across the Minch to Loch Broom on the mainland. But the boatmen flatly refused to cross the open sea, insisting that if the least gale of wind blew up they would all perish. While the argument was going on they saw two men-of-war sailing northwards up the Minch, and that ended the dispute. To avoid observation by these ships they made for the deserted island of Euirn, where they landed, and climbed a slope to observe the men-of-war. Some thought they were English, some French. The Prince vainly tried to bribe the boatmen to sail towards the ships in the guise of fishermen and find out if they were French, in which case they were to make signals. The ships sailed on out of sight, Charles and his party re-embarked and sailed southwards along the island. They then saw two more ships and to be on the safe side they put ashore on the island again. There they found a hut used by fishermen on their visits from Stornoway and plenty of cod and ling in great piles on the shore. They found an earthen pitcher left behind by the fishermen and, with the brandy and sugar they had together with water from the good springs on the island, they brewed warm punch, Charles drinking often to 'the Black Eye' by which Donald MacLeod thought he meant the French King's second daughter. (On the following 1 August, according to Patrick Grant of Glenmoriston, the Prince was heard to speak 'much to the praise of one of the daughters of the King of France' and to drink her health.) Donald also reported that the Prince spoke affectionately of the King of France and expressed his confidence in his desire to help him, but that whenever he talked on this subject he always used to add: 'A King and his Council are very different things'.

During their stay on the island of Euirn Charles tried his hand at cooking, demonstrating how to make use of butter that was much the worse for travelling and baking a cake of meal and cow's brains. They left on 10 May to return to Scalpa, but, finding that Donald Campbell had left home, they put out to sea again. They sighted a ship outside Finsbay, Harris, and in trying to escape from it came within sight of another in Loch Maddy, North Uist. On the 11th they put into Loch Uskevagh, in Benbecula, and went ashore just in time to avoid a fierce gale. On the way they had been reduced to eating a dish of meal and salt water, a new experience for Charles. However, as Donald MacLeod said, 'never any meat or drink came wrong to him, for he could take a share of every thing, be it good, bad, or indifferent, and was always chearful and contented in every condition'. Here they caught and ate crabs before being driven inland by the heavy rain to look for shelter. They found a hut belonging to a cowherd of Clanranald's and stayed there three nights. They sent one of the boatmen to inform Clanranald of their arrival, and on the 14th Clanranald arrived with wine, beer, biscuits and trout: 'never a man was welcomer, to be sure,' remarked O'Sullivan. The next day Clanranald returned home and sent the Prince some badly needed shirts, some pairs of stockings, a pair of shoes and a silver cup. The shirts were particularly welcome, as he had only three left: he had originally had six, but had given the other three to O'Sullivan and O'Neil. On the 14th a servant of Clanranald's piloted them to a little island in Loch Skiport, where he thought they would be safer, but the next day a Government man-of-war entered the Loch, and they were off again. This time the pilot brought them to Coradale in South Uist, where they lived until 5 June in 'a hut better than ordinary' and Charles diverted himself with hunting and fishing. From Coradale Charles sent Donald MacLeod in Donald Campbell's boat to the mainland, with letters to Lochiel and Murray of Broughton containing a request for information on the state of affairs and for cash and brandy. He was away for eighteen days, returning with no money (Murray saying that he had none to give, though he had a substantial sum of French gold on him) but with two ankers of brandy which he had bought with difficulty at a guinea each. He had met Lochiel and Broughton at the head of Loch Arkaig. (A number of Jacobite leaders had met at Murlaggan, near the head of Loch Arkaig, after Culloden to discuss plans. They included Lochiel, wounded in both ankles, Broughton, Glenbucket, Clanranald, Colonel John Roy Stewart, among others. Later, with the advance of the Earl of Loudoun into Lochaber, they dispersed.)

Macdonald of Boisdale, Clanranald's brother, lived only a few miles away from where Charles had taken refuge, and he sent O'Sullivan to him both for advice and to show that he had confidence in him even though Boisdale had not come out in the rising. Boisdale assured O'Sullivan that he would serve the Prince to the utmost of his power and promised to help him get a ship from Stornoway. But he would not go immediately to the Prince, on the grounds that this might discover his whereabouts. It was at this time that Charles heard of the arrival of the French ships that had picked up Sir Thomas Sheridan and others, and could not understand why they had not made some inquiry for him. Charles and Boisdale agreed on a regular correspondence (Boisdale using the name of Johnston and Charles being Sinclair), which would inform Charles of what was going on in Uist. Clanranald visited him and brought him a complete Highland outfit, of which he was badly in need as his old vest, coat and breeches were badly torn and covered with soot. 'When the Prince got on his highland Cloaths,' says O'Sullivan, 'he was quite another man. "Now," says he leping, "I only want the Itch to be a compleat highlander."' During his stay at Coradale Charles was troubled by dysentery (a 'bloody flux'), which he attributed to drinking milk. He therefore gave up milk, and stuck to water when he could not get spirits, and recovered.

On the whole Charles's period at Coradale was one of the happiest during his months as a fugitive. He shot and fished. 'His royal highness,' says Alexander Macdonald, who visited the Prince with Boisdale and others on 10 June, 'was pretty oft at his diversion through the mountain, papping down perhaps dozens in a day of muircocks and hens, with which this place abounds; for he is most dextrous at shooting all kinds of fowl upon wing, scarce ever making a miss.' He had convivial drinking sessions with a number of Macdonalds, notably Hugh Macdonald of Balshair, who has left an account of the Prince at this time. And Lady Margaret Macdonald, wife of Sir Alexander Macdonald of Sleat, had a romantic attachment to the Prince (whom she had never met) and his cause, although her husband was on the Government side, and sent him messages and newspapers by Macdonald of Balshair. Balshair's account of meeting Charles at Coradale describes his dress as 'a tartan short coat and vest of the same, got from Lady Clanranald, his night cape linen, all patched with suit [soot] drops, his shirt, hands and face patchd with the same, a short kilt, tartan hose and Highland brogs, his upper coat being English cloath'. His first action on seeing Balshair was to call for a dram, 'being the first article of a Highland entertainment'. The drink was followed by a meal, after which they settled down to a serious bout of further drinking. As conversation became 'more free', Balshair ventured to ask Charles if he would take it amiss if he told him what were the chief objections against him in Great Britain, and the Prince said 'no':

I told him that Popery and arbitrary government were the two chiefest. He said it was only bad constructions his enemys pat on't. 'Do you 'no, Mr. M'Donald,' he says, 'what religion are all the princes in Europe of?' I told him I imagin'd they were of the same establish'd religion of the nation they liv'd in. He told me then that they had litle or no religion at all. Boystill [Boisdale, who was present] then told him that his predecessor, Donald Clanranald, had fought seven sett battles for his, yet after the restauration, he was not ound by King Charles at Court. The Prince said, Boystill, Dont be rubbing up old sores, for if I cam home the case would be otherwise with me. I then says to him, that notwithstanding of what freedome wee enjoy'd there with him, wee cou'd've no access to him if he was setled at London; and told us then if he had never so much ado, he'd be one night merry with his Highland freinds. Wee continued this drinking for 3 days and 3 nights. He still had the better of us, and even of Boystill himself, notwithstanding his being as able a boulman [bowlman, i.e., drinker], I dare say, as any in Scotland.

But the net was closing. The Government authorities now knew that Charles was in South Uist. Detachments of the 'independent companies' of MacLeods and Macdonalds had landed at Barra early in June and in the middle of the month the men from Skye came to South Uist and more MacLeods landed on Benbecula and encamped near Rossinish. And all the time Government ships were patrolling the coasts. It was time for Charles to be off on his wanderings again. On 6 June he sailed for the island of Wiay (Ouia), off Benbecula, where he stayed four nights. 'From thence the Prince and O'Neil, with a guide, went to Rushness [Rossinish], where Lady Clanranald was,' as Donald MacLeod reports. 'Donald and O'Sullivan were left at Ouia, where they abode two nights after the Prince had got off to Rushness by land. The third night after the Prince had been at Rushness, he got information that it was advisable he should go back again to the place from whence he had come: but he knew not well what to do, as the boats of the militia had been all the time in the course between Ouia and Rushness.' Donald MacLeod and O'Sullivan, learning of Charles's predicament, managed to reach him at night by boat and brought him south again towards Coradale: bad weather forced them to put into Ushinish Point, two and a half miles north of Coradale, and they spent the night in a cleft in a rock, with the enemy less than two miles away. That night they sailed to Cilistiela in South Uist and on 15 June they reached Loch Boisdale in safety, only to learn that Boisdale had been taken prisoner (in spite of his not having joined the rising). Charles 'skulked' (to use the favourite word of both the Jacobites and their enemies in describing the activities of Jacobites after Culloden) by Loch Boisdale until the 20th, receiving presents of brandy and other necessaries from Lady Macdonald of Boisdale.

Government ships were everywhere. Captain Rowe in the *Baltimore* together with the *Raven* had entered Loch Boisdale on 15 June. On the 16th the *Tryal* arrived at Barra, escorting a company of Guise's Regiment commanded by Captain Caroline Scott, already notorious for his cold-blooded cruelty in hunting down Jacobites. At dawn on the 21st, as O'Sullivan vividly narrates, 'we see a man running down the hill to us as fast as it was possible to go. We go to meet him, judging there must be some thing extraordenary, as far as he cou'd see us, he makes a sign to us to go off, lookelly our tente was just down, as it was the custom every morning in those latter days. This man tells us, that all the boats of the seven men of War were coming towards the land, full of soldiers, that they were not landed when he parted from Boise-dels house, & that he did not doubt but they were informed of the place where the Prince was.' Captain Scott's men and a landing party from the *Baltimore* had landed, 700 in all, of whom 150 had been 'sent to kill Cattles' and the rest were 'chearching & rumeging for armes and the Spanish money that was said to be hid in Boisdels house'. The Prince and his companions embarked in frantic haste in order to sail up Loch Boisdale. The boatmen, in their haste to be gone, wanted to leave their provisions. ' "A Gad" sayd the Prince, "they shall never say that we were so pressed, that we abandoned our meat," & goes him self & takes a quarter of mutton & a boul of meal that was left.' As they pushed off from shore they heard shots, but they got safely up to the top of the loch. From there the only way of escape lay across the hills to the west side of South Uist. The fewer his companions the greater his chance of escape, so Charles now reluctantly took leave of O'Sullivan, Donald MacLeod, and the boatmen. O'Sullivan, according to his own account, burst into tears and the Prince embraced him ' & holds him in his arms for a quarter of an hour'. For Donald MacLeod, too, it was 'a woeful parting indeed'. The Prince paid off the boatmen – 'a shilling sterling a day, besides their maintance,' and gave Donald a draught of sixty pistols drawn on John Hay of Restalrig. (Donald was never able to present it.) 'They parted with a resolution to meet again at a certain place by different roads,' and, with Neil MacEachain as a guide, Charles and O'Neil crossed the hills to a hut near Ormaclett, about three miles from Milton.

At Milton Flora Macdonald, daughter of the deceased Macdonald of Milton, was on a visit to her brother. Her mother had married again after her first husband's death, and her second husband was another Macdonald, Hugh Macdonald of Armadale in Skye, who was now a captain in Macdonald of Sleat's independent company which was in South Uist in search of the Prince. According to O'Sullivan, Captain Macdonald 'announced his movements to friends of ours so that the Prince might always have due warning of them'. But it was his step-daughter who was Charles's real saviour. O'Neil had met Flora Macdonald before, and meeting her at Ormaclett by a happy accident he asked her if the independent companies were to pass that way the next day, as he had been informed. O'Neil himself takes up the tale:

> The young lady answered in the negative, saying they would not pass till the day after. I then told her I brought a friend to see her. She with some emotion asked if it was the Prince. I answered in the affirmative and instantly brought him in. We then consulted on the immediate danger the Prince was in, and could think of no more proper or safe place or expedient than to propose to Miss Flora to convey him to the Isle of Sky, where her mother lived. This seem'd the more feasable, as the young lady's father being captain of an independent company would afford a pass for herself and servant to go visit her mother.

Thus was proposed the famous expedient of disguising the Prince as a maid so that he could go with Flora to her home in Skye. At first

Flora was very reluctant to co-operate in such a hare-brained and dangerous scheme. But O'Neil 'remonstrated to her the honour and immortality that would redound to her by such a glorious action; and she at length acquiesced, after the Prince had told her the sense he would always retain of so conspicuous a service'. Flora herself gave her own account to Dr John Burton of York, who took it down as she spoke:

After Miss MacDonald (with some difficulty) agreed to undertake the dangerous enterprize, she set out for Clanranald's house [on the west coast of Benbecula], Saturday, June 21st, and at one of the fords was taken prisoner by a party of militia, she not having a passport. She demanded to whom they belonged? And finding by the answer that her stepfather was then commander, she refused to give any answers till she should see their captain. So she and her servant, Neil MacKechan, were prisoners all that night.

Her stepfather, coming next day, being Sunday, she told him what she was about, upon which he granted a passport for herself, a man-servant (Neil MacKechan), and another woman, Bettie Burk, a good spinster, and whom he recommended as such in a letter to his wife at Armadale in Sky, as she had much lint to spin. If her stepfather (Hugh MacDonald of Armadale) had not granted Miss a passport, she could not have undertook her journey and voyage. Armadale set his stepdaughter at liberty, who immediately made the best of her way to Clanranald's house and acquainted the Lady Clanranald with the scheme, who supplied the Prince with apparel sufficient for his disguise, viz. a flower'd gown, a white apron, etc., and sent some provisions along with him.

O'Neil tells what happened next:

She promised to acquaint us next day when things were ripe for execution, and we parted for the mountain of Corradale. Next day at 4 in the afternoon we received a message from our protectrix telling us all was well. We determined joining her immediately, but the messenger told us we could not pass any of the fords that separated the island we were in from Benbicula, as they were both guarded. In this dilemma a man of the country tended his boat to us, which we readily accepted of; and next day landed at Benbicula, and immediately marched for Rushnish, the place of our rendezvous, where we arrived at midnight, and instead of our protectrix found a guard of the enemy. We were constrain'd to retreat four miles, having eat nothing for 34 hours before.

Several changes of plan and considerable going and coming followed. Eventually Charles found a hiding place under a rock in Benbecula and then in an abandoned hut, where he was visited by Lady Clanranald and Flora, who was staying with her. Flora stayed at the Clanranald house until 27 June; during this period O'Neil went frequently between the house and the Prince's hiding place. On the morning of 28 June they heard that Major-General John Campbell of Mamore had landed with 1,500 men to join up with Captain Scott's men, making 2,300 men in all. When Lady Clanranald was visiting Charles she heard that Captain John Ferguson (an Aberdeenshire naval officer with a deep hatred of Highlanders and a justified reputation for cruelty) with an advance party of General Campbell's men were at her house and that 'Ferguson had lain in her bed the night before'. She hurried home and was cross-examined by Ferguson about where she had been. General Campbell arrived and joined in the suspicious cross-examination. Lady Clanranald insisted that she had been visiting a sick child. 'Both the General and Ferguson asked many other questions, such as where the child lived, how far it was from thence? etc., but they could make nothing out of the lady fit for their purpose.' Nevertheless, she was arrested soon afterwards, but by this time the Prince, with Flora and a number of companions, had got away.

It was on the 28th that a French cutter arrived at South Uist with the intention of taking off the Prince, not knowing that he was now 'skulking' on Benbecula. Some days later they took off O'Sullivan, who was fatigued and hungry and suffering from exposure. The cutter was pursued by a Government man-of-war from Barra and had to make for Norway, where O'Sullivan hoped to be able to find a neutral ship that would come back and search for the Prince.

The Prince and his party left as soon as they heard that General Campbell and Captain Ferguson were at the Clanranald house. They crossed Loch Uskevagh and on the north side of the loch Charles changed into his woman's clothes, to become the Irish maid Betty Burke. Flora Macdonald later told a number of people 'that when the Prince put on women's cloathes he proposed carrying a pistol under one of his petticoats for making some small defence in case of an attack. But Miss declared against it, alleging that if any person should happen to search them the pistol would serve to make a discovery. To which the Prince replied merrily: "Indeed, Miss, if we shall happen to meet with any that will go so narrowly to work in searching as what you mean they will certainly discover me at any rate."' But 'Miss' was adamant, and Charles had to do without his pistol and made do with 'a short heavy cudgel, with which he design'd to do his best to knock down any single person that should attack him'. Flora was also adamant in refusing to allow Charles to take O'Neil with him, insisting that his safety depended on his having the minimum number of people with him and saying that 'she could more easily undertake the preservation of one than of two or more'. Charles and Flora eventually sailed with five others, Neil MacEachain, John Macdonald (at the helm), Alexander Macdonald, and two other boatmen.

They set sail for Skye at eight o'clock on the evening of the 28th. Flora Macdonald told Dr Burton about the journey:

> They had not rowed from the shore above a league till the sea became rough, and at last tempestuous, and to entertain the company the Prince sung several songs and seemed to be in good spirits.
>
> In the passage Miss MacDonald fell asleep, and then the Prince carefully guarded her, lest in the darkness any of the men chance to step on her. She awaked in a surprize with some little bustle in the boat, and wondered what was the matter, etc.

She told some other friends that when she awoke she found the Prince leaning over her with his hands spread about her head, to protect her from being hurt by one of the men, who was 'obliged to do somewhat about the sail', stumbling over her in the dark. Among the songs sung by the Prince during the passage, Flora told Dr Burton, was 'The King shall enjoy his own again', the old song with which the supporters of Charles I had cheered themselves during his last troubled years and which was later sung by the supporters of the restoration of Charles II before being adopted by the Jacobite cause after 1688. We can imagine Charles singing to the sleeping Flora as their boat crossed on the turbulent waters of the Minch:

> *. . . For who better may*
> *Our high sceptre sway,*
> *Than he whose right it is to reign:*
> *Then look for no peace,*
> *For the wars will never cease*
> *Till the king shall enjoy his own again.*

Fog descended and held up their progress for a while, for they were afraid to approach the coast of Skye unawares, knowing it to be closely guarded. But soon a breeze sprang up and dispersed the fog and on the morning of the 29th they made Vaternish Point in the north-west of Skye. They sailed close to the shore, but seeing a number of armed men rushing out of a guard house and shouting at them to land at their peril, they changed course and sailed across the entrance to Loch Snizort to a point just north of Kilbride which is still called Prince Charlie's Point. As they left Vaternish Point they were fired on by the soldiers on shore, but no one was hit.

After they had landed Flora left the Prince by the boat and she set out with Neil MacEachain for the house of Sir Alexander Macdonald, whose wife Margaret had such a passion for Charles and for the Jacobite cause. Sir Alexander himself remained on the Government side; nevertheless, Charles had a special feeling for the Macdonalds and felt, as another Alexander Macdonald put it, that he was 'sure to meet with greater favour among the worst of his men than among the cold MacLeods'. But he was in fact in terrible danger. At Sir Alexander's house Flora found a Lieutenant MacLeod, an officer of militia, who was there with a number of men (and the rest of his command nearby) in search of the Prince. She had to make polite conversation with the lieutenant while Lady Macdonald conferred with Macdonald of Kingsburgh, who happened to be visiting the house at the same time and whom she knew she could trust. She also managed to send a message to Donald Roy Macdonald, brother of Macdonald of Balshair in North Uist, who was then (as one of those involved later reported) 'at a surgeon's house, two miles off, under cure of a wound he had received through his foot at the battle of Culloden'. She asked him to come to her as quickly as possible. Captain Roy Macdonald later gave his account of events to Bishop Forbes, who wrote it down:

Immediately the Captain set out upon the surgeon's horse, and when near Mouggistot [Mugstot, now Monkstadt, Sir Alexander Macdonald's house] he spied Lady Margaret and Kingsburgh walking together, and talking in a serious way, above the garden. When he came near them he dismounted, and Lady Margaret, upon seeing him, stept aside from Kingsburgh to meet the Captain and to speak with him, spreading out her hands and saying, 'O Donald Roy, we are ruined for ever.' Upon this, he asked what was the matter? Her ladyship answered that the Prince was landed about a quarter of a mile from the house, and that if he should have the misfortune to be seized there they would be affronted for ever, mentioning a circumstance that distressed her much, because it made the case the more perplexed, and made her altogether at a loss how to behave in the matter, which was that Lieutenant MacLeod was at that very instant in the dining room with Miss Flora MacDonald (she having left the Prince in women's cloaths on the spot where he had come ashore); and, which rendered the case worse and worse, that the Lieutenant had three or four of his men about the house with him, the rest of his command being only a small distance from the house, as he was

employed to guard that part of the coast of Sky, particularly to en-
quire at every boat that should come from the Long Isle if there
were any rebels on board, etc. Kingsburgh coming directly up to
them, they began to project what was fittest to be done, all of them
agreeing that Lieutenant MacLeod's presence, with the whole of
his command so near, threw a number of difficulties in their way, and
made the case full of dangers, if not desperate.

They considered many alternative courses of action, but 'all choices
were bad, the Prince's situation having a most dismal aspect'. At
length Captain Roy Macdonald suggested that the best course would be
for the Prince to go overland the fifteen miles or so to Portree, on the
other side of Skye, and from there to cross the Sound of Raasay to the
island of Raasay where he might seek protection from MacLeod of
Raasay, known to be a devoted Jacobite. This was agreed, and Kingsburgh sent Neil MacEachain to bring Charles (who was still on the
shore) to an agreed place at the back of a hill about a mile from Mugstot.
There Kingsburgh eventually joined them and took the Prince to his
house. Flora caught up with them on the way. Bishop Forbes later
collected an account of what happened from Kingsburgh, Flora
Macdonald and others.

When the Prince came to Kingsburgh's house (Sunday, June 29th)
it was between ten and eleven at night; and Mrs. Macdonald [Kings-
burgh's wife], not expecting to see her husband that night was making
ready to go to bed. One of her servant maids came and told her
that Kingsburgh was come home and had brought some company
with him 'What company?' says Mrs. MacDonald. 'Milton's
daughter, I believe,' says the maid, 'and some company with her.'
'Milton's daughter [i.e. Flora, whose father, in Scottish style, is here
called by the name of the property he owned],' replies Mrs. Mac-
Donald, 'is very welcome to come here with any company she
pleases to bring. But you'll give my service to her, and tell her to
make free with anything in the house; for I am very sleepy and cannot see her this night.' In a little her own daughter came and told
her in a surprize 'O mother, my father has brought in a very odd,
muckle, ill-shaken-up wife as ever I saw! I never saw the like of her,
and he has gone into the hall with her.' She had scarce done telling
her tale when Kingsburgh came and desired his lady to fasten on her
bucklings again, and to get some supper for him and the company he
had brought with him. 'Pray, goodman,' says she, 'what company is
this you have brought with you?' 'Why, goodwife,' said he, 'you
shall know that in due time; only make haste and get some supper in
the meantime.' [Mrs Macdonald asks her daughter to fetch her the

keys, but the daughter says she is too frightened of 'the muckle woman walking up and down in the hall'.] Mrs. MacDonald went herself to get the keys, and I heard her more than once declare that upon looking in at the door she had not the courage to go forward. 'For,' said she, 'I saw such an odd muckle trallup of a carlin, making lang wide steps through the hall that I could not like her appearance at all.' Mrs. MacDonald called Kingsburgh, and very seriously begged to know what a lang, odd hussie was this he had brought to the house; for that she was so frighted at the sight of her that she could not go into the hall for her keys. 'Did you never see a woman before,' said he, 'goodwife? What frights you at seeing a woman? Pray, make haste, and get us some supper.' ... When she entered the hall, the Prince happen'd to be sitting; but immediately he arose, went forward and saluted Mrs MacDonald, who, feeling a long stiff beard, trembled to think that this behoved to be some distressed nobleman or gentleman in disguise, for she never dream'd it to be the Prince, though all along she had been seized with a dread she could not account for from the monent she had heard that Kingsburgh had brought company with him.... Immediately she importun'd Kingsburgh to tell her who the person was, ... Kingsburgh smiled at mention of the bearded kiss, and said; 'Why, my dear, it is the Prince. You have the honour to have him in your house.' 'The Prince,' cried she. 'O Lord, we are a' ruin'd and undone for ever! We will a' be hang'd now!' 'Hout, goodwife,' says the honest stout soul, 'we will die but ance; and if we are hanged for this, I am sure we die in a good cause. Pray, make no delay; go, get some supper....

Mrs Macdonald protested that she had nothing but eggs and butter and cheese, to which Kingsburgh replied that that was better fare than the Prince had had for some time. Charles in fact enjoyed his supper, and called for a dram afterwards, 'for,' said he, 'I have learn'd in my skulking to take a hearty dram'. He then took out a cracked and broken pipe wrapped about with thread and asked Kingsburgh if he could have some tobacco, for he had also learned to smoke in his wanderings. Kingsburgh took the broken pipe from him to keep as a souvenir and gave him a new one together with a supply of tobacco. They spent a convivial evening. 'Kingsburgh became so merry and jocose that putting up his hand to the Prince's face, he turned off his head-dress which was a very old clout of a mutch or toy; upon which Mrs MacDonald hasted out of the room and brought a clean nightcap for him.'

Charles lay late the next morning, and Flora was in an agony of anxiety lest he should not get away in time. At last they got him up. Kingsburgh – in his own account, given to Bishop Forbes – 'was at pains to represent to the Prince the inconveniency and danger of his being in female dress, particularly from his airs being all so man-like, and told him that he was very bad at acting the part of a dissembler. He advised him therefore to take from him a suite of Highland cloaths with a broadsword in his hand, which would become him much better'. However, he thought it wiser that he should leave the house in his woman's clothes 'lest the servants should be making their observations' and change when he got to the edge of a wood. Mrs Macdonald got her daughter to help the Prince dress as Betty Burke for the last time.

> When Miss MacDonald ... was a dressing of him, he was like to fall over with laughing. After the peeness, gown, hood, mantle, etc., were put on, he said, 'O, Miss, you have forgot my apron. Where is my apron? Pray get me my apron here, for that is a principal part of my dress.'
> Kingsburgh and his lady both declared that the Prince behaved not like one that was in danger, but as chearfully and merrily as if he had been putting on women's cloathes merely for a piece of diversion.

In July 1747 Bishop Forbes asked Kingsburgh a number of questions about Charles's behaviour while he was with him in Skye. He reported some of the difficulties the Prince had with his female costume:

> Asked further. If it was true that the Prince lifted the petticoats too high in wading the rivulet when going to Kingsburgh, and that honest MacKechan hastily called to him to beware? He said, 'It is a fact; and that MacKechan cried, 'For God's sake, Sir, take care what you are doing, for you will certainly discover yourself;' and that the Prince laughed heartily, and thanked him kindly for his great concern.'

Patrick Grant, who was with Charles in Glenmoriston in the latter part of July, made it clear in a conversation with Bishop Forbes in October 1751 that the Prince when in Highland dress wore nothing under his kilt. The whole passage is of interest:

> Patrick Grant remarked that the Prince walked so nimbly in the daytime that few persons could keep up with him. But then he was as bad at it in the night time, for, not being used with such rough and plashy footing as is commonly to be found in the hills, braes, and glens of the Highlands of Scotland, he was every now and then (through the darkness of the nights) slumping into this and the other clayhole or puddle, insomuch that very often he would have been

plashed up to the navel, having no breeches, but a philabeg [kilt], and when he had arrived at any place to take a little rest, he would have taken a nook of his plaid and therewith have rubbed his belly and thighs to clean them the best way he could.

Charles duly changed into Highland clothes at the edge of the wood and then took a sad farewell of Kingsburgh. He wept, and his nose bled, which alarmed Kingsburgh, but Charles reassured him. 'Alas! Kingsburgh, I am afraid I shall not meet with another Macdonald in my difficulties,' were the Prince's last words to his loyal host. Soon afterwards Captain Ferguson came to Kingsburgh's house, and after cross-examining both Kingsburgh and his wife and daughter took him and his daughter away as prisoners.

Charles went on foot with Neil MacEachain and a guide provided by Kingsburgh to Portree, where Flora also went, on horseback, by a different path. At Portree he took leave of his preserver. Flora, in the account of her adventures which she gave Bishop Forbes, says nothing of any emotional scene on this occasion – in striking contrast to the accounts given by several of the Prince's male companions on the occasion of their parting with him: we remember, for example, O'Sullivan's loud weeping and long embrace. Flora was a hard-headed and highly competent young woman who managed her part of the affair very successfully. There was no suspicion of a romance between her and the Prince. O'Neil is the one who seems to have been a bit in love with her. Flora was arrested on her way back to her home in Armadale and taken on board Captain Ferguson's sloop, the *Furnace* – though fortunately General Campbell was there at the time and saw that she was treated with the 'utmost respect'. She was taken to London and imprisoned in the Tower, but was released under the Act of Indemnity of 1747. She married Allan Macdonald in 1750, and in 1774 they emigrated to North Carolina. But they returned to Skye in 1779, disapproving of the revolt of the American colonies. She was twenty-four years old at the time of her adventure with the Prince. Their association lasted in all no more than twelve days.

While Charles was with Kingsburgh, Donald Roy Macdonald was in Portree trying to get in touch with one or more of the sons of MacLeod of Raasay, so that he could find out where their father was. He was able to find the eldest son John and the third son Murdoch (who had been wounded at Culloden), and it was with these two, together with Captain Malcolm MacLeod, second cousin of MacLeod of Raasay, and two boatmen, John Mackenzie and Donald MacFrier, that the Prince crossed the few miles to Raasay in a small boat on 1 July. They stayed two days on the island, where they found the houses burned by Government troops and the whole island too narrow and confined for safety. Charles insisted on returning to Skye, so back they went on the evening of the 2nd. Malcolm MacLeod tells what happened:

> They had not well left the shore till the wind blew a hard gale, and the sea became so very rough and tempestuous that all on board begged he would return; for the waves were beating over and over them, the men tugging hard at the oars, and Captain MacLeod laving the water out of the little boat. The Prince would by no means hear of returning, and to divert the men from thinking on the danger he sung them a merry Highland song. About nine or ten o'clock the same night they landed at a place in Sky called Nicolson's Rock, near Scorobreck, in Troternish. In rowing along they found the coast very bad and dangerous, and when they came to the Rock the Prince was the third man that jump'd out among the water and cried out, 'Take care of the boat, and hawl her up to dry ground,' which was immediately done, he himself assisting as much as any one of them. The Prince had upon him a large big coat, which was become very heavy and cumbersome by the waves beating so much upon it, for it was wet through and through. . . . They went forwards to a cow-byre on the rock, about two miles from Scorobreck, a gentleman's house. In this byre the Prince took up his quarters, . . . Here they took some little refreshment of bread and cheese they had along with them, the cakes being mouldered down into very small crumbs.

Charles wanted to go south on Skye to Strathaird, the Mackinnon country, and he asked Malcolm MacLeod to be his guide. MacLeod tried in vain to persuade him to go by sea, which would be safer, but he insisted on going by land, though it was a journey of nearly twenty miles over extremely rough country, and considerably longer than that by the indirect routes they would have to follow for the sake of safety. They set out on the night of the 3rd, in spite of Captain MacLeod's warning that if they travelled by night they might 'fall into dangers and inconveniences for want of knowing well where they were.' 'The Prince,' as MacLeod reports, 'proposed to pass for the Captain's servant, the better to conceal him, and that he should be named Lewie Caw, there being of that name a young surgeon lad (who had been in the Prince's service) skulking at that time in Sky, where he had some relations. The Captain advised the Prince, since he had proposed being his servant, to walk at some distance behind him; and if at any time he happened to meet with any persons and to converse with them, as he was well known in the island, that the Prince should show no concern on his face, but sit down at a small distance, when he should happen to talk with any folks'. This Charles readily agreed to do. It was an arduous journey. Captain MacLeod gives some vivid details:

> The Captain, happening to see the Prince uneasy and fidging, took him to the back of a know [hillock], and opening his breast, saw him troubled with lice for want of clean linen, and by reason of the coarse odd way he behoved to live in, both as to sustenance and sleep. He said, he believed, he took fourscore off him. .... He used to say that the fatigues and distresses he underwent signified nothing at all, because he was only a single person; but when he reflected upon the many brave fellows who suffered in his cause, that, he behoved to own, did strike him to the heart, and did sink very deep with him.

MacLeod and the Prince had an argument about drinking cold water when he was hot. Charles denied that it would do him any harm, adding: 'If you happen to drink any cold thing when you are warm, only remember, MacLeod, to piss after drinking, and it will do you no harm at all. This advice I had from a friend abroad'. MacLeod says that 'the Prince was always sure to observe this direction'. Among the other remarks MacLeod reported as having been made to him by Charles on this journey was this: 'MacLeod, do you not think that God Almighty has made this person of mine for doing some good yet? When I was in Italy, and dining at the king's table, very often the sweat would have been coming through my coat with the heat of the climate; and now that I am in a cold country, of a more piercing and trying climate, and exposed to different kinds of fatigues, I really find I agree equally with both. I have had this philibeg on now for some days, and I find I do as well with it as any the best breeches I ever put on. I hope in God, MacLeod, to walk the streets of London with it yet.'

When they were approaching Strathaird, MacLeod suggested that the Prince had better disguise himself now that he was coming to a region where he was known, since Mackinnon and his men had been out in his service. Charles suggested blacking his face, but MacLeod reasonably objected that this would be more likely to arouse suspicion than to dispel it. 'The Prince then pulling off the periwig and putting it into his pocket took out a dirty white napkin and desired the Captain to tye that about his head, and to bring it down upon his eyes and nose. He put the bonnet on above the napkin and said, "I think I will now pass well enough for your servant, and that I am sick with the much fatigue I have undergone".' But MacLeod insisted on still further disguise, because the Prince had such a distinctive face and was incapable of 'dissembling his air'.

In Strathaird they ran into two of Mackinnon's men who had been out in the rising: they recognized Charles, and 'wept bitterly to see him in such a pickle'. MacLeod warned them to keep quiet before parting with them. His aim was to bring the Prince to the house of his brother-in-law, Captain John Mackinnon. When he arrived there, leaving the Prince at a little distance, he found that John Mackinnon was not at home, but his wife, Malcolm MacLeod's sister, assured him 'that no party she knew of was in that corner' and invited him, together with 'Lewie Caw', to stay. On Mackinnon's return home, MacLeod told him the true identity of Lewie Caw, making Mackinnon promise not to reveal his knowledge by any special treatment of him. 'But he was no sooner entred the house than he could not hold his eyes from staring on Lewie, and very soon he was forced to turn his face away from the Prince and to weep.' The Prince played with the Mackinnons' little boy Neil, 'carrying him in his arms and singing to him, and said, "I hope this child may be a captain in my service yet".'

The problem now was to get a boat to take Charles to the mainland. The islands were altogether too dangerous, and were being searched. (It had been, in fact, a mistake to leave the mainland in the first place. It was much easier to avoid discovery on the mainland than in Uist, Skye or Raasay.) The old Laird of Mackinnon himself promised to bring his boat, and Malcolm MacLeod now proposed, since the Prince had met old Mackinnon, that he (Mackinnon) should be in charge of all further operations while MacLeod himself returned to his own people to avoid suspicion. Charles agreed to MacLeod's departure with the greatest reluctance. They parted at Elgol, from where the Prince sailed for the mainland. Malcolm MacLeod tells what happened:

When the Prince was about stepping into the boat, about 8 or 9 at night [on 4 July], he turned to Malcolm and said, 'Don't you remember I promised to meet Murdoch MacLeod at such a place?' 'No matter,' said Malcolm, 'I shall make your apology.' 'That's not enough,' said the Prince. 'Have you paper, pen and ink upon you MacLeod? I'll write him a few lines. I'm obliged so to do in good manners.' Accordingly he wrote him the following words:

'Sir, – I thank God I am in good health, and have got off as design'd. Remember me to all friends, and thank them for the trouble they have been at. – I am, Sir, Your humble servant,

JAMES THOMSON

Elliguil, July 4th, 1746.'

(The text of the letter as we have it is clearly not in Charles's own spelling. Slightly differing versions exist.)

Before finally parting with Malcolm Charles gave him the letter and then asked him for a light for his pipe, for he intended to smoke on his voyage across to the mainland. 'Malcolm took some tow out of his pocket, and snapping one of the guns held the tow to the pan and kindled it. Then putting it to the mouth of the pipe he blew and the Prince smok'd. But the cuttie being exceedingly short, Malcolm scarred the Prince's cheek with the tow.' The Prince presented Malcolm with a silver buckle and ten guineas, the latter of which he had great difficulty in making him accept. Malcolm made his way back to Raasay, where parties of Government troops had landed and were 'rummaging' the island. He was eventually captured by a party of MacLeods loyal to the Government, taken to Portree, sent to Edinburgh on the sloop 'commanded by that cruel, barbarous man, John Ferguson of Aberdeenshire,' and acquitted himself so adroitly at his subsequent interrogation that no one could prove anything against him and he was freed on 4 July 1747 (exactly a year after parting from the Prince), under the Act of Indemnity of that year.

The next morning Charles and the Laird of Mackinnon, with John Mackinnon and four boatmen, reached the south shore of Loch Nevis, a sea loch which lies between North Morar and Knoydart on the mainland. They spent three nights in the open, and then rowed up the loch along the coast. They were challenged by a party of militia on shore, who ordered them ashore, but they refused to obey and were pursued by five men in a boat, whom they managed to out-row. They crossed the loch and landed on the north side, where they climbed a hill to reconnoitre and saw the boatload of militia returning from their unsuccessful pursuit. After Charles had slept for three hours on the hill they came down again, re-embarked and crossed to the south side of the loch, landing near Mallaig. They then set out for the house of Macdonald of Morar, some seven or eight miles away. They arrived at Morar's house just before dawn the next day, but the house had been burned by Captain Ferguson and Morar was living with his family in a little hut. His wife, who was Lochiel's daughter, recognized Charles at once, and met him with a flood of tears and some warmed-up cold salmon. Morar led the travellers to a nearby cave and then went to look for young Clanranald, to whom he was related, but he returned without having found him. At this point it was decided that old Mackinnon should return home, so he set off accordingly, only to be taken prisoner on the way (he was released in 1747). Charles, together with John Mackinnon and a young local guide provided by Morar, moved on south to the house of Angus Macdonald of Borrodale where he had stayed on his very first landing on the mainland and which seemed to have some special fascination for him. He found that his house too had been burned by Captain Ferguson and Angus Macdonald was living with two men in a nearby hut. John Mackinnon formally committed the Prince to Angus Macdonald's care and returned to the boat to sail for home, only to be taken prisoner near Elgol by a party of militia (he too remained a prisoner until July 1747).

Charles stayed at Borrodale with Angus Macdonald from the 10th to the 16th of July. From there he sent a letter by Angus's son John to Alexander Macdonald of Glenaladale asking him to come to Borrodale and discuss future plans. Then, hearing of the capture of old Mackinnon, he moved four miles eastward to an inaccessible cave where, with Angus Macdonald and another son of his called Ranald, he awaited the arrival of Glenaladale. Glenaladale arrived on the night of the 15th. The next day, Angus Macdonald having received a letter from his son-in-law saying that rumours of the Prince's presence there were circulating, they prepared to find another refuge. Angus Macdonald's son-in-law had prepared a hiding-place between Loch Eilt and Loch Beoraid, and there they went. As soon as they had arrived there they received information that General Campbell, with six men-of-war and a large body of troops, had anchored in Loch Nevis. They sent two men to Loch Nevis to observe General Campbell's movements, but before they could return they learned that Captain Scott was in the lower part of Arisaig. At this point the story is taken up by young Clanranald:

His royal highness and the small company that was with him, finding upon this information that Clanranald's country was surrounded on all sides by the troops, and that in all probability there could be no further security for his person in that country, it was resolved that his royal highness should leave it with the utmost dispatch, especially since it was impossible to join young Clanranald, the enemy being already between them and the place where he was. Accordingly he sets out, accompanied only by Major MacDonald of Glenaladale and his brother (Lieutenant John MacDonald), and the other Lieutenant John MacDonald, junior, Boradale's son, being obliged to part with Angus MacDonald of Boradale, and his son-in law (Angus MacEachine), ... that they might the more easily pass undiscovered by the guards on their way, and by twelve o'clock [on the 18th] they came to the top of a hill in the outmost bounds of

Arisaig called Scoorvuy, where having taken some refreshment it was thought proper to send Lieutenant John MacDonald (Glenaladale's brother) to Glenfinin, the outmost bounds of Clanranald's country, and Major MacDonald of Glenaladale's property, as well for intelligence as to bring two men Glenaladale kept still on guard there, and appointed them to meet him about ten o'clock at night on the top of a hill, above Locharkaig in Lochiel's country, called Scoorwick Corrichan [this must be the mountain Sgor nan Coireachan, which looks down over Glen Dessary and Loch Arkaig from the west: it is over 3,000 feet high, yet they apparently arranged to meet at the top of it].

Making for the rendezvous, Charles and his companions came to the mountain Fraoch Cuirn, which they climbed, in order to see what was happening in the neighbourhood. They saw cattle in motion, and Major Macdonald of Glenaladale went to see what this meant. He discovered 'some of his own tenants removing with their cattle from the troops, who by this time, to the number of five or seven hundred, had come to the head of Locharkaig, in order to inclose his royal highness in Clanranald's country, while the search was going on very narrowly within it'. This meant that they had to alter their course. They sent a messenger to Glenfinnan, who returned with word that a hundred of the Argyllshire militia were at the foot of the very hill where they then were. They set out northwards without waiting for their promised guide, Donald Cameron of Glenpean, but luckily they ran into him late that night. Marching over mountainous country at night, with the enemy's camp-fires visible everywhere 'without the help of a prospective glass', they pushed on towards the head of Loch Hourn. The enemy camps were 'in a direct line pitched from the head of the Lochiel in Lochiel's country to the head of Loch Uirn [Hourn], dividing Knoydart of that part of MacLeod's country called Glenealg'. These camps were 'within half a mile's distance of one another, their sentries being placed within call of one another, and patrols going about every quarter of an hour to keep their sentries alert, that so his royal highness might be surely catched should he attempt to pass through them'.

They had several very narrow escapes. Hiding during the day, they moved at night. At the top of the mountain Druim Chosaidh, west of Loch Quoich and south of Loch Hourn, 'they observed the fires of a camp directly in their front, which they could scarcely shun,' at Glen Cosaidh. 'However, being resolved to pass at any rate, they came so near without being observed as to hear them talk distinctly; and ascending the next hill, no sooner was his royal highness at the top than he and his small party spied the fires of another camp at the very foot where they were to descend. But turning a little westward they passed between two of their guards betwixt one and two o'clock in the morning of July 26th [actually, 21st].' They had escaped the net. Major Macdonald of Glenaladale later recorded a critical moment on this day:

... we were climbing up the hill immediately above the camp, the night being very dark and the hill very steep. Donald Cameron being guide was foremost, the Prince was after him, and I followed in his rear, and my brother and cousine after me, and crossing a small rivulet that gushed out of a spring, as I think, and glyded over a precipis att the very place we crossed it, Donald Cameron crossed first, the Prince next, and in crossing, missed a step, and 'tis altogether probable he would fall down the precipis, which we took to be very high, if he had not been very full of life, and that I caught hold of one arm and Donald Cameron of the other and recovered him in a tryce.

They pushed on northwards towards Glen Shiel, 'Seaforth's country,' where they ran into a Glengarry man 'who that morning had been chased by troops (they having killed his father the day before) from Glengary to Glensheil'. Major Macdonald of Glenaladale knew him, and they decided to employ him as a guide since Donald Cameron had to return 'to take care of his wife and weans'. The intention had been to push north to Poolewe, where they had heard that some French vessels had been seen. But then they heard that there had been only one French ship, and it had already come and gone. A change of course was therefore planned, southwards to join Lochiel, and it was on this course that the Glengarry man would be able to guide them. It was while these matters were being discussed that Charles and his companions escaped capture by a fortunate accident. Having set off, as usual, late at night, Glenaladale suddenly missed his purse and went back with John Macdonald (Borrodale's son) to look for it. They found it a quarter of a mile back, but the gold which he had received from the Prince was missing. They reflected that it might have been stolen by a little boy who had been sent by one Gilchrist MacCrath (with whom they had lodged the night before) to bring them milk, so they went back more than a mile to MacCrath's house 'and intreated him to oblige the boy to restore the purse, which he did to a trifle. They returned by a different road from what they had gone before, and came to the Prince, who was in great pain for them, fearing they might have been intercepted by an officer and two private men that pass'd under arms by the place where his royal highness was in their absence;

which made him reflect how much the hand of Providence guided him in all his ways, and particularly in this late lucky accident of losing the purse, which stopped them in their progress: whereas if they had pursued their journey they would inevitably have fallen in with these persons, in which case any thinking person may easily judge how fatal the consequence of such a meeting might have proved.'

In the event, they moved east, not south, from Glen Shiel to Glen Cluanie, then struck north from the western end of Loch Cluanie across wild mountainous country to the western end of Loch Affric before turning east along the northern shore of Loch Affric and through Glen Affric to Strath Glass where they turned north to climb Beinn Acharain. This was the most northerly point they reached, on 4 August. Before reaching Beinn Acharain, while they were on the slopes above Loch Cluanie, they came to the cave of Coir a' Chait, which lies in the high pass between the mountains of Garbh Leac on the west and Sgurr nan Conbhairean on the east (both over 3,600 feet). There they found the famous Glenmoriston men – John Macdonald, Alexander Macdonald, Alexander Chisholm, Donald Chisholm and his brother Hugh, Gregor Macgregor, Patrick Grant and Hugh Macmillan – living in the cave in a somewhat Robin Hood manner, raiding and plundering military parties when they got the opportunity. They welcomed the Prince and, in Alexander Macdonald's account, 'making a bed for him, his royal highness was lulled asleep with the sweet murmurs of the finest purling stream that could be, running by his bedside, within the grotto, in which romantic habitation his royal highness pass'd threedays [24th to 27th of July], at the end of which he was so well refreshed that he thought himself able to encounter any hardships'. He left on 28 July, accompanied by the Glenmoriston men, for another cave, where they spent four days. But, in Glenaladale's words, 'being informed that one Campbell (factor to Seaforth in Kintale, and captain at that time of a company of militia) had gathered a throng herdship of cattle and pitched his camp within four miles of them, it was then resolved his royal highness should remove his quarters'. So they moved north again. It was while he was in the mountainous country north and west of Strath Glass that Charles awaited the return of a further express he had sent to Poolewe, and received confirmation that the only French ship that had been there had come and gone. (There is some conflict among contemporary sources as to when Charles first learned this and there is accordingly some doubt as to the precise motivation of the change of course he decided on 23 July.) There seemed no point now in pushing further north, especially as they now learned from their spies that the

Government troops had returned to their camp at Fort Augustus so that there was now a chance of crossing the Great Glen and joining Lochiel in Badenoch.

So, still with the Glenmoriston men, they came south again across Glen Affric and by 12 August were at the western end of Glenmoriston. On 14 August they reached the swollen River Garry in heavy rain. 'Two of the company went first to try if they could wade the water, and they found it passable, even though it came up to their very middle. Whereupon, his royal highness and the rest of his party entering the water, they forded it safely, and, travelling about a mile from the water of Gary, the night being very dark, they were obliged to pass it on the side of a hill, without any cover, though it rained excessively.' The next day, still in heavy rain, they crossed the hills to the slopes above Achnasaul at the north-eastern end of Loch Arkaig, where they had arranged to meet messengers they had sent out. 'There' (it is still Glenaladale's account) 'they pass'd the day in a most inconvenient habitation, it raining within as without it. Towards the afternoon they began to despair of their expresses, and, being entirely run out of provisions of any kind and being quite strangers to the situation in Lochiel's country for the present, they began to concert what should be done, when, in the midst of their concert, the expresses came to them and brought word to the Major [Glenaladale] that Cameron of Cluns could not wait upon him that night, but had directed him to lodge all night in a certain wood within two miles of them, where he would come to them next morning.' They went to the place indicated, and, one of the Glenmoriston men having shot a large deer, feasted there 'most deliciously'. Charles sent a message to Macdonald of Lochgarry, who joined them that evening.

Just over two miles away, on the other side of the River Arkaig, was Achnacarry, the seat of Lochiel, whom Charles was hoping to meet. But they found that Achnacarry House had been burned down, and Lochiel was 'skulking' some twenty miles away, equally anxious to get news of the Prince. Hearing that Charles was by Loch Arkaig, Lochiel sent his brother Dr Archibald Cameron and Mr John Cameron, formerly Presbyterian chaplain at Fort William, to seek him out. Charles's messenger to Lochiel met Lochiel's messengers soon after they had set out, and also ran into two French officers who were looking for the Prince. Charles's messenger would not reveal his master's whereabouts to anyone but Lochiel, but he did tell Dr Cameron that he had 'business of the utmost consequence'. Dr Cameron brought the messenger, together with the two French officers, to Lochiel, and the next day Lochiel sent his brother to Charles. John Cameron met them on the way, and accompanied them to the small hut where the Prince was staying. He has left a description of how Charles looked: 'He was then bare-footed, had an old black kilt coat on, a plaid, phila-beg and waistcoat, a dirty shirt and a long red beard, a gun in his hand, a pistol and durk by his side. He was very cheerful and in good health, and, in my opinion, fatter than when he was at Inverness'.

Charles was anxious to go to Lochiel, but he had learned from the newspapers that the Government troops were looking for him in the region where Lochiel was, so he decided to stay where he was for a few days. Macdonald of Lochgarry and Dr Cameron returned to Lochiel, and Glenaladale and the faithful Glenmoriston men also left. The Prince stayed in his hut with the sons of Cameron of Clunes and after a few days John Cameron went with them to Clunes (less than two miles east of Loch Arkaig, near the shore of Loch Lochy) to seek intelligence.

John Cameron has left a vivid account of the kind of life Charles led throughout this period of his wanderings – sleeping rough, eating and drinking when he could, always on the alert for red-coats. He stayed in the region of Loch Arkaig altogether from the 17th to 27th of August, and then received a message from Lochiel that he would be safe where Lochiel himself was 'skulking', in Badenoch. So he set off for Badenoch on the 27th, with Lochgarry and Dr Archibald Cameron who had come to guide him and accompanied by John Cameron, Clunes's son Sandy, and three servants. It was a tough journey, and they travelled, as usual, at night. Their route took them north-east parallel to the south side of Loch Lochy and south-east of Loch Oich to the Pass of Corrie-yairack, then south across a shoulder of Creag Meaghaidh (3,700 feet) to the west end of Loch Laggan, then south again across Ben Alder Forest to a spot below Ben Alder overlooking Loch Ericht. The next day Charles was taken to Meall Mor a few miles away where he finally met Lochiel, still lame from his wound at Culloden. Donald Macpher-son, Cluny Macpherson's youngest brother, who was present at the meeting (which took place probably on 3 September) later gave an account of it:

The joy at the meeting was certainly very great and much easier to be conceived than express'd. However, such was his Royal Highness circumspection that when the other would have kneeld at his coming up to him he said, 'Oh! no, my dear Locheil,' claping him on the shoulder, 'you don't know who may be looking from the tops of yonder hills, and if they see any such motions they'll immediately

conclude that I am here, which may prove of bad consequence.'
Locheil then ushered him into his habitation which was indeed but
a very poor one as to the accomodation and make.

The Prince was 'gay, hearty, and in better spirits than it was possible
to think he could be,' and joined merrily in the feast that had been
prepared for him – 'with plenty of mutton newly killed, and an anker
of whiskie of twenty Scotch pints, with some good beef sassers made
the year before, and plenty of butter and cheese, and besides, a large
well cured bacon ham; provisions formerly laid in for Locheil by Mac-
Pherson of Breackachie, younger'. Donald Macpherson's account
continues:

> Upon his entry he took a hearty dram, which he pretty often called
> for thereafter to drink his friends healths; and when there were some
> minch'd collops dress'd with butter for him in a large sawce pan
> that Locheil and Cluny carried always about with 'em, which was
> all the fire vessels they had, he eat heartily, and said with a very
> chearful and lively countenance, 'Now, gentlemen, I leive like a
> Prince,' tho' at the same time he was no otherwise served than by
> eating his collops out of the sawce pan, only that he had a silver
> spoon.

Charles stayed two days with Lochiel, and then, Cluny Macpherson
having joined them, he took him to a place above the Alder Water
(Uisge Aulder) 'where the hut or bothie was superlatively bad or
smockie'. After two or possibly three nights there he was taken by
Cluny to his own extraordinary 'cage' further up Ben Alder. Cluny's
house had been burned in June by Government forces, and, in the words
of Captain John Macpherson of Strathmashie, 'they burnt not only the
house itself with such office-houses as were near it, but all the houses
that they apprehended belonged to it at a good distance from it. It was
a most pretty, regular, well-contrived house as any benorth the river of
Tay: double, built in the new way, only about two years before,
pavilion roof'd with two pretty pavillions joined to it by colonades,
and consisted of eighteen rooms'. By contrast, he was now living in
accommodation described by Donald Macpherson:

> It was really a curiosity, and can scarcely be described to perfection.
> 'Twas situate in the face of a very rough high rockie mountain
> called Letternilichk, which is still a part of Benalder, full of great
> stones and crevices and some scattered wood interspersed. The
> habitation called the *Cage* in the face of that mountain was within a
> small thick bush of wood. There were first some rows of trees laid

down in order to level a floor for the habitation, and as the place was steep this rais'd the lower side to equall height with the other; and these trees, in the way of jests or planks, were entirely well levelled with earth and gravel. There were betwixt the trees, growing naturally on their own roots, some stakes fixed in the earth, which with the trees were interwoven with ropes made of heath and birch twigs all to the top of the Cage, it being of a round or rather oval shape, and the whole thatched or rather covered over with foge [moss]. This whole fabrick hung as it were by a large tree, which reclined from the one end all along the roof to the other, and which gave it the name of the Cage; and by chance there happen'd to be two stones at a small distance from other in the side next the precipice resembling the pillars of a bosom chimney, and here was the fire placed. The smock [smoke] had its vent out there, all along a very stonny plat of the rock, which and the smock were all together so much of a colour that any one could make no difference in the clearest day, the smock and stones by and through which it pass'd being of such true and real resemblance. The Cage was no larger than to contain six or seven persons, four of which number were frequently employed in playing at cards, one idle looking on, one becking, and another firing bread and cooking.

Donald Macpherson the younger of Breackachie in Badenoch, who described himself as having been 'provisor for the Prince during the time of his skulking in Badenoch', later told Bishop Forbes some interesting details of Charles's stay there – which was not 'between two and three weeks' as Breackachie said, but from the 2nd to the 13th of September. He said that although during this period the Prince was about ten miles from Lord Loudoun's army, yet his presence in Badenoch was never suspected. 'Lochiel had been crippling about in his wounds for several months in Badenoch,' he said, 'and it was known to several Macphersons that Cluny, Lochiel, Dr. Cameron, etc., were together in Badenoch, but then these Macpherson's never once hinted to any person that they knew of any such thing; and when the Prince came to Cluny and Lochiel in Badenoch, it was known to none but to themselves and those that were with them; even the foresaid Macphersons never once suspecting that the Prince had ever come down the country to Cluny, Lochiel, etc. None were admitted to see Cluny, Lochiel, etc., but young Breakachie and any such as they themselves ordered or allowed him to introduce to them.' Breackachie said that Cluny was preparing to make an elaborate 'subtarrenean house' as winter quarters for the Prince when news came of the arrival of two French ships on the west coast, 'to which ships the Prince travelled on foot, being about

100 English miles, even though at that very time he was troubled with a looseness or flux'.

At first there was a plan to send Breackachie and John Roy Stewart to the east coast to hire a ship there that would take off the Prince, Lochiel, Cluny and their immediate companions. Then news came of the French ships in the west. What had happened was that after much activity by the Prince's friends in France and a series of unsuccessful attempts on the part of a number of French ships to reach Scotland and find the Prince, two St Malo privateers, *L'Heureux* of thirty-four guns and *Le Prince de Conti* of thirty guns, entered Loch Boisdale in South Uist in the afternoon of 4 September and sent their boats ashore with armed parties to question people about the Prince's whereabouts. But they found no one. They continued to land men and make inquiries the next day, and found a number of inhabitants whom they told of their intentions. One of these was the same Captain Macdonald of Clanranald's regiment who had been in the eight-oared boat in which the Prince had crossed to Benbecula from the mainland on the night of 26 April, and he offered to come on board and serve as pilot. Macdonald piloted the ships across the Minch to Loch nan Uamh, a route familiar enough by now in Jacobite story, and they lay in the loch from the 6th to the 19th of September. While there they boarded the small Glasgow ship the *May*, which was sheltering in the loch, and took her captain and crew prisoner. The master of the *May* had mistaken the two French ships for English men-of-war. They were flying British colours, which at first frightened off John Macdonald of Borrodale and other Jacobites waiting on the shore. But eventually contact was made with the Prince through Cameron of Clunes who sent one John Macpherson alias John McColvain to find Cluny; Macpherson had the good fortune to run into Cluny and Dr Cameron on the way from the Cage to Loch Arkaig on some private business (perhaps to do with gold hidden there). Cluny immediately provided a guide to take John Macpherson to the Cage, where he arrived about one o'clock in the morning on 13 September. On the same day the Prince set out for Loch nan Uamh.

By the 15th the Prince and his companions had crossed Glen Spean and Glen Roy and were on their way to Lochiel's burnt seat of Achnacarry. Their great problem was to cross the River Lochy. Donald Macpherson describes the scene:

> ... they came to the river Lochy at night, being fine moonshine. The difficulty was how to get over. Upon this Cluns Cameron met them on the water side, at whom Lochiel asked how they would get

over the river. He said, 'Very well, for I have an old boat carried from Locharkaig that the enemy left unburnt of all the boats you had, Lochiel.' Lochiel asked to see the boat. Upon seeing it he said, 'I am afraid we will not be safe with it.' Quoth Cluns, 'I will cross first and show you the way.' The matter was agreed upon. Cluns upon reflection said, 'I have six bottles of brandy, and I believe all of you will be the better of a dram.' This brandy was brought from Fort Augustus, where the enemy lay in garrison, about nine miles from that part of Lochy where they were about to cross. Lochiel went to the Prince and said, 'Will your Royal Highness take a dram?' 'O,' said the Prince, 'can you have a dram here?' 'Yes,' replies Lochiel, 'and that from Fort Augustus too' Which pleased the Prince much that he should have provisions from his enemies, etc. He said, 'Come, let us have it.' Upon this three of the bottles were drunk. Then they crossed the River Lochy by three crossings, Cluns Cameron in the first with so many, then the Prince in the second with so many, and in the last Lochiel with so many. In the third and last ferrying the crazy boat laked so much that there would be four or five pints of water in the bottom of the boat, and in hurrying over the three remaining bottles of brandy were all broke.

They spent the 16th in Lochiel's ruined house and set off that night for Glencamgarry, at the west end of Loch Arkaig, where Cluny Macpherson and Dr Cameron were waiting for them and had prepared food and shelter. On the 18th they set out, unusually, by daylight, and on the 19th 'arrived at the shipping'. All this time Government troops, imagining that Charles had managed to get to the east coast, were looking for him there and had laid an embargo on all shipping from east coast ports in Scotland.

Amid all the difficulties that Charles encountered during his five months as a fugitive, "tis a question,' mused Donald Macpherson, 'if at all he pass'd so much of his time anywhere so private and secure as he did that he spent in Benalder, being always within the circumference of six miles'. But the most extraordinary thing about the Prince's behaviour during these gruelling months, in virtually every minute of which his life was in danger, was his stamina and his cheerfulness. Though he occasionally got angry and (more rarely) ill-tempered, there is no record at all, among the many accounts given later by his companions of the various stages of his adventures, of any scenes of petulance and sulkiness of the kind that we know of in earlier as well as later phases of Charles's career. He sang, he danced, he joked, he found all sorts of ways of cheering and encouraging his weary companions. He often lacked both food and sleep for days and nights on end, was often wet to the skin for whole days, his clothes were frequently tattered and lousy, and he suffered intermittently from dysentery. Charles was essentially an extrovert and an outdoor man. In indoor scenes of policy-making and intrigue he was impatient and suspicious. Even when he held court in Holyrood after the Battle of Prestonpans he seems to have been less the gracious and confident Prince Charming than legend makes him out to have been. In a sense, his period as a fugitive was his finest hour. John Cameron's account of the Prince's wanderings is obviously coloured by his own devotion, but its conclusion is worth quoting:

> I have told you what I was witness to or informed of by such as I could absolutely depend upon. I shall only add that the Prince submitted with patience to his adverse fortune, was chearful, and frequently desired those that were with him to be so. He was cautious when in the greatest danger, never at a loss in resolving what to do, with uncommon fortitude. He regretted more the distress of those who suffered for adhering to his interest than the hardships and dangers he was hourly exposed to. To conclude, he possesses all the virtues that form the character of a HERO and a GREAT PRINCE.

Cluny Macpherson and Macpherson of Breackachie did not go aboard *L'Heureux* with Charles and other 'skulking gentlemen' who assembled on the shores of Loch nan Uamh on learning that the French ships were there. They preferred to return to the security of Cluny's Cage. With Charles went Lochiel and his brother Dr Cameron, Lochgarry, and John Roy Stewart. (Cameron returned to Scotland in 1753 to further another Jacobite plot and was arrested and hanged.) 'Twenty-three gentlemen and a hundred and seven men of common rank' are said to have sailed with him in the two ships. According to a contemporary newspaper report, 'the gentlemen, as well as the commons, *were seen to weep*, though they boasted of being soon back with an irresistible force.'

Lachlan McLean, master of the *May* and a prisoner on board *L'Heureux*, recorded what happened on the evening of the 19 September. 'About six in the evening, after sitting to supper, a message came from *Le Conti*, upon which Colonel Warren [who commanded the two French ships] and the Captain of the Frigate got up in a great hurry, got on their best clothes, ordered us on board our Vessell with our chests where we remained guarded by their men and an officer until two next morning the 20th, when Colonel Warren and one of his officers came on board of us ... he too was in top spirits, telling us plainly that he had now got the Prince (meaning the young Pretender) on board with Lochiel.' The ships sailed between two and three o'clock that morning. Charles was first taken aboard *Le Prince de Conti* and was then transferred to *L'Heureux*, from which he wrote a short letter to Cluny Macpherson telling him of his safe embarkation: 'Thanks to God I am arrived safe aboard the vessell, which is a very clever one, and has another alonst with her as good, the first is of 36 guns and the second 32.'

And so, in the dark of that early morning in September, Bonnie Prince Charlie sailed south-west out of Loch nan Uamh and into the Atlantic to leave Scotland forever but to leave behind in Scotland, to which he had brought some glamour and immense suffering, a strange and lingering memory of gaiety and courage and a sense of a noble cause nobly lost.

CHAPTER FIFTEEN

Exits and Entrances

AT NOON on Monday 29 September (or 10 October New Style, which we shall now use for events on the Continent) *L'Heureux* anchored off Roscoff, in Brittany, and Charles went ashore in the ship's boat, with cheers from both *L'Heureux* and *Le Prince de Conti* and a salute of twenty-one guns from each ship. Colonel Warren wrote to James in Rome: 'I have the happiness to advise your Majesty of my wished for success in meeting His Royal Highness the Prince on the continent of Scotland, and bringing him safe back to France, ... 'tis scarce to be imagined what a crowd of dangers he has run thro' by sea and land, but Providence has been visibly in special care, and will doubtless in time complete his wishes. ... I congratulate your Majesty on this happy event, ...'

An account of Charles's reception in France, 'as related by persons at Paris in letters to their friends in Great Britain', was published in London in 1749 and is also included in the Lockhart Papers. No sooner had news of the Prince's landing reached Versailles, we are told, 'than the Castle of St Antoine was ordered to be prepared for his reception, and his brother accompanied by several young noblemen went to meet him, and conducted him directly to Versailles, ... The King of France, Louis the fifteenth, immediately quitting the Council which was sitting on affairs of moment, went to receive him, and as he advanced, took him in his arms with every mark of tender affection, and said '*Mon très cher Prince, je rends grace au Ciel qui me donne le plaisir extrême de vous voir arrivé en bonne santé après tant de fatigues et de dangers. Vous avez fait voir que toutes les grandes qualités des Heros et des Philosophes se trouvent unies en vous; et j'espère qu'un de ces jours vous recevrez la recompense d'un merite si extraordinaire*'. ('My very dear Prince, I thank God who gives me the great pleasure of seeing you arrive in good health after so many fatigues and dangers. You have shown that all the great qualities of Heroes and Philosophers are united in you, and I hope that one of these days you will receive your reward for such extraordinary merit.') But in fact whatever King Louis may have said to Charles, he and the Prince had very different objects in view. Louis and his ministers were perfectly prepared to grant Charles a pension to enable him to live quietly on the Continent; but, the Forty-five having served their purpose, they did not contemplate any further military action and certainly did not intend to provide French help for another attempt by Charles to put the Stuarts back on the British throne. But such another attempt was precisely what Charles had in mind. He arrived back in France in high spirits, greeted his brother Henry with joy and affection, which was reciprocated, and set about building up his image in Paris as the gay and irrepressible hero whose endurance of fantastic dangers after the defeat of his first great plan to regain the throne for his father was the guarantee that the next one would succeed. But he knew he needed a French force for that success, and this is what Louis had no intention of providing. Charles would be useful as a Stuart pensioner whom he could use if and when it suited him to embarrass the British Government; but that was all.

Charles's first visit to Louis at Versailles after his return was made 'as it were *incog*', as the pamphlet of letters from Paris puts it, but ten days later he decided to pay a formal visit, setting out from St Antoine with a procession of coaches, the first containing 'the Lords Ogilvy and Elcho, the venerable Glenbucket and Mr Kelly', the second 'the young Chevalier himself, Lord Lewis Gordon, and the eldest Locheil as master of the horse; two pages richly dressed lolled on the boot, and ten footmen in the livery of the character assumed by the young Chevalier, walked on each side'. Other followers were in a third coach, and behind, on horseback, came young Lochiel and some others. The Prince himself was gorgeously dressed. 'His coat was rose-coloured velvet embroidered with silver and lined with silver tissue; his waistcoat was a rich gold brocade, with a spangled fringe set on in scollops. The cockade in his hat, and the buckles of his shoes were diamonds; the George which he wore at his bosom, and the order of St Andrew which he wore also tied by a piece of green ribbon to one of the buttons of his waistcoat, were prodigiously illustrated with large brilliants; in short he glittered all over like the star which they tell you appeared at his nativity.' He supped with the King and the royal family, and he and his followers were 'magnificently entertained'. The letter-writer continues: 'I should not have mentioned these particulars, but to shew you that the French Court took all imaginable pains to lull the young Chevalier into forgetfulness of the breach of past promises, and perswade him that his concerns would now be taken into immediate consideration.'

But troubles were not long in developing. In the first place, in spite of the warm reunion between Charles and his brother Henry, it soon became clear that they were very different both in temperament and point of view. On 31 October Henry wrote to James that though Charles's love for him was undoubted, 'that is all'. Charles was, he said, completely under the sway of the clique he had around him, and he mentioned Kelly in particular as one from whom he expected difficulties. He said that Colonel O'Brien (a French-born Irishman in the French service whom James had appointed his Envoy and representative to the Court of France in 1745, and who at the end of 1746 was to be created Earl of Lismore by James) and Cardinal Tencin were trying to restrain the Prince, but the Prince had no confidence in them. Henry also refers to Charles's disapproval of his (Henry's) way of life, about which he often attacked him, though 'in a loving way', and of Charles's desire to have his brother make himself more popular. He deplores Charles's 'ill understood systeme of pretended popularity' which he sees as the source of all their troubles.

Charles settled down in his luxuriously-furnished mansion in the Faubourg Saint-Antoine to a life of conspicuous hedonism. He played up to the applause of the Paris crowds, in the theatre, at concerts, at parties, in the street. He espoused the cause of the French Queen and the Dauphin against the King and his mistresses: the Queen, Marie Leszczinska, who was related to his own mother, developed a tenderness described by a correspondent in Paris as 'maternal' for the Prince: 'and I have been told by several about Her Majesty, that whenever he came to court ... she used to keep him in conversation for whole hours together and make him recite to her and the Ladies who were with her, all his adventures, the detail of which seldom failed of drawing tears from her eyes'. But it was a cousin of the Queen, Marie Jablonowska, who had married the Prince de Talmond in 1730 and was already nearly forty years old, who established a really close association with and dominance over him. The Princesse de Talmond almost certainly became Charles's mistress some time after this, thus triumphing over the many great ladies of Paris who were fighting over him. But it must again be emphasized that Charles was not a very highly-sexed person: he was attractive to women and he liked to be liked, especially now when the courting of popularity in Paris was part of his deliberate policy. The charm that the Princesse de Talmond had for him was at least as much social and intellectual as sexual: she and the Duchesse

D'Aiguillon (whose witty vitality as well as her high social connections gave her the entrée everywhere) introduced him to the *philosophes* and for the first time this quite unintellectual young man moved in the most 'advanced' free-thinking circles of the day. This did not strengthen his religious principles, which were never as strong as those of his father and brother, but it helped to develop his self-confidence and his determination to work for his own policy according to his own rules.

Messages came from King Louis offering a settled pension: since these were verbal and not in writing, Charles treated them with lofty disdain, on one occasion writing to his father that O'Brien had received from the clerk of the Marquis D'Argenson (Louis's secretary of state for foreign affairs from 1744 to 1747) a verbal message 'making a most scandalous arrangement for us' (it was in fact for a pension of 12,000 francs a month and a house for himself and his brother). Charles's letter continued: 'I find it, and am absolutely convinced of it, that the only way of delyng with this Government, is to give as short and smart answers as one can, at the same time paying them in their own Coin by Loding them with sivilities and compliments, setting apart business, for that kind of vermin, the more you give them, the more thel take, as also the more room you give them, the more they have to grapple at, which makes it necessary to be Laconick with them, ...' When D'Argenson put the proposal in writing, Charles replied in terms of lofty obscurity.

Charles was unfair to D'Argenson, who admired him and was doing his best to be of help. (Incidentally, the Marquis D'Argenson must be distinguished from his brother, the Comte D'Argenson, secretary of state for war, who was also involved in Charles's affairs: some biographers of the Prince have confused the two.) He did not admire Charles's brother Henry, whom he considered to be 'quite Italian' and to be crafty, superstitious and jealous of Charles, and though this view may well have been prejudiced it appeared to have been borne out later when in May 1747 Henry, without telling Charles, suddenly returned to Rome to accept a Cardinal's hat, thus striking a mighty blow at the Stuart cause and alienating his brother completely. As for Louis, he was not ungenerous in the help he offered, which included commissions in the French army and substantial pensions to the exiled leaders of the Forty-five in accordance with their military rank. But Charles was no more disposed to accept this solution than was Lochiel, whose rank of brigadier and colonel rated 4,000 livres a year but who preferred to either commission or pension an immediate French military expedition to prevent the destruction and depopulation of the Highlands resulting from Hanoverian policy after Culloden. Lochiel urged Charles to press for the necessary French assistance, which Charles did again and again, but in vain: the most he could get for Lochiel was command of a French regiment, which Lochiel said he would accept for Charles's sake, but he preferred 'to share in the fate of the people I have undone, and if they must be sacrificed to die along with them. It is the only way I can free myself of the reproach of their blood.' Lochiel died in 1748: he is perhaps the most attractive character of all Charles's supporters.

Cardinal Tencin appears to have thought of an original solution to Charles's problems. According to the anonymous Paris correspondent he visited Charles to propose that 'the Ministry might find some expedient to gratify him with the succours he demanded, provided that in case of a restoration to the Crown of Great Britain, the kingdom of Ireland were yielded up and made a province to France, as an equivalent for the expence the Government must necessarily be at in such an undertaking. But scarcely had the Cardinal finished what he had to say when the young Chevalier started from his seat, and not able to contain how much he was irritated, cryed out "*Non, Monsieur le Cardinal, tout ou rien! point de partage!*"'

By 1747 Charles had got nowhere. It was now suggested that he should marry, as a Stuart heir was important: it was clear that he had no chance of obtaining one of Louis's daughters, though this was his original intention, and several other ladies were thought of. But Charles was prepared to wait: 'My opinion is I cannot yet marry unless I get the King's dauter, which is in vain to ask at present, and am afraid will always be the same' and proposed that Henry should marry the daughter of Prince Radziwill. Of course Henry had other plans, though as yet they were unsuspected by Charles, who continued to criticize Henry's strict way of life.

The correspondence between Charles and his father in the early months of 1747 reveals a growing rift between the two. In February James wrote at length reviewing Charles's conduct over the years, deploring his refusal of a pension from Louis, and worrying lest Charles is attempting to gain popularity in England by neglecting his Catholic religion. Charles now left Paris for Lyons, and then went to Avignon. He discovered that Henry was planning to visit Spain, and was annoyed because he had not been told. He was equally secretive in deciding to go to Spain himself: Henry, he wrote him, should not go lest they might appear not to be acting in concert. Meanwhile, James worried about what Charles was up to and wondered whether he had been expelled from France by Louis. But he sent him 15,000 livres. Charles reached

Spain and managed to obtain an interview with Ferdinand VI, newly succeeded to the throne. Ferdinand was polite but quite unhelpful: he had not the slightest intention of assisting Charles and made it clear that his most urgent desire was that Charles should leave the country at once. So, frustrated once again, Charles was back in Paris in March.

On 10 April 1747 Charles wrote to his father deploring as 'a melancholi thing this Affair of Murray the Secretary' and saying that there was some reason to suspect that 'he was in a click with Lord George' (quite untrue, of course). He continues:

I have received a civill note from Count d'Argenson, in which he desiers I should give him an adress by which he can be always able to communicate to me his masters pleasure without its ever being suspected. which I did, giving him a cant name to be sent under cover to Waters jounior, so that now everything is at their door. I am seeking out for a cuntry house near the town where I shall be able to brese a little fresh air, and be a porte for any business that may happen. . . . I have got a cold in my head a little troblesom, but of no consequence, God willing.

On the 17th he writes again, saying that his cold is better. He goes on: 'It gives me great concern to see . . . how unesy y^r Majesty was, and not approving my Conduct'. There are clear differences between father and son about which advisers to trust and about money matters. James is also worried about differences between the brothers, but Charles reassures him: 'Your Majesty may be absolutely shure what any little coldness or broalie that may ever hapen to be betwixt us is nothing, but venting one anothers spleen, which, God nose, we have occasion enough to have, seeing every day so many follise of our own people, besides strangers'. James was now prematurely old, and querulous as ever: he had quite given up hope of a restoration, at least for himself. He wrote his 'Dearest Carluccio' a long letter of 17 April complaining about those whom Charles chooses to confide in (especially Kelly) and at the same time urging him not to act on his own: 'To do all one's self is impossible, and to act always of one's own head is both presumptuous and dengerous'. He would like Charles to leave Paris, and he would 'prefer Rome either to Avignon or Switzerland'. He talks of Charles's visit to Spain: 'I am in hopes your journey thither will be of no ill consequence, provided you manage your matters in a proper manner on your return to Paris, where, I think, you should have equally in your view the solliciting another expedition, and the endeavoring to make your situation as little bad as possible in case of Peace'. He expects no success in the matter of the expedition, and urges Charles to cultivate the good will of Louis and his Ministers. 'I hope you will no longer refuse accepting the pension that was offerd to you, and continue to remain either in or about Paris till an expedition or a Peace sends you from thence.' James clearly anticipated that when France and Britain made peace, as they were shortly to do, a condition of the peace treaty would be Charles's banishment from France, and he wants Charles to prepare for this: 'Should you continue not to accept the pension now offerd you by the King of France, you would run the risque, I am affrayd, of getting nothing from him after a Peace, and in that case without you were to return to live with me at Rome, you know I have not the wherewithall to maintain you elsewhere, whereas if you once accept the pension, I hope it would be continued to you whereever you may be.' This long, sad, troubled letter ends with thanks 'for your kind token of the China Box, which is really very pretty'. Charles replied in a few lines, taking up none of his father's points. 'I am thank God in good health, but wou'd be yet better iff I had occasion again to be in action.' Charles clearly could not accept his father's unheroic assessment of the situation.

Charles's insistence on playing a lone hand had by now upset nearly everyone with whom he had any relationship, from his father to the French ministers. It was at this low ebb in his fortunes that Henry struck the fatal blow of deciding to enter the Church. He slipped quietly out of Paris, on 29 April, even, it is said, having invited Charles to supper that night, leaving the Prince to wait for him in vain in a brightly illuminated house with the servants all ready to serve the meal. Charles feared that Henry might have been assassinated. Three days later Charles received the letter Henry had written him on the 29th, saying he was going to Rome for a fortnight to see his father and that he needed a change of air anyway. But he never returned. He had long felt a religious vocation, and now he was about to be created a Cardinal, given the Church of Santa Maria in Campitelli, and in virtue of his rank granted precedence immediately after the Dean of the Sacred College (a position he was eventually to hold himself). Later, he received other honours, including the episcopal see of Frascati. There is no need to doubt Henry's sincerity, or indeed his competence in the performing of the duties of his religious offices. But clearly he had made up his mind that the restoration of the Stuarts was a lost cause. That the next Stuart heir after Charles was now not only a zealous Catholic but a Cardinal of the Church, and of course by that token a celibate, undermined all Charles's plans and hopes. James informed Louis XV of the news on 9 June, and Charles on the 13th. He said that he and Henry had consulted the Pope, and Henry had been promised a Cardinalate. James's letter to Charles was anxious and placatory; he knew that Charles 'might probably not approve' this step. Charles was furious. He vowed never to return to Rome, and kept the vow until after his father's death in 1766. Poor James never lost his mournful affection for his 'dearest Carluccio', but Charles seems now to have lost whatever feeling for his father he may have had. He felt betrayed.

Another blow was soon to fall. The War of the Austrian Succession was coming to an end, and representatives of the belligerents met at Aix-la-Chapelle to settle the terms of peace. Fearing what might happen, Charles issued a public protest (in French) on 16 July 1748:

> We protest . . . against all the conventions that may be stipulated in the said assemblies, so far as they shall be contrary to engagements already entered into by us.
>
> We declare by these presents that we regard, and will always regard, as null, void, and of no effect, everything that may be statuted or stipulated which may tend to the acknowledgment of any other person whatsoever as sovereign of the kingdom of Great Britain, besides the person of the most high and most excellent prince, James the Third, our most honoured lord and father, and in default of him, the person of the nearest heir agreeably to the fundamental laws of Great Britain.

It was, of course, a completely empty gesture. Among the clauses of the Peace of Aix-la-Chapelle was one which bound France to recognize the House of Hanover and to expel Charles. For James, the whole thing must have had a familiar ring: the same thing had happened to him at the Treaty of Utrecht in 1713. But Charles was made of different stuff and, unlike his father, was not content to be a docile 'rover'. He refused to leave Paris.

Charles's response to the proceedings at Aix-la-Chapelle was deliberately outrageous. He flaunted his relations not only with the Princesse de Talmond, who was probably now his mistress, but also with other noble ladies who fought for his attentions. 'The Prince is amusing himself with love affairs,' wrote the Marquis D'Argenson in July. 'Madame de Guéménée almost seized him by force: they quarrelled after a ridiculous scene. He lives with the Princesse de Talmond: he is furious and obstinate in everything. He wished to imitate Charles XII and stand a siege in his house. Madame de Talmond has dissuaded him.' D'Argenson wrote a play for private performance, *La Prison du Prince Charles Edouard Stuart*, in which he portrayed the Princesse de Talmond and the Duchesse D'Aiguillon as fighting over the Prince like fish-wives. Louis proposed that Charles retire to Fribourg in Switzerland and offered him a generous pension and other inducements, 'but the young Chevalier continuing to live as a person regardless of what he was doing,' reported a Paris observer, 'the King ordered Cardinal Tencin to acquaint him with the necessity there was for his departure'. Charles paid no attention. He expressed publicly his pleasure at the victories of the British fleet, and had medals struck with his head on one side and a ship on the other, and the motto *Amor et Spes Britanniae*. He ignored further urgings from Louis to leave for Switzerland, and ostentatiously bought new furniture for his house. 'Among other things,' says the Parisian correspondent already referred to, 'he sent to the King's goldsmith, who had been employed by him before, and ordered him to make a service of plate to the value of an hundred thousand crowns, to be ready against a particular day, which the goldsmith promised not to fail in; but it so happened that immediately afterwards he received orders to prepare such a large quantity for the King's use against the same time, that he found it impossible to comply with both, upon which he waited on the young Chevalier and intreated he would allow him some days longer, telling him the reason; but he would not admit of the excuse, insisting on being first served, as he had given the first orders.' When Louis heard this he probably imagined that Charles's hurry was in order to have the plate ready in time for his departure, so he agreed that the goldsmith should attend to the Prince's order first. But Charles had still no intention of leaving Paris. Instead he used the new plate in a magnificent entertainment that he gave for the Princesse de Talmond 'and above thirty others of the nobility of both sexes and several foreigners of distinction.' Where he got the money for all this remains a mystery: he would take nothing for himself from Louis.

In dissociating himself from the French king and from the other members of his own family Charles may well have been deliberately seeking to gain popularity in England. This was D'Argenson's view, and he considered the policy a shrewd one. It certainly secured the Prince great popularity in Paris. But of course Louis could not tolerate such behaviour indefinitely: the British Minister was putting increasing pressure on him to get rid of Charles in accordance with the terms of the peace treaty. Louis appealed to James to put pressure on Charles, which he did, but to no avail. Charles counted on the fact that his popularity in Paris would prevent the French King from taking any active steps to expel him. A mingling of ideas he had picked up from the *philosophes* and recollections of his faithful Highlanders led him to consider himself a species of Noble Savage, and he noted down some *'Maximes d'un Homme sauvage'*. Louis got more and more exasperated at Charles's behaviour. He kept sending the Duc de Gevrès to him to insist on his leaving, but Charles treated him with contempt: if the King had a message for him, he said, he could give it to him himself. Meanwhile – *'Pardonnez moi, j'ai quelques affaires'*, and he left the room, 'leaving the Duke in the greatest consternation'. Louis then sent the Comte de Maurepas to Charles, to tell him that if he would not leave voluntarily he would be forcibly expelled. But Charles replied, 'with the greatest disdain': *'Les ministres! les ministres! Si vous voulez m'obliger, Monsieur le Comte, dites au Roi votre maître que Je suis né pour rompre tous les projets de ses ministres.'* ('Tell the King your master that I was born to smash all his ministers' plans.') This, as the Paris observer noted, 'was plainly setting them at defiance.'

Louis was reluctant to expel Charles by force, but now he had no option. He finally signed the order for his expulsion on 10 December 1748, remarking as he signed that it was difficult for a King to be a true friend: *'Pauvre Prince! qu'il est difficile pour un Roy d'être un veritable ami!'* The plan to seize and expel Charles was immediately known all over Paris, and Charles was informed of it. He paid no attention, exclaiming 'Pish – pish – an idle rumour! They know I will obey my father'. He was to be seized on his way to the Opera. The anonymous Paris correspondent gives an account of what happened, given him by one of the officers involved in the operation:

Having concerted the measures for executing their orders, the officers who were to have a share in it were commanded to repair to Monsieur de Vaudreuil's, Major in the Guards, on Tuesday morning before day, in order to prevent their being perceived, and the Duke de Biron caused ten ells of crimson silk cord to be procured for the purpose of binding their intended prisoner. In the course of Tuesday the eleventh of December, the Duke ordered twelve hundred men of his regiment to invest the Palais Royal [the passage leading to the Opera House in the Palais Royal had been chosen as the best place to make the seizure]; the serjeants of the regiment, armed with cuirasses and scull-caps, had directions to be in the passage to the Opera-house and in the entrances of the houses bordering upon it, the serjeants of grenadiers were ordered to seize the young Chevalier; two companies of grenadiers took post in the courtyard of the kitchens, where the Duke de Biron, disguised and in a coach, waited to see the success of the enterprise; the mousquetaires had orders to be ready to mount on horseback; the *guét* (or armed police) were distributed in all the neighbouring streets; troops were posted upon the road from the Palais Royal to Vincennes; hatchets and scaling ladders were prepared and locksmiths were directed to attend in order to take the young Chevalier by escalade in case he should throw himself into some house, and there resolve to stand a siege; ...

Several people sent Charles notes warning him of the plot, and it is said that even as he passed through the Rue St Honoré on his way to the Opera he heard a voice saying: 'Prince, return, they are going to arrest you, the Palais Royal is beset'. But he paid no attention, and went on:

and in alighting from his coach at the passage of the Opera-house, he found the guards doubled, with their bayonets fixed, and the *guét* turning passengers out of the streets and making the coaches file off; and he was surrounded by six serjeants dressed in grey cloaths, as if they had been servants desirous to get a sight of him, a popular curiosity to which he had been much accustomed. A serjeant in uniform now advanced, under pretence of dispersing the mob, which was the signal agreed upon, and at that instant two serjeants seized him by the arms behind, two confined his hands, one clasped him round the middle, and another seized his legs. [He was taken through a gate at the end of the passage which opened into a courtyard, and there formally arrested in the King's name and disarmed.] Monsieur de Vaudreuil then went to the Duke de Biron's coach to give an account of what had passed, and informed him of the young Chevalier's being disarmed without resistance; but the Duke judging that for greater security he should be bound, the order to that effect was executed in the presence of M. de Vaudreuil, who made his excuses to the young Chevalier, by assuring him that these precautions were taken from regard to his person and solely to prevent him from making any attempt upon himself. ... Both his arms and legs were tied, and he was bound with so many cords that looking disdainfully upon them, he asked ' Have you not enough now?' and M. de Vaudreuil answering 'Not yet,' the young Chevalier darted at him a menacing look. This operation being terminated, he was put into a hired coach that waited in the courtyard of the kitchens, ...

Charles was taken to Vincennes, where he was kept under guard until the following Sunday, when he was escorted to Beauvoisin on the frontier between France and Savoy, and from there he went to Chambéry, where he spent three days and wrote several letters, and then on to the papal city of Avignon.

Paris was shocked at this treatment of a guest of France. It is said that 'the Dauphin went to the royal apartments and in the full levee took the liberty of condemning the step that had been taken, with a vehemence, which however just, was thought too presuming'. Satirical verses attacking Louis and praising Charles were freely circulated:

> De l'amitié des rois exemple mémorable,
> Et de leurs intérêts victime déplorable,
> Tu triomphes, cher prince, au milieu de tes fers;
> Sur toi dans ce moment tous les yeux sont ouverts. ...

(Memorable example of the friendship of kings, and lamentable victim of their selfishness, you triumph, dear prince, in the midst of your chains; on you at this moment all eyes are turned.)

There was talk of expelling the Princesse de Talmond to Lorraine, but in the end all that happened was that one of her servants was arrested, on which she wrote to Louis's minister Maurepas: 'Sir, the King's laurels are in full bloom, but, as the imprisonment of my lackey cannot add to their glory, I beg you to release him'. The officious Walton reported to London that Madame de Talmond now joined Charles at Avignon, but such evidence as exists indicates that she did not follow the Prince at this time.

At Avignon Charles went to the house of Mrs Hay (Lady Inverness), and stayed there until the house of the Marquis de Rochefort was made ready for him. He was cordially welcomed by both the Archbishop and the Vice-Legate of Avignon, but managed to alienate the former by his strange diversion of introducing boxing matches and prize fights into the city. Such sports had been forbidden by an edict of Sixtus V at the end of the sixteenth century, and the Archbishop felt it his duty to put a stop to them. The dispute between Charles and the Archbishop on this matter was referred to the Pope for arbitration, and His Holiness naturally upheld his predecessor's edict. As a result, Charles broke off all intercourse with the anti-pugilistic Archbishop. He did, however, make the acquaintance of the Infante Don Philip of Spain, who was on his way to the Duchy of Parma which had been awarded him at the Peace of Aix-la-Chapelle: they met at a masked ball given by the Vice-Legate.

But it was all of very short duration. The British Government were determined that Charles should be driven to Rome, and threatened the Pope with the bombardment of Civita Vecchia if he did not order Charles out of Avignon. Under pressure, Benedict XIV issued the required order, and this time Charles complied. On 28 February 1749 he rode out of Avignon with his equerry Henry Goring to lead a mysterious life of hiding and wandering until his return to Rome on his father's death in 1766. Andrew Lang's examination of the Stuart Papers at Windsor and his unravelling of mysteries in his book, *Pickle the Spy*, throw some light on these years of secret movement and disguises, but leave many matters still unsolved. There is a curious parallel between the wandering years, when he was pursued by secret agents and would-be assassins, and those months in Scotland after Culloden when he was a fugitive from the redcoats. We know that in spite of the constant danger and the great physical hardships Charles found a certain exhilaration in the hand-to-mouth existence of a hunted fugitive in Scotland. Whether in this second and much longer period of wandering, when he was not continuously in the same kind of desperate danger but must often have been in black moods of frustration or despair, he ever felt the kind of happy excitement he felt at times during his Highland wanderings we cannot tell. Perhaps he did, on one of his more daring or more hopeful escapades. But all the time he was running downhill psychologically and physically.

Walton, trying as usual to collect information about Charles to pass to London, could do nothing but report unconfirmed rumours, and at one point said that many people at Rome, not having heard anything from him, gave out that he was dead. The British envoy at Florence, Sir Horace Mann, wrote in August 1750, 'notwithstanding the utmost diligence and infinite pains I have taken to discover where the Pretender's eldest son conceals himself, all my correspondents at Rome persisting in the same story, that the Pretender himself [James] nor any of his adherents there knew anything of him'. He adds that Cardinal Albani had been told by Charles's brother Henry 'that the Pretender, his father, now and then received a letter from him, sometimes by one and sometimes by another, with news of his health only; but that those letters were never dated nor any mention made of the place whence they came, adding that the father was quite in despair'.

Charles had arranged for his correspondence to be addressed to him under an assumed name at the banking house of Waters and we know that on 6 March 1749, he arranged to call for his letters there. In early April he was at Lunéville, in Lorraine, presumably with the Princesse de Talmond, who had estates there. The father of the Queen of France, Stanislaus I of Poland, who had abdicated in 1735 but retained his title and received the duchies of Lorraine and Bar, now kept his court at Lorraine. There was wild talk of putting Charles on the Polish throne and of a Radziwill marriage. But Charles was soon in Paris again, once more with the Princesse de Talmond, who seems to have concealed him there. On 26 April he was in Strasbourg and he was in Venice in May, but the Venetians expelled him on the 25th: Charles appealed in vain to Maria Theresa to intervene. 'What can a bird do that has not found a right nest?' he wrote to a correspondent. 'He must flit from bough to bough.' It must be remembered that the Peace of Aix-la-Chapelle required the expulsion of Charles not only from France but from every secular state in Europe: the Hanoverian Government were determined to force him back to Rome, and Charles was equally determined not to go.

He was in Paris again at the end of June, and it must have been now that he began his relationship with Mademoiselle Ferrand des Marres, a highly intelligent young woman who had been of help to the philosopher Condillac in developing his psychological theories. Mademoiselle Ferrand had written an account of a brigand called Cartouche, and Charles wrote to her presenting himself for her sympathy as a kind of Cartouche, and arranged for her to receive his correspondence from Waters (addressed to 'Mr John Douglas'). Mlle Ferrand was a close friend of the widowed young Madame de Vassé, and both lived in the secular wing of the Convent of St Joseph in the Rue Dominique. There also lived the sixty-year-old Marquise de Deffand, that formidable wit whose famous salon had attracted Voltaire, Montesquieu, Fontenelle and others and who since 1747, wittily malicious as ever, had been holding court every night in her yellow drawing-room. The Princesse de Talmond also took rooms in the convent, and it is believed that Charles used to visit her at night by a secret staircase. There was a Jacobite atmosphere in the convent, for Madame du Deffand's guests included several French intellectuals sympathetic to the Jacobite cause as well as the Jacobite brother-in-law of the Duke of Berwick, whose name was Bulkeley. It seems fairly clear that the Princesse de Talmond, Mademoiselle Ferrand and Madame de Vassé, who were all attracted to Charles and formed a trio of helpers, arranged for him to stay secretly at the Convent of St Joseph on his visits to Paris, though the tradition that he stayed hidden for three years in the room of Madame de Vassé is a palpable exaggeration of the facts. But there is good reason to believe that there were occasions when Charles listened in concealment to some of the best conversation in Paris, including talk about himself.

There appears to have been some jealousy between the Princesse de Talmond and Mademoiselle Ferrand. A close friend of Madame de Vassé told the German diplomat Baron von Grimm (who wrote it all down afterwards) that she had been obliged to get rid of the Prince because of the violent scenes between him and Madame de Talmond. There are notes and memoranda in existence which do indeed suggest that Charles and the Princesse sometimes quarrelled. At the same time she was of great help to him: 'Mademoiselle Luci', as he called her, not only obtained books for him (*Joseph Andrews* in both English and French and a French translation of *Tom Jones*, all of which he himself asked for – uncharacteristically, for he was not much of a reader) but also seems to have been a channel between him and the French King, who was now engaging in devious diplomatic activity unknown to his ministers.

Charles was in and out of Paris at this time. He was anxious to find out what was happening in Britain, and to get money from Jacobites there. Attempts were made to find and bring the gold hidden at Loch Arkaig, but it had been tampered with and had caused dissension, confusion and betrayal in the Highlands. Charles sent Henry Goring to England at the end of July 1749 to see what was happening to the Jacobite leaders there and to try and raise money, and he was followed by Balhaldy, who visited London to no avail. Goring was told that Charles had better make his peace with France and get rid of his present advisers, and when Charles promised to give up a number of these, including the faithful George Kelly, he received £15,000 of which he sent part to support those of his followers who were living at Avignon.

In spite of discouraging messages from England, Charles felt that the situation was changing in his favour. George II's eldest son, the Prince of Wales, was openly at war with his father, and was said to be in communication with Jacobites: there is even a suggestion that he toyed with the idea of giving up the succession to the British throne to Charles, keeping the Empire for himself. (As he died in 1751, before his father, nothing came of these supposed plans.) In April 1749 Dr William King, Principal of St Mary Hall, Oxford, had made a speech in Latin in the Sheldonian Theatre at the opening of the Radcliffe Library in which he obliquely but unmistakably expressed his Jacobite views, introducing six times the word *redeat* ('may he return') in his peroration, to the applause of his audience. Some months later Dr King attended Lichfield Races in order to sound out the views of Midland squires and made a list of 275 gentlemen. About the same time a new Jacobite medal was struck in silver and bronze, with Charles's bust on one side and on the other a withered tree from which shot forth a vigorous young branch, with the word *Revirescet* ('it will flourish again') beneath. And in France Charles was distributing small silver tokens bearing his profile and the words *Laetamini Cives* ('Citizens rejoice!'). On 3 June 1750, Charles asked Dormer, his agent at Antwerp, to procure 26,000 muskets and other weapons. A month later he asked his father for a renewal of his commission as Regent. Clearly, something was in the wind.

What happened next is described by Dr King in his *Political and Literary Anecdotes*:

> September, 1750. – I received a note from my Lady Primrose [Jacobite daughter of Peter Drelincourt, Dean of Armagh, and widow of the third Viscount Primrose], who desired to see me immediately. As soon as I waited on her, she led me into her dressing-room, and presented me to – [the dash indicated Charles]. If I was surprised to find him there, I was still more astonished when he acquainted me with the motives which had induced him to hazard a journey to England at this juncture. The impatience of his friends who were in exile, had formed a scheme which was impracticable; but although it had been as feasible as they had represented it to him, yet no preparation had been made, nor was anything ready to carry it into execution. He was soon convinced that he had been deceived; and therefore, after a stay in London of five days only he returned to the place from whence he came.

Charles had left Antwerp on 12 September and was in London on the 16th; on the 22nd he left for Paris. What exactly his object was remains unclear, though it may well have been connected with what was later to develop as the Elibank Plot. Joseph Forsyth, who was a guest of Charles's brother the Cardinal Duke of York at Frascati during the last years of Henry's life, describes in his *Remarks ... during an Excursion in Italy* a meeting at a house in Pall Mall attended by Charles, the Duke of Beaufort, the Earl of Westmorland and others at which the restoration of the Stuarts was discussed – the last time English Jacobites met together formally to discuss such a proposition. Many years later, talking to Gustavus III of Sweden on 6 December 1783, Charles told some details of his visit. He perambulated London with one Colonel Brett, and actually inspected the defences of the Tower, deciding that a gate might be blown in with a petard. Sir Walter Scott, who as a member of the Commission appointed to examine the Stuart MSS had read them carefully, including some that have since been lost, mentions in his introduction to *Redgauntlet* 'wild schemes' that had been drawn up by some desperate Jacobites at this time, including 'the surprisal of St James's palace, and the assassination of the royal family'. (This may well be a reference to the Elibank plot, rather than to something separate planned for 1750.) But according to Joseph Forsyth Charles always insisted that no violence was to be done to the Elector of Hanover (as the Jacobites always called George II) or any member of his family.

What Charles wanted the 26,000 muskets for remains obscure. He offered the meeting at Pall Mall to lead a rising if 4,000 men could be mustered, but this was not taken seriously. Whatever the precise motive of his astonishing visit to London, he was persuaded to leave quickly, and nothing concrete appears to have been done to advance the cause.

Charles took one action in London, however, which he clearly thought was in his own interest and in the interest of the Jacobite cause. He was formally admitted a member of the Church of England 'in the new church in the Strand' (probably St Martin-in-the-Fields, though it might have been St Mary-le-Strand or St Clement Danes). Charles himself explained his act in a draft proclamation of 1759:

> In order to make my renountiation of the Church of Rome the most authentick, and the less liable afterwards to malitious interpretations, I went to London in the year 1750; and in that capital did then make a solemn abjuration of the Romish religion, and did embrace that of the Church of England as by Law established in the 39 Articles in which I hope to live and die.

There is something pathetic about this belated attempt to placate the anti-Catholic feeling which over seventy years before had been responsible for his grandfather's loss of the throne and which was still freely drawn on in Government propaganda during the Forty-five. Unlike his father and his brother, Charles was not a man of strong religious principle: we remember that when drinking with his Highland cronies in Coradale in June 1746 he had told Hugh Macdonald of Balshar that the princes of Europe had little or no religion at all. Henri IV of France had believed that Paris was worth a mass and successfully gave up his Protestantism for his throne; Charles's father might have made a successful deal of that kind in the reverse direction; perhaps even Charles himself could have done it at an earlier stage. ('Captain Donald Roy M'Donald ... used ... to tell me [it is Bishop Forbes speaking] that when in England with the army, he himself took the freedom to speak to Keppoch and some others about the Prince's joining in Divine service with a Protestant clergyman, importuning them to use their influence with the Prince for that purpose, for that he was persuaded such a measure would do him much service, especially among the English.') But it was too late now. The only result of Charles's change of religion was to increase dissension in the ranks of the Jacobite exiles.

Charles returned to his life of secretly moving about Europe. He still kept in touch with the Princesse de Talmond – the *Reine de Maroc*, Queen of Morocco, as he now called her, though with what implication is unknown – but their relationship was drawing to an end. We lose sight of Charles altogether at the end of September, until we see him in Berlin in February 1751; Frederick the Great received him politely; he had sympathy for the Jacobite cause and employed the Earl of Marischal as his ambassador to Paris in order to spite the Hanoverian Government; but he could offer no active help. Charles then disappears again, and we get nothing but tantalizing glimpses of him in various disguises. He turns up briefly in Paris in March, but for the most part he remained in hiding. He asked Mademoiselle Ferrand to get him a copy of Racine's *Athalie* and Richardson's *Clarissa*, and she advised him against reading certain fashionable rubbishy books on psychology. Mademoiselle Ferrand and the Princesse de Talmond wrote letters to each other in terms of dignified hostility, and Charles made copies of them. Exactly what kind of life he was leading, what games he was playing and fantasies he was indulging in, we do not know.

Reality of a kind breaks in with the Elibank Plot. Lord Elcho in his Journal says that the moving spirit in the plot was Alexander Murray, Lord Elibank's brother. Murray, says Elcho, 'had made the Prince believe that he had got sixty men together in London, who had sworn to attack St James's and assassinate all the Royal Family at a time'. The Prince was then to come from Flanders and 'offer himself to the English nation'. But it is impossible to believe that Charles approved the assassination of the royal family, which represented a kind of violence to which he was consistently opposed. But something was clearly afoot. Dr Archibald Cameron was sent to the Highlands to coordinate action there. Elcho says that Murray's courage failed him when he reached London, and he returned to Paris. The capture and subsequent execution of Dr Cameron put an end to the plot. The fact is that the British Government had known all along what was going on from a spy in the Jacobite camp.

In *Pickle the Spy* Andrew Lang identified this spy as Alastair Ruadh Macdonell, young Glengarry, and the evidence is generally considered conclusive. Pickle was in communication with the powerful Government statesman Henry Pelham from November 1752, writing him regular reports of the state of the plotting. Not that he knew any details, but he knew that the first blow was to be struck in London and that only after that was there to be a rising in Scotland. He named Alexander Murray and Charles himself as the originators of the plot. In fact, Alderman Heathcote was to be in charge of the details in London. Murray and Henry Goring were several times in England on business connected with the plot, and Thomas Carte, the Jacobite historian who went by the name of Phillips, carried messages. In Scotland, James Keith was to land at the head of a Swedish force which was to meet Scottish Jacobite leaders at Crieff market. (It was to arrange this that Archibald Cameron was sent to Scotland.) An unsigned memorandum among the Stuart Papers at Windsor gives precise details of the London end of the plot: sentries were to be placed at St James's Palace and in the surrounding park, two or three thousand picked men were to be assembled in Westminster but lodged in separate houses so as not to arouse suspicion, and at the time arranged they were to gather at specified places, the Palace was to be seized by one group and the Tower, if it did not yield to a summons to surrender by another, was to have its gates blown in. Was this plan drawn up by the Colonel Brett with whom Charles had discussed the blowing in of a Tower gate with a petard?

The date originally fixed for the plot was 10 November 1752, but Pickle wrote later to say that he had seen Charles and the date had been postponed, though no definite later date seems to have been settled on. Plans were being made throughout the winter of 1752–53. The arrest of Archibald Cameron on 23 March 1753 seems to have been one reason for the abandonment of the plot. The Government did not wish it to be known that they had a spy in the Jacobite camp and thus knew exactly why Cameron was in Scotland, and to protect their source of information they had Cameron tried and executed for his part in the Forty-five – a procedure which sent a shiver of horror through the country. But the Government preferred to be thought cruel rather than to expose their knowledge. Archibald Cameron was thus the last participator in the rising of 1745 to be executed. His wife petitioned George II desperately for her husband's life, but he brutally rebuffed her and indeed had her put in prison to prevent her annoying him with her pleading. However, he exercised regal clemency in having Cameron hanged without being cut down and disembowelled while still alive.

There appear to have been other reasons for the abandonment of the Elibank Plot in addition to Cameron's arrest. One was probably the realization by Charles and his advisers that the sympathetic Frederick the Great had no serious intention of helping, as was expected. The other was the intense Jacobite suspicion of Clementina Walkinshaw, who had got in touch with the Prince in Ghent in the spring of 1752 and had been living with him since November – from the very time, that is, that Pickle the Spy began his correspondence with Pelham. Many Jacobites, who were aware that there was a leakage of information, were convinced that Clementina was the source, and this seemed all the more plausible since she had an elder sister in the service of the Hanoverian Princess of Wales at Leicester House. She was now pregnant, and Charles – though he clearly had not initiated the relationship – was loyal to her: as Pickle wrote to his employers, 'the Pretender keeps her well, and seems to be very fond of her'. Charles would not tolerate any interference with his private life, and the Jacobite suspicions of his mistress did him and his cause nothing but harm. But it really did not matter: with the collapse of the last practical scheme devised within Britain for the restoration of the Stuarts to the throne, the cause was lost anyway. It hardly needed the ascent to the British throne in 1760 of George III, grandson of George II, native-born Englishman and proud Briton, to emphasize that the day of the Stuarts was well and truly over.

CHAPTER SIXTEEN

King Charles III

EXACTLY how and in what circumstances Charles and Clementina Walkinshaw came together late in 1752 can only be surmised. It may be that they had met when Charles was in London in September 1750. Clementina may then have accompanied Lady Primrose when she crossed to the Netherlands. At any rate, there is reason to believe what Charles's daughter told Louis XV in 1774 – that an uncle of Clementina's obtained for her the stall of a Canoness in one of the Chapters of the Austrian Netherlands (these were educational institutions for young ladies with aristocratic family connections). The death in October 1752 of Mademoiselle Ferrand and Charles's widening breach with the Princesse de Talmond left him in need of another confidential female agent. It seems reasonable that, if Charles indeed made the first move in proposing reunion with Clementina, he was thinking of this, and that it was because he considered her as a promising agent that he arranged to meet her in Paris. But however things developed, they were soon living together, at first very contentedly. She accompanied him on his European wanderings. On 29 October 1753, their daughter – the only child Charles was ever to have – was baptized Charlotte in the Church of Our Lady of the Fountains at Liège. On 12 November Charles wrote to Goring: 'I have wrote to Avignon for to discard all my Papist servants. . . . I shall still maintain the two gentlemen and all the Protestant servants on the same footing as usual. My mistress has behaved so unworthily that she has put me out of patience and as she is a Papist too, I discard her also!!!' He adds in a P.S. that she had told him that she had friends who would maintain her, 'so that, after such a declaration, and other impertinencies, makes me abandon her'. He asks Goring to find out who her friends are and arrange for her to be delivered to them. On the same day he wrote to Stafford and Sheridan (the 'two gentlemen' of the preceding letter) at Avignon ordering them to 'discard all the Roman Catholic servants that are in the house, as I am not able to maintain them any more'. He suggested that they might go to Rome and get assistance from James Edgar, his father's secretary.

But Charles did not dismiss Clementina at this time, perhaps for the very reason that so many of his supporters were urging him to do so. There is a story told by Dr William King in his *Anecdotes* that the English Jacobites sent over one Macnamara to Charles to plead with him to get rid of his mistress and that Charles refused, saying that although he had no regard for Miss Walkinshaw and could see her removed without concern he would not permit those who called themselves his adherents to dictate to him about his private life. On this, says Dr King, Macnamara burst out: 'What has your family done, Sir, thus to draw down the vengeance of Heaven on every branch of it through so many ages?' (Scott used this story in *Redgauntlet*.)

Desperate for money and for a place to stay, hunted by Hanoverian spies, Charles flitted from place to place with his mistress and child. Goring had turned against him, reproaching him bitterly for living with a woman whom he considered a spy. (Archibald Cameron's widow wrote to James Edgar in January 1754 naming Young Glengarry as the spy; yet Goring persisted in believing that it was Clementina.) The Earl of Marischal also turned against him, accusing him of threatening to publish the names of those English Jacobites who had protested against his way of life and had advised him to repudiate Clementina. Charles replied in a cold, sad letter, repudiating the charge as a 'damned lie'. He was now abandoned by 'the only friend that I know of this side of the water'. He added: 'My heart is broke enough without that you should finish it. . . .' He was indeed a broken man. All the strength and vigour of character that he could call upon in times of danger and excitement, all the gay confidence of ultimate victory that he could express so appealingly when he had supporters around him on whom to exercise his persuasive charm, were now gone. This outdoor extrovert could not survive a situation that called for endless shabby indoor concealments contrived without hope. Courage turned to irascibility, determination to bad-tempered obstinacy, conviviality to a solitary love of the bottle.

In 1759 a faint ray of hope appeared. In the midst of the Seven Years' War (1756–63), waged between Frederick the Great of Prussia and an alliance whose chief members were Austria, France and Russia, with Britain this time on the side of Prussia, there was a prospect of a French expedition against England, and, in the hope that this would involve a Jacobite rising, Charles drafted a proclamation which protested his right as lawful heir to the throne and emphasized that he had given up his Roman Catholicism:

The Roman Catholick religion has been the ruin of the Royal Family, the subversion of the English Monarchy and Constitution, in the last century, did like an earthquake raise up that fatal rock on which it split. In that religion was I brought up and educated as other Princes are with a firm attachment to the see of Rome. Had motives of interest been able to make me disguise my sentiments upon the material point of religion I should certainly in my first undertaking in the year 1745 have declared myself a protestant, it was too evidently my interest so to doe to leave a doubt with any person. As to the motive which dissuaded me from it, it was no other than a persuasion of the truth of my religion. The adversity I have suffered since that time, has made me reflect, has furnished me with opportunity of being informed, and God had been pleased so far to smile upon my honest endeavour, as to enlighten my understanding and point me out the hidden path by which the finger of man has been introduced to form the artfull system of Roman Infallibility.

Iff it was greatly my interest when last amongst you to appear to be a protestant, it was surely as much against it after my misfortune and during my Exile to become realy one; that motive however had no weight with me in a matter of so great concern.

Then comes the paragraph, quoted in the preceding chapter, which gives an account of his being received into the Church of England in London in 1750, followed by a paragraph which asserts his claim 'as a protestant Prince' and promises the redress of grievances. The whole thing is a pathetic document, and in any case it was soon rendered useless by the British victories of Admiral Boscawen at Lagos and Admiral Hawke at Quiberon Bay which put an end to the Duc de Choiseul's plan to effect a junction between the Toulon and Brest squadrons which would then proceed to Le Havre and convoy a fleet of transports across the Channel.

Charles had been in Basle in 1755 and 1756, living with Clementina and his daughter under the name of Thompson. The Earl of Marischal, now Governor of Neufchâtel, would have nothing to do with the Prince, and spoke of him 'with the utmost horror and detestation, and in the most opprobrious terms,' if we are to believe the report of Arthur Villette, the English Resident at Berne, who also reported that Lord Elcho 'had heartily repented his folly and rashness' in joining Charles. Charles then spent some time in the attractive Duchy of Bouillon, then ruled by his cousin Charles Godfrey de Latour d'Auvergne, who had married Charles's mother's sister. He achieved a reconciliation with Madame de Pompadour, with whom he had quarrelled, hoping unrealistically that her friendship at this stage would be politically helpful. Then we find him in Brest and Boulogne, concerned with the planned French invasion of England. His father was pressing him strongly to send Clementina away. Pressure was also being put on Clementina to leave him. In June 1760 she wrote to James's assistant secretary Andrew Lumisden from Boulogne a strange letter: 'I do not choose to say any more to you,' she wrote, 'but that before 1745, I lived in London, in great plenty, was between that and 1747 undone, and am now in a strange poor place, starving indeed'. The suggestion that Clementina was 'undone' between 1745 and 1747 in the sense that she had been seduced by Charles is patently absurd, though this has not prevented some biographers of Charles from making it: but perhaps she had been seduced, and even had a child, by someone else? 'I was bred to business about White Hall, and could be of use to Him, were there not unluckily an obstacle in the way, which has done Him no service, and me great hurt,' the letter continues. Was the obstacle her sister Catherine? Or was it (as Compton Mackenzie has suggested) that she had been previously mistress of an important man who had used her as a spy for his own ends and had even borne him a child? This would explain the persistent story that Clementina had borne Charles an earlier child who had died young. The naïve romanticizing of the sex-life of the under-sexed Charles in which the folk imagination has indulged for generations (there are still totally absurd stories of ille-gitimate children he fathered in Scotland in 1745–46 floating about in Aberdeen and elsewhere) may have resulted in the obscuring of some important events in Clementina's past. Whatever that past was, she moved into an unknown future on 22 July, 1760, when she fled with her seven-year-old child in a hired coach to Paris, never to return to Charles.

Clementina left Charles at Bouillon, where in a little château in the wooded valley of the Semois he had been in a sort of a way re-creating his Highland life, shooting and fishing during the day and drinking at night. But his drinking was heavier than it had ever been in the High-lands: night after night he was carried drunk to bed. Clementina was ignored or abused. For her it had become an impossible existence. Lord Elcho, whose reports are generally malicious and therefore suspect, says that she took to drink as well.

Meanwhile, James was old and ill and knew he had not long to live. He kept writing to Charles pleading with him to come and visit him at Rome, even (on 3 March 1760) sending 12,000 livres for his expenses. But Charles refused. It was while he was resisting pressure from all sides to go to his father at Rome that Clementina Walkinshaw left him.

She wrote:

Sir:

Your Royalle Highness cannot be surprised at my having taken partty when you consider one repeated bad treatment I have matte with these eight years past, and the Dealy risque of loosing my life. Not been able to bear any longer such hardships, my health been altered by them has obliged me at last to take this Desperate Step of removing from your Royalle Highness with my child which nothing but the fear of my life would ever have made me undertake any Thing without your knowledge. Your Royalle Highness is to great and just when you refflect not to think that you have push'd me to the greatest extremiti, and that there is not one woman in the world that would have suffer'd so long as what I have done. However it shall never hinder me from having for your Royalle persone all the attachment and respect, and I hope in time coming by my conduct to merit your protection and friendship for me and my child I put myself under the care of providence which I hope wont abbandone me as my intentions are honest and that I never will doe a dirtty action for the whole world I quite my Dearest prince with the greatest regret and shalle always be miserable if I dont hear of his welfair and happiness. May God Almighty bliss and preserve him and prospere all his undertakings which is the earnest wish of one how will be till Death my Dearest Prince.

Your most faithfull and most obedient Humble servant

Clementine Walkinshaw

There is one thing I must assur your R:H: that you may not put the Blame on innocent people that there is not one soul ether in the house or out of it that knew or has given me the smallest help in this undertaking nor anybody that ever you knew or saw.

According to Lord Elcho, Clementina later described to him in detail the terrible life Charles had led her, beating her frequently and at the same time displaying great jealousy: 'he invariably surrounded their bed with chairs placed on tables, and on the chairs little bells, so that if anyone approached during the night, the bells would be set a-ringing'.

Charles seemed more concerned to get back his child than his mistress. He wrote to John Gordon, Rector of the Scots College at Paris: 'I shall be in the greatest affliction untill I guett back the child, which was my only comfort in my misfortune'. Andrew Lang prints a letter 'From Jones the servant' which gives a vivid picture of the pursuit of Clementina:

... They (Gordon and Bodson) both came to my room and told me to go to the Lady's lodging and see to amuse her untill such time as they had an order to take up the chylde. I went to her lodgings but she was gon out, I waited untill she came back. She seemed much syrprazed at seeing me. I reasoned the matter with her but all to no purpose. She told me that she would sooner make away with herself than go back, and as for the Chylde she would be cut to pieces sooner than give her up. I stayed in the Lady's Room until ten and a half. She sent for a coach to go out. I asked if she would allow me to accompany her and the Chylde. She told me yes, wee set out and at a little distance from the lodgings, the coach stopt, there came a gentleman well-drest and two others ... and told the Lady to come out and to go with the other coach. I came out allong with them. I asked the Lady if there was place for me; the Gentleman answered in Ruff manner 'No Sir, go about your business if you have any.' They set off in a coach and four horses, which, Sir, seemed to me to be hired horses, the Gentleman was a Frenchman as far as one could judge. I followed them as far as I was able but lost sight of them.

The pursuit went on for a month. But it was all to no avail. Clementina was at the Convent of the Nuns of the Visitation, under the protection of King Louis and the Archbishop of Paris and pensioned by James.

Charles was furious with everybody – Clementina, Louis, his father. James wrote to him at Bouillon on 8 September trying to explain matters and to calm him down:

I have now been four weeks, My Dear Son, without receiving your usual letter to Edgar, which gives me great uneasyness, and the more that I am affrayed that you have at present suspicions of me, which I do not deserve, and which I shall now here endeavour to remove with all the brevity I can. You could not doubt to be sure of the desire I had that Mrs Walkinshaw should be no more with you, both from the letter I writt to you on her subject, and the message I had before sent you upon it by Lumisden, tho' I had been Long before informed of her being with you, which could not be otherways, the Fact being so publick, and making so much noise, as you must know better than myself; But it is very true at the same time that she had no order from me to leave you. It was many months before that I had undoubted Informations of her desire to Leave you, to satisfy her own conscience in the first place, and to stop the mouths of those to whom she knew she was obnoxius and suspected, and Lastly to give her Daughter in a Convent a Christian and good Education: And it is very true that I did what I could to encourage her to endeavour to obtain your permission and consent to Leave you, tho' I could not disapprove much Less oppose so reasonable and pious desires. After she had Left you, she writt herself to implore my Protection, and to seek a subsistance for herself and her Daughter to enable her to execute the Laudable Intention she entertain'd . . .

James goes on to stress the importance of providing a proper education for the child, impossible 'in the uncertain and ambulatory Life you Lead', saying that 'if you have a true Love and tenderness for her, you should preferr her good education to all other considerations'. He himself is weak, he says, and has had a return of his coughing,

but O My Dear Child could I but once have the satisfaction of seeing you before I dy, I flatter myself that I might soon be able to convince you that you never could have had a more tender Father than myself, nor a truer friend wholly taken up with all that may conduce to your temporal and Eternal Happiness. . . .

This is a moving glimpse of the sad old Chevalier de St George, who was now entering the final years of a life of exile. His tragedy is less spectacular than that of his son, but no less real. The mixture of melancholy and kindness in his character is not unattractive, though not calculated to stimulate active and enthusiastic loyalty. Charles, however, showed no compassion for the old man; he was brooding angrily over his own real and fancied injuries: he never replied to his father's letter. And on 25 October, when George II died, Charles took no notice. (The story that he was present in disguise at the coronation of George III on September 1761, and let fall a white kid glove from the gallery in response to the ritual challenge by Dymock, the Champion of England, in defence of the right of the newly-crowned king, is a romantic fiction, as apparently are all other stories of Charles's later visits to England or Ireland. Scott, who used a version of the coronation story in *Redgauntlet*, admitted in his note that it was 'probably one of those numerous fictions which were circulated to keep up the spirits of a sinking faction'.) Charles had by now alienated virtually all his supporters, the latest being Alexander Murray (of the Elibank Plot) whom he now dismissed on suspicion of having assisted Clementina's flight. Murray's brother, Lord Elibank, wrote to Charles on 29 December in anguished reproach. 'Your Royal Highness is resolved to destroy yourself to all intents and purposes. Everybody here talks of your conduct with horror, and from being once the admiration of Europe you have become the reverse. . . . You have banished all your father's subjects.' On the same day that this letter was written James wrote to the Maréchal de Belle-Isle contrasting Charles's affectionate behaviour to him before 1745 with his present conduct and pleading with the Maréchal to urge Charles to visit him at Rome. The day before, Clementina Walkinshaw had written him a letter curiously combining reproach and affection:

Nothing in this world can be more sensible to me than this fattale separation. I can't express to you, my Dearest prince, how much my heart suffers on this account. I am affraid you ar untirly out of Humour with me. It is certain I have committed a fault which nothing but Despair could ever have push'd me to that extremity, but if Your Royal Highness will consider that in your violent passions I always ran the risque of loosing my life as unluckily as I was the victime everything that Desobliged you, which made me think that certainly you had some pick against me which allone has been the cause of the Desperate Step I undertook. I can assure you, my Dearest prince, that I had nothing else in view but your honour and glory, and one principal object, which was the childs education, . . . She will always be yours, but my ambition is that she should doe you honour. She has all the happie disposition in the world for that, and it would have been a thousand pities to have neglected them. She is already making great progreuss in her reading Both in lattine and french and she has a vast Dessire to be able to writ to her Dear papa which I hope she will do in a few months. I shall now, my Dearest prince, plead your forgiveness. I know that you have a good heart; and as you ar great, I hope you ar just, and I flatter myself you wont forget the sacrifice I made to you of my honour and the presiouse pledge I have with me. . . . I would be vastly happie, my Dearest prince, if I could have the satisfaction of hearing from you and that your Humanity and goodness would forgive me, I am vastly uneasie to hear about your health; for the love of god take great care of it . . . I think that all the eyes of europe are fixt upon you at present, and that there is a vast number of reports upon your account which I have done all in my little power to contradict, as I would rather Dye ten thousand Deaths than lett word slipp from my mouth that would Doe you the smallest injury or hurt, and what ever may be your way of thinking or actting towards me, I shall never ceass wishing your Royall Highness al manner of happiness and that everything that is good and great may for ever attend my Dearest Prince, . . .

Charles did not reply, nor did he answer her letter of 13 February 1761, when she once again explained the reasons for her flight: 'You pushed me to the greatest extremity, and even despair, as I was always in perpetual dread of my life from your violent passions'. She had heard reports 'that you are not yourself, that your head is quite gone'. There were widely circulated rumours about both his physical and his mental health, and apparently there was some justification for them. Yet he had only just passed his fortieth birthday. John Gordon wrote to reproach him for neglecting to take exercise and for not taking solid food. Charles's reply ignored the reproach and the advice but includes the strange sentence: 'My attachment to our country is strong, but my Scotch Blud is to high after all the Insultes to apply more to them that Refused a Little Childe in my Concine (?)'. He refers to his father coldly as 'The Old Gentilman' and thinks he should exert himself 'to be father of his Subjects ... Being more in power than even the first of his subjects'.

But James was beyond exerting himself. He had long been a sick man, and as early as 1756 had been given a papal dispensation 'to drink either broth or chocolate before he communicates, on account of his habitual indisposition of stomach'. In October 1762 – scarcely three weeks after the death of his faithful secretary James Edgar – he had suffered a paralytic stroke and the last three and a half years of his life were spent in almost total passivity; he died quietly, 'with his usual mild serenity in his countenance' as Lumisden reported, at 9.15 p.m. on 1 January 1766.

It was only when he received definite news at Bouillon that his father was dying that Charles decided at last to return to Rome. He let it be known to the Vatican that 'after having been so long in such hidden retirement as to cause many people to think him dead', as Cardinal Albani put it in writing to Sir Horace Mann in November 1765, he was now anxious to settle in Rome. 'To these requests,' the Cardinal continued, 'His Holiness has replied that he will see him again with much pleasure, that he will be treated in accordance with his distinguished rank, and that he can reckone, after his father's death, upon the revenues which have already been settled for the Cardinal his brother. But with regard to his being recognized as King, the Pope neither can nor will take upon himself the responsibility of admitting such a claim; His Holiness will act in this respect as the other sovereigns.'

Charles left for Rome on 30 December but he did not reach the city until after his father's death. James was given a magnificent royal funeral, but this did not mean that the authorities who arranged it were prepared to recognize his son as King Charles III. The Cardinal of York, with whom after years of total estrangement Charles now re-established a fraternal relationship, exerted himself to achieve papal recognition of his brother's claim, but to no avail. The British Government initiated feverish diplomatic activity throughout Europe to make sure that no country recognized Charles, but it was hardly necessary. In spite of the fact that both the French and the Spanish ambassadors to the Holy See supported the Cardinal of York's application for his brother's recognition, the prestige and power of Britain, increased after her successes in the Seven Years' War, together with the almost total eclipse of the Jacobite movement, made any recognition of Charles quixotic and unrealistic. Louis XV disowned his ambassador's action and reprimanded the ambassador. Clement XIII did indeed agree to put the question of Charles's recognition to the congregation of Cardinals, but they returned an overwhelming negative. 'I have now the satisfaction to inform your Grace,' wrote Sir Horace Mann to the Duke of Richmond on 24 January, 'that the consultation whether it was expedient for the Pope to acknowledge the present Pretender under the title which his Father usurped, was held the 13th, and the result was that the Pope could not *per ora* grant what was demanded. This sentence has greatly displeased Cardinal Stuart and his friends, among the most zealous and active of whom were the public ministers whom I mentioned in my last letter, and who I should think would not be able to justify their conduct to their own Courts if it was taken notice of.'

Charles was able to muster a few loyal Jacobites who treated him as though he were King – some Irish in the French service, some long exiled Scots, some unsuccessful English gentlemen of fortune – but his pretence at maintaining a royal style at the Palazzo Muti, where he was now re-established, was patently hollow. Most people in Rome treated him as they treated other members of the aristocracy, not in any way as a king. The Rectors of the English, Scottish and Irish Colleges at Rome were part of the small minority who did treat him with the deference due to royalty, and for this flouting of a papal decision they were banished from Rome. By order of the Pope the royal arms which James had placed over the door of the Palazzo Muti were taken down. So it was a thoroughly unkinged Charles who settled down to live once again in the palazzo where he had been born and where he had spent his childhood. He no longer lacked money, however. His brother resigned to him his pension from the Pope of 20,000 crowns together with all the savings James had left him in his will.

Back in Britain, the diminishing number of the faithful tried to cheer themselves by writing to each other reports of what was going on in

Rome. They had pretty well dwindled to a handful of non-juring Scottish bishops (i.e. those who had always refused to swear allegiance to the House of Hanover) and the Laurence Oliphants of Gask, father and son, who had been out in the Forty-five, had escaped to Sweden after Culloden and had been allowed to return in 1762. In their correspondence they referred to Charles as 'cousin Peggie' or sometimes just 'the young lady'. 'What do you hear of the young lady that has made her escape out of her nunnery?' asked Oliphant of Bishop Robert Gordon on 20 January 1766, and the Bishop replied that she was well; 'nor have I the least suspicion of her not supporting her character with her usual firmness and dignity, notwithstanding what may at any time be reported by an slanderous, lying, and malicious race of men'. This tiny band of friends stubbornly refused to believe any ill of their hero. 'Have compassion on poor cousin Peggie,' writes Bishop Gordon in March 1767 to Oliphant, who has heard with sadness that his 'favorite lady is for certain a papagee', 'and believe not every report tho appearances, she confesses, may be sometimes against her, and these, magnified in every respect to her disadvantage'. Later they discuss marriage possibilities for Charles, and when he finally does marry they exchange news of the welfare of the couple. It is all rather silly and at the same time rather touching; most touching of all is the determined way in which Bishop Forbes transcribed and kept extracts from these letters in the massive collection of Jacobite material he entitled *The Lyon in Mourning*. (The younger Oliphant of Gask lived until 1792 and never recognized the House of Hanover: on Charles's death he recognized Henry IX and declared that if Henry died he would recognize the King of Sardinia, who was the senior descendant of Henrietta, Duchesse d'Orléans, daughter of Charles I.)

Charles's improved financial position, which he owed to his now affluent brother, did not do Clementina Walkinshaw any good. She wrote to Andrew Lumisden (who had succeeded James Edgar as James's secretary in 1764 and remained in the extremely difficult position of Charles's secretary) about support from Charles, but Lumisden, writing of course without his master's knowledge, assured her that 'his passion must still greatly cool before any application can be made to him in your behalf'. A rumour that Charles and Miss Walkinshaw had been secretly married greatly distressed the Cardinal Duke of York, who wrote to Waters in Paris asking him to get an affidavit from the lady to the effect that she and Charles had never married. The unfortunate Clementina, doubtless under financial pressure, signed the required document on 9 March 1767:

Whereas I, Clementina Walkinshaw, a native of Scotland, has heard a report spread about that Charles, heretofore Prince of Wales, and now the Third of that name King of Great Britain, etc, is married to me, grounded on the connection the public think the said Prince and now King had formerly with me: I, the beforementioned Clementina Walkinshaw, do voluntarily and upon my oath before God my Creator, and before the here subscribing witness, Mr John Waters standing so at my request, [swear] that such a report of marriage, or anything relative to the least tendency of that kind, is void of all foundation; and that I never gave the least room, either by word or writing, to such a falsehood, spread abroad by enemies to me I suppose, as likeways evidently to the said King Charles the Third, my sovereign. . . .

Charles remained adamant in refusing to assist Clementina financially: his brother supported her and her daughter.

Clementina tried to reach Charles through their daughter Charlotte, who, presumably on her mother's prompting, now wrote a series of letters in French to 'Mon Auguste Papa', signing herself 'Pouponne'. But Charles ignored these too. One of them was accompanied by a letter from Clementina giving proud details of their daughter's progress in singing, music, dancing, geography and history. When in 1772 Clementina heard of Charles's marriage, she had Charlotte write again to her father, this time to offer her congratulations: 'C'est avec le plus profond respect Mon Auguste Papa que je prends la liberté de vous faire mon complimens sur votre établissement . . .' She goes on to appeal to her august papa to establish communication with her, since at present all that she gets from being his daughter is despair; she is without means and without prospects and consequently condemned to lead *la vie du Monde la plus malheureuses et la plus Misérables* [sic]'. Charles replied through John Gordon that he would receive Charlotte into his household on condition that she would have nothing more to do with her mother; Charlotte refused the condition; and that put an end to this particular chapter in the story of Charles's relation with his daughter. The story was to have an unexpected ending, as we shall find later. We must now return to 1767.

In May 1767 we get a glimpse of Charles at Rome in a letter from William Hamilton, English envoy at Naples, to Lord Shelburne, secretary of state for the southern department:

The Pretender is hardly thought of even at Rome; the life he leads is now very regular and sober, his chief occupation is shooting in the environs of Rome, and the only people he can see or converse with are his few attendants, ... The pension his father had of £1200 a year from the Court of Rome is now granted to the Cardinal, but as he was not in the least want of any addition to his income, he gives it to the present Pretender, and it is said, allows him £1800 a year more out of his own income. ...

To give your Lordship a strong picture of this unfortunate man, I will finish my despatch with transcribing part of a letter from an English lady ... who has been always attached to that family, ...

'I have at last seen —— in his own house; as for his person it is rather handsome, his face ruddy and full of pimples. He looks good-natured and was over-joyed to see me – nothing could be more affectionately gracious. I cannot answer for his cleverness, for he appeared to me to be absorbed in melancholy thoughts, a good deal of distraction in his conversation and frequent brown studies.... He has all the reason in the world to be melancholy, for there is not a soul goes near him, not knowing what to call him. He told me time lay heavy upon him. I said I supposed he read a good deal. He made no answer. ...'

William Hamilton's testimony to Charles's sobriety is not borne out by the evidence of other witnesses. His brother wrote several times 'to deplore the continuance of the bottle'. 'I am persuaded we should gain ground,' he wrote in another letter to an unknown correspondent, 'as to everything, were it not for the nasty bottle, that goes on but too much, and certainly must at last kill him'. Charles himself sometimes wrote strangely. In February 1767 he wrote to his brother of the necessity of his (Charles's) remaining in Rome and showing himself out of mourning, 'and, I may say, of ragged clothes, as well as my servants'. He adds mysteriously: 'What is in my breast cannot be divulged until I have occasion. God alone is judge.' But it does seem that he pulled himself together in May. He was reconciled to the Pope and decided to give up his hermit-like life and go out into Roman society, even though it was as Count of Albany rather than Charles III. But at the end of the year he quarrelled with Lumisden and dismissed him, together with other of his gentlemen with whom he had also quarrelled. They had refused to accompany him in his carriage when they considered him to be in no fit state to make a public appearance.

The evidence about Charles's drinking is conflicting. He does seem to have controlled it for a while on going out again into society, and thereafter to have indulged in intermittent bouts. He was still fond of hunting, and when the season allowed he returned to the scenes of his boyhood hunting activities around Albano. There is a picture of him at the end of the 1760's by a not unduly sympathetic lady eyewitness:

The Pretender is naturally above middle size but stoops excessively; he appears bloated and red in the face; his countenance heavy and sleepy, which is attributed to his having given in to excess of drinking; but when a young man he must have been esteemed handsome. His complexion is of the fair tint, his eyes blue [his eyes were in fact brown: this makes one wonder how accurate an observer the lady was], his hair light brown, and the contour of his face a long oval; he is by no means thin, has a noble person, and a graceful manner. His dress was scarlet, laced with broad gold lace; he wears the blue riband outside of his coat, from which depends a cameo antique, as large as the palm of my hand; and he wears the same garter and motto as those of the noble order of St. George in England. Upon the whole, he has a melancholy, mortified appearance. ... At Princess Palestrina's, he asked me if I understood the game of *Tarrochi*, which they were about to play at. I answered in the negative; upon which, taking the pack in his hands, he desired to know if I had ever seen such odd cards? I replied that they were very odd indeed. He then, displaying them, said, 'There is everything in the world to be found in these cards – the sun, the moon, the stars; and here,' says he, throwing me a card, 'is the Pope; here is the devil; there is but one of the trio wanting, and you know who that should be!' I was so amazed, so astonished, though he spoke this last in a laughing good humoured manner, that I did not know which way to look; and as to a reply I made none.

Charles left Rome for Pisa in the summer of 1770, to take the baths there on the advice of his doctors. He went by Florence, where he was lavishly entertained, but as Count of Albany not as King Charles. He then proceeded to Pisa, and after some weeks there returned to Florence, where he had been so well received. But by now the Grand Duke had become alarmed at possible English reaction to Charles's reception in Florence, and ordered that he should be ignored. The resulting change in the treatment he now received from the Florentines enraged him, and with characteristic obstinacy he determined to settle there permanently. Sir Horace Mann, British envoy in Florence, duly reported all this to his Government. In vain, wrote Sir Horace, Charles's friends tried to persuade him to change his mind, afraid 'that his violent temper, heated by the wine he was always taking, might induce him to commit some great irregularity in public of which the Government would be obliged to take notice'. It was only when his brother the Cardinal applied the strongest pressure that Charles gave up his scheme and left Florence: the Cardinal, after all, provided his income. He went back to Pisa where he stayed for a while before returning to Rome.

On 29 May 1771 we find Charles writing from Rome about a secret trip to Paris he proposed to take under the name of Douglas, with one servant. His brother is not to know. In August he was in Siena and by the end of the month was in Paris, staying with a tailor called Didelot at the Hôtel de Brunswick, off the Rue Saint-Honoré. The object of Charles's secret departure from Italy (which baffled and upset the watchful Sir Horace Mann) was marriage. The idea emanated from the French King and the Duc d'Aiguillon, who found the prospect of a Stuart heir to trouble the British Government highly agreeable. The Duc de Fitzjames was instructed to write to Charles offering him a pension of 40,000 crowns a year if he would marry someone found suitable for him. The plan was originally for Charles to marry a young lady cryptically called 'Miss Speedy', who is now known to have been Princess Marie-Louise Ferdinande, daughter of the Prince of Salm-Kyrburg; she was only eighteen, and burst into tears on learning what was proposed for her. Colonel Edmund Ryan, an Irish colonel in the French service who was acting as Charles's agent in this matter (much as Charles Wogan had acted for his father more than fifty years before) very properly took the view that it would be barbaric to press the matter further, and continued his search. After a number of false alarms he discovered at the end of December that the widowed Princesse de Stolberg would be happy for Charles to marry her daughter Louise, and Louise would be happy too. Louise's father, Gustave Adolphe, Prince of Stolberg-Gedern, came of an old and distinguished family recently raised to princely rank, while her mother, a daughter of Maximilien Emmanuel, Prince of Hornes and Lady Charlotte Bruce, was allied to the Bruces in Scotland, the Montmorencys and Créquis in France, the Orsini in Italy and the Gonzagas and Medinas in Spain – enough blue blood, it was agreed, for a Stuart without a throne. Prince Gustave Adolphe had been killed fighting for Austria at the Battle of Leuthen in 1757, leaving his twenty-four-year-old widow to bring up four daughters with no money. The Empress Maria Theresa helped the family, and obtained a nomination for Louise, the eldest child, to the Chapter of Sainte Wandru at Mons, one of those aristocratic educational institutions in the Austrian Netherlands referred to on p. 264. She had her earliest education in a convent and at fourteen had entered Sainte Wandru. She had left there at sixteen and had then moved about in society with her mother in search of a husband. She was now almost twenty and, as Ryan reported, had 'a good figure, a pretty face, and excellent teeth, with all the qualities which Your Majesty can desire'. The Princesse would have been equally happy to give her fifteen-year-old third daughter to Charles, but the Duc de Fitzjames thought Louise more suitable and Charles himself wrote that he preferred the elder. Louise was a self-possessed, sophisticated young lady, with no illusions about the world. Even a nominal crown had its attractions – and who could be sure that it might not be made a reality? She would have financial security and, at least in a limited circle, a sort of regal state. All the evidence points to the fact that she was no innocent young victim dragged reluctantly to the bed of a middle-aged drunkard. She knew exactly what she was doing, and was glad to do it. She was annoyed at various legal and theological difficulties which were raised and insisted on their being overcome at once in her impatience to assume her new position. They were overcome; and the wedding took place by proxy in Paris on 28 March, in great secrecy. Colonel Ryan then escorted Louise to Venice, and from there they sailed to Ancona. Charles and his bride met at Macerata on 17 April, Good Friday, and the real wedding took place the same day, thanks to the good offices of Cardinal Marefoschi, at the Marefoschi Palace. The Princesse had made it a condition that the marriage should take place and be consummated on the very day that Charles and Louise first met. And so it happened. Charles, who usually paid attention to omens and prophecies, does not appear to have been troubled by the ill omen of the day.

CHAPTER SEVENTEEN

The End of the Story

CHARLES and his bride entered Rome on Wednesday, 22 April 1772. The Cardinal Duke of York had arranged a magnificent processional entry through the Porta del Popolo. They drove to the Palazzo Muti, where the delighted Louise heard her husband and herself greeted as King and Queen by the faithful Jacobites of the household. Soon after their arrival the Cardinal called on his sister-in-law and presented her with a snuff-box set in diamonds in which was a draft on his banker for 40,000 crowns. Charles sent to inform Cardinal Pallavicini, the papal secretary of state, of the arrival of the 'King and Queen of England', but the Vatican ignored the announcement. Clement XIV – he had been elected Pope in 1769 – thought it politic to maintain his predecessor's refusal to recognize Charles's royal claims. Louise had to be content with hearing herself addressed as 'Your Majesty' within the Palazzo Muti. But though they refused to see the couple as King and Queen the people of Rome were well enough disposed to the newly-weds. The Pope was perfectly happy to show them every consideration except the recognition they both wanted, and everywhere they were received, entertained and treated with courtesy and consideration.

The marriage began well. Charles gave up his heavy drinking and recovered some of his former charm. Louise, receiving visitors but (being in her own view royal) not returning their visits, driving about the streets of Rome with the Prince by day and attending concerts or formal parties with him in the evenings, was thoroughly enjoying her new position. Blonde, blue-eyed, with a slightly *retroussé* nose and a complexion *'d'une blancheur éclatante'* (as the Swiss writer Charles Victor de Bonstetten described her), she became known as the 'Queen of Hearts' and expected men to fall in love with her. Young Thomas William Coke, doing the Grand Tour after leaving Eton, fell for Louise in Rome and aroused tender feelings on her part. Bonstetten was a visitor at the Palazzo Muti in 1774 and in his *Souvenirs* gives us a sympathetic picture of the miniature court there: *'on était là avec le roi et la reine d'Angleterre, entourés de trois à quatre chambellans ou dames d'honneur; tout cela embelli par les charmes et la gaité de la reine'*. He was impressed enough to call the couple 'the King and Queen of England' and to talk of the charms and gaiety of the Queen. He too fell for Louise, and retained an affection for her throughout the rest of his life: they corresponded regularly. Bonstetten had with him in Rome a fellow-Swiss by the name of Schérer, who fell in love with Lucille de Maltzam, one of Louise's maids of honour.

The only fly in the ointment in this promising stage of the marriage was Clementina Walkinshaw, who turned up in Rome with her daughter early in 1773 in the hope of now obtaining from Charles the support she had long sought. We have already seen the letter that Charlotte wrote her father in April 1772. This seems to have been the beginning of a campaign. But it proved unsuccessful. Clementina and her daughter were ordered to leave the city, and the Cardinal provided money. Charles's harsh treatment of his daughter was presumably the result of his resentment at the way Clementina was deliberately making herself a nuisance to himself and his new wife. Charles never saw Clementina in Rome – indeed, they never saw each other again anywhere after her original flight from him. She lived until 1802, pensioned, after James's death, by the Cardinal Duke of York. She spent the last ten years of her life in Switzerland and died at Freiburg.

Charles's reformation did not last. He grew more and more resentful at Rome's refusal to accord him royal honours, and withdrew from society to brood and drink. The irrepressible Sir Horace Mann wrote home on 11 December 1773, that, after 'having abstained from any great excess in wine' for some time after his marriage, Charles 'has given in to it again as much as ever, so that he is seldom quite sober, and frequently commits the greatest disorders in his family'. Charles tried again to persuade the Pope to recognize his royal status, writing to Cardinal Marefoschi that it was for the Pope to set the example in this, and then all others would follow. But the Pope remained unmoved. Enraged, Charles decided to abandon Rome, vowing that he would never enter its gates again.

He went with his wife to Leghorn, then to Siena (where, according to a wholly imaginary story put about in the middle of the nineteenth century by two romantic and self-deluding brothers known as the Sobieski Stuarts, Louise gave birth to a son: she never in fact bore any children, and since the whole purpose of the marriage was to provide a Stuart heir there would have been no reason to conceal it if she had borne Charles a son). In October 1774 Charles went to Florence, determined to settle there in spite of the coldness of Leopold, Grand Duke of Tuscany (and second son of Maria Theresa) who once again did not want to offend the British Government. In Florence he thought he would be able to live more economically. Prince Corsini provided a palazzo, and the couple settled down to a Florentine existence. Louise had remained for a while in Rome, but by the end of the year she had joined her husband in Florence. In a fit of anger at the refusal of the French court to afford him the regal dignities on which he insisted, Charles refused his French subsidy, but his shrewdly practical wife managed secretly to have the money paid to her from 1775. Charles knew nothing about this until ten years later, when he wrote to the Comte de Vergennes that by her 'adroit insinuations' she had contrived to persuade King Louis to leave him in total want and had obtained 600,000 francs that were rightly his without his knowledge. Louise had made up her mind about how she wanted to live and how she was going to manage it. She delighted in the company of young men, and she enjoyed her flirtatious correspondence with Bonstetten.

There is an interesting picture of Charles in March 1775 given in a letter written from Pisa by a Scottish visitor:

We went to Florence from this place on the 18th of last month and arrived the same night. The next morning I was told Prince Jarlagh [Charlie] was in town. I made an impatient ramble till I found out that he had a servant who could speak English, who proved to be a rank Highlander, John Stewart of the family of Ardvolich. He has been with his royal master ever since the year 1745. He is the upper domestick. We were happy to meet each other. I asked if it was possible I could say in my own country I had spoken to his master. He replied, there was no difficulty and desired me to come next morning, the 22d, and I should obtain my request. Accordingly I came at 9 o'clock, time enough to breakfast with Mr. Stewart before Prince Jarlagh could be seen, which was 11; when Mr. Stewart called me upstairs, and introduced me into his dressing-room; where seeing him before me, I kneel'd down. He kindly gave me his right hand, which I did myself the honour to kiss, saying, 'it was the loyalty of my parents to his royal family that emboldened me to presume this attempt.' He asked me what family I was of. I answered, 'Of the house of Glenbucky; that the late Alexander was a near relation to me.' He spoke a few words more in which he said, 'My lad, I wish you well,' and then retired. He looks old in complexion and is pretty stout in person.

Charles avoided the lively salons of Florence and preferred solitary walks by the Arno or drives with his wife through the city. He explored churches and palaces and gardens. He went frequently to the theatre, where he sometimes slept in his box. He visited places of public assembly and hung about on the outskirts of balls and gatherings. When he encountered the Grand Duke and Duchess, they refused to recognize him. Though he gave out that he and his wife wished to be called the Count and Countess of Albany, his deep inward rage at being refused recognition as a king, together with his inability to do anything at all about it, produced continuous psychological disturbance. He drank more and more, Cyprus wine being his favourite tipple, and on more than one occasion was seen in public (sometimes at the theatre) the worse for liquor. Louise received calls; flirted; wrote amorously and yet in curiously schoolgirlish fashion to Bonstetten that he was the man '*le plus créé pour captiver mon coeur, mon esprit et mon âme*' and about how much she wanted a lover who loved only her. She told him that her passion was now Montaigne, and that she read one of his essays every morning. She had decided, she said, to give up being a queen; she was tired of her husband's insistence on royal treatment, and would have preferred '*oublier toutes grandeurs et devenir tout à fait républicain*', she wrote. This enthusiasm for republicanism was, of course, a passing mood. Normally she was strongly behind Charles in his regal claims. But she was getting bored, and she was becoming thoroughly discontented with her husband. Unable to get through to him in direct conversation, she wrote him a letter on 5 June, 1775:

Since your Majesty won't listen to reason when one speaks and since you have decided to be sulky with me because I don't want go for a walk in June at a time when the heat is excessive, I humbly represent to your Majesty that my health suffers a great deal from great heat and that consequently your Sacred Majesty is too just and too good to expose anybody for your own pleasure not only to illness but even to the least suffering in the world. I know your loyal heart and your sensitive soul, and it would be cruel to make a poor woman run about the streets in terrible heat (*courir les rues par une chaleur horrible*) just because your Majesty is bored in his room. You suggest this, Sir, thinking that it will soften your first proposal that I should get up at seven in the morning after having gone to bed at two hours after midnight – but that must be a joke of your Majesty's, otherwise one would have to believe you were in your dotage. You are not yet as old as that, Sir, but it certainly would do you no honour in the world to have people imagining that you, who have always had the reputation of a gallant (*qui avez toujours passé pour un gaillard*), had degenerated to the point when you did not want to spend more than a few hours in bed with a young woman who is pretty and who loves you. But if your Majesty continues to sulk as you have been doing, I shall feel obliged to justify myself before the public for being the innocent cause that the Royal Face is not shining as gloriously as usual and that its beautiful eyes are clouded. I shall circulate among all my friends the memorial that I have attached to this letter, of which I have already sent your Majesty a copy and in which I have set out the facts as well as I can, and believing that my cause is good I hope that they will do me justice. I am, Sir, with profound devotion,

the Humble Half of your Majesty
Louise R.

This is not the letter of an innocent girl married to a tyrant. It is a cleverly malicious attack on a sick and unhappy man where it will hurt most. This is not to say that Charles's treatment of Louise was in any way admirable. But Charles was ill and suffering: he had had an attack of asthma; he was threatened with apoplexy and had been prescribed 'bleedings and emetics'. The following year he grew worse. His legs grew swollen and painful and he suffered almost continually from sickness in his stomach. A persistent cough developed. He lost his appetite. But though medical advice prevailed on him to lessen his drinking during the day, he continued to drink heavily in the evenings. He was frequently seen drunk at the theatre, or if not drunk at least (as Sir Horace Mann reported) 'in a drowsy posture'. 'Two days ago,' wrote Mann in September 1776, 'a couch was made for his Box [in the theatre], for him to lay at full length; on this he slept the greater part of yesterday evening'. But visitors, and Louise, came and went to and from the box as usual. Charles always took her with him. 'He is jealous to such a degree that neither there or at home, she is ever out of his sight. All the avenues to her room, excepting through his own, are barricaded.' The reasons given by Charles for this, Mann adds, is that the succession must never be in doubt.

Louise's letters to Bonstetten grew more outspoken. 'I prefer an agreeable man to the most grand lord who would bore me.' And again, more emphatically: 'You are charming, seductive, agreeable, and that is always the same refrain after I have talked of you for two hours. But what is nicest of all is to be able to say to you yourself when I am writing to you what it would be impossible to say if you were here'. But Bonstetten stayed in Switzerland, and the Countess of Albany had to come to terms with the fact. 'There remains still at the bottom of my heart a fire not fully extinguished which it needs only you to re-light.' Shortly afterwards she writes that she is consoling herself with another. But until she became deeply and permanently involved with that other it seems that her epistolary affair with Bonstetten was an important part of her emotional life. There was a moment in the course of their correspondence when she more than hinted that her husband's death would leave her free to marry him:

> Quasi quasi j'ai vu le moment, il y a deux jours, que j'allais devenir la maîtresse de mon sort; la mort, la maladie, ennemies des mortels, se promenoit sur la tête de mon seigneur et maître, mais, grace a Dieu, l'heur n'était pas encore venu.

(Two days ago I almost saw the moment arrive when I would become mistress of my fate; death and disease, enemies of mortals, walked over the head of my lord and master, but, thank God, the hour had not yet arrived.)

With that deft turn at the end of the sentence, interposing that 'grace a Dieu', she barely managed to retreat from the suggestion that she was waiting impatiently for her husband's death. But the sentence is even more ambiguous than this, for she does not write 'l'heure n'était pas encore venue' but 'l'heur n'était pas encore venu'. Now this may well be her uncertain French grammar, for there are many mistakes of gender in her letters (her native language was German), and the English rendering just given assumes that she meant 'l'heure', but she may indeed have meant 'l'heur', a now obsolete word meaning luck or chance.

In 1777 Charles gave up the palazzo provided by Prince Corsini and bought the Palazzo Guadigni (later San Clemente) in the Via San Sebastiano: it still has the weather vane he erected, which shows 'C R 1777' – his last royal gesture. It was in this year and in this house that Louise first met the twenty-seven-year-old poet and dramatist Vittorio Alfieri.

Whether the affair between Louise and Alfieri was a grand romantic passion between a captive heroine and a fairy-tale liberator or a sordid intrigue between a bored young woman and a histrionic *poseur* is a matter of opinion. Alfieri's passion for Louise seems to have been genuine enough, yet at the same time curiously *voulu*: he wanted some-one to play Beatrice to his Dante, and he interpreted his feeling for Louise in the light of his literary needs and his fondness for high romantic gesturing. He had already had some passionate affairs in the course of the travels he undertook after leaving his native Piedmont. He had fallen deeply in love with a married woman in Holland, and later became involved with another married woman in London, an involvement which resulted in a duel with Lord Ligonier, the injured husband, a divorce, and the necessity for Alfieri to leave England. Returning to Turin in 1772 he fell in love with the Marchesa Turinetti di Prie. In 1777, eager to establish himself as a tragic dramatist in Italian after having written his first two tragedies in French, and finding that his Piedmontese background and much travel abroad had combined to weaken his powers of expression in Italian, he came to Florence in order to improve his Italian style. He was also looking for someone whom he could love with perhaps less of the wild romantic passion of his earlier affairs but with more literary and artistic feeling. He found her in Louise, as he recorded ten years later in his *Memoirs:*

At the end of the previous summer, which I spent at Florence, I had often accidentally met a charming and beautiful lady whom it was impossible not to see and pay attention to, since she was both a foreigner and of high rank ... A soft gleam in her dark eyes combined (and this is very rare) with a very white skin and fair hair emphasised her beauty, with which it was difficult not to be impressed and vanquished. She was twenty-five years old, with a great interest in the fine arts and in literature, a temperament of gold and, in spite of the ample ease provided by her position, plagued by painful domestic circumstances which left her little opportunity to achieve the happiness and good fortune she deserved. This was altogether too much to be resisted.

Alfieri goes on to tell us that in the autumn he was taken by an acquaintance to visit her, and soon found himself smitten, but in a way quite different from his three previous affairs. This *'gentilissima e bella signora'* gradually came to dominate his every thought and feeling and in two months he realized that this was an intellectual passion as well as a passion of the heart and that 'instead of finding in her, as in all ordinary women, an obstacle to literary glory, a distraction from useful work and what one might call a diminishing (*rimpicciolimento*) of [his] thoughts', he found in her 'both stimulus, comfort and example towards all good work'. That autumn he wrote his first sonnet to her:

Negri, vivaci, e in dolce fuoco ardenti
Occhi, che date a un tempo e morte e vita, ...

(Black, lively and sweetly burning
Eyes, that give at the same time both death and life, ...)

Louise had by this time built up a little salon round herself and Charles, though continuously watchful, allowed her to receive her friends. Alfieri began his visits to Louise perfectly properly as the conventional *cavaliere servente* accepted by Italian society at the time. For a while Charles had no suspicions, and remained unaware of the frustrations and quiet plottings that went on between his wife and his guest while they watched him doze off and hoped that the Cyprus wine he had so lavishly imbibed would keep him fast asleep for some time. (The fact that this is a stock situation going back to Ovid and that Alfieri wrote a poem in this tradition describing the adulterous couple waiting for the husband to fall fast asleep so that they could enjoy their love does not mean that it did not happen: this was a case of life imitating art, an activity at which Alfieri was adept.) Inspired by Louise, Alfieri wrote his tragedy *Maria Stuarda*, about Mary Queen of Scots. He was happy, he wrote later, in the affection of his beloved, and would have been in a state of perfect tranquillity if she had not been continually upset 'by her querulous, unreasonable and constantly drunken old husband'. Alfieri used to come to the Palazzo Guadigni in the evenings and sometimes dine there; Charles was always present 'or at best in the next room'. A crisis was inevitable sooner or later, and it came on St Andrew's Day (30 November), 1780. Charles had been drinking to the patron saint of Scotland and, according to one report, entered her room in an intoxicated state, accused her of adultery, physically attacked her, ravished her and ended by attempting to strangle her; she was rescued by servants who heard her screams. These lurid details were happily communicated to his Government by Sir Horace Mann, but, though apparently there had been what Alfieri calls '*una violenta scena baccanale*' it is impossible for fairly obvious reasons to accept all the details put about by Louise to justify her desertion of her husband shortly afterwards. As so often happens with men who drink a great deal, he was probably less often stupefied by drink than observers believed. He must have seen more than Louise and her lover thought, and something in particular must have happened to provoke a violent fit of anger and jealousy on St Andrew's Night. Interestingly enough, Louis Dutens, a French Protestant Pastor in the service of the British Embassy at Turin, who was in Florence at the time and gives a full account of how Louise came to leave Charles in his *Mémoires d'un voyageur qui se repose*, says nothing of the St Andrew's Night affair, and Alfieri is less detailed in his account than Mann's report would lead us to expect. He simply says that after the St Andrew's Night scene Louise, in order to free herself from Charles's horrible treatment, was finally compelled to look for a way to escape from his tyranny and save her health and her life. Whatever actually happened, the crisis was predictable: even if Charles had remained blind to what was going on, Louise wanted freedom to make love with Alfieri in less frustrating circumstances.

Alfieri was now determined to liberate his Beatrice from what he called 'the tyranny of an unreasonable and perpetually drunken master'. With the help of Signora Orlandini, Irish-born widow of a General Orlandini and now mistress of an Irishman called Gehegan, Alfieri – 'already practised in the art of laying plans by the habit of composing tragedies', as Dutens puts it – and Louise devised a scheme for her escape. It was not easy, for Charles kept a watchful eye on his wife: 'he never left her alone, and when he had to allow her out of his sight, he locked her up', says Dutens. But Charles was outwitted. The idea was that Louise should go to visit the Convent of the *Bianchette* ('Little White Nuns') to inspect their lace-making. The convent was in the Via del Mandorlo (now the Via Giusti), not far from the Palazzo Guadigni. That morning Signora Orlandini was invited to breakfast at the Palazzo, and the proposal to visit the convent was made by her, as pre-arranged. Louise dutifully said she would be glad to go if her husband had no objection: Charles had no objection, but, as was anticipated, he insisted on going too. The three drove to the convent door, and there they found Gehegan, who 'happened' to have gone for a ride that way. Gehegan escorted the ladies up the steps to the door, while Charles, who was thoroughly out of condition, panted behind. He rang the bell. The door opened, the two ladies hastily entered, and the door was shut again. When Charles got to the door Gehegan complained that the nuns had been so rude as to shut it in his face. 'Wait a minute,' said Charles. 'They'll open it for *me*.' And he rang. There was no reply, and he rang again. There was still no reply, and he banged on the door with his fists. Eventually the Mother Superior opened the grille and calmly informed Charles that the Countess of Albany had sought refuge in the convent and would remain there under the protection of the Grand Duchess. There was absolutely nothing that Charles could do, except rage in vain protest before getting back into his carriage and returning to the Palazzo Guadigni.

On 9 December Louise wrote to her brother-in-law the Cardinal asking his help, and on the 15th he replied giving his approval to what she had done ('the fact that your action was made with the approval of the Court guarantees the integrity of your motives') and recommending that she retire to the Ursuline Convent in Rome, for which his father had had 'une prédilection particulière'. The next day the Pope wrote, recognizing that Louise had 'borne with patience so many strange and sad vicissitudes' and informing her that if she had really decided on a separation for 'ragioni giustissime' ('most just reasons') he would, in agreement with the Court of the Grand Duke, arrange for the Papal Nuncio to provide protection for the journey to Rome. Both the Cardinal and Pope imagined that Louise was seeking to retire to a life of religious meditation: the Cardinal thanked Heaven that Louise's sorrows had moved her to an edifying life, but hardly dared to hope that Heaven's purpose would stretch to the conversion of Charles.

Louise's journey from Florence to Rome had a certain comic-opera quality. To make sure that Charles would not be able to hinder the escape, the carriage in which she travelled with Lucille de Maltzam was escorted by armed footmen on horseback, while others watched the Palazzo Guadigni to make sure that nobody came out; Alfieri himself, with Gehegan, both disguised as coachmen and armed with pistols, sat on the box of Louise's carriage. The escort accompanied Louise only a certain distance on the road to Rome, until there was no more risk of pursuit; then Alfieri returned to Florence to avoid scandal. In Rome Louise was warmly welcomed by her brother-in-law, and she was received into the Ursuline Convent with every papal mark of approval. 'The mould for any more casts of Royal Stuarts has been broke,' wrote Sir Horace Mann triumphantly, 'or what is equivalent to it is now shut up in a Convent of Nuns, under the double lock and key of the Pope and Cardinal York, out of the reach of any dabbler who might foister in any spurious copy. Historians may now close the lives of that family, unless the Cardinal should become Pope, and that would only produce a short scene of ridicule.'

There were further comic-opera scenes in Florence. On 9 December Gehegan wrote to Charles saying that he had heard repeatedly a report to the effect that Charles had threatened to have him shot 'for no other reason that I know of than because I had the honour of handing your amiable Consort out of your carriage, and thence up a flight of stairs . . .' If the report was true, Gehegan assured Charles that anybody he employed on such an errand 'will be received as he merits'. According to Dutens, Charles sent an apology by one of his gentlemen. Some time later Gehegan wrote again, this time on behalf of Alfieri. 'Many persons who have the honour of dining at your table, say that you are pleased to *speak of Comte Alfieri* in the most unbecoming manner of which he, though now at Naples, has had notice. It is said, Sir, that you call him a seducer, and attribute to him the separation between you and your most amiable Consort, whereas it is notorious to all Florence, that her

state of health and daily sufferings, forced her to that extremity. ...
Count Alfieri, conscious of his innocence, and justly surprised as well as
irritated at such a calumny, has prayed me, Sir, as his friend, to know
from you whether such a report be true, and if such is your opinion of
him; he being determined if you persist, Sir, in holding this language,
to return in the speediest manner to Florence to *Demand Satisfaction*
for so gross an injury.' It is not known what answer, if any, Charles
returned to this epistle.

Louise, meanwhile, had no intention of remaining shut up in a
convent. 'She has obtained leave to go abroad whenever she pleases
without the least constraint,' wrote Sir Horace Mann on 23 January
1781. 'She had a long audience of the Pope in the Sacristy of a Church,
Cardinal York treats her with the greatest civility, and has made her
the most generous offer, and she goes frequently to dine with him at
Frascati, where he commonly resides.' She had completely won over
her brother-in-law, and could do what she pleased with him. In March
she left the convent to live in an apartment of the Cancelleria, the
Cardinal's official residence (though he generally resided in his bishopric
of Frascati). Alfieri had gone to Naples, awaiting an opportunity to join
Louise in Rome. By assiduous cultivation of the appropriate ecclesiasti-
cal authorities and transforming himself into what he called an *'uomo
visitante, riverenziante e piaggante'* ('reverential and flattering visitor') in
his contacts with 'these priestlings (*'pretacchiuoli'*) who managed to
make such a mess of the Countess's affairs', he obtained permission to
stay in Rome. He settled at the Villa Strozzi on the Esquiline, to divide
his time between his mistress, his tragedies, and his horses, for which he
had a passion. The Cardinal, still under the influence of his scheming
sister-in-law, cut Charles's allowance by half and gave her the balance;
she also obtained a pension of 20,000 crowns from France. Her only
problem now was to be able to leave Rome and embark on a life of
perfect freedom with her lover. The Cardinal expected her to stay in
Rome, and had not the faintest idea that she was mis-using the independent position he had provided for her in that city to prosecute her
affair with Alfieri. Louise had brought Alfieri and the Cardinal together
by sending the poet to him with a present of a beautiful copy of Virgil,
having noted, as she wrote in a letter, that his library lacked a Virgil.
Charles demanded in vain that Alfieri should be banished from Rome.
The Pope replied that he wished he had many gentlemen of equal
merit in the city.

For two years Louise and Alfieri lived at Rome and successfully
carried on their love affair. Alfieri would visit her at the Cancelleria

to read her his latest verses and make love. For him it was a period of great creativity and real happiness; for her, though she certainly enjoyed being the inspiration of a famous poet, Rome was a temporary stopping place on the road to a fuller freedom whose attainment remained a problem. For her old and sick husband in Florence, pleading in vain with the Pope through his envoy Count Corsini for the return of his wife and the restoration of his full pension, life now seemed to have nothing whatever to offer. Mann wrote on 25 March 1783, that Charles was dangerously ill, and there is evidence of this in the fact that his will is dated 23–25 March 1783. On 30 March he formally legitimated his daughter Charlotte, who was still living in her French convent. The Cardinal Duke of York, hearing that his brother was critically ill, travelled to Florence, but stopped at Siena to send a courier to find out if he was still alive. Somehow, the weak and broken man, old beyond his years, survived an illness so grave that he was given the last Sacraments (he had quietly resumed his Catholic faith at least as early as the mid-1760's), and when his brother arrived he was able to give him his side of the story of Louise and Alfieri. Henry's eyes were opened: he realized at last how he had been taken in by his sister-in-law and her lover. Sir Horace Mann once again rubbed his hands over the turn of events. 'The tables are now turned,' he wrote. 'The cat, at last, is out of the bag. The Cardinal of York's visit to his Brother gave the latter an opportunity to undeceive him, by proving to him that the complaints laid to his charge, of ill-using her were invented to cover a Plot formed by Count Alfieri who, (by working up Tragedies, of which he has wrote many, is most expert, though he always kept behind the curtain,) had imposed upon the Great Duke, the Pope, and the Cardinal, and all those who took her part.'

The Cardinal was enraged, both because he had been imposed upon and because his natural puritanism – his acquaintance Gorani records that he was unpopular in his diocese of Frascati for his bitter opposition to the most innocent pleasures and his wish that 'everyone should spend his life in church' – had been outraged. He at once obtained from Pius VI (who had been Pope since 1775) an order expelling Alfieri from the Estates of the Church. Alfieri left Rome for Siena protesting ironically that he did not understand why his advances to the Countess of Albany could have upset anybody, least of all the Count of Albany and the Cardinal Duke of York, for the former had made him welcome daily at his house while the latter had always seemed to be pleased when the Countess dined with him [the Cardinal] in Rome or Frascati. After a stay in Siena he wandered about for a while both in Italy and abroad, lamenting in his poetry the fate that had torn him from the side of her

> *Ch'a ogni nobile impresa impulso e norma,*
> *Mi aiutava a innalzar i pensier miei;*
> (Who to every noble undertaking, impulse and principle
> Helped me to elevate my thoughts.)

Louise retired to Genzano, an attractive resort town in the Alban hills some seventeen miles south-east of Rome, and consoled herself by copious self-expression in letters to Alfieri's friend Francesco Gori. She represents herself as unhappy and melancholy, unable to live without her lover, tormented lest he turn to another, recognizing the moral dubiety of looking for happiness through somebody else's death yet declaring that is in fact what she does. They are strange letters, and though they are often histrionic they seem convincing enough as the record of a genuine state of mind. They provide ample evidence of Louise's character, at once scheming and hysterical, vulgar and romantic.

At this point in the drama a new character appears on the stage. Gustavus III, King of Sweden, man of letters, historian, crusader against political corruption, who had asserted his power over the estates in the interests of reform and made himself an absolute ruler out of an idealistic patriotism, is a curiously attractive character in spite of his odd mixture of reforming energy and damaging eccentricity. He was travelling in Europe in 1783 under the name of Count Haga and met Charles that year in Florence. He was moved by the plight of a prince who less than forty years before had made all Europe ring with his daring bid to establish his father on the British throne and he exerted himself to put Charles's affairs in order. This involved both a re-arrangement of Charles's finances and a formal separation between him and Louise. Gustavus made friendly contact with Louise through a member of his suite, Baron Carl Sparre. Among the letters from Louise to Sparre in the University Library of Upsala is one dated simply 'Wednesday, three o'clock', in which she asks Sparre to thank 'Mr le Comte d'Aga' (i.e. King Gustavus) for the interest he had shown the previous day both in the Count of Albany's situation and in her own. Another letter to Sparre says she is sending her marriage contract and a note from her husband, to be passed on to Gustavus. She adds: 'I beg you to have the kindness to put the final touch to your goodness by ordering Stuart [Charles's servant John Stuart] not to touch the diamonds before I have this letter of my husband's. [These are the Sobieski diamonds, which she took with her when she left Charles.] If he does not give me the document I desire, I shall keep the diamonds at Rome. After all, the Count of Albany can be very pleased that for a legal fiction I renounce an allowance of 4,000 *écus* and the enjoyment of these diamonds, which he can dispose of as he wishes.' She did in fact give up quite a lot for her freedom, which was formally arranged through the good offices of Gustavus. Horace Mann once again wrote home to give the news:

> For this single point ['an amicable divorce *a mensa et thoro*, and liberty to reside where she pleases'] she has sacrificed every other advantage. She has given up her Pin-money, which by her marriage contract was fifteen thousand french Livres per Annum, as likewise four thousand Crowns (or 1,000 stg.) which the Cardinal since their separation stopped for her maintenance, out of the pension of 10,000 Crowns which the Court of Rome always allowed to their Father, the disposal of which the present Pope left to the Cardinal, who gave his Brother only five thousand, but now the whole is to be given to him, to whom likewise the Cardinal gives up all the furniture in the House at Rome with the Plate and his share of the jewels that were brought into their Family by the late Pretender's wife the Princess Sobiesky, *excepting the great Ruby*, and one of a lesser size, that was pawned to the King of Poland by that Republick, ... Count Albany by the above means will now have a clear Income of ten thousand Crowns from Rome, besides which he has in the french fund 54,000 Livres per Annum: The Countess by relinquishing her Pin-money and part of the Roman pension receives nothing at present from her Husband's Family, but on the separation from her Husband the Court of France allows her a pension of 60,000 Livres and at his death by her Marriage Articles she will have a Dowry of 6,000 Roman Crowns.

Louise, as her letters to Sparre clearly show, was delighted by the settlement. '*Que d'obligations ne vous dois je pas,*' she wrote him as matters were drawing to a conclusion, '*je ne pourrai le reconnaitre qu'en vous allant voir en Suede. Oh oui oui j'irai je vous en donne ma parole d'honneur, souvenez vous, quoique femme, j'y suis fidele comme un homme*'. ('The number of obligations I owe you I can only acknowledge properly by going to see you in Sweden. Oh yes yes, I shall go, I give you my word of honour; remember that though I am a woman I am as faithful as a man.') She was clearly flirting with the Baron: her last letter to him that we have concludes 'looking forward to seeing you, I shall wait for you as late as you care to come'. She seems to have made a conquest: in a letter to her secretary Sparre expresses regret that he cannot pay a last call on the 'adorable Princess' and talks in extravagant terms of his submission, admiration and homage. But of course it was all part of the gallantry of the age, and probably neither of them meant much by their epistolary effusions. Certainly as soon as she got the opportunity Louise went joyfully to her reunion with Alfieri, in the castle of Martinsburg near Colmar in Alsace, lent for this happy occasion by Lucille de Maltzam, who clearly thought it would be better for the couple to be out of Italy at this new turn in their fortunes. The story of Louise's subsequent life with Alfieri is no part of the life of Charles. After Charles's death they never married, but lived together first in Paris and then, when things were made difficult for them there, in Italy again, settling down in Florence at the end of 1793 in the Casa dei Gianfigliazzi on the south bank of the Arno. They were in London in 1791, when Louise was presented at Court by her relative on her mother's side Lady Ailesbury, and tried unsuccessfully to get a pension from George III. (This might have freed her to marry Alfieri: if she married him she risked forfeiting the pension of 60,000 livres from the French Court.) Alfieri died in 1803, and Louise stayed on in Florence with the French artist François Xavier Fabre. She died in Florence in 1824. Some have seen her as a romantic heroine who managed to ensure the triumph of love over circumstance, and certainly she was visited in later life by people who found her story very romantic. To others she was a vain, scheming, conscienceless, histrionic woman, who had no real generosity in her make-up. Her letters reveal her as more the latter than the former, but one must remember her unusual history.

'*Le vieux de Florence est surement devenu imbecile*' – 'the old man of Florence is now quite senile' – was his wife's cruel remark when the negotiations for a settlement were being carried on, and though he had not lost his wits in any literal sense, he was now a confused and lonely old man. He was very ill again in January 1784, but once more he recovered. One of his few pleasures was still music, and the musician Domenico Corri used to spend an occasional evening with him and play the harpsichord while Charles played the 'cello. He also practised on the bagpipes. He always kept a pair of loaded silver-mounted pistols on a table. It is said also that he kept a chest of £12,000 in gold under his bed, in case it was needed for any new attempt at a Jacobite restoration. But he did not really believe in that, nor indeed in much else. He was conscious most of all of loneliness, and in July 1784 he sent for his daughter Charlotte, now legitimated and given the title of Duchess of Albany, to join him at Florence. (The Cardinal had opposed both the legitimation and the title, but Charles had replied to his brother's protest that she had been recognized by himself, the King of France, and the Pope, and she was Royal Highness everywhere.) Charlotte arrived in October.

'She is goodness itself,' recorded the French traveller Charles Dupaty in his *Lettres sur l'Italie en 1785*: 'but it is the kind of goodness that is not commanded by reason but flows from the heart, possessing grace and charm and compelling adoration, a goodness which implies so many virtues and parades none of them'. Charlotte was certainly both good-natured and capable and, bearing her father no malice for his long neglect of her, set herself to make his last years as comfortable as possible. In a series of letters to her uncle the Cardinal she gradually won his confidence and affection: she disabused him of any illusions he may have retained about Louise and, what was more important, reconciled the two brothers. It was entirely due to her patient efforts that Charles and Henry met near Perugia in October 1785 and resumed after almost a lifetime the friendship of their childhood and youth.

Charles made much of his daughter. On St Andrew's Day 1784 he gave a banquet for her and invested her with the Green Ribbon of the Order of the Thistle. He seems to have thought of her as his heir, for he proposed to have medals struck for her, the design for one of which shows a storm-tossed ship approaching the English coast, flying a flag bearing the Stuart arms, with the motto *Pendet salus spe exigua et extrema* ('Deliverance depends on a small, last hope'). The Comte de Vergennes, the French foreign minister, through whose good offices Charles had got the documents legitimizing Charlotte under the name of the Duchess of Albany registered by the Paris Parliament, wrote to her on 16 November to announce that Louis XVI had granted her father a pension of 60,000 livres, with a reversion in her favour of 10,000 livres at his death. Everything was set to enable Charles to live out the remainder of his life in dignity and order. Charlotte watched over his drinking and tried to protect him from excitement which might prove fatal. She was not always successful. A Mr Greathead called on one of Charles's better days and was received by him. They talked alone in the evening and Greathead turned the conversation on the events of 1745-46. As the Prince recalled the experiences of that year – the early victory, the march into England, the retreat from Derby, Culloden, the months of hiding from his enemies in the heather – he got more and more animated and finally, when he talked of the butchery of his Highlanders and the terrible details of the execution of those condemned to death, his voice broke and he collapsed in a fit on the floor. Charlotte, hearing what had happened from an adjoining room, rushed in to assist her father. 'Oh sir,' she exclaimed to Mr Greathead, 'what is this? You must have been speaking to my father about Scotland and the Highlanders. No one dares to mention these subjects in his presence.' It is said that Charles used to burst into tears on hearing the tune 'Lochaber no more', sung by some condemned Jacobites as they were in jail awaiting execution.

With Charles reconciled to his brother the Cardinal and on good terms with the Pope, there was no reason why, as the Cardinal suggested, he should not return to Rome, and though the doctors of Florence tried to keep such a valuable patient in their city, Charlotte was able to arrange for the removal. They set out for Rome on 2 December 1785, the Cardinal meeting them on the way at Viterbo. Once again Charles was installed at the Palazzo Muti, where he had been born almost sixty-five years before. He was very weak now, unable to walk easily because of greatly swollen legs, troubled by dropsy and asthma, and often, as he himself put it, 'bothered in the head'. Yet he still had his good days. On one of these, when he was receiving visitors, the name of M. de Vaudreuil was announced. This was the nephew of the officer who had arrested him at the Opera House in Paris, and the name sounded with shocking familiarity in Charles's ears: once again he fell down in a fit.

On 7 January 1788, Charles had the first of a series of strokes, from which he never fully recovered consciousness. Charlotte was herself seriously ill of a liver complaint (perhaps cancer), so that she was not informed of her father's desperate condition until the 11th. But she exerted herself to relieve her father's dying hours, and he died in her arms – on 31 January as was officially stated but a tradition says on 30 January, the official date being one day later to avoid coinciding with the ill-omened anniversary of the execution of Charles I. His brother, now in the eyes of loyal Jacobites King Henry I of Scotland and IX of England, conducted the funeral service of King Charles III of England, Scotland, France and Ireland (as Charles was called once more in death) at Frascati, where his tomb is in the Cathedral, the Pope having refused to allow it to be held in Rome.

Charlotte did not long survive her father. A fall from a horse at Bologna on 14 October 1789 exacerbated the illness from which she had been suffering for some time and for which she had recently had an unsuccessful operation, and she died on 17 November. She was never officially recognized as Charles's heir, so her death unmarried was not regarded as dynastically significant. She led a strange life, and there now seems no doubt that during her years in France she bore three children to a French prelate. Robert Burns commemorated her in 1787, the year after he had won fame for the Kilmarnock edition of his poems (it would be pleasant to think that Charles heard of the new Scottish poet who was to do so much for Jacobite song, but it is highly improbable that he did):

> This lovely maid's of noble blood,
>   That ruled Albion's kingdoms three;
> But Oh, Alas! for her bonie face!
>   They hae wrang'd the lass of Albanie! ...
>
> Alas the day, and woe the day,
>   A false Usurper wan the gree,
> That now commands the towers and lands,
>   The royal right of Albanie.
>
> We'll daily pray, we'll nightly pray,
>   On bended knees most ferventlie,
> That the time may come, with pipe and drum,
>   We'll welcome home fair Albanie.

As for Charles, his life and fortunes had already been and were still to be the subject of innumerable Scottish songs that reflected the ways in which he had captured the popular imagination, but it was in the Gaelic-speaking Highlands that the note of personal grief was sounded most clearly on the news of his death. It is heard in *An Suaithneas Ban* (*The White Cockade*) by William Ross which is described by John Lorne Campbell as 'at once the Prince's only true elegy and the last genuine Jacobite poem composed in Scotland'. Campbell's translation of the opening stanzas runs as follows:

> As I walked across the hill
> On Sunday, and a friend with me,
> We read together a letter's news
> No joyful tale we gathered there.
>
> Ancient Scotland! a tale of woe
> Every sea-wave breaking brings,
> That thy royal heir is now in Rome
> Earthed in chest of polished boards.
>
> Heavily I sigh each day,
> Oft my thoughts are far away;
> False the world, and sad the fate
> That all flesh is to death a prey. ...

Epilogue

'HENRY IX, King of Great Britain, France, and Ireland, Defender of the Faith, Cardinal Bishop of Frascati' read one side of a medal that the new Stuart claimant had struck, while the other, more realistically, read '*Non desideriis hominum, sed voluntate Dei*' (Not by the desires of men, but by the will of God). The Cardinal King was a rich man, and could afford to maintain a regal pomp in his daily habits, something he did out of principle in spite of his generally ascetic temperament. He does not seem to have maintained any correspondence with British Jacobites, and little is known about his political views. His royal claims had no effect whatever on the course of history, and for all the regal habits that he maintained in his social life he led a dull if comfortable existence until the outbreak of the French Revolution removed the source of much of his wealth, which came from revenues in France and Spain as well as Italy. He survived in Frascati with diminished resources until the French occupation of Rome in February 1798, when he fled to Naples and then crossed in a British warship to Messina: there is a tradition that Nelson entertained him to dinner in his flagship together with the King and Queen of the Two Sicilies and Sir William and Lady Hamilton. From Messina he went to Corfu, and then to Venice for the conclave which met there on 30 November 1799, to elect Cardinal Chiaramonti pope as Pius VII. He was now in a state of complete destitution. Cardinal Borgia wrote to the British M.P. Sir John Hippisley, Baronet, asking him to use his influence to help the impoverished Cardinal. 'It is greatly afflicting,' he wrote, 'to see so great a personage, the last descendant of his Royal House, reduced to such distressed circumstances, having been barbarously stripped by the French of all his property'. *The Times* wrote sympathetically of him on 28 February 1800: 'The malign influence of the Star, which had so strongly marked the fate of so many of his illustrious ancestors, was not exhausted, and it was peculiarly reserved for the Cardinal of York to be exposed to the shafts of adversity at a period of life when least able to struggle with misfortune. At the advanced age of seventy-five he is driven from his episcopal residence, his house sacked, his property confiscated, and constrained to seek his personal safety in flight, upon the seas, under every aggravated circumstance that could affect his health and fortunes'. The result of Sir John Hippisley's intervention and the kind of public sympathy represented by the article in *The Times* was a pension of £5,000 awarded to the Cardinal by the British Government with the warm approval of King George III. He returned to Frascati in June 1800, when the political situation in Italy was calmer, and lived there until his death on 13 July 1807.

Henry IX's heir was a matter of the purest theory. In his will he named as his heir Charles Emmanuel IV, King of Sardinia, senior descendant of Charles I's daughter Henrietta who had married Philippe Duc d'Orléans and whose daughter Anna Maria had married Victor Amadeus II of Sardinia, and after his death claims of the most academic kind were made for the descendants of Charles Emmanuel's brother, Victor Emmanuel I. By this time Jacobitism other than as a historical sentiment was confined to the occasional eccentric antiquary. In the sentimental sense many people were Jacobites who were completely loyal to the reigning house. George IV himself had Jacobite sympathies and thirty-one years after the death of Bonnie Prince Charlie contributed to the cost of Canova's graceful monument in St Peter's, Rome, to James III and his two sons, described in the Prologue. Opposite this monument above the door that leads to the stair up to the dome, is the memorial tablet to Charles's mother.

As the visitor stands and looks from the monument to the sons to the memorial tablet to the mother, he may perhaps reflect that both Clementina and Henry fittingly receive their commemoration in Rome, where in one way or another they both in the end belonged. But Charles? The total time he spent in Scotland amounted to almost exactly one year, but surely it is to Scotland that he belongs. It was Scotland that gave him his army and his legend. It was largely Scottish history from 1688 – Killiecrankie, Darien, Glencoe, the Union, the conflict between patriarchal and feudal order in the Highlands – that gave the Jacobitism of Charles's time an emotional base. He set out in 1745 to regain the throne for his father and so for himself, and he never gave up the royal claims of his house. But, born in Rome though he was, ill-educated as a potential British monarch, ignorant of so much in Scottish history, society and language, he managed in asserting his personal claims in Scotland to strike something deep in the Scottish imagination, so that even those Scots who did not come out for him in 1745 and who actually opposed him felt something of his appeal. For English Jacobites, their Jacobitism was a form of High Toryism. But Scottish Jacobites were different. Troubled by an apparent conflict between self-interest and national feeling, vaguely aware that the economic advantages of the union with England might have to be paid for by a loss of national institutions and a dilution of national culture (however that was to be defined), many Scotsmen saw in Bonnie Prince Charlie a symbol of something they felt deeply but were unable to describe. This is not to minimize the conflict and misunderstanding between the Lowlands and the Highlands in the eighteenth century. It is true that Lowlanders often regarded Highlanders as alien barbarians. And it was the Highlanders who composed most of Charles's army and bore the brunt of the suffering after Culloden: it was their society that was destroyed afterwards, their dress and customs that were banned, their land that was 'cleared' for sheep (though often by their own chiefs). But the Lowlands too cherished the story of the Prince in song and legend. His appeal, in a sense, was to the conscience. Many who would not have wanted to see him win felt that nevertheless he stood for something they ought to have valued. Burns, who called himself a 'sentimental Jacobite', understood this, combining as he did a romantic feeling for the lost cause of the House of Stuart with democratic egalitarianism; Walter Scott understood it too, and showed in Waverley's predicament and in Redgauntlet's obsession both the appeal and the dangers of a Jacobitism which, however attractive, was in the last analysis an anomaly and an anachronism – even worse, an irrelevance.

So it is right to remember Bonnie Prince Charlie, as he himself did so often and so vainly in those long sad years of decline, as he was in the Highlands, persuading the reluctant chiefs by sheer charm of personality, raising the standard in Glenfinnan, riding proudly through Perth, entering Holyrood after the victory of Prestonpans, even scrambling over rocks and heather to elude the watchful redcoats or eating and drinking in a cave with the faithful Glenmoriston men. This was the idealized Prince Charlie, and the folk memory was right to cherish it.

And if we stand in Glenfinnan looking up at his lonely monument, or walk through the still infinitely mournful battlefield of Culloden, or listen to a Scottish folksong or dance tune in some way associated with him, or even look at some of the ridiculous tartanry laid out in Edinburgh or Inverness for tourists, we may perhaps catch a glimpse of some of the contradictory feelings awakened in the Scottish consciousness by this strangely fated man.

Bibliography

There is abundant printed material on the Jacobite movement and on the Forty-five rising and its aftermath, much of it eighteenth-century. It is these eighteenth-century sources that have been chiefly used in this study, though modern secondary sources have also been consulted, especially when they print letters or other primary material not previously available. The following is a select list of the works used, in the order of the chapters of this book to which they are related:

CHAPTER I

Journal du Marquis de Dangeau, avec les additions inédites du Duc de Saint-Simon. Ed. F. S. Feuillet de Conches, Paris, 1854–60.

The Chevalier de St George and the Jacobite Movements in his Favour [An anthology of contemporary sources]. Ed. C. S. Terry, London, 1901.

The Laws and Acts Made in the First Parliament of Our most High and Dread Sovereign James VII. Edinburgh, 1731. (Separate title-pages for each of the two sessions, and for the following three items which form part of the same book.)

The Acts and Orders of the Meeting of the Estates of the Kingdom of Scotland Holden and begun at Edinburgh, March 14, 1689. Edinburgh, 1731.

The Laws and Acts Made in the First Parliament of Our Most High and Dread Sovereigns William and Mary. Edinburgh, 1731. (Separate title-pages for each of the nine sessions.)

The Laws and Acts of Parliament of Our Most High and Dread Sovereign, Anne. Edinburgh, 1731. (Separate title-pages for each of the four sessions.)

The Jacobite Movement: The First Phase. Sir Charles Petrie, Bt. London, 1948.

Bishop Burnet's History Of His Own Time. 3 vols. London, 1725.

The Life and Times of John Maitland, Duke of Lauderdale. W. C. Mackenzie. London, 1923.

Scottish Kings. Gordon Donaldson. London, 1967.

The History of Scotland. J. Hill Burton. Vols. VII and VIII. Edinburgh, 1898.

CHAPTER 2

The Loyal Clans. Audrey Cunningham. Cambridge, 1932.

The Massacre of Glencoe, being a true narrative of the Barbarous Murther of the

Glenco-men in the Highlands of Scotland.
. . . London, 1703.

Annals and Correspondence of the Viscount and the 1st and 2nd Earls of Stair. Ed. J. M. Graham. London, 1875.

The Massacre of Glencoe. John Prebble. London, 1966.

The Union of England and Scotland. James Mackinnon. London, 1896.

Scotland and the Union. W. L. Mathieson. Glasgow, 1905.

The Company of Scotland Trading to Africa and the Indies. G. Pratt Insh. London, 1932.

CHAPTER 3

Memoirs of the Affairs of Scotland, from Queen Anne's Accession to the Throne to the Commencement of the Union of the Two Kingdoms of Scotland and England. [George Lockhart of Carnwath]. London, 1714.

The Lockhart Papers, containing the Memoirs and Commentaries upon the Affairs of Scotland from 1702 to 1715, by George Lockhart, Esq. of Carnwath, . . . 2 vols. London, 1817.

Minutes of the Proceedings in Parliament, 1706–7. [The copy in the author's possession is a – perhaps unique? – sewing together of all 89 numbers of the daily minutes of Scotland's last Parliament, printed by Andrew Anderson in Edinburgh in the course of the Parliament's sitting. At the front is Her Majestie's Most Gracious Letter to the Parliament of Scotland together with His Grace the Lord High Commissioner, and the Lord High Chancellor their Speeches, Edinburgh, 1706: this is a separate pamphlet which has been sewn in with the minutes.]

A Short Account of Scotland, being A Description of the Nature of that Kingdom, and what the Constitution of it is in Church

and State [The Rev. Thomas Morer]. London, 1702.

A Discourse upon the Union of Scotland and England [George Ridpath]. London, 1702.

The Speeches by a Member of the Parliament which began at Edinburgh the 6th of May 1703 [Fletcher of Saltoun]. Edinburgh, 1703.

The Political Works of Andrew Fletcher, Esq. of Saltoun. Glasgow, 1749.

A Diary of the Proceedings in the Parliament and Privy Council of Scotland, May 21, MDCC – March 7, MDCCVII. Sir David Hume of Crossrigg. Edinburgh, 1828.

Andrew Fletcher of Saltoun. W. C. Mackenzie. Edinburgh, 1935.

Seafield Correspondence from 1685 to 1708. Ed. James Grant. Scottish History Society. Edinburgh, 1912.

Letters Relating to Scotland in the Reign of Queen Anne by James Ogilvy, First Earl of Seafield, and Others. Ed. P. Hume Brown. Scottish History Society. Edinburgh, 1915.

CHAPTER 4

The Secret History of Colonel Hooke's Negotiations in Scotland in Favour of the Pretender in 1707 . . ., written by Himself. London, 1760.

Mémoires du Comte de Forbin. 2 vols. Amsterdam, 1730.

The History of the Late Rebellion Rais'd against His Majesty King George by the Friends of the Popish Pretender [Peter Rae]. Dumfries, 1718.

Lovat of the Forty-Five. W. C. Mackenzie. Edinburgh, 1934.

The History of the Late Rebellion, with Original Papers and Characters of the Principal Noblemen and Gentlemen Concern'd in it, by the Reverend Mr Robert Patten. London, 1717.

Inglorious Rebellion: The Jacobite Risings of 1708, 1715 and 1719. C. Sinclair-Stevenson. London, 1971.

The Jacobite Rising of 1715. John Baynes. London, 1970.

Memoirs of the Insurrection in Scotland in 1715. The Master of Sinclair. Edinburgh, 1858.

The Jacobite Relics of Scotland, collected and illustrated by James Hogg. 2 vols. Edinburgh, 1819–21.

Major Fraser's Manuscript, 1696–1737. Ed. Alexander Fergusson. 2 vols. Edinburgh, 1839.

The Jacobite Movement: The Last Phase. Sir Charles Petrie. London, 1950.

The Jacobite Attempt of 1719, Letters of James Butler, Second Duke of Ormonde . . . Ed. William Kirk Dickson. Scottish History Society. Edinburgh, 1895.

Underground Catholicism in Scotland. P. F. Anson. Montrose, 1970.

CHAPTERS 5–14

The Jacobite Court at Rome in 1719 from Original Documents at Fettercairn House and at Windsor Castle. Ed. Henrietta Tayler. Scottish History Society. Edinburgh, 1938.

The Life and Times of Prince Charles Stewart. A. C. Ewald. London, 1878.

Prince Charles Edward. Andrew Lang. London, 1900.

Prince Charlie and His Ladies. Compton Mackenzie. New York, 1935.

The Rising of 1745, with a Bibliography of Jacobite History 1689–1788. [An anthology of contemporary sources.] C. S. Terry. London, 1900.

Le Prince Errant: Charles-Edouard le dernier des Stuarts. L. Dumont-Wilden. Paris, 1934. [English translation as The Wandering Prince, by W. B. Wells, London, 1934.]

Highland Songs of the Forty-Five. Ed. J. Lorne Campbell. Edinburgh, 1933.

Collected Papers on the Jacobite Risings. R. C. Jarvis. Vol. I. Manchester, 1971.

Wade in Scotland. J. B. Salmond. Edinburgh, 1938.

Scotland in the Age of Improvement. Ed. N. T. Phillipson and Rosalind Mitchison. Edinburgh, 1970.

Memorials of John Murray of Broughton 1740–47. Scottish History Society. Edinburgh, 1898.

1745 and After. [O'Sullivan's narrative and letters.] Ed. A. and H. Tayler. London, 1938.

Memoirs of the Chevalier de Johnstone. Translated from the Original French MS of the Chevalier. Aberdeen, 1870.

Lord George Murray and the Forty-Five. Winifred Duke. Aberdeen, 1927.

The Jacobite General. [Lord George Murray.] Katherine Tomasson. London, 1958.

The Autobiography of Alexander Carlyle of Inveresk. Ed. J. Hill Burton. Edinburgh, 1910.

The Woodhouselee MS. A Narrative of Events in Edinburgh and District During the Jacobite Occupation, September to November 1745. Edinburgh, 1907.

Itinerary of Prince Charles Edward Stuart W. B. Blaikie. Scottish History Society. Edinburgh, 1897.

The Lyon in Mourning or a Collection of Speeches Letters Journals etc. relative to the

Affairs of Prince Charles Edward Stuart, by the Rev. Robert Forbes A.M., Bishop of Ross and Caithness 1746-1775. Ed. Henry Paton. 3 vols. Scottish History Society. Edinburgh, 1895-6.

The History of the Rebellion in the Year 1745. John Home, London, 1802.

The History of the Rebellion, MDCCXLV and MDCCXLVI. Andrew Henderson. London, 1753.

History of the Rebellion of 1745-6. Robert Chambers. 6th edition. Edinburgh, 1847. [1st edition 1827].

A Short Account of the Affairs of Scotland 1744-46, by David, Lord Elcho. Ed. Evan Charteris. London, 1907.

Battles of the '45. Katherine Tomasson and Francis Buist. London, 1962.

A Full and True Collection of All the Proclamations and Orders published by the Authority of Charles, Prince of Wales, . . . 2 vols. Glasgow, 1745-6.

A Plain Authentick and Faithful Narrative of Several Passages of the Young Chevalier from the Battle of Culloden to his Embarkation for France. . . . 3rd ed. London, 1765.

Ships of the '45: The Rescue of the Young Pretender. John S. Gibson. London, 1967.

The Prisoners of the '45. Ed. Sir Bruce Seton and J. G. Arnot. Scottish History Society. Edinburgh, 1938-9.

Journal et Mémoires du Marquis d'Argenson. Ed. J. B. Rathery for the Société de l'Histoire de France. Paris, 1859 ff.

Political and Literary Anecdotes of his own Times. W. King. London, 1819.

Pickle the Spy. Andrew Lang. London, 1897.

The Companions of Pickle. Andrew Lang London, 1898.

La Contessa D'Albany e Il Salotto del Lungarno. Carlo Pelligrini. Naples, 1951.

Rime. Vittorio Alfieri, ed. F. Maddini. Asti, 1954.

Vita de Vittorio Alfieri da Asti, scritta da esso. Ed. Luigi Fasso. 2 vols. Asti, 1951.

The Decline of the Last Stuarts. Ed. Lord Mahon. [Sir Horace Mann's reports from Florence.] London, 1845.

Mémoires d'un voyageur qui se repose. Louis Dutens. Paris, 1806.

Lettres sur l'Italie en 1785. Charles Dupaty. Paris, 1796.

The Life and Letters of H.R.H. Charlotte Stuart, Duchess of Albany. F. J. A. Skeet. London, 1932.

Life of Cardinal York. B. W. Kelly. London, 1899.

Index

If you have enjoyed this Pan book,
you may like to choose your next book from
the titles listed on the following pages

Battles of the '45 50p

Katherine Tomasson & Francis Buist

Illustrated

'Gentlemen, I have flung away the scabbard'
Prince Charles Edward

On 23rd July 1745 Prince Charles Edward arrived in Scotland with nine companions, few arms and little money. The news aroused both dismay and enthusiasm amongst his supporters, but they twice defeated the numerically superior and better disciplined government armies before the Duke of Cumberland exacted a terrible revenge at Culloden.

'This is history as it should be written'
Books and Bookmen

'So vivid it is as if the authors were giving an eye-witness account'
Edinburgh Tatler

'As effective and careful an account of the campaign as could be hoped for . . . the impartiality does not dim the vivid colours or the fierce gallantry that enliven the story'
Times Literary Supplement

The Steel Bonnets 95p

George MacDonald Fraser

The Story of the Anglo-Scottish Border Reivers

'In the making of Britain, between England and Scotland, there was prolonged and terrible violence, and whoever gained in the end, the Border country suffered fearfully in the process. It was the ring in which the champions met; armies marched and counter-marched and fought and fled across it; it was wasted and burned and despoiled, its people harried and robbed and slaughtered, on both sides, by both sides. Whatever the rights and wrongs, the Borderers were the people who bore the brunt; for almost 300 years, from the late thirteenth century to the middle of the sixteenth, they lived on a battlefield that stretched from the Solway to the North Sea. War after war was fought on it, and this, to put it mildly, had an effect on the folk who lived there. . . . By the sixteenth century robbery and blood feud had become virtually systematic, and that century saw the activities of the steel-bonneted Border riders – noble and simple, robber and lawman, soldier and farmer, outlaw and peasant – at their height.'

from the Introduction

These and other Pan books are obtainable from all booksellers and newsagents. If you have any difficulty please send purchase price plus 7p postage to

PO Box 11 Falmouth Cornwall

While every effort is made to keep prices low, it is sometimes necessary to increase prices at short notice. Pan Books reserve the right to show new retail prices on covers which may differ from those previously advertised in the text or elsewhere.